Invisibility and Influence

LATINX: THE FUTURE IS NOW
A series edited by Lorgia García-Peña and Nicole Guidotti-Hernández

Books in the series
Jason Ruiz, *Narcomedia: Latinidad, Popular Culture, and America's War on Drugs*

Rebeca L. Hey-Colón, *Channeling Knowledges: Water and Afro-Diasporic Spirits in Latinx and Caribbean Worlds*

Tatiana Reinoza, *Reclaiming the Americas: Latinx Art and the Politics of Territory*

Kristy L. Ulibarri, *Visible Borders, Invisible Economies: Living Death in Latinx Narratives*

Marisel C. Moreno, *Crossing Waters: Undocumented Migration in Hispanophone Caribbean and Latinx Literature and Art*

Yajaira M. Padilla, *From Threatening Guerrillas to Forever Illegals: US Central Americans and the Cultural Politics of Non-Belonging*

Francisco J. Galarte, *Brown Trans Figurations: Rethinking Race, Gender, and Sexuality in Chicanx/Latinx Studies*

Invisibility and Influence

A Literary History of AfroLatinidades

REGINA MARIE MILLS

University of Texas Press ◆ *Austin*

Copyright © 2024 by the University of Texas Press
All rights reserved
Printed in the United States of America

First edition, 2024

Requests for permission to reproduce material from this work should be sent to permissions@utpress.utexas.edu

♾ The paper used in this book meets the minimum requirements of ANSI/NISO Z39.48-1992 (R1997) (Permanence of Paper).

Library of Congress Cataloging-in-Publication Data

Names: Mills, Regina Marie, author.
Title: Invisibility and influence : a literary history of AfroLatinidades / Regina Marie Mills.
Other titles: Latinx (Series)
Description: First edition. | Austin : University of Texas Press, 2024. | Series: Latinx : the future is now | Includes bibliographical references and index.
Identifiers: LCCN 2023031039 (print) | LCCN 2023031040 (ebook)
 ISBN 978-1-4773-2913-9 (hardcover)
 ISBN 978-1-4773-2914-6 (paperback)
 ISBN 978-1-4773-2915-3 (pdf)
 ISBN 978-1-4773-2916-0 (epub)
Subjects: LCSH: Autobiography—African American authors. | Autobiography—Latin American authors. | Autobiography—Hispanic American authors. | Autobiography—Caribbean authors. | Black people—Latin America—Biography—History and criticism. | Racially mixed people—United States—Biography—History and criticism. | Racially mixed people—Caribbean Area—Biography—History and criticism.
Classification: LCC PS366.A88 M55 2024 (print) | LCC PS366.A88 (ebook) | DDC 810.9492—dc23/eng/20231206
LC record available at https://lccn.loc.gov/2023031039
LC ebook record available at https://lccn.loc.gov/2023031040

doi:10.7560/329139

For my mother, Scarlet

Contents

Acknowledgments **ix**

Introduction: (Life) Writing against Mestizaje **1**

1. Arturo Schomburg, Pura Belpré, and the "Racial Integrity" of Auto/biography **21**

2. Jesús Colón, the New York Young Lords, and "Observe and Participate" Autobiography **47**

3. AfroLatinidad as Creative Destruction: Piri Thomas's Life Writing as a Theorization of Violence **75**

4. Call-and-Response AfroLatinidad: Spirituality, Race, and Gender in Marta Moreno Vega's and Lourdes Casal's Life Writing **103**

5. Queer AfroLatinidades: Monstrosity and Reclaiming Black Latinx Girlhood in Jaquira Díaz's *Ordinary Girls* and Ariana Brown's Verse Memoirs **127**

Epilogue: Science, Spirituality, and Changing Notions of Ancestry in AfroLatinx Narratives **153**

Notes **161**
Bibliography **204**
Index **229**

Acknowledgments

I cannot believe that a work to which I dedicated seven years of my life is actually in print. *Invisibility and Influence* would never have been possible without the support of many people and institutions. I'll start at the project's beginning: the University of Texas at Austin. Mil gracias to my dissertation committee, Jim Cox, Dave Vázquez, Jennifer Wilks, and John Morán González. A lot of love to the writing group I had with fellow UT grads Sequoia Maner and Anne Stewart (though I know I often turned in the sloppiest work). The work of Kevin Quashie pervades many of these chapters (and work beyond the book), and that's all because of Sequoia. Thanks to Anna Crain and Holly Schwadron in UT's Rhetoric and Writing Department. The dissertation that I defended was finished in the Assistant Director's office during spring break 2018; that office always made me feel safe and supported. Thank you both so much for that.

Thank you also to the archives and fellowships that supported this work, especially the chapters on Piri Thomas, Arturo Schomburg, Jesús Colón, the Young Lords Party, and Lourdes Casal. Thanks to the Schomburg Center for Research in Black Culture, which I visited as a 2017–2018 New York Public Library Short-Term Fellowship recipient. The original items that I describe and analyze in chapters 1 and 3 of this book are held in the Manuscripts and Archives Division at The New York Public Library. My gratitude to El Centro de Estudios Puertorriqueños, who supported my research at the Centro Library and Archives with a Dissertation Summer Fellowship in 2017. The original items that I describe and analyze in chapter 2 of this book are held at the Centro Library and Archives at Hunter College (CUNY). While I had planned return visits to these archives and additional visits to the CUNY Dominican Studies Institute, among others, the COVID-19 pandemic foiled those plans. I do want to thank Jessica Holden and the

University Archives and Special Collections of the Joseph P. Healey Library at University of Massachusetts, Boston, who sent me digitized copies of Lourdes Casal's work in *Nuestro* magazine, which I discuss in chapter 4 of *Invisibility and Influence*. In addition to these archival fellowships and support, I want to thank Kerry L. Hayne and the Summer Institute on Tenure and Professional Advancement (SITPA) at Duke University, through which I was a SITPA Scholar from 2019–2021. Their professional and financial support is much appreciated, and I am truly glad I could connect with my SITPA mentor, Judith Madera.

Thank you to those who supported me at my current institution, Texas A&M University, including the Department of English and the programs in Latino/a and Mexican American Studies and Africana Studies. I appreciate the financial support provided through start-up funds, conference funding, and summer research assistantships. At Texas A&M, I want to especially give a shout out to Felipe Hinojosa, Ira Dworkin, Emily Johansen, Shona Jackson, Vanita Reddy, Maura Ives, Darrel Wanzer-Serrano, Sonia Hernandez, Juan Alonzo, Alain Lawo-Sukam, and Nancy Plankey-Videla. Thank you to the ADVANCE Scholar Program at Texas A&M; my internal mentor, Sonia Hernández; and my external mentor, Elena Machado Sáez. Un abrazo muy fuerte to Marcela Fuentes, who came in as tenure-track faculty with me back in 2018 and without whom I do not think I would have kept my sanity. You are a queen, and I know we will always have each other's backs.

I have been fortunate to teach and learn from thoughtful graduate students at Texas A&M. Thank you first to the students in my fall 2020 and fall 2022 "Latinx Life Writing" graduate courses, for which I was able to rehearse older arguments and realize new ones for this book. I was fortunate to receive support for summer graduate assistantships, and this work can be keenly felt in *Invisibility and Influence*. My gratitude to my summer 2021 graduate research assistant, Anneke Snyder, whose influence can most be felt in the introduction. I rewrote my first real version of the introduction that summer, one of a few rewrites during the course of this book-writing process. While the introduction is now half as long as it was in 2021, and a lot of the quotations and references have been moved to the endnotes, the sources that Anneke found for me to review and our discussions on those sources helped shape the way I framed this book. My summer 2022 graduate research assistant, Joseline González-Ajanel also greatly influenced my chapter 1 and chapter 4 revisions as well as publications that will hopefully be out by the time you read these words.

The pandemic left me at home playing a lot of video games, but also, it connected me to people in ways I never had been before. Zoom writing sessions made this book possible, and I want to thank the many people who wrote with me virtually. In particular, Omaris Zamora spearheaded a Zoom writing group that got me through the worst of the pandemic, which included: Ashley Coleman Taylor, Melissa Valle, Zaire Dinzey-Flores, Karishma Desai, Shantee Rosado, Yalidy Matos, and Jeffrey Coleman (apologies for anyone I missed on this list). Thank you also, Jeffrey, for the lovely ballpoint pens, with which I have written many letters over the last few years. My eternal gratitude to Manuel Cuellar, Trent Masiki, Sheela Jane Menon, Domino Renee Perez, Jim Cox, Ira Dworkin, Rachel Lim, Kim McCoy Coleman, Matt King, Guadalupe Escobar, Jennifer Caroccio Maldonado, and Renee Hudson, all of whom either wrote in community with me, read some of my work along the way, or both. My first attempt at the introduction for this book was as a paper for the 2021 ACLA panel "After Race, Too: New Alignments in Comparative Racialization, Multiracialism, and Post-racialism," so thanks to Lynn Itagaki and Rafael Pérez-Torres for organizing that space. For sharing professional or emotional support (or both), thanks to Dave Vázquez, Suzanne Bost, Lee Bebout, Sujey Vega, Domino Perez, Frederick Luis Aldama, Carlos Kelly, Phill Penix-Tadsen, Kishonna L. Gray, Nalini Iyer, and Rachel Gonzalez-Martin.

I had two other key forms of support in the final stretches of this process. First, attending the Transnational Dialogues in Afro-Latin American and Afro-Latinx Studies NEH Summer 2022 Institute at the University of Pittsburgh helped me think through conceptions of mestizaje transnationally and gave me the opportunity to meet incredible scholars such as Vanessa K. Valdés, Jennifer A. Jones, Petra Rivera-Rideau, Sherwin K. Bryant, Reighan Gillam, and Nancy Raquel Mirabal. You will find many of the scholars we engaged with during that two-week period in this book. The Institute was organized by Michelle Reid-Vazquez, managed by Shawn Alfonso-Wells, and coordinated by Israel Herndon. Thank you all for two weeks I will never forget. Second, thank you to Denison University and the Politics and Public Affairs (PPA) Department for sponsoring me as an Affiliated Scholar in Spring 2023. Denison provided library and office privileges during my visits to Columbus when I was on teaching leave so I could finalize the manuscript.

I have been so fortunate to be a University of Texas Press author, and I give my deepest thanks to my editor, Kerry Webb. Her unrivaled patience as I completed the manuscript and revisions during the pandemic was a godsend. Thank you to series editors Lorgia García-Peña and Nicole Guidotti-Hernández, whose comments on the proposal and the completed manuscript were thorough and kind. I admire their scholarship but also their work outside the academy, and it is an honor to be part of the "Latinx: The Future Is Now" series they helm, alongside several amazing scholars. Thank you to the anonymous readers for their generative comments on my proposal, sample chapters, original manuscript, and revised manuscript.

Last, but not least: family. I am lucky to been accepted into two families—my birth family in northern Virginia and Guatemala and a chosen family in Austin, TX. Thank you, Domino, Jim, and Ewan, for giving me a place to call home in Texas. At your house, I can be myself unapologetically, and for that, I will forever be grateful. I am not a religious person, but I often think that my mom connected us so that she knew I would be taken care of in her absence. Thank you also to the family I was born into—my mom, Scarlet; my dad, Brian; and my six siblings. One of the hardest choices in my life was moving out west after college, but I know in my heart that I wouldn't be the person I am today if I had not made that choice. However, I am glad to come home and to know that, even if you don't always understand what I do, that you love and support me and are excited when I succeed. To my dad, who has confronted many challenges and is living proof that it is never too late to change paths and pursue your dreams. He taught me to strive and push myself to be better. To my sister Scarlet Ann, who will always answer my calls, sends me amazing book recommendations, and will never say no to playing a *Splatoon* or *League of Legends* session with me when I need it. To my brother Derek, who is patient with me when I talk about video games from a literary perspective and who I admire endlessly for his compassion and kindness. To my brother Daniel, whose resilience and hard work is inspiring. To my brother B. J., for preparing me for a years-long writing project with our years-long quest to finish *Tales of Graces*. To Patrick and Stephanie, who I will always love.

My mom, who died suddenly and far too young in 2015, drives my work. I know she would be so proud of me. It breaks my heart that she has missed her children's weddings, graduations, and life-defining accomplishments since her passing. She loved ceremonies of achievement and throwing a great party after, so I know she would have hosted a wild book party for me. She (and my dad) never doubted that I would write a book one day. I love you and miss you every day, Mama Bear. Thank you also to my maternal family in Guatemala, who always asks about my book and who loves me even though I know I am not the perfect Guatemalan granddaughter, niece, or cousin.

Lastly, to the love of my life, Anthony. If I saw myself the way you see me, I would be the most confident, successful, amazing person in the world and somehow have a Nobel Prize. You never let me put myself or my work down. Thank you for being my number one fan, for being there for me even when I'm trying to tough it out on my own. I love the family we have created together, us two. Te amo mucho, mi cielo.

Introduction: (Life) Writing against Mestizaje

Positionality, Double-Dutch, and AfroLatinx Memoir

Veronica Chambers begins her memoir with a flashback to her girlhood, grounding the memoir in her memories of double-dutch. Double-dutch establishes both the joy of Black girlhood and the complicated game that being Afro-Panamanian entails.[1] Veronica compares double-dutch to the excitement and "invitation" that, for boys in her neighborhood, was represented by "Air Jordans" or "a car idling before a drag race."[2] The sport, competition, and spectacle of double-dutch gives "double-dutch girls [. . .] our own prance."[3] The girls' prance is a performance that builds joy and community but also provides a way for girls to push each other to better themselves and their skills. Double-dutch also acts as a metaphor for Veronica's life as a Black Central American girl (and later, woman). Writing in the post–Civil Rights Movement, with the belief that Black women had opportunities never before available, Chambers explains, "It wasn't a question of whether we'd make it in, we'd conquered that years before. The challenge was to prove how long we could jump."[4] Double-dutch is divided into two acts—the entrance and the maintenance. AfroLatina women have made strides to be seen and to enter all facets of society. However, like double-dutch, it is an exhausting endeavor, where your stamina will be tested; as she writes, beyond the tricks, "the real feat is longevity."[5] In comparing AfroLatinidad to double-dutch, the challenge is to see how long you can stay visible, under your own terms, before you trip and no longer have control. Each rope represents obstacles, like sexism and anti-Blackness, that always seem to circle back.

Double-dutch, as Chambers describes, makes "your legs feel powerful and heavy,"[6] highlighting Afro-Caribbean girls' physical power and mental dexterity but also the weights that remain and grow heavier as time passes. "In the rope, if you're good enough, you can do anything and be anything you want,"[7] she claims, but in the end, the rope always wins. However, "there is a space between the two ropes where nothing is better than being a black girl. The helix encircles you and protects you and there you are strong."[8] Here, Chambers points us to the power and protection in the liminal space of the moving jump ropes. The image of a helix, two or more entwined strands dancing around each other (like the double-helix of DNA), forms a protective cocoon. The helix is also an image of intertwining lines, struggles, and identities. The memoir promises to show us the strands that influence who Chambers imagines herself to be at the intersection of "black," "Panamanian," and "girl." While she makes no claims to Central Americanness in this brief first chapter on double-dutch, the book itself lays claim to Black Central Americanness, as she admires her mother's Panamanian Spanish and waxes nostalgic about Panamanian dishes.

Playing double-dutch sets up many of the major themes and concerns that follow Veronica through the memoir, namely the disparate worlds of girls and boys (and similarly disparate treatment), the desperate desire for her mother's love, and the exploration and troubling of Blackness.[9] As a Black woman of Central American–Caribbean parentage,[10] Chambers's life narrative negotiates US and Panamanian experiences of Blackness,[11] and particularly the invisibility of Central American Blackness. *Mama's Girl* is prefaced by an excerpt from Audre Lorde's poem "Black Mother Woman." In addition to setting up the central mother-daughter conflict, the poem also introduces the memoir's approach to constructing the self. Lorde writes, "I learn from you / to define myself / through your denials."[12] By prefacing her memoir with this excerpt, Chambers points to the importance of denial and invisibility as influences on her self-construction.[13] Beyond the speaker's eyes are "a squadron of conflicting rebellions," which Lorde evokes in the double-dutch hurdles described above. *Mama's Girl* is about mother-daughter conflict, yes, but also about the conflicting ideas of Blackness, girlhood, and identity that Veronica's mother—and Veronica's life experiences—provide.[14]

Chambers's memoir is one of the few texts marketed towards adults that focuses on an Afro–Central American experience in the United States.[15] While Chambers has, since her success with *Mama's Girl*, written fiction, nonfiction, and young adult (YA) books with Afro-Panamanian characters, such as *Marisol and Magdalena* (1998) and *Quinceañera Means Sweet 15* (2001), this work remains one of few memoirs that provides insight into girlhood from an Afro–Central American perspective.[16] She focuses particularly on her ambivalent relationship with her mother (this relationship eventually grows to be strong and affectionate) and, like in Jaquira Díaz's *Ordinary Girls* (discussed in chapter 5), on the emotional, financial, and physical violence Veronica suffers at the hands of her mother, father, stepmother, and the poor neighborhoods in which she grew up. There is very little scholarship discussing Chambers's memoir,[17] though the book was commercially successful, with favorable reviews in *Kirkus* and the *Los Angeles Times*.[18] However, the book is rarely discussed as a Latina memoir, or even as an AfroLatina memoir.[19]

I start this book with Veronica Chambers's *Mama's Girl* (1996) because the memoir has stayed with me since I first read it in 2013. In my first year of graduate school, I compiled a list of every book by a US–Central American writer that I could find, and *Mama's Girl* was one of them. It is the first memoir I think of when I wonder or am asked why I decided to write AfroLatinx literary studies scholarship.[20] As a white Guatemalan American, I have seen Guatemala's fraught relationship to Blackness and experienced my own conflict with ethnoracial identity. Guatemala, and Guatemalans, go beyond rejecting Blackness to outright denying its existence in Central American spaces. As Vielka Cecilia Hoy asserts, "Central America suffers from the same national identity dilemmas that much of Latin America is plagued with—namely, where to place Blackness in whitening ideologies."[21] *Mama's Girl* made clear to me the stringent denial of Blackness that underlies Guatemalan ladino identity,[22] an iteration of mestizo identity that emphasizes Spanish ancestry and rejects Indigenous culture.[23] In fact, more enslaved Africans were transported to Latin America and the Caribbean, including Central America, than to Anglophone territories in the Americas, so the relative denial of Blackness is clearly ideological rather than demographic.[24] The belief that the African diaspora came primarily to North America means that the Blackness of Central American history, and of Latin America more broadly, is not only erased but denied entirely by ladinos.[25] Diaspora Blackness has been rendered invisible, even as it is also foundational to US Latinidad and Latin Americanness. Media and news articles have now "discovered" the presence and influence of AfroLatinx peoples. It is now common to see articles with titles such as "These Afro-Latino Actors Are Pushing Back against Erasure in Hollywood" or "Afro-Latinos and Black History Month."[26] However, claiming that AfroLatinidad is just now being recognized is itself a failure of recognition. The colonizer paradigm of discovery has haunted AfroLatinx communities and conceptions of AfroLatinidad.[27] Rather than position this book as a discovery of AfroLatinx writers, my aim is to provide a deeper look at their continued influence and the ways they used life writing to engage the distortions of visibility that they encountered across the last century.

Argument and Contributions

This book studies the development of AfroLatinx life writing in the United States, demonstrating how a century's worth of US AfroLatinx writers have defined themselves and generated a rich array of AfroLatinidades. These AfroLatinidades arise from negotiations of visibility—the distorted images from media and history books, the hypervisibility of Blackness and Brownness, and acts intended to forcibly erase Black Latinx narratives. Navigating US (white) American, Black, and Latinx-mestizo perceptions, or what Juan Flores and Miriam Jiménez Román term "triple-consciousness,"[28] AfroLatinx writers have been hypervisible as either Black writers or Latina/o/x writers, but not in terms of the distinctive AfroLatinx community that they constitute. Because of their need to navigate ethnoracial and sociohistorical expectations alongside their own particularized situations, AfroLatinx writers have adopted and innovated on the genre of life writing. *Life writing* is a capacious term, including any manner of life narratives, whether presented through traditional outlets like the biographies and memoirs distributed by New York City publishers, memoirs-in-verse that may be self-published or sold through independent presses, or more experimental works, such as those that try to tell the life stories of organizations and political movements.[29] While this genre has often been seen as a uniquely individualistic one, representing the extraordinary, I argue that AfroLatinxs primarily use life writing to make claims about community and to find belonging. In doing so, these writers provide readers with a wide range of AfroLatinidades, rather than a monolithic AfroLatinidad that folds into the narrative of mestizaje.

I define AfroLatinidades as social, cultural, and political constructions based in the embodied experiences of Black Latinxs. Like Omaris Z. Zamora, I assert that AfroLatinidades are first and foremost an embodied experience, not an abstract one.[30] These concrete realities, I argue, influence conceptions of identity and belonging, as well as their relationships to other important facets of being such as sexuality, gender, religion, and politics. The AfroLatinidades I trace in this monograph reject the myth of racial democracy and the idealization of mestizaje as a tool for diversity, inclusion, and solidarity. While not all AfroLatinx people create such defiant conceptions of AfroLatinidad, the AfroLatinidades this book outlines call out the white supremacist and anti-Black implications within Latinidad and Latin American constructions of identity.[31] AfroLatinidades call attention to the realities of living in a Black body, where "Black" does not automatically equate with "US Black." Thus, to construct an AfroLatinidad is to point out how US narratives of Blackness dominate and erase other forms of diaspora Blackness[32] *and* how white and light-skinned Latinxs dominate and erase other forms of Latinidad. AfroLatinidades, then, arise from the negotiation of invisibility, visibility, and hypervisibility. This focus on visibility, a concept well theorized within Black studies and US–Central American studies,[33] is particularly pertinent to AfroLatinxs, since they reside in a space that appears to reject the Black/white binary by claiming Brownness, mixedness or mestizaje, or racial democracy and inclusion, while also continuing anti-Black political, social, and cultural constructions of Latinoness and Latin Americanness.[34] In AfroLatinx studies, as Jennifer A. Jones delineates, visibility generally refers to work that highlights the absence of AfroLatinxs from Latinx or Black Studies.[35] In *Invisibility and Influence*, I engage the visibility spectrum as a lens for analysis.

AfroLatinidades place diaspora Blackness (in its many iterations) at the center of AfroLatinx identity and sense of belonging. When I say that an AfroLatinx life writer constructs a conception of AfroLatinidad, I am making a claim about how the writer constructs their own self-identity and their sense of belonging within larger communities. That is, they construct an AfroLatinidad by bringing to light the distortions and erasures they must navigate, within themselves and in the world around them, that renders their presence both invisible and hypervisible. AfroLatinidades, as imagined by these life writers, reside in the body and how that body navigates narratives of visibility, such as the idea that Blackness is perpetually foreign to Latinidad or that Latinidad is an "off-white" identity.[36] These AfroLatinx writers claim that having a Black body concretely changes their experience within Latinx communities, US Black communities, and non-Latinx white communities.

Building on the germinal work of scholars and activists such as Miriam Jiménez Román, Juan Flores, Agustin Lao-Montes, and the Black Latinas Know Collective, this book argues that the authors' texts must be understood not simply as Latinx or Afro-diasporic life writing but as AfroLatinx. Their writing must therefore be considered to collectively comprise a literary history of these communities as well as being creative interventions into discourses on race, politics, spirituality, queerness, and more. While this study focuses on AfroLatinx life writing primarily based in the United States and

Puerto Rico,[37] this writing is hardly limited to US borders. Some life narratives are set outside of the United States, even if they are written within it. Furthermore, these writers are consistently tied to literary, political, and spiritual traditions outside of the continental United States: from Lucumi in Cuba, to art and tourism in Puerto Rico, to the politics of race in Hispaniola. These "cultural remittances," as Flores calls them in *The Diaspora Strikes Back* (2009), show how US AfroLatinx literature continually converses with Latin American and Caribbean history, culture, and politics.

Invisibility and Influence contributes to the fields of AfroLatinx studies, Latinx studies, Black studies, and life writing studies. In particular, this study aims to add to conversations by scholars that have already made a strong case for AfroLatinx studies as a field of its own, such as Lorgia García-Peña, Miriam Jiménez Román, Juan Flores, Silvio Torres-Saillant, Yomaira C. Figueroa-Vásquez, Vanessa K. Valdés, Omaris Z. Zamora, Paul Joseph López Oro, and the Black Latinas Know Collective. This book is one of the first to focus entirely on AfroLatinx life writing,[38] and in doing so, I claim this work as literary scholarship that considers the differences and commonalities of an approach to life writing from and on the ethnoracial margins. Angela Davis in *Lectures on Liberation* says that if one wants to understand freedom, one must read literature by Black writers.[39] I argue that if you want to understand life writing, you must read AfroLatinx life writing, as these writers must reckon most deeply with the literary, rhetorical, and political strategies one engages to construct the self and, particularly, to construct the self in the context of community. In addition, since their identity refuses to fit into dominant frameworks, these writers must theorize the very concept of identity.

Another contribution of *Invisibility and Influence* is to place Black studies' concepts and theories into conversation with Latinx Studies and Caribbean studies, as Lao-Montes and Jossianna Arroyo have suggested, respectively.[40] Latinx studies in particular has much to gain by paying more attention to diaspora Blackness within Latin America and North America. I integrate AfroLatinx life writing into the idiom of visibility, invisibility, and hypervisibility, one that has been especially strong in Black studies (e.g., Nicole Fleetwood, Audre Lorde) and US–Central American studies (e.g., Arturo Arias, Claudia Milian, and Yajaira Padilla). I build from the work of Urayoán Noel's study of Nuyorican poetry, which also thinks beyond the binary of invisibility and visibility,[41] as he does with the concept of "*blurred visibility.*"[42]

My study contextualizes mestizaje as a visibility structure, one that AfroLatinx life writing actively negotiates.[43] In fact, Hoy's conception of AfroLatinidad as "negotiating among invisibilities" inflects my focus on the self-conscious and purposeful engagement of visibility narratives.[44] Negotiation entails more than discussion, but the active working through of tension and disagreement. These AfroLatinx life writers work through the tensions of visibility structures like mestizaje. There has been limited scholarship examining mestizaje from a critical, literary studies perspective rather than a social scientific or legal perspective.[45] While there is significant research that shows a debate between the potential good and ill of mestizaje narratives, these life narratives by AfroLatinx people living in the US generally position themselves *against mestizaje* based on their lived experiences.

Lastly, I depend heavily on woman-of-color feminist scholarship, which I believe is foundational to both life writing studies and AfroLatinx studies, including my work in the first three chapters of *Invisibility and Influence*, which are focused primarily on AfroLatino male writers (Arturo Schomburg, Jesús Colón, the Young Lords Party, and Piri Thomas). For example, in discussing Afro–Puerto Rican writer and archivist Arturo Schomburg, thinking through the similarities between him and Afro–Puerto Rican folklorist and librarian Pura Belpré calls attention to the masculinist power structures that have marginalized AfroLatina voices. In addition, this woman-of-color feminist analysis points towards the erasure of the representation of domestic and spiritual realms of AfroLatinx life by AfroLatino male writers. A woman-of-color feminist framework provides insight into the work of writers of all genders and sexualities, as woman-of-color feminism is a comprehensive theory of social existence, and the writing of men can and should be examined through this framework.

Methods and Scholarly Genealogy

This book considers how life writing is a tool for navigating the terms of visibility and its distortions, one which also provides a space to witness the interior and exterior factors that allow for different conceptions of AfroLatinidades to rise and fall. Each chapter illuminates how AfroLatinx life writing negotiates living at the intersection of hypervisibility and invisibility, particularly in the context of dominant and even hegemonic conceptions of mestizaje in Latin America, the Caribbean, and the United States. AfroLatinx hypervisibility is created through white supremacist ideas that highlight skin color, gender, sexuality, and institutional expectations of Brown illegality and Black criminality. AfroLatinx invisibility stems from the repression and erasure of Brown and Black labor, whether it be cultural, economic, physical, or domestic. While AfroLatinxs navigate societal definitions and expectations around Blackness, Latinidad, and other vectors of identity such as class, sexuality, and gender, their life writing reveals how they also shape those definitions. As Lesley Feracho argues, "for the marginalized in particular, the process of self-definition includes a search for tools of empowerment. Among the tools at their disposal, writing serves as a means of reconstructing an identity in which women are subjects, navigating sociocultural and economic forces that objectify them."[46] Through life writing, these AfroLatinx writers—on the margins of US Blackness, Latin American mestizaje, and US Latinidad—make visible erased or denied histories, forces, cultures, and practices. They also strive to be visible on their own terms and to counter distorted images from dominant sources.

While visibility has often been lauded as an uncritical good, critical race and ethnic studies scholarship has often cautioned against this view. More representation does not always equal better representation. Who controls how, when, and to what purpose communities of color are visible? Refusing to be visible can be just as empowering for people of color, AfroLatinx people in particular. The scholarship of Carole Boyce Davies, Saidiya Hartman, Dixa Ramírez, and the Latina Feminist Group, for instance, reflects concerns about whose life stories are told, how legible they are, and why they are being invoked. As Ramírez writes in the Dominican context, "Equally important to being legible and visible have been Dominican strategies of refusal, that is of refusing the terms necessary for their legibility in dominant histories and narratives."[47] At times, scholars argue that AfroLatinxs just want to be seen or to bridge the gap between (US) Black and (white) Latinx communities.[48] But, as Yomaira Figueroa asserts, visibility is not enough and often not even the goal.[49] *Invisibility and Influence* demonstrates how life writers mobilize hypervisibility and invisibility for themselves (for example, in pursuit of African diasporic spirituality) or try to find liberation from constraining forms of visibility based in respectability politics, isolating individuality, or mestizo nationalism.

Black studies and US-Central American studies have provided substantial theorization of the spectrum of visibility, particularly the power of distortion and invisibilization. Audre Lorde said in 1977, "Within this country where racial difference creates a constant, if unspoken, distortion of vision, Black women have on one hand always been highly visible, and so, on the other hand, have been rendered invisible through the depersonalization of racism."[50] In *Troubling Vision*, Nicole Fleetwood argues "that the visible black body is always already troubling to the dominant visual field," and thus declares, "Blackness troubles vision in Western discourse."[51] In US–Central American studies, Claudia Milian has argued that "the theoretical directions and dimensions that mark Central American–Americanness [are] unnameability, invisibility, awkwardness, and off the hyphen status."[52] Arturo Arias's landmark 2003 article on Central American invisibility in the US discussed not only how invisibility was imposed on this community but also how it has been deployed as a "strategic non-identity."[53] These scholars all emphasize both the structuring force of the visibility spectrum as well as how visibility can be a tool used against or in the interest of a particular writer. In AfroLatinx life writing, visibility and invisibility can be a problem to be fixed, a dangerous position, or an opportunity.

In Latinx studies, we should consider mestizaje as a visibility structure that calls attention to and privileges some aspects of ancestry while erasing others. AfroLatinidades trouble the US Black/white binary as well as Latin American and Caribbean notions of hegemonic mestizaje, notions that imagine themselves more tolerant of skin color differences. Mestizaje discourses, particularly in Latin America and the Caribbean, often combine a pseudobiological comment on racial mixture with metaphors of cultural blending or inheritances, usually for nationalist purposes.[54] As Alicia Arrizón argues in her keyword article on the term, *mestizaje* has different meanings in different contexts. However, she also argues that in spaces that experienced Spanish and US colonialism, "it is imperative to understand mestizaje as the product of a history formed by cultural encounters, colonial difference, and the 'whitening' of the Indigenous/Black subordinated colonial subject."[55] In Mexican philosopher and educator José Vasconcelos's *La raza cósmica* [*The Cosmic Race*], mestizaje was represented as racial pillars on which the best of the non-European cultures (African, Indigenous, Asian) could be extracted alongside the supposedly elevated and civilizing nature of European whiteness, to create a national Mexican identity.[56] In this dominant conceptualization of mestizaje, the mestizo represents the best of all cultures. While the idea that a predominantly Spanish mestizo culture, with a few worthwhile African diasporic and Indigenous practices thrown in, represents the best of Latin America has been contested,[57] it still holds substantial power throughout Latin America.[58] US Latinx conceptions of mestizaje replicate some of the Latin American narrative, particularly the focus on Brownness.[59] Chicana feminist conceptions in particular champion the unique nature of Latinx culture and linguistic mixture (as a mixture of Indigenous, Spanish, and at times, African cultures), epitomized by Gloria Anzaldúa's oft-cited "mestiza consciousness."[60] However, those who advocate for mestizaje's utility insist that Latinx mestizaje, sometimes equated with Latinidad,[61] can also be a powerful tool for political solidarity. Whether by defining mestizos as "disenfranchised, marginal, and impure" subjects,[62] or by a shared affect of "feeling brown," or an "ethics of the self" used by people of color "who don't feel quite right within the protocols of normative affect and comportment,"[63] mestizaje becomes a tool of hope, a way to make something good from a shared history of forced and violent mixture, leading to political solidarity against Euro-white oppression in the United States. This, in essence, is what drove the Chicano Movement. Thus, deployments of Chicana/x mestizaje often rely on feelings of "dislocation," "multiple subjectivities," "a persistent oscillation between presence and absence, resistance and capitulation, agency and victimhood, power and fatigue."[64] Rafael Pérez-Torres, through his concept of "critical mestizaje," demonstrates the ways that Chicanxs use the concept to theorize embodiment, politics, and desire not only through race but ideology (like those around gender and sexuality).[65] However, even in a panethnic Latinx context, mestizaje as "Latino exceptionalism," as Miriam Jiménez Román phrases it, posits Latinos as exceptional (both ideologically and racially) but also acts to exempt them from racialized prejudice or discrimination.[66]

Advocates of mestizaje are rarely able to sufficiently theorize the place of African (or Asian) diasporic realities in their conceptions. The anti-Blackness of mestizaje and Latinidad has been increasingly well documented by AfroLatinx studies scholars.[67] Therefore, I use the term *mestizaje* with its extractive nature, focus on the Spanish/Indigenous conflict, and colonial power inequities at the fore. As Lourdes Martínez-Echazábal writes,

> the idea of mestizaje or transculturation was and is guided by the dictates of power. If we agree that "culture" acts as a form of institutional power, then the alleged exchange and mutual assimilation (whether culturally, psychological, racial, or all of the above) between colonizer and colonized, exploiter and exploited, rich and poor, European and non-European, East and West, or North and South can never be true transculturation, for such relations will always be mediated by privilege and assigned value.[68]

I evoke mestizaje to point to its limits. The AfroLatinidades that this book examines make visible the lie that mestizaje is a give-and-take mixing of colonized and colonizer culture, since this is no more grounded in historical reality than the one-drop rule was in the US South. Mestizaje (and related labels like "ladino," "racial democracy," and "racial inclusion") claims to make visible the multiethnic and multiracial roots of Latin America but does so by imagining those ethnic and racial foundations as part of an imagined Latin American past and not the present.[69] As Pérez-Torres writes, "the social and historical exigencies of the mestizo body bind it to the inequitable discourses about racial, class, gender, and sexual hierarchies," which limits its transformative potential.[70] If that is the case, then AfroLatinx life writing emphasizes these limits and refuses to recuperate mestizaje as a saving grace. Both the US refusal to see beyond a Black/white binary, and the Latin American and Caribbean blindness to the clear social, political, and economic realities that privilege whiteness are distorted visions that erase the systems of power that determine narratives of racialization.[71] In defining AfroLatinidades as negotiations of traits, practices, and experiences that distort one's visibility through exaggeration or erasure, I argue that the writers in this book use life writing to take control over how they are seen. In their writing, white supremacy in the United States, Caribbean, and Latin America leads to conditions of hypervisibility and invisibility, as does religion, sexuality, gender, and radicalism. Michel-Rolph Trouillot declares in *Silencing the Past* that "the ultimate mark of power may be its invisibility."[72] These writers, through naming these conditions of visibility, also make visible the structures of power and oppression that others ignore.

Some of the power structures that these AfroLatinx life writing texts grapple with include the "heroic men" tradition of biography, mestizaje, masculinism and heterosexism, and religion. Their choice of the life narrative medium also reflects their concern for the connection between content and form. In this way, many of the texts examined in *Invisibility and Influence* align with the definition of testimonio. Most testimonios are acts of collaboration and translation, whether from Spanish or an Indigenous language to English or from the context of the past to the present. Through a testimonio,[73] as defined by Sidonie Smith and Julia Watson, "the narrator intends to communicate the situation of a group's oppression, struggle, or imprisonment, to claim some agency in the act of narrating, and to call on readers to respond actively in judging the crisis."[74] One might argue that US AfroLatinx life writing does not fit the definition of testimonio as it coalesced in 1960s Latin America, because as it is written primarily from US spaces and in English, the authors are not mediated through translators, and nor are they always radicals resisting government oppression.[75] However, institutional structures, archives, ideologies, and sociocultural expectations *do* mediate the writers and their narratives. According to Avery F. Gordon, "as a concept, mediation describes the process that links an institution and an individual, a social structure and a subject, and history and a biography."[76] The Latina Feminist Group, in *Telling to Live*, similarly argue for their work as testimonio.[77] Also anticipating skepticism in using this term, they argue that what makes something testimonio is how content and process mediate each other.[78] The politics of life writing informs the choices of story and discourse, or what a narrative says and how it says it. AfroLatinx life writing is a form of testimonio in that it must mediate power structures that attempt to place it as either Black or Latinx writing, but also in that it must navigate the invisibility and hypervisibility that formal and informal institutions impose on AfroLatinxs.

Discussions of visibility and power are also core concerns of life writing studies as a field. Life writing studies and the term *life writing* itself, which came into popularity in the late 1980s and early 1990s, as Craig Howes notes, is grounded in feminist theory, taking seriously how women without access to the publishing industry have documented their lives.[79] Coming in the wake of work like Gloria Anzaldúa's *Borderlands / La Frontera* (1987) and Audre Lorde's *Sister Outsider* (1984, but including earlier speeches and writings), life writing studies contends that life writing can itself be an act of theorization.[80] That is, life writing is more than the concrete life experience of one person; it represents the shared questions and struggles facing a community of people. The very term "life writing" extends beyond the male-centric limitations of biography/autobiography to life narratives outside of the published mainstream, seeing quasi-public and even private material as life narrative in order to be "more inclusive of the heterogeneity of self-referential practices."[81] However, the Eurocentric lens of academic feminism has rarely allowed scholars to interpret women of color's experience as they do white women's.[82] While notable exceptions exist, such as the work of Joanna Braxton, Jocelyn Moody, and Annette Angela Portillo,[83] feminist life writing studies frequently exemplifies "the assumption that whites provide the theory whereas black women could only provide more examples."[84] As Margaret Homan argues, racialized women's lives are often seen as specific rather than universal and thus cannot be the basis of theoretical abstraction. People of color and particularly woman-of-color feminists, in their own life writing and their analyses of life writing, have long viewed first-person narratives and traces in the archives as acts of theorization. Woman-of-color feminist life writing studies reflects ideals such as the personal as a reflection of communal realities, the refusal to treat men's and cisgender experience as neutral or a preferred norm, the recognition of difference as a wellspring rather than an impediment to connection,[85] and solidarity through difference. My hope is that this book will also help elevate woman-of-color feminist voices within life writing studies as a field.

In choosing life writing as the primary genre through which I examine US AfroLatinx invisibility and influence, I have chosen to engage with a literary form historically questioned for its value in literary studies. Is it a genre at all? Is it self-indulgent? Is it unreliable? The fact that women, enslaved people, independence and sovereignty activists, and marginalized communities have used this category of writing, through publication when possible and desired, and frequently through private or less public means, is central to why those in power have denigrated this category of writing. Despite the rich archive of Black, Latinx, and AfroLatinx life writing and scholarship on life writing, life writing studies is often viewed as a white or Eurocentric critical tradition.[86]

Earlier work in the study of life narrative—when it was known as biography studies, autobiography studies, and later auto/biography studies—was unapologetically Eurocentric and white supremacist, even rejecting the ability of "non-Western" people to create life writing. In 1956, Georges Gusdorf claimed "that autobiography is a uniquely Western genre of life narrative, only possible in a culture with a historical notion of time and a concept of the individual."[87] That is, Gusdorf excluded non-Western people and people of color from this genre, indicating that nonwhite people did not share the cultural beliefs necessary for such writing. This imagining of life narrative, to Gusdorf and his ilk, celebrates exceptional individuals and documents the Great Men of History.[88] His assumption is that the ability "to turn back on one's own past, to recollect one's life in order to narrate it, is not at all universal" for people of color but "seems so natural to us [the 'Western man']."[89] Maureen Perkins and Benjamin Nathans argue that "the belief that 'genuine autobiography' is possible only under certain cognitive preconditions" continues in mainstream life writing studies into the twenty-first century.[90] Thus, the choice of AfroLatinxs to take up life writing, a field in which people of color's writing has sometimes been viewed as inferior or excluded from authentic auto/biography altogether, is a challenge to white supremacist thought. Their challenge stems not from conforming to Great Man theories but rather from these writers' choice to focus on how their stories are part of larger AfroLatinx histories. By using these life stories to claim belonging, rather than to convince others they are a credit to US and Latin American histories, AfroLatinx life writers fill gaps in official histories and paint a portrait of the heterogenous AfroLatinidades that have flourished and continue to do so.

Historically, Latinx studies scholarship on life writing has depended heavily on Chicana feminist mestizaje, namely the work of Gloria Anzaldúa and Cherríe Moraga. In particular, their term "theory in the flesh," discussed in a brief transition between sections in the iconic woman-of-color feminist anthology *This Bridge Called My Back*, has generated substantial scholarship of its own, including an entire edited collection.[91] Theory in the flesh was defined as "where the physical realities of our lives—our skin color, the land or concrete we grew up on, our sexual longings—all fuse to create a politic born out of necessity."[92] This brief description, alongside Anzaldúa's concepts of *autohistoria* and *autohistoria-teoría* (terms whose definitions are easier to find outside of Anzaldúa's writing), often has carried the theoretical weight of Latinx studies work on life narratives. Autohistoria, according to Anzaldúa, is "the story of the self, and the story of the culture," which "brings theory into the personal anecdote."[93] While this framework has been, and continues to be, incredibly powerful for woman-of-color and Chicana and Latina feminists, putting this theory alongside other ideas of theorization through life narrative can strengthen our analysis. This view that life narrative is an act of theorization, as I have shown, is part of a larger scholarly tradition, not only an Anzaldúan concept.

In addition, a narrow focus on Anzaldúa can provide problematic readings of AfroLatina/x writing and experiences.[94] For instance, how mestizaje has been deployed has often erased even Anzaldúa's attempts to highlight colorism within Chicanx communities. While her work certainly could speak more to what she briefly refers to as "afromestizaje" in *Borderlands / La Frontera*,[95] her autohistoria, "La Prieta," also reflects on the preference for whiteness in Tejanx communities, as the first line expresses her Mamagrande's fear that she will find "the sign of indio, or worse, of mulatto blood" on baby Gloria.[96] However, she never returns to or names this anti-Blackness explicitly. Her choice to rarely elaborate on references to anti-Blackness may be why her work has often been mobilized for thinking through a Brown aesthetic and material condition without much thought to how Brownness often imagines itself in anti-Black ways, as Ren Ellis Neyra suggests.[97] Depending primarily on Anzaldúa (and Moraga) can lead to homogenous understandings of Latinx life writing and its political and literary deployment. Indeed, in chapter 5, I analyze Ariana Brown's poetry collection, *We Are Owed.* (2021), which questions Chicana and Latina feminists' tight embrace of Anzaldúa's *Borderlands / La Frontera*,[98] alongside scholarship that questions and revises borderlands theory to speak to AfroLatinx experiences, such as Lorgia García-Peña's *The Borders of Dominicanidad*.

The investment in Chicanx-focused mestizaje makes Chicana feminism alone insufficient as a lens for AfroLatinx life writing, so this book incorporates a broader base of woman-of-color feminist theorists, who similarly consider the blurred lines between life stories and scholarship. Trinh T. Minh-ha, Carole Boyce Davies, and Rosamond King all advocate for interdisciplinary methods that encourage conversations across and within communities of color as a form of resistance against political and theoretical homogenization.[99] Similarly, The Latina Feminist Group's concept of *papelitos guardados* and Carole Boyce Davies's concept of "the collective life story," alongside Anzaldúa's autohistoria-teoría, consider life writing an act of theorization as well as a means of rejecting individualistic or Great Man narratives. Both also emphasize the power of visibility narratives. For example, the Latina Feminist Group uses papelitos guardados to describe their life narrative collection. It is a term with multiple meanings: "protected documents, guarded roles, stored papers, conserved roles, safe papers, secret roles, hidden papers, safe roles, preserved documents, protected roles."[100] In thinking about AfroLatinx life writing as papelitos guardados, one can examine how they reflect on questions of identity, the visibility spectrum and its weaponization, and memory. bell hooks's conception of inhabiting the margins as a radical space embraces discussions of visibility across identities of difference and beyond the body of the text.[101]

One way in which *Invisibility and Influence* embraces marginality is to engage the authors' archives when possible. By looking at drafts of their work, contextual pieces of these authors' lives, and even unpublished memoirs and projects, I demonstrate how even unpublished life writing has provided theorizations of AfroLatinidad and AfroLatina/o/x relationships to US Black, US Latinx, and Latin American communities. What is the relation of invisibility to the margins? Being marginal is a form of visibility, after all. And in some contexts, the reader's marginal marks stand out all the more as commentary, as reflections on an interior. In chapters 1, 2, and 3, the importance of the margins is taken quite literally through the use of archival findings, such as drafts of Piri Thomas's *Down These Mean Streets*. The relative lack of archival material for AfroLatina writers versus AfroLatino writers in my study further proves the masculinism that has dominated conceptions of AfroLatinidad. However, within my examination of AfroLatina writers, I have also seen how these writers have found other archives beyond libraries and universities through which to examine AfroLatina spirituality, heritage and ancestry, and queerness.

Lastly, this is a literary studies project that is concerned with the relationship between content, form, and politics. While scholars such as Ralph E. Rodriguez take to task Latinx literary studies for being more concerned with content over form, this book argues that AfroLatinx authors' creative interventions are made possible only through their engagement with the political, historical, and cultural circumstances surrounding them.[102] Thus, I approach these texts through socioformal analysis, defined by Paula M. L. Moya as literary criticism that attends "to the social dimension of literary form by describing how the thematic and formal features of a text mediate the historically situated cultural and political tensions expressed in a work of literature."[103] One cannot evacuate the politics of AfroLatinx life writing, since those politics also drive the authors' literary choices. In fact, as Barbara Christian declared in "The Race for Theory," "I am inclined to say that our theorizing (and I intentionally use the verb rather than the noun) is often in narrative forms, in the stories we create, in riddles and proverbs, in the play with language, because dynamic rather than fixed ideas seem more to our liking."[104] Here, Christian points to an essential principle of Black feminism: life narrative as theory. The conflation of theory and narrative does not evacuate the lyricism, linguistic playfulness, and experimentation of these stories. AfroLatinx life narratives reflect the dynamism of AfroLatinidades through the choices they make in navigating a sense of self in community, the politics of visibility, and the genres in which they write.

Chapter Summaries

The chapters of *Invisibility and Influence* consider the following questions: How do AfroLatinx writers define and relate to in/visibility and hypervisibility? How does this relation make itself clear through the structure of life stories, the literary and vernacular traditions they employ, and the metaphors by which they compare their journeys to build community and identity? Proceeding in a generally chronological order (starting in the 1910s and ending in 2021), each chapter demonstrates the ways in which AfroLatinx life writers argue against mestizaje, while also offering an alternative view of AfroLatinidad based in literary-political projects. While the first three chapters focus on AfroLatinidades constructed by Afro–Puerto Ricans, the last two chapters and epilogue also highlight life writing by Afro-Cuban, Afro–Mexican American, and Afro-Dominican writers.

While the archival, political, and historical importance of Arturo Alfonso Schomburg's writings are without question, the literary importance of these life writings has been overlooked. Thus, chapter 1, "Arturo Schomburg, Pura Belpré, and the 'Racial Integrity' of Auto/biography," examines the life writing of Arturo Schomburg, the Afro–Puerto Rican bibliophile whose writing spanned the 1910s to the 1930s. I illustrate the ways in which Schomburg's writing negotiated the boundary between history and biography to reject white supremacy and reclaim AfroLatino "racial integrity," while also establishing some literary strategies whose use continued for decades. As a biographer, Schomburg wrote some of the first works published in the US about historically significant Afro-Hispanic and AfroLatino figures and recovered the voices of US Black writers, such as Phillis Wheatley. In addition, his own life often bleeds into these biographies and histories, making some of these works auto/biographical. Using Schomburg's auto/biographical and biographical writings, I argue that Schomburg advocates that Black communities are the foundations of Spain and the Américas, not marginal to them, even if there have been tangible efforts to make those histories invisible. In addition, I consider his recovery work of Phillis Wheatley as well as how his work paralleled that of Pura Belpré, an Afro–Puerto Rican librarian contemporary. Though Belpré's archive is smaller and affected by her time away from the New York Public Library after her marriage, I examine her writing as a way of considering the circumstances that led Schomburg's work to be more visible and studied. This chapter, like chapters 2 and 3, depends on literary analysis of published texts as well as archival findings from the Schomburg Center for Research in Black Culture (SCRBC) and Hunter College's CENTRO, the Center for Puerto Rican Studies.

As I argue in chapter 2, "Jesús Colón, the New York Young Lords, and 'Observe and Participate' Autobiography," for Jesús Colón and the Young Lords, anti-Blackness existed in Puerto Rico long before US imperialism, and that anti-Blackness is in fact what drove (and still drives) Puerto Rico's continued status as a colony. Latin American and US colonialism, through the practice of slavery, as Sherwin Bryant argues, constructed Blackness as an identity incapable of individual or national sovereignty.[105] Thus, in maintaining the importance of dismantling anti-Black attitudes in the continental US and on the island as well as embracing the Blackness of puertorriqueñidad, the Young Lords believed that to fight against US colonialism one had to dismantle anti-Black structures and nationalist stories that erased Black Caribbean influence. The writers examined use life writing to craft Afro–Puerto Rican socialist identities and futures. While Colón's *A Puerto Rican in New York* (1961), and other sketches drawn from his posthumous collection *The Way It Was* (1993), are individual attempts to tell a collective story (and thus, often double down on the male perspective as a universal perspective), the Young Lords' collaborative *Palante: Young Lords Party* (1971) shows the tension between Afro–Puerto Rican masculinist ideas versus Third World feminist ideals in defining Afro–Puerto Rican lives and futures.

Chapter 3, "AfroLatinidad as Creative Destruction: Piri Thomas's Life Writing as a Theorization of Violence," engages violence as an analytic lens through which to negotiate AfroLatino visibility, building on the work of Viet Thanh Nguyen, Saidiya Hartman, and Nicole Guidotti-Hernández. The chapter answers Guidotti-Hernández's call in *Unspeakable Violence* (2010) to examine the victimization and simultaneous complicity of marginalized groups in the violence of identity creation. I contend that Thomas's trilogy memoirs, like those of W. E. B. Du Bois, provide "an autobiography of a[n ethno-]race concept": a personal narrative and sociological reflection on AfroLatino masculinity focused on the shaping power of violence. This chapter depends on the use of archival fragments to delineate Thomas's conception of AfroLatinidad as "creative destruction," which is the lens through which he frames his boyhood struggles to understand his ethnoracial identity and relationship to his father as well as his later enactments of misogynist and antiqueer violence.

While the first three chapters examine the more masculinist models of AfroLatinidades offered by AfroLatino life writers from the 1920s through the 1970s, the final chapters focus on AfroLatina and queer AfroLatinx life writing that rejects and rewrites masculinist models for AfroLatinidades based in spirituality, folklore and monstrosity, and genetic ancestry. In chapter 4, "Call-and-Response AfroLatinidad: Spirituality, Race, and Gender in Marta Moreno Vega's and Lourdes Casal's Life Writing," I discuss AfroLatina authors Marta Moreno Vega and Lourdes Casal, who center domesticity and spirituality to combat the ways their lives are pushed to the periphery. For Moreno Vega and Casal, Yoruba multiplicity and adaptation are celebrated over mixture. As J. Lorand Matory asserts, "the self is the convergence of multiple beings—a manifestation of the ritually engineered balance among those beings,"[106] rather than a mixture that absorbs or rejects only some components. For these AfroLatina writers, diasporic Africanity, and its attendant feminist spirituality (rather than a pure Africanity or a nation-based Blackness), grounds itself in dispersal and the coincidence of the divine and ordinary rather than in a mixture that requires trade-offs, usually in favor of Europe over Africa. Their model is additive. Their relationship to Afrodiasporic religions, mysticism, Christian religions, and espiritismo performs what I term "call-and-response AfroLatinidad." The call-and-response structure of these narratives mirrors espiritista and Lucumi practices (like drumming) and posits AfroLatinidad as a dynamic conversation among ideas of Blackness and Latinidad, rather than a power struggle or mixture.

In chapter 5, "Queer AfroLatinidades: Monstrosity and Reclaiming Black Latinx Girlhood in Jaquira Díaz's *Ordinary Girls* and Ariana Brown's Verse Memoirs," these queer AfroLatinx writers navigate the spectrum of visibility by reckoning with monstrosity, a concept frequently used against queer communities of color. Adopting Saidiya Hartman's concept of "waywardness" as well as monster theory, I illuminate Díaz's conception of queer AfroLatinidad in relation to the legend of La Llorona, true crime stories, and reclamations of Black Latinx girlhood. While Brown's verse memoirs, *Sana Sana* (2020) and *We Are Owed.* (2021), depend on sociohistorical grounding, critical fabulation (per Hartman), and a call for a postnationalist AfroLatinidad, she, too, ultimately calls for Black Latinx girls to find love with one another. Both writers—through Díaz's centering of Afro-Boricua Jaqui and other girls of color's stories and Brown's numerous poems centering a six-year-old Ariana—use the life writing genre to argue for the authority and necessity of queer Black Latinx girls' stories. Díaz and Brown reject Puerto Rican, Tejano, and Mexican narratives of mestizaje and jibaridad, respectively, which have historically painted queer, AfroLatinx women as freaks and monsters. Thus, their AfroLatinidades reclaim monstrosity, rewriting and fleshing out one-dimensional narratives of mythic figures: La Llorona (Díaz) and Gaspar Yanga (A. Brown).

The epilogue concludes *Invisibility and Influence* through an interrogation of Raquel Cepeda's memoir, *Bird of Paradise: How I Became Latina* (2013), and its spiritual sequel, the documentary film *Some Girls* (2017). Cepeda's work, which brings together memoir and commercial DNA-ancestry tests, represents new and challenging questions for the field of life writing studies as well as AfroLatinx studies and critical race studies.

CHAPTER 1

Arturo Schomburg, Pura Belpré, and the "Racial Integrity" of Auto/biography

Introduction

Arturo Alfonso Schomburg (1874–1938) never published a memoir of his own. However, he wrote many biographical essays that often brought his own life and connections to bear. As Marlene Kadar writes, "Life Writing comprises texts that are written by an author who does not continuously write about someone else, and who also does not pretend to be absent from the [Black, Brown, or white] text himself/herself."[1] While Schomburg's essays focused on influential figures, Schomburg himself never pretends to be absent from the text, as he reflects on the process of researching these biographies or on the potential impact that this information could have had on a young Arturo. Schomburg often inserted himself into the biographical essays he wrote, positioning his encounter with archival texts alongside his identity and experiences as an Afro–Puerto Rican in the US and abroad. He blurred the lines between the abstract and concrete as well as the individual and the community, and he challenged definitions of Americanity and Blackness without dismissing the importance of identity and belonging.

Schomburg's importance to Black studies and archival studies is without question. In fact, since I wrote the first version of this chapter in 2017, there has been an explosion of publications on Schomburg.[2] Earlier work by Jossianna Arroyo, Jesse Hoffnung-Garskof, and Adalaine Holton analyzed his Masonic writings as well as his importance as a historian and bibliophile.[3] Lorgia García-Peña, Lisa Sánchez González, and Vanessa K. Valdés have examined his political and archival achievements.[4] García-Peña posits Schomburg as the first to articulate the field of ethnic studies. Sánchez González positions Schomburg's work as a struggle against "paperlessness," the conflict born from colonization and archival erasure. She also argues that we must decolonize the ways in which we study him and recognize his work as part of a tradition with Édouard Glissant and Sylvia Wynter.[5] In Valdés's consideration of representative Schomburg writings as crónicas, she argues that his work is an act of archive building and "the acknowledgement of Afro-Latinx contributions to the hemisphere."[6] This chapter would not be possible without the important contributions on the archival, political, and historical significance of Schomburg's writings. However, my focus is the literary importance and strategies of these life writings, following the work of Holton and Valdés,[7] as well as how these biographical essays illuminate a theory of life writing. I illustrate the ways in which Schomburg's writing negotiated the boundary between history and biography to reject white supremacy and reclaim AfroLatino "racial integrity." Through what I term "auto/biographies of racial integrity," Schomburg weaves his subject-position as an Afro–Puerto Rican man into the supposed objectivity of biographies. In doing so, he argues that white subjectivity masked as neutral observation perpetuates the white supremacist orientation of American biography. Schomburg's life writing also reflects a masculinist bias that has permeated the study of early AfroLatinx writing in the United States.[8]

Before analyzing Schomburg in more detail, I want to begin with an Afro-Boricua contemporary of Schomburg: Pura Belpré. The limited scholarship that exists on Belpré focuses on her trailblazing work as a children's librarian—which advocated strongly for bilingualism and Spanish-language programming—and her folktales for youth. In Belpré's writing for children, Lisa Sánchez González argues, Belpré avers both the innocence of children and their desire to know that who they are and where they come from are valuable.[9] She was not writing for historical associations or professors but rather for Puerto Rican children and children of color generally who faced the deprecation of their cultures at every turn.[10] While Belpré was focused on the local as a way of making systemic changes, Schomburg was focused on the global. His creation of what would become one of the largest and most influential collections of African diaspora art, literature, history, and cultural objects reflects that diasporic mindset but also the realities of his life as an AfroLatino man, which afforded him certain privileges and access not available to women like Belpré.[11] Sánchez González's biography of Belpré suggests that her career and writing were hampered by her marriage in 1943. For example, while Belpré claims to have had plenty of time to write, Sánchez González notes that she published little during her two decades outside the workforce.[12] This could have been because of her decision, encouraged by her husband, to leave the New York Public Library (NYPL), or perhaps because publishers were less eager to publish her work at that time, which focused on Puerto Rican girl protagonists.[13] Either way, the fact that there has been wider (if still not wide) focus on Arturo Schomburg reflects the gendered prejudice and discrimination that makes finding AfroLatina life writing and scholars of the time period especially difficult. Belpré's experience reflects the societal limitations imposed on (and expected of) Afro–Puerto Rican women, as well as the lack of opportunities afforded to them. While she wrote essays "often composed in the vein of memoir,"[14] these were not published, and in fact, the essays I will discuss here were likely written in the 1960s and 1970s, far after Schomburg's time.[15] However, much of this writing reflects on Belpré's experiences during the 1920s to mid-1940s in addition to her return to library work in the 1960s, which lasted until her death in 1982.

While Belpré's work as a librarian, purveyor of Puerto Rican folklore, and children's advocate have begun to come to the fore through the work of Sánchez González, Victoria Núñez, and Marilisa Jiménez García, the auto/biographical aspect of her work, particularly her essays, has been underexplored. Thanks to the work of Sánchez González, a treasure trove of published (but previously difficult to find) and unpublished works have been made available in the collection *The Stories I Read to Children* (2013).[16] As Jiménez García argues in her recent work on the connection between children's literature and US empire in Puerto Rico, one should examine Schomburg alongside Belpré, as they were contemporaries (though Schomburg died younger and decades earlier, in 1938).[17] Further, Jiménez García asserts that Belpré and Schomburg are "the AfroLatinx foundations" of youth literature.[18] However, Belpré's auto/biographical work, as Sánchez González argues, does not announce itself as an Afro-diasporic project the way that Schomburg's does.[19] Her dependence on folklore often propagated mestizaje narratives and "mythic versions of cultural fusion."[20] However, I begin here with a close reading of a selection of Belpré's auto/biographical work, because while she does often align with a mestizaje discourse that fails to meaningfully incorporate the influence of Africanity, she uses a similar strategy to Arturo Schomburg in these essays: the insertion of her own feeling of erasure as an entry point to counteract that erasure.

Belpré's experience as an Afro–Puerto Rican woman in the white-dominated worlds of libraries and folklore displays itself through her writing's focus on visibility and naming. As Sánchez González argues in "Pura Belpré: Her Life in Pictures,"[21] Belpré, like Schomburg and Jesús Colón (another contemporary), was "a darker shade of brown, and therefore must have suffered racialized discrimination not only in the larger US society but also within the Puerto Rican community itself."[22] Like Schomburg, Belpré reflected a "tradition of Afro-Boricua literacy, autodidactism, and community-based education, in the face of racial discrimination and erasure."[23] In addition, while she may not have a center named after her, Belpré's work, subsumed under the monolithic name of the New York Public Library, certainly influenced the representation of Puerto Ricans, Black and white, as well as multiracial and multilingual communities throughout the city. For example, while Belpré often forwarded Puerto Rican culture as a mixture of Spanish, Taíno, and African cultures,[24] she frequently did so in ways that highlighted the nonwhiteness of Spain and Puerto Rico. For example, in "The Folklore of the Puerto Rican Child," her description of Puerto Rican folklore names Spain's history of occupation and multiculturalism, which speaks aloud a North African history often unspoken.[25] She declares, "Just as Spain is one of the important sources of our folklore, so is Africa."[26] Schomburg similarly points to this history of African presence in Spain, in his essay "In Quest of Juan de Pareja," discussed later in this chapter.

The importance of seeing herself in institutions recurs in her auto/biographical writing. In "The Art of Writing for Children" (undated), she begins with an anecdote: as part of her training as a children's librarian, she read all the fairy tales on the shelves and recalls the heartbreak she felt when she found no Puerto Rican folktales or representation.[27] This structure of an anecdote of invisibility mirrors Schomburg's introduction to "José Campeche 1752–1809," in which Schomburg similarly reflects on the "conspiracy of silence" regarding the Afro–Puerto Rican painter. Both authors insert themselves and the moment in which they recognized the erasure or forced invisibility of their culture. While Belpré does not name Blackness as an explanation as Schomburg does in his essay, it is reasonable to believe that she is aware of the ethnoracial dimension of this erasure. For example, while brief, an undated archival fragment that Sánchez González titles "Fragment on Racism and Children's Fiction" demonstrates Belpré's concern for the depiction of race and racism in children's literature. She mentions excluding books from bibliographies for classrooms if they are "marred by racial slurs." This is not limited solely to the N-word but also the use of slurs to demean Black children's hair.[28] Her curatorial work as a librarian and her auto/biographical writing recognized the multifaceted machinations of white supremacy. Belpré's "The Art of Writing for Children," like Schomburg's essay on Campeche, identifies institutional invisibilization of Puerto Rican culture and then acts to counter this invisibility. While the rest of this chapter focuses on Schomburg and his auto/biographical approach to recording AfroLatinx and hemispheric Black life, I want to emphasize the impact that Belpré made on Puerto Rican folklore and children's literature. Due to her position as an Afro–Puerto Rican woman librarian and writer, Belpré's influence cannot be *under*stated and yet, due to scholarly and archival practices that privilege men, it often has. Nevertheless, Belpré and Schomburg's rhetorical move—calling attention to moments of erasure—suggests a shared concern of early twentieth-century AfroLatinos/as that helped drive the construction of an AfroLatinidad focused on a celebratory visibility.[29] Auto/biographies of racial integrity like "The Art of Writing for Children" negotiate the boundary between history and biography to reject white supremacy and fight for the inclusion of AfroLatino/a voices in US and hemispheric American history.

White Biography, Black Biography: Schomburg's Negotiation of Competing American Traditions

Schomburg's writing responded to US white and Black Americans' attempts to define an American tradition of biography, a literary conflict waged from the 1850s through the Harlem Renaissance. Early works, like Ralph Waldo Emerson's biographical collection *Representative Men* (1850) and Benjamin Franklin's perpetually-in-progress autobiography, *The Autobiography of Benjamin Franklin* (1771–1790), attempted to establish what it meant to be American and the values that American life writing should hold. US Black historians and writers were also creating their own histories, biographies, and autobiographical pieces to counter Eurocentric and white supremacist definitions of Americanness and to craft a Black American tradition of auto/biography and history. Such works included Martin Delany's *The Condition, Elevation, Emigration, and Destiny of the Colored People of the United States* (1852), William Wells Brown's *The Black Man: His Antecedents, His Genius, and His Achievements* (1863), Pauline Hopkins's series *Famous Men of the Negro Race* (1900–1901), the work of Schomburg's mentor John Edward Bruce (namely "The Making of a Race" [1922]), Carter G. Woodson's *The Negro in Our History* (1922) and *Negro Makers of History* (1928), and W. E. B. Du Bois's *The Negro* (1915) and *The Gift of Black Folk* (1924).[30] As Scott E. Casper notes, "commercial publishers and religious tract societies produced hundreds of book-length biographies every year from the 1830s on."[31] These collections generally held up individuals as exemplars of a national or racial character.[32]

While never writing a full-length autobiography or any biographical collections, like the above scholars did, Schomburg published essays in important publications of the day serving Black readers, such as *The Crisis* and *Opportunity*, from the early 1910s through the 1930s. These readers were often imagined as male; for example, the editorial page of *The Crisis*, the official publication of the NAACP, averred it would "stand for the rights of men, irrespective of color or race."[33] However, as Valdés notes, the two venues had very different approaches to the issues that Black people faced, as represented through the "catastrophic" *Crisis* and the "decidedly more optimistic" *Opportunity*.[34] In fact, Schomburg's earlier writing would appear more frequently in *The Crisis*, while his later work appeared more in the National Urban League's *Opportunity*. Neither venue was a purely academic one (unlike Woodson's *Journal of Negro History*, for example), and his choice to publish in these more popular sources shows his dedication to making knowledge of the achievements of Black men accessible to all.[35]

Schomburg's auto/biographies of racial integrity look to expand American biography beyond US whiteness and US Blackness to a hemispheric Americanness that recognized influential Afro-Hispanic and AfroLatino figures alongside other Great Black Men (and a few women). This chapter shows the ways in which Schomburg's Afro–Puerto Rican identity influenced and structured his writing and how he attempted to influence how the genre represented race, culture, and transnationalism. His writings also reflect what Cathy Park Hong entitles "minor feelings," a concept grounded in visibility and perception, since, as she writes, "it's clear that *how* I am perceived inheres to *who* I am."[36] Schomburg writes always through perception, through the "triple-consciousness" of US Black, white Latinx, and white EuroAmericans,[37] recognizing how historical and biographical narratives by non-AfroLatinos determine AfroLatino visibility and recognition (or in this case, erasure). As Hong writes about how she "struggled to prove myself into existence,"[38] Schomburg, too, engages life narratives to counter AfroLatino/a invisibility and prove AfroLatino/a existence. His auto/biographies of racial integrity use both his own exceptional life and the life of other Afro-diasporic people "to move beyond the stereotypes [and] express [his] inner consciousness."[39] Through these sketches of exceptional AfroLatino lives, Schomburg wishes to combat stereotypes and present his own Afro–Puerto Rican experience.

Through the insertion of his own life experiences, his use of archival documents that centered Black voices (such as court testimony from the Boston Massacre trial), strategic appeals to white authority, and reversing linguistic and narrative expectations around race, Schomburg developed an AfroLatino auto/biographical tradition distinct from US Black and US white traditions. Like other masculinist conceptions of AfroLatinidad would do (see chapter 2), Schomburg identified Afro-diasporic communities as reflective of the American revolutionary spirit. For Schomburg, Crispus Attucks was the first American revolutionary. However, Schomburg also recovered and collected the work of Afro-diasporic women and, I argue, forwarded Phillis Wheatley as the progenitor of American poetry. Schomburg's auto/biographies of racial integrity identify Africanity as the foundation of a hemispheric American literature and history.

From the nineteenth century to the present, many have argued, as Scott E. Casper puts it, that "biographies were not good literature and they were bad history."[40] The scholarly study of biography has either been denigrated, as biography is not "real" literature, or based in conservative values. As Casper notes, "biography had a double-edged relationship with *history*" that could "reinforce larger master narratives" or challenge them.[41] Craig Howes points to the history of biography studies, and the defenders of biography, as directly in opposition to life writing studies. These scholars tend to see life writing studies as ideologically driven, an extension of feminist studies. Defenders of biography still tout the supposed objectivity of the genre, more in line with history than literature.[42] For Casper, lack of attention to biography is because "nothing about it seems subversive. It seems the paramount genre of dominant liberal individualism and self-made manhood, the genre *against* which women's or working-class fiction protested."[43] In thinking of life writing as a critical practice, Kadar appears to exclude most biographies, suggesting perhaps that the "auto" of autobiography is central to life writing studies.[44] While Casper recognizes that indeed there have been subversive uses of biography, he does not trace this history. I view Schomburg's biographical essays as a genre that straddles this line of the great-man liberal individualist model of biography and the subversive tradition that protests it.

Born a year after the 1873 abolition of slavery in Puerto Rico,[45] Schomburg came to New York City at the age of seventeen, in 1891.[46] Schomburg was an active part of the Antillean independence movement,[47] collaborating with other Puerto Ricans and Cubans against Spanish colonialism and cofounding the Las Dos Antillas (the Two Antilles) political club. However, this revolutionary movement fell away in 1898, when the United States took control of Puerto Rico and Cuba.[48] In 1901, the Insular Cases were decided by the US Supreme Court, making Puerto Rico into an "unincorporated territory," or, to borrow from Marcelo Svirsky and Simone Bignall, a "colonial state of exception."[49] Schomburg was a stalwart supporter of Puerto Rican independence, though he also wrote articles that supported American intervention in Panamá and Cuba.[50] In 1917, the US granted Puerto Ricans a liminal US citizenship with the freedom to migrate between the island and the continental United States (often referred to as "the mainland") and, if they were in the continental US, to vote. Schomburg lived in New York City

(Harlem and Brooklyn) after his migration, becoming an integral part of the culture and community for US Black and Afro-Caribbean people.

Schomburg devoted his life to studying, collecting, and writing African diasporic history. He was a member of two major historical associations, the American Negro Academy (ANA) and the Negro Society for Historical Research (NSHR); he was the president of the former and cofounder of the latter. Both societies limited membership (to fifty and twenty members, respectively) and excluded women. In both associations, Schomburg's focus on AfroLatino and Afro-Hispanic history made him an anomaly. According to Schomburg biographer Elinor Des Verney Sinnette, "Schomburg was the only presenter before the American Negro Academy who consistently reminded the membership of the role of blacks in Spain, Central America, and the West Indies."[51] The NSHR focused on building a collection of Afrodiasporic materials, and unlike other Black history organizations, was open to lay historians and community intellectuals.[52] As Adalaine Holton argues, Schomburg believed "an archive of black history [was] vital to Afrodiasporic subjectivity and the future of Afrodiasporic peoples."[53] In 1926, Schomburg sold his impressive collection of over ten thousand books, manuscripts, images, art, newspapers, and other materials to the New York Public Library. This material was housed in the 135th Street Branch of the NYPL as the Schomburg Collection.[54] Schomburg remained in association with and, for a time, employed by the NYPL, continuing to build the collection until his death in 1938. The building was renamed the Schomburg Center for Research in Black Culture in 1972 and designated as one of four NYPL research libraries.

In his day and in the scholarly debate about his life that followed, Schomburg's identity and his community commitments have been continually dissected.[55] As Valdés notes, this dissection usually tries to "make sense of his interest in black history."[56] Historically, Schomburg has been known primarily for this Harlem Renaissance bibliophile role and, inaccurately, for having interests aligned primarily with US Black people. But Schomburg's Afro–Puerto Rican identity was never a secret, even if friends and scholars have continually questioned his Blackness and puertorriqueñidad. As reported by Sinnette, his mentor Bruce asserted that Schomburg was not as Black as other Black Americans, calling him a "half-breed" with "dual minds" who did not "think as black" as important Black historians, such as Alexander Crummell.[57] The scholar Winston James made the opposite claim, arguing that Schomburg "actively supported and identified with black nationalist aspirations, and with the struggle of African-Americans."[58] The Afro–Puerto Rican feminist Angela Jorge, in a footnote to her important tract on the place of Afro–Puerto Ricans in the feminist movement, offers Schomburg as an example of a Black Puerto Rican "lost to the Puerto Rican community." The note, like most writing on Schomburg, contradicts itself, suggesting that he joined the Black community but also "continued to identify with the Puerto Rican community." Ultimately, she blames Schomburg's invisibility on Puerto Ricans who have not historically "claimed" him.[59] Fortunately, recent work in AfroLatinx studies has begun to provide us a richer picture of Schomburg's life and his political, cultural, and intellectual investments.[60] Rather than arguing that Schomburg was "more" Black than Puerto Rican or vice versa, this chapter focuses on how Schomburg's life writing navigated the spectrum of invisibility and hypervisibility. Through essays that mix the biographical and autobiographical, Schomburg argues for the importance of his migrant Black Latino identity to his theorization of life writing and his strategies for depicting marginalized Afro-diasporic figures.

I first examine Schomburg's theorizations of Black history and biography, focusing specifically on his iconic speech to teachers on the need for Black history, specifically an endowed chair for Black history, and his essay in *Survey Graphic*, later reprinted in Alain Locke's *The New Negro* (1925). I read his speech as a revision of, rather than revolution against, the genres of history and biography as they had been defined by white scholars at the time. In the final section, I look at the ways in which Arturo Schomburg developed "auto/biographies of racial integrity." Through these auto/biographies, Schomburg revised late British colonial and early American history to put African subjects at their center. He establishes Phillis Wheatley as the first American poet and restores agency and influence to Crispus Attucks and the Black men who testified against the soldiers who committed the Boston Massacre, making Afro-diasporic Blackness central to the American revolutionary spirit. Furthermore, his narratives reclaim AfroLatino and Afro-Hispanic excellence by inserting AfroLatino men into the Great Man narrative of history and integrating race pride with archival research.

Schomburg Theorizing Black History and Biography

Much of Schomburg's thinking about his connection to a hemispheric Black history was reflected in his biographical essays and recollections of archival encounters. As Adalaine Holton argues, Schomburg anticipated what Antoinette Burton calls "archive stories," or narratives about how historians encounter, create, and experience archives.[61] In fact, in several auto/biographies, Schomburg places himself and his joy of discovery at the center of the narrative. As Barbara Caine notes, the term *auto/biography* uses the slash to visually indicate the blurred lines between the life being written about and the connections and investments of the biographer.[62] As Sánchez González posits, "[Schomburg's] essays always negotiate the historical 'we,' the meta-critical third person, and his own personal involvement with the issues, figures, and histories he discusses."[63] Thus, I use the terminology of *auto/biography* to reflect Schomburg's proud insertion of his own subjective experience into his essays about objective historical figures and events.[64] That is, these biographies are always also autobiographical and forward his subjective experiences in the archive in order to center the Black archivist subject and call attention to the emotional and biographical frames that determine our encounters with the archive.

Schomburg sets out his theory of biography and history most clearly in his celebrated July 1913 lecture to "the Teachers' Summer class at Cheney Institute," entitled "Racial Integrity: A Plea for the Establishment of a Chair of Negro History in Our Schools and Colleges, etc.," which was published soon after by the NSHR. As Margarita Castromán Soto notes, "Racial Integrity" has been analyzed far less than Schomburg's "The Negro Digs Up His Past" in *The New Negro*. She writes, "Curiously, this earlier essay—less beholden to dominant intellectual trends like New Negro ideology—theorizes archival approaches that are more tightly aligned with Schomburg's actual practice than the essay for which we know him best."[65] Castromán Soto identifies "Racial Integrity" as the origin of the "Black archival turn" and makes a compelling argument for the essay's thoughtful development of the archive as and beyond repository.[66] In my analysis, I will treat the essay as a theorization of the use of auto/biography towards a hemispheric Blackness and the construction of an AfroLatinidad of celebratory visibility.

"Racial Integrity" argues for the creation of Black studies programs that allow Afro-diasporic people to create their own archives and knowledge rather than depending on the current status quo, which privileges race pride histories with little documentation. Schomburg walks the line between a radical overhaul of current historiographical methods and dependence on current standards of historical evidence. Regarding the purpose of his paper in the field of history and biography, Schomburg states, "The object of this paper is not to revolutionize existing standards, but simply to improve them by amending them." Rather than revolutionizing, he wants "the practical history of the Negro Race, from the dawn of civilization to the present time" to be incorporated into history.[67] In situating his plea for Black history, Schomburg suggests that Black history could be added to the dominant historical narrative as it had been written by white scholars. This would appear to encourage an "inclusion" model of Afro-diasporic history, where Black-created histories could be included with white-created histories. However, at the same time, he realizes that white historians' work has primarily created narratives more concerned with maintaining white supremacy than providing human histories. Indeed, he suggests that the current "histories" only really work when telling the stories of white people and "bear no analogy to our [African-descended people's] own"; thus, it is imperative to build "a course of study in Negro History and achievements" that speaks to students of African descent.[68] Schomburg makes a similar argument to begin "The Negro Digs Up His Past," stating, "The American Negro must remake his past in order to make his future."[69] To remake the past, he—as Schomburg's vision is decidedly masculine—must revise the genre of biography, with certain underlying ideologies.[70] Schomburg advocates for a Black history curriculum and for institutional support for Black scholars and scholarship, particularly because he believed that the current history of Afro-diasporic people was woefully understudied and misrepresented due to its domination by white scholars and white supremacist ideology.

Schomburg describes his own approach to history and biography as one that "will inspire us [African-descended people] to racial integrity" and counter these white supremacist histories.[71] In his speech, he defines "racial integrity" in the context of the achievement and historical struggle of Jewish people. He writes, "We need it [racial integrity] more than the Jews who though not a practical nation, live in theory a nation of most powerful intellects. They live on the very groups of nations who destroyed them; and this concentration of force, energy, power and vitality has made them a combination of forces to be relied on." That is, he calls to the resilience of Jewish peoples to maintain their culture, language, and histories in the face of unceasing attempts at erasure. In following their example, Schomburg argues that Afro-descendents must "cling to their customs and traditions, no matter where they live" whether it be in "Timbuctoo" (Mali in West Africa) or South America ("the Andean mountains").[72] This vision is decidedly hemispheric, including Afro–Latin American contributions. He advocates a history of Afro-diasporic people *by* Afro-diasporic people, "written by our men and women."[73] He asks, "Where is our historian to give us, [sic] our side view and our chair of Negro History to teach our people our own history. We are at the mercy of the 'flotsam and jetsam' of the white writers."[74] In describing the work of white writers as trash, floating in the sea, Schomburg suggests that these white historians' work is anchored in nothing; it is under-researched garbage far from the realities of Afro-diasporic life. Schomburg, however, does not argue that access to elite education is needed to counter the trash bin of history. He emphasizes that these new historians must come from all classes and backgrounds, and that one must not depend solely on the elite to revise and make visible this expansive Black history.[75] This statement is also an act of projection that reflects Schomburg's own self-directed training as an archivist, collector, and writer. Beyond access to educational institutions, Schomburg suggests that restoring the "racial integrity" of the genre of biography means expanding not only the class backgrounds of Black historians but also showcasing the heterogeneity of Black experiences. Valdés defines Schomburg's use of "racial integrity" as "a conception whereby peoples of African descent achieve a sense of unification, as opposed to fragmentation and division."[76] My own definition diverges slightly from this; while I agree that Schomburg's auto/biographies of racial integrity seek Afro-diasporic unification, it is not in opposition to fragmentation. Indeed, Schomburg celebrates the heterogeneity of Blackness and asks readers to think about how we connect through difference. Like Gloria Anzaldúa's conception of the mosaic or Audre Lorde's advocacy of difference as a wellspring rather than obstacle,[77] auto/biographies of racial integrity celebrate the distinct history of Afro-Hispanic, AfroLatino, and other Afro-diasporic communities.

Schomburg saw the act of recovery work, particularly in the field of biography, as a natural and healthy urge for those in the marginalized and misrepresented field of Black history. In an unpublished biography on Cyrille Charles Auguste Bissette, Schomburg writes, "It is natural that an enthusiast about a relatively unknown writer should come to feel that the influence of the man about whom he is concerned has been unduly minimised. It is equally natural that he should set about to rectify the historical injustice by demonstrating the influence of his subject upon the future development of ideas."[78] By establishing his anger as natural, rather than an impediment to objectivity, Schomburg establishes the auto/biography of racial integrity as an expected response to marginalization and oppression—a corrective to history produced through the lens of white supremacy. In doing so, he hoped to provide the intellectual basis to address the erasure of Black achievement, render visible Black influence, and imagine Black and AfroLatino history that did not revolve around whiteness.

Schomburg's auto/biographical essays often focus on men in war, religion, or fine arts (e.g., painting), areas that have often privileged men and excluded women. However, his unpublished work also recognized that African diasporic biography had to extend beyond those realms. For example, in a proposal for an unpublished cookbook of the African diaspora, Schomburg includes not only the recipes but the people who made, and made famous, those recipes.[79] The book is equal parts cookbook and biography of

Afro-diasporic cooks in history.[80] He states as its purpose: "To include personality sketches of many other famous Negro cooks—past and present—[. . .] To show that the well-known colored cooks are exceptional partly because their names are known whereas the true creative impulse as in all folk arts, is vested in anonymous thousands."[81] This stated purpose reflects a desire to lift up the names of Black chefs marginalized by the white cooking and publishing world. It also promises that doing so reflects the larger "creative impulse" of Afro-diasporic communities, imagining it as a kind of folk art. Schomburg hopes that these "sketches" (a term Afro–Puerto Rican communist Jesús Colón would use for his own memoir in 1961) will provide the contours of the larger contributions of the Black diaspora. To reappropriate Flor Piñeiro de Rivera's assertion about the Schomburg Center for Research in Black Culture, Schomburg's auto/biographical writing and his contribution to the fields of history and biography are "a monument to Africanness, to Americanness in its hemispheric sense, to Caribbeanness, and to Puerto Ricanness."[82] In his auto/biographies, Schomburg brings an AfroLatino aesthetic and lens to the genre, even when not writing specifically about AfroLatino and Afro-Hispanic subjects.

Schomburg's Auto/biographies of "Racial Integrity"

The auto/biography of racial integrity is a set of practices and structures that unites Schomburg's writing. These practices argue that Africanity is constitutive of Americanity—predating Toni Morrison's similar claim in *Playing in the Dark* (1992)—and highlight AfroLatino and Afro-Hispanic excellence. Schomburg ties subjectivity ("racial patriotism"[83]) with objectivity (facts), using the Great Man narrative of history. Schomburg's conception of AfroLatinidad, I contend, was not tied entirely to his Afro–Puerto Rican identity but to a larger sense of connectedness among people of African descent in the Hispanophone Caribbean and the Americas. The auto/biography of racial integrity finds Afro-diasporic connection through difference, but also works to render visible Black influence (particularly AfroLatino and Afro-Hispanic) that has been denied in white histories.

Revising America's Beginnings

Schomburg intricately weaves his subject-position as an Afro–Puerto Rican man into his mission to restore global Black narratives. His work critiques biographies and histories that centered whiteness and subscribed to white supremacist notions of savagery and civilization. In his own auto/biographical essays, Schomburg embraces subjectivity and the work it does for the writer and reader of Afro-diasporic life writing, in line with many woman-of-color feminist ideals that question the objectiveness of objectivity and encourage the inclusion of individual experience and emotion.[84] For example, in "Racial Integrity," Schomburg describes slave narratives as "a collection of facts mingled with pain,"[85] but he does so without denigrating the necessity of these emotions and in fact describes them as "invaluable." Schomburg's writing on colonial North America leading up to the American Revolution often depends on primary sources and expert testimony but also rethinks America's beginnings for the purpose of advancing Black civil rights and includes his own "candor and pathos."[86] Through his writing on Phillis Wheatley and Crispus Attucks, Schomburg highlights the foundational Africanity of American literature and the American spirit.

In his introduction to a reprinting of Wheatley's *Poems and Letters* (1915), Schomburg conjectures that Wheatley is the progenitor of American poetry and thus implies that the experience of enslaved Black people in the Americas is foundational to American literature.[87] Schomburg has often been credited for recovering Phillis Wheatley's poetry, and he worked diligently to track down copies of her published work and to collect pieces that Wheatley had owned.[88] In his "An Appreciation," which prefaces Wheatley's poetry collection, Schomburg makes an argument similar to that presented by Toni Morrison in her seminal work of literary criticism, *Playing in the Dark*. Morrison argues that "a real or fabricated Africanist presence was crucial to [white American authors'] sense of Americanness."[89] Africanism is, for Morrison, a constructed Black presence used as a means for white writers to explore "the terror of freedom."[90] For citizens of the young United States, the Black population was a "surrogate" for exploring issues of human freedom, even as Black people legally lacked full humanity in the American imagination.[91] Schomburg, on the other hand, looks at an African woman's use of poetry, particularly poetry patronized and supported by British colonizers, in order to point towards the African beginnings of the American literary tradition rather than offer insight into white exploration of American identity. Schomburg pretends to offer no opinion of his own (strange for what is explicitly named "an appreciation"), saying that he "offer[s] no defense as to the merits of Phillis Wheatley's poems" and instead offers the reader the opinions of several commentators including such white canonical figures as Thomas Jefferson.[92] Despite his claims to the contrary, he uses these experts to craft the argument that Phillis Wheatley, an enslaved African woman, shaped an American literary identity at a time when "American literature was in its swaddling clothes" and under attack as a pale imitation of British literature.[93] Schomburg does not go so far as to explicitly claim Wheatley's supreme status as the first great American poet, due partly to the fact that she published her first works before the official establishment of the United States, through a British press. However, Schomburg strongly asserts that "[her] poetry was as good as the best American poetry of her age."[94] Schomburg's title, "An Appreciation," reflects the two purposes of this biography. The term *appreciation* itself has multiple meanings: one is to recognize or give thanks to. In this essay, Schomburg gives thanks to Wheatley's poetic contributions. However, another meaning is to increase in value, such as when a stock appreciates in value. Thus, by prefacing his work in this way, he does more than take a humble stance, he also makes an argument: that Phillis Wheatley's poetry has only grown in value. That from this African poet, American poetry could spring. Schomburg's championing of Wheatley's work also shows that while he imagined the hemispheric Black historian as male, he recognized the role of men *and* women in this history.

Similarly, in "Crispus Attucks—Free Patriot," published in the *New York Amsterdam News* in 1935, Schomburg restores Black voices to a key story of the American Revolution—the Boston Massacre.[95] Like *The Crisis* and *Opportunity*, this venue was (and is) a Black-owned and -operated newspaper with a storied history that, at the time, served a large readership of Black and other people of color throughout the United States.[96] In this article, Schomburg uses historical documents to establish Attucks's status as a "mulatto" seaman from the West Indies, and he includes Black men's testimony in court as his central evidence, rather than the work of white historians. In doing so, Schomburg makes apparent the Afro-Caribbean foundations of the American revolutionary spirit and shows that Black men crafted the legal narrative of what occurred at the Boston Massacre. First, he deduces Crispus Attucks's origins in Nassau, Bahamas, arguing against claims by white historians that Attucks was a fugitive slave and instead portrays him as a world traveler building capital for the British empire.[97] Halfway through the article, Schomburg includes the testimonies of "Newton Prince a free Negro," "Andrew," and "Cato" (the latter two were servants) against the British soldiers in their murder trial. Indeed, Schomburg uses the respected testimony of these three Black men to counter the judgment of Chief Supreme Court Justice Roger B. Taney, who infamously wrote in the *Scott v. Sanford* decision that "the African race" "had no rights which the white man was bound to respect."[98] Schomburg makes this explicit when he praises that the English judges, "unlike Chief Justice Taney, did not rule they [the Black witnesses] had no right anybody was bound to respect."[99] He provides the word-for-word testimony of these Black men—the actual interrogation by the lawyer to the witnesses, with little to no editing. For example, "Andrew, Mr. Oliver Wendell's servant" is asked, "Q. 'Do you know who this stout man was that fell in and struck the Grenadier?' A. 'I thought, and still think it was the mulatto who was shot.'"[100] Schomburg provides Andrew's testimony as evidence that Attucks was an active agent in the struggle, contesting white historians' attempts to diminish Afro-diasporic people's historical influence in America's first days. By disproving claims that Attucks was a fugitive slave or a hapless victim of the Boston Massacre, Schomburg centers African participation in the physical and legal story of the American Revolution. These men's stories were solicited and heard by a court of law, and they should play a significant role in the narrative of the Boston Massacre. For Schomburg, Attucks and the Black men who shared his story were foundational to the American Independence movement.

Schomburg challenges the Taney decision to make similar claims about the essential role of Black people in colonial and early America in the unpublished work, "Free Negroes in the Formation of the American Republic."[101] In Section III of this document, Schomburg takes on the argument that the US Constitution was never intended to apply to Black people. Schomburg argues, using primarily the dissenters in *Scott v. Sanford*, that the Constitution is not an inherently white supremacist document.[102] He quotes Justice John McLean, who indicates that "the Government was not made especially for the colored race, yet many of them were citizens of the New England States and exercised the right of suffrage when the Constitution was adopted."[103] He also quotes, at length, Justice Benjamin Robbins Curtis, who pointedly argues that "'it is not true in point of fact that the Constitution was made exclusively for the white race.'"[104] He points to the fact that in five of the first thirteen states, free Black men "'possessed the franchise of electors.'"[105] It follows then, for Justice Curtis, that, if these Black men were citizens, then the Preamble of the Constitution must have been "'ordained and established by the people of the United States'"—Black and white. Again, through the use of white experts and legal definitions of citizenship, Schomburg makes African diasporic people political actors who were meant to be participants in the rights and responsibilities outlined by the US Constitution.

In all of Schomburg's pieces on colonial and newly independent America, his language subverts the way in which colonial and Early American history usually characterizes white and African people, namely by using objectification to refer to white people and the language of partnership to talk about Black people. For example, the article on Crispus Attucks, despite claiming to focus on the first victim of the revolutionary period, actually begins long before the Boston Massacre, offering an overview of the British empire and its attempts to colonize North America. In Schomburg's framing, America cannot be so easily separated from its British imperial roots. In describing Britain's Caribbean colonies, he starts by describing the migration of white British subjects to the islands. However, Schomburg's word choice makes these white British people passive objects. For example, he recounts that ships came to colonies such as Jamaica, Barbados, and St. Lucia "and landed their precious human cargo of whites," describing white people in the objectifying and property-focused manner more common to white historians' descriptions of enslaved Africans.[106] In the published version on Crispus Attucks, Schomburg describes Black people as "African contingents," there "to help develop the newly acquired colonial possessions."[107] While Schomburg moves on to talk in more detail about the widespread practice of slavery in British colonies throughout the Caribbean and Central America, this introduction to African people as "contingents" characterizes them as team members or soldiers, people who were an intricate part of the development of colonized territory. In doing so, Schomburg reclaims African agency, albeit by problematically aligning Black people with the colonizers, and underlines their importance to the history of economic development in the Caribbean, an argument that Schomburg makes in other venues, namely "The Economic Contribution by the Negro to America."[108] However, in the earlier draft of "Crispus Attucks—Free Patriot," Schomburg goes further than arguing that Africans helped to develop the colonies—he argues that the "African contingents" were also part of "the enjoyment of a national providence."[109] In addition to its religious sense of divine intervention, the *Oxford English Dictionary* has just as many economically focused definitions for "providence"—for example, definition one includes "foresight; anticipation of and preparation for the future; prudent management, government, or guidance" and "regard for future needs in the management of resources; thrift, frugality."[110] In insisting that they "enjoy" the "national providence," Schomburg insists that African people were more than labor and actually shaped the colonial future. Schomburg asserts that "long before the year 1770, a large number of blacks were employed in her Majesty's dominion" and "were considered subjects amenable to English discipline and protection," again emphasizing Black people's legal rights.[111] In laying out the history of the British empire leading up to Attucks's patriotic death, Schomburg provides context for understanding Attucks's Caribbean background and the active, if problematic, role that people of African descent played in developing that empire.

In the final section leading up to the actual Boston Massacre, Schomburg cements the idea that early America is inseparable from Africa and the

Caribbean. In discussing the iconic beginnings of New England, he refers to the "white Pilgrims" and the "black Pilgrims" brought over by the *Mayflower*,[112] revising the mythic history of this vessel and asserting that it played a role in the forced migration and enslavement of African people.[113] While there is currently no clear evidence that the *Mayflower* was a slave ship,[114] Schomburg makes this assertion and lays claims to the Pilgrim mantle for Black enslaved people to highlight the ways in which the *Mayflower* passengers who colonized New England were crucial in developing the slave-based economy of the Caribbean and the American colonies.[115]

AfroLatino Excellence and the "Great (Black) Man" Narrative

Schomburg's pride in his Afro-diasporic roots radiates from his writing. In an unpublished essay for a prospective "magazine devoted to the racial groups of the Antilles," Schomburg states, "It seems appropriate for me to mention that men of African descent have filled most every position of trust with dignity and propriety that can be mentioned by any person."[116] The rest of the manuscript, entitled "Some Notable Colored Men from the West Indies," lists the accomplishments of Afro-Caribbean men in the realms of journalism, government, publishing, and a host of other fields. This never-published article, while less polished than other, more well-known articles he wrote, reflects Schomburg's investments. The masculinist focus of his history clearly stands out, as does his belief that auto/biographical work can be a balm for histories of racial discrimination and erasure. For Schomburg, "a group tradition must supply compensation for persecution, and pride of race the antidote for prejudice."[117] By using the term "antidote," Schomburg suggests that history based in race pride can act as a solution. The term's medical valence also implies healing. For Schomburg, the auto/biography of racial integrity was one step in the process of healing from white supremacist policies and attitudes.

Schomburg's travels to the Dominican Republic, Cuba, Panamá, and Spain provided him an entryway for revising the history of the Americas and restoring AfroLatino history.[118] According to Ralph Waldo Emerson, in the introduction to his biographical work *Representative Men*, "other men are lenses through which we read our own minds."[119] Similarly, Schomburg's auto/biographical essays provide insight into his mind: the way he imagines his own existence and his conception of AfroLatinidad. These narratives often come out of concrete symbols—such as seeing a monument or plaque or finding a painting of an important man of African descent in the Americas. In "General

Antonio Maceo," published in *The Crisis*, an obscured monument in a newspaper picture begins Schomburg's investigation into Maceo's life. He writes, "Only the base of the monument was visible as printed in the American illustrated papers. This fact has caused me to write of the figure left out of the picture."[120] Here, the statue of Afro-Cuban General Maceo stands in for the marginalized Afro-Caribbean man.[121] Writing from his own marginality as a space of "counter hegemonic discourse,"[122] Schomburg positions himself as the man who will move the statue, and the man it represents, out of the margins into the forefront of hemispheric American military history. Despite his claims to want to avoid hagiography, as he professes in "The Negro Digs Up His Past," Schomburg describes General Maceo as "glorious" and one of the "greatest captains of antiquity" and adds "no man of military standing in the whole of America [. . .] can excel the exploits of Antonio Maceo."[123] In his writing, Schomburg makes Maceo into a legend and a man beyond reproach—"always above suspicion"—whose excellence is not limited to Cuba but moves beyond the island: as a military man, Maceo was "the ablest and noblest of American born Cavalry leaders, unsurpassed by any which the New World has produced."[124] This focus on military history, of course, also ends up providing a limited sense of Afro-Caribbean excellence, focused on spaces in which men have been centered and women sidelined. The repeated emphasis on Maceo as a historical figure of the Americas works to tie his achievements to Afro-diasporic men in Cuba, the Caribbean, and all of North and South America. He refuses to align "America" with the US, and in doing so, refuses the imperialist claim within that language that makes everything "American" of the United States. Schomburg creates a transnational connection, offering Maceo as an example of global Black excellence, of hemispheric American excellence, while also emphasizing his achievements in their Afro-Caribbean context.

Maceo's marginalized monument resembles the unassuming plaque dedicated to José Campeche, whose image bookends Schomburg's auto/biographical essay on the accomplished Afro–Puerto Rican painter. As discussed in this chapter's introduction, in "José Campeche 1752–1809,"[125] Schomburg begins by sharing his own story of growing up and walking by Campeche's plaque each day without knowing the man's significance.[126] He observes, "Imagine a boy living in the city of his birth and not knowing who was the most noted native painter! It is true the fact was recorded on a marble tablet duly inscribed and placed on the wall of a building where it could easily be read."[127] Schomburg begins with a nationalist connection, imagining a Puerto Rican boy in San Juan being unaware of a "native painter" of accomplishment. In this sense, "native" means "Puerto Rican," eliding discussion of Indigenous erasure while also stressing Puerto Rico's status as a nation, despite its technical status as a Spanish colony at the time. Schomburg wants to astonish the reader that a hometown hero could remain unknown to a local resident. However, it becomes clear that the "conspiracy of silence" enabled by Spanish white supremacy has robbed the Afro–Puerto Rican painter "full recognition and [. . .] the fame his genius merited."[128] Like he does in his appreciation of Phillis Wheatley, Schomburg allows (white) Spanish colonial experts to sing the painter's praises: "Rafael María de Labra y Cabrada, the most notable representative of the Spanish-American colonial possessions [. . .] asserted that the greatest painter of the island, one worthy of note, was the mulatto José Campeche of San Juan."[129] In ending the auto/biographical essay, Schomburg notes that the Catholic Church saved his home on Cruz Street, including the small marker honoring Campeche. Quite literally, the building and the plaque are "a gift," an economic outlaying to maintain the space. However, Schomburg's characterization of "the building with the marble table" as "a gift" also reflects his own appreciation of having a space dedicated to Afro–Puerto Rican achievement.[130] Beyond monuments and memorials as inspiration for his writing, Schomburg was also driven to provide visual records of AfroLatinidad in his published essays.[131] For instance, the essay on Maceo includes a portrait of the general in military uniform as well as a clear picture of his imposing monument in Cuba.[132] In his work on Campeche, Schomburg includes both a painting of the artist and a painting that Campeche created. In doing so, he documented the AfroLatinidad of his subjects and underscored their contributions to military history, the fine arts, and other fields.

Finding paintings or archival documents that verify his own claims to a historical figure's Blackness, especially if these claims were contested, are often highly emotional moments in Schomburg's essays. For example, "In Quest of Juan de Pareja," published in *The Crisis*, is as much about Schomburg's experience of the Africanity of Spanish history as it is about Juan de Pareja. Schomburg leads the reader on a tour of Spain, mapping out the pervasive presence of people of African descent: "I walked up the hill to the Alhambra and saw in the sunshine the legacies of that civilization, which grew luxuriantly like an exotic plant native, yet foreign, to Spain."[133] Again, we see Schomburg use "native" in a way that subverts the depiction of Blackness as perpetually foreign. While recognizing Afro-Hispanics as migrants to Spain, Schomburg underscores the long, but denied, history of African influence in Spain—a legacy that is "native, yet foreign." Schomburg tells us that while he enjoyed viewing a "copy of the Mona Lisa by da Vinci" that was more stunning than the one kept in the Louvre, he had really come to the Prado, Spain's primary art museum, based in Madrid, to view a painting by the enslaved Afro-Spanish painter, Juan de Pareja.[134] Schomburg's claim that a work by Juan de Pareja would trump one by the Renaissance great elevates the Afro-Spanish painter's work. Of course, while Schomburg can easily view da Vinci's work, he must overcome obstacles, such as the closure of a section of the museum due to repairs, to see Pareja's "The Calling of Matthew." As reward for his persistence, Schomburg gets to view the image and a portrait of Pareja completed by Diego Velázquez, Pareja's enslaver, who taught him to paint.[135] According to the Prado's director, this one-of-a-kind canvas "is the only picture of Pareja that we have and we prize it as among the rarest of the collection."[136] In experiencing Pareja's painting, Schomburg "sat in reverent silence [. . .] and was glad of the opportunity thus given [him] to see this work and to tell [his] people in America of this further claim back in the 17th century to a place in the republic of arts and letters."[137] Schomburg's experience is one of awe, of a silence that was not conspiratorial or harmful, as it had been in his writing on Campeche. Here, he uses "reverent" to show deep respect and solemnity for a masterpiece. Schomburg's silence is respectful, reflective, and even joyful, suggesting Kevin Quashie's concept of quietude.[138] Unlike silence, which is suppressive and withholding, quiet is a retreat to the interior, a space with creative and liberatory possibilities.[139] Schomburg's "reverent silence" celebrates the ability to claim "a place in the republic of arts and letters" for an Afro-Spanish man, restoring the racial integrity to generations of Afro-diasporic people. However, as Holton notes, the essay's ending also feels stilted and, perhaps, disappointed.[140] While Schomburg gets to enjoy the piece, he must do so alone, as the piece is not publicly visible. The title of the piece frames his journey to see the painting as a quest, but at the end of the quest, the treasure remains sequestered, unable to be touted and appreciated by the AfroLatinos, like him, looking for themselves in art history.

    As he does in his essays on early America, Schomburg also places men of African descent at the beginning of Spanish America, focusing particularly on their history before slavery. In doing so, Schomburg offers the reader a history of AfroLatinidad not entirely subsumed by slavery. For example, in "Notes on Panamá and the Negro," published in *Opportunity*, he starts by stating that when the first Spaniards landed in Panamá, they found a colony of people of African descent "who had lived in the vicinity for a period of time unknown to the oldest of the clan. [. . .] How these sons of Africa came to this place will perhaps never be known."[141] Though the history of how these Black Panamanians arrived on the isthmus has been lost, or more likely, denied, Schomburg reminds the reader that slavery was not the natural condition of Afro-diasporic people but was imposed on them later.[142] Schomburg crafts the migratory history of Blackness in Panamá, though again from a masculinist perspective. He points to the first enslaved people brought by Balboa to Panamá to develop roadways and transportation along the Pacific coast as "the precursors of the present day gigantic undertaking of the Panama Canal," in which Black West Indians provided most of the labor, finishing the Canal in 1914.[143] After establishing these beginnings, Schomburg retells the history of enslaved Black Panamanians to emphasize a history of Afro-Panamanian resistance and maroon or palenque communities (communities established by fugitives from slavery).[144] In fact, he points toward maroon communities that succeeded in gaining recognition for their political leadership, such as the town of Palenque, led by "Luis of Mozambique."[145] In an essay ostensibly about the first American-born bishop of the Catholic Church, Schomburg recasts early Afro-Latin American history as more than enslavement. These people of African descent were foundational to the development of the isthmus and resisted Spanish oppression, ultimately governing themselves. This revisionist history rejects the white supremacist histories of the Americas that Schomburg reviled.

Schomburg also ties Afro-Latin American and Afro-Hispanic history to US AfroLatino history, creating a hemispheric American history. Sometimes Schomburg's writing points out AfroLatino influence for ironic purposes to undermine white supremacy. One particular example occurs in Schomburg's essays on the Negro Brotherhood of Sevilla, one of many "religious brotherhoods for enslaved and free Africans who were excluded from participating in the white brotherhoods" that supported each other culturally, financially, and medically.[146] In two articles published in *Opportunity*, Schomburg comments that the robes of the Negro Brotherhood look just like those of the Ku Klux Klan and suggests that the KKK must have based their costume off of this organization's. He argues, "To all appearances the American organization copied the dress of those believers in Christ. Not even in garments, it seems, is the American order original. They are evidently copied faithfully from a very sacred brotherhood'"[147] and "to all intents and purposes the KKK are splendid imitators of the Negroes [sic] dresses."[148] By emphasizing this comparison, he portrays the KKK as unoriginal imitators of Black excellence. Despite their claims to white Protestant superiority, white supremacists are wholly unable to prove that superiority, as even their fashion choices are knockoffs of a Black Catholic organization. In a scholarly tone, Schomburg ribs the KKK and their self-importance. He denigrates the white supremacist organization at the same time that he points to the foundational influence of Afro-Hispanic people globally and in the United States.

Just as Schomburg makes a connection between African Spain and the US, he translates the *Dred Scott* decision in the US across the Caribbean to Cuba, comparing the impact of Chief Justice Taney's majority opinion to that of Amendment 17 in Cuba, which disallowed the creation of race-based parties.[149] In his article in *The Crisis*, "General Evaristo Estenoz," Schomburg focuses on the Afro-Cuban founder of the Independent Colored Party (Partido Independiente de Color, or PIC) in Cuba, a political party founded in 1908 comprised primarily of Afro-Cuban veterans of the Cuban War of Independence to advance the interests of Afro-Cubans. Like he did in his writing on General Maceo, Schomburg characterizes Estenoz as a military great, deserving of praise and imitation. However, Schomburg talks about more than his military career, pointing to his success in growing a political party "capable of thwarting the prearranged plans of the whites" and his success printing a related newsletter.[150] Schomburg shifts his shining description of Estenoz to the obstacle that faces him: Amendment 17. By comparing the law, which was meant to curb the influence of Afro-Cubans in the political system after the 1912 uprising led by the PIC,[151] to the *Dred Scott* decision, Schomburg makes visible how anti-Black political attitudes and practices travel across borders. He writes that Amendment 17 is "an unconstitutional law, as infamous and despicable as the American Dred Scott Decision" that "deprives the Negroes of Cuba of political character and independence."[152] Beyond showing the transnational nature of anti-Blackness, Schomburg also suggests that US anti-Black racism and specifically the nation's use of the *Dred Scott* decision (along with the Platt Amendment) has negatively influenced Cuban politics. Schomburg's reference to *Dred Scott* reflects a common assertion by Puerto Ricans that racism is an import from the US, though his critique is more thoughtful. He does not argue that racism did not exist in Cuba previously; in fact, as Valdés argues, "Schomburg ends his essay debunking the myth of racial unity that had been circulated within Cuba at the conclusion of the nineteenth century."[153] Rather, he argues that white Cubans were adopting the methods of US white supremacists and cautions those who want to believe in a mestizaje myth of color blindness. In this way, the essay makes visible the political and military contributions of Afro-Cuban men as well as the multiple anti-Black policies and attitudes that impede Afro-Cuban political equality.

Schomburg uses his auto/biographical writing to trace a lineage of Afro-Hispanic and AfroLatino men, particularly those who were the first to accomplish particular milestones in the Americas. Through historical figures like Estevanico, the Negro Brotherhood of Sevilla, and Bishop Victoria y Luna, Schomburg lauds AfroLatinos for being the first Americans, of any color, to accomplish these landmarks. As José M. Irizarry Rodríguez writes, "through storytelling testimonios of success, [Schomburg and other early Puerto Rican writers] hoped to guide their compatriots through perilous new circumstances and to strengthen community."[154] In "The Negro Brotherhood of Sevilla," Schomburg begins his discussion of the unique Spanish brotherhood by mapping out the traveling of Africanity, beginning in the fourteenth century.[155] Standing in the chapel that was home to this Black brotherhood, he reflects on his place in the larger history of the African diaspora: "I looked down on the marble flooring and read the inscribed marble slab and pictured mentally the early coming to America of the Negro race, their great unrewarded services in the opening of the virgin forests, scaling the heights and making pleasant the avenues for others to follow."[156] He stresses the role of "the Negro race" in making the Americas a place that could be developed and enhanced. Like in his biography of Crispus Attucks, he depends on an erasure of Indigenous presence ("virgin forests") but adds Black people alongside white European (Spanish and British) explorers. Still, he does so since he sees Afro-diasporic people as essential to the beginnings of the Americas, "unrewarded" for their work through monetary compensation or historical recognition but just as important to the American pioneering spirit (as problematic as it may be).

In the cathedral, he thinks back to the beginnings of the Americas, which for Schomburg, is not Columbus but rather Estevanico, the African man enslaved by the Portuguese that sailed to America along with Álvar Núñez Cabeza de Vaca, their story partially told in Cabeza de Vaca's *La relación y comentarios* (Relation of Álvar Núñez Cabeza de Vaca).[157] Schomburg

> contemplat[es] the services of Estevanico in the discovery of the Seven Cities of Cíbola in Arizona; these who were with Diego Colon at Hispaniola and rebelled against injustices during the year 1515, in fact all those who followed the Spanish Conquistadores in their voyages of discoveries over the Andes, many to be frozen to death, or with Hernan Cortes few to be pierced by Indian arrows viewing the expansive waters of the Pacific Ocean.[158]

In this reflection, Schomburg recounts the story of Estevanico, placing him at the center of several important historical events. He was one of the first men of African descent in North America. And in his second expedition to the Americas, he is said to have discovered the city of Cíbola, though he also died during the journey. Beyond this named individual, Schomburg also recognizes the many unnamed and invisibilized Africans who traveled, rebelled, and died in the Americas alongside well-known Spaniards like Cortés, restoring, in a small way, their place in the history of the Americas.

Schomburg's essay on the achievements of Francisco Xavier Luna y Victoria also stands out for its treatment of its subject alongside Schomburg's joy of archival discovery.[159] The setting in modern-day Panamá demonstrates the widespread influence of AfroLatino and Afro-Hispanic men, alongside Estevanico and the Brotherhood of Negroes, spanning North, Central, and South America in addition to Spain. Luna y Victoria was the first person born in the Americas to attain the rank of bishop in the Catholic Church. Schomburg, based on his research in the Archive of the Indies in Sevilla, Spain, declares that "Francisco Xavier Luna y Victoria, native of the country [the Americas], a man of color, [. . .] had ascended in the hierarchical scale of the church by his meritorious virtues."[160] His essay is based on reading and holding "the very documents belonging to Francisco Xavier Luna y Victoria!" including the diploma which certified his status.[161] Schomburg's excitement, reflected by a rarely used exclamation point, comes from the ability to point to documentation that white supremacy was not yet fully embedded in the Americas at the beginning of European contact with Indigenous peoples. Schomburg reiterates his characterization of Luna y Victoria as "American-born," celebrating a moment in which a man of African descent is the first man of any ethnic or racial identity to be a "first." That is, Schomburg avoids writing about Luna y Victoria's accomplishment as that confined only to Afro-diasporic people, often using passive voice to note the "[hemispheric] American-born" part, then the man-of-color distinction: "Thus it happens that the person to enjoy the great distinction of being the first American-born made a Bishop in America and the great honor of being the founder of a University, is the Negro noted herein."[162] Beyond his influence in the Catholic Church, Luna y Victoria was also the founder of "the University of Saint Xavier, which flourished for many years in its benevolent services for humanity and ranked as one of the few that existed in those early days in America."[163] His influence on one of the first bodies of higher learning in the Americas again points to the influential standing of AfroLatino men in the Americas, not only in religious or political positions but also in education and scholarship. The essay comes full circle to Schomburg's own life and mission: to educate AfroLatino and other Afro-diasporic men of the foundational nature of Africanity in the Americas and in so doing cultivate a sense of pride in AfroLatino history and themselves for sharing in it.

Conclusion

For Arturo Alfonso Schomburg, AfroLatinidad was embedded in the history of the Americas, and his auto/biographical writing was driven by a pride in his Afro–Puerto Rican identity. He set out to prove that nearly every important historical event was driven or influenced by Afro-diasporic people. His AfroLatino lens impacted all of his writing—for better, in centering the distinct history and accomplishments of AfroLatinos and Afro-Hispanics, and for worse, in creating biographical works that elided the roles of Afro-diasporic women in education, politics, and the arts (with the exception of Phillis Wheatley). Schomburg felt that objective truth could only be ascertained with subjective passion and believed that race pride and the drive to build the archive were a natural response by Black and Afro-diasporic historians and biographers to combat white supremacy. He was also never afraid to imagine what lay in the gaps and silences of the historical record in regard to ethno-race, though he often failed in regard to gender. Many of his essays were uncritically laudatory, though this was understandable in the Jim Crow era in which Black humanity was constantly questioned in the popular media and academia. Schomburg chose to write about Afro-Hispanic and AfroLatino (male) personalities that reflected the same marginalization he felt within US Black, white, and Puerto Rican spaces. Though his lens was limited by his focus on Great Men, Schomburg worked hard to revise US biography and history into a hemispheric American history that centered AfroLatino resistance, innovation, and achievement. In addition, the strategies he used—the insertion of his own life experiences, the use of archival documents that centered Black voices, strategic appeals to white authority, and reversing linguistic and narrative expectations around race—continued to influence AfroLatino life writing in the twentieth century.

CHAPTER 2

Jesús Colón, the New York Young Lords, and "Observe and Participate" Autobiography

Introduction

The liminal status of Puerto Ricans as simultaneously American citizens and racialized migrants influences both the representation of Puerto Rico and Puerto Rican literary history.[1] Puerto Ricans, especially Afro–Puerto Ricans, have long critiqued and organized around the issues that have arisen from their colonial and racialized status.[2] Radical nineteenth-century Afro-Caribbean journalists—such as Sotero Figueroa (1851–1923),[3] cofounder of the exile newspaper *La Patria*, and Francisco Gonzalo "Pachín" Marín (1863–1897),[4] a poet and journalist who died fighting for Antillean independence from Spain—created and used newspaper outlets to publish creative, political work. In her article on Marín and Nuyorican poet "Tato" Laviera, Laura Lomas argues, "the critique of racism, colonialism, and poverty that disproportionately affects darker-skinned Latinas/os, constitutes one of the unfinished projects that twentieth-century poets inherited from their nineteenth-century predecessors."[5] Like Figueroa and Marín, Afro–Puerto Rican communist Jesús Colón (1901–74) and the Young Lords Party (YLP, 1969–1972)[6] are best known for their radical politics and their impact on the ethnic and alternative press.[7] Some have questioned the literary value of Colón and the Young Lords' work due to its overt politics.[8] However, I argue that Colón and the New York Young Lords' English-language life writing transforms nineteenth-century Afro–Puerto Rican struggles into a twentieth-century Afro–Puerto Rican literary tradition.

For Jesús Colón and the Young Lords, anti-Blackness existed in Puerto Rico long before US imperialism and has been and remains a major driver of Puerto Rico's continued status as a colony. Their writing confirms that Latin American and US colonialism, through the practice of slavery, as Sherwin

Bryant argues, constructed Blackness as an identity incapable of individual or national sovereignty.[9] Thus, in maintaining the importance of dismantling anti-Black attitudes in the continental US and on the island as well as embracing the Blackness of puertorriqueñidad, Colón and particularly the Young Lords asserted that to fight against US colonialism one had to dismantle anti-Black structures and nationalist stories that erased Black Caribbean influence.[10] These writers used life writing to craft Afro–Puerto Rican socialist identities and futures. Both Colón's *A Puerto Rican in New York* (1961) and other sketches drawn from his posthumous collection *The Way It Was* (1993), as well as the Young Lords' collaborative autobiography *Palante: Young Lords Party* (1971), reflect on the connections between gender, race, and labor. Thus, these life narratives constructed an AfroLatinidad based in an Afro–Puerto Rican socialism that countered the dominant jíbaro image of Puerto Rico and instead centered a diasporic Black identity. The AfroLatinidades highlighted in this chapter call attention to the realities of living in a Black body where "Black" does not automatically equate to "US Black." In addition, the AfroLatinidades crafted by Colón and the YLP write against the Puerto Rican mestizaje narrative of jibaridad often used to cement anti-Black attitudes and histories. The AfroLatinidades that spring from *Palante* and Colón's sketches arise from the negotiation of invisibility, visibility, and hypervisibility.

In the previous chapter, I examined Arturo Schomburg's theorization of auto/biography and his work in imagining a hemispheric American auto/biographical genre in which colonial African American, AfroLatino, and Afro-Hispanic men (and a few women) were central to American history. In doing so, he navigated how white conceptions of Blackness as inferior, as a one-dimensional figure only fit for History in its hypervisible marker as "slave," had invisibilized AfroLatino and Afro-Hispanic men in biographical and historical narratives. In this chapter, I present a different negotiation of AfroLatino/a invisibility and hypervisibility: a revolutionary and intellectual tradition of AfroLatinidad based in radical politics and collective notions of identity. Unlike Schomburg, these writers looked less to revise biography and history to include Great Black Men; however, like Schomburg, Colón and the Young Lords Party also saw themselves and their writing as part of a hemispheric American tradition. As with the previous chapter, I bring together the life writing of these writer-organizers with archival findings, in this case from the papers of Jesús Colón and various Young Lords, held at CENTRO, the Center for Puerto Rican Studies at Hunter College.

Jesús Colón, the Afro–Puerto Rican journalist and communist, and the Young Lords Party represented their distinct AfroLatinidad through what I term the "observe and participate" autobiography. "Observation and participation" was a community recruitment strategy, originally described by Cha Cha Jiménez, the founder of the Young Lords Organization (YLO) in Chicago, to which the New York Young Lords originally belonged. Pablo "Yorúba" Guzmán has testified to the phrase's lasting power, which conveys the necessity of organizers observing their community, identifying its needs, and then acting on those observations.[11] This strategy of recruitment and activism has been used by Afro–Puerto Ricans in other settings as well. For example, Lisa Sánchez González describes Pura Belpré's work with the New York Public Library (see chapter 1) as "entrenching herself in the community's everyday life, assessing the needs and desires of the community from that vantage point, and organizing events that respond to these needs and desires in convenient locations and in creative ways."[12] In addition to their actions, Jesús Colón's and the New York Young Lords' life writing reflects the spirit of the "observe and participate" model.

In addition to its use as a political recruitment strategy, I use this term "observe and participate" to evoke the ethnographic model of participant observation. Danny L. Jorgenson states that participant observation "is distinguished from other methods for researching human existence by the investigator's participation in the lives of those being studied while making observations and otherwise collecting information."[13] In this method of human research, sociologists and anthropologists embed themselves in a subculture or society and participate, whether actively or passively, in the practices (routine and ceremonial) of a group or culture. Participant observation is made up of three parts: the participation, the observations, and the analysis of both the practices observed and experienced and the notes taken by the researcher.[14] In this way, participant observation attempts to recognize that the researcher and their perception of a cultural practice are a necessary component of the analytic process. Though, in practice, participant-observers may not always reflect deeply on how their own cultural background and beliefs inform their analysis of another's traditions, this ethnographic method focuses on making visible one's own presence and influence on the community in which they have entered. Similarly, I argue that "observe and participate" autobiography reflects both political organizing and ethnographic qualities, as it encourages reflection on the needs of the community, how an individual fits into and makes an impact on that community, and the manner by which those conclusions are conveyed.

The "observe and participate" literary form emerges from a strand of socialist, pro-independence politics for which race, culture, colonial status, and gender were constitutive components and employs a litany of literary choices such as intertextuality, representation, and characterization as well as rhetorical appeals to authenticity and accessibility. To represent a range of AfroLatina/o/x experiences, these "observe and participate" autobiographies refuse to offer a representative person of color to stand in for all who struggle for freedom. These life narratives emphasize heterogeneity within social and political movements, and privilege the community over the individual. Rather than dwell on exceptional lives, Colón's sketches and the Young Lords' *Palante* represent the ordinary, even when those lives were not exemplary.[15] These writers believed that Afro–Puerto Ricans did not need to be "humanized" by making visible only extraordinary people. Representing former gang members, recovering addicts, and people who worked themselves to the bone without ever moving up the economic ladder, Colón and the New York Young Lords represented a nuanced picture of the racial politics of the United States, Boriquén (the island of Puerto Rico), and Boricuas (those from it).[16]

The "observe and participate" autobiography highlights how race, ethnicity, gender, and histories of migration are negotiated to create AfroLatina/o/x identities. While the YLP's political and rhetorical influence has gained increasing attention,[17] scholars have not studied the YLP in conjunction with Colón, despite their shared politics. In reading their life writing together, I argue that Colón and the New York Young Lords' collective autobiographies compose a revolutionary *literary* tradition of AfroLatino/a life writing shaped by radical politics and communal production. "Observe and participate" life writing is a literary form based on a model of socialist, pro-Independence, anti-racist political recruitment.[18] It has three components: narratives that challenge the cultural myth of Puerto Rican racial harmony through intertextuality and juxtaposition; a political conversion narrative that centers an observer becoming a political participant, using street vernacular and orality to claim authenticity and accessibility; and a structure that forces the reader to become an observer of injustice and that, by the end, challenges them to become an anti-racist participant. Colón and the New York Young Lords juxtapose literary texts and narratives about race to displace the myth of racial harmony and make visible its roots in Puerto Rican and US traditions of anti-Blackness. The YLP and Jesús Colón claimed an Afro-diasporic political and cultural pride that was conspicuously absent from other Puerto Rican socialists and nationalists of the time. The "observe and participate" autobiography provided a means to rethink the relationship among puertorriqueñidad, Africanity, Americanity, and visibility, with the goal of building organizations and narratives that not only included Afro–Puerto Ricans but prioritized issues of race and gender. Drawing from the revolutionary cultures of the tabaqueros (cigar workers), Pedro Albizu Campos's Nationalist Party, and Third World feminism, these writer-organizers represent an Afro–Puerto Rican socialist literary tradition that continues to influence literary and political actors in the twenty-first century.

Before moving into the analytic sections below, I provide brief biographies of each writer-organizer and their context, as part of my argument depends on seeing how the Young Lords follow and adapt Colón's thematic and literary choices and thus continue a radical Puerto Rican construction of AfroLatinidad.

Contextualizing Jesús Colón and the New York Young Lords

Jesús Colón's experience as a journalist and Communist organizer led him to view life writing as an opportunity to give voice to marginalized subjects: Afro–Puerto Ricans and, of course, the worker.[19] Colón's biography intersects with key moments in Puerto Rican history. He was born only three years after the US acquisition of the island in 1898, during a time when Puerto Ricans were struggling to come to terms with the sudden loss of hard-fought-for governmental autonomy from Spain.[20] As nationalist resistance mounted, the United States was increasingly pressured to clarify the status of Puerto Rico. Colón claims to have arrived in the US as a stowaway in 1917,[21] the year the Jones-Shafroth Act incorporated Puerto Rico as a territory and a restricted form of US citizenship was granted to Puerto Ricans.[22] Colón began his career in journalism writing for Spanish-language outlets, which he continued from 1923 until the 1950s when he joined *The Daily Worker*, the New York City–based organ of CPUSA. From that point, he published his journalism primarily in English. In *The Daily Worker*, Colón wrote a recurring column, "As I See It from Here," which detailed his encounters and observations about racism, Communist organizing, and moments of universal brotherhood.[23] As Edna Acosta-Belén and Virginia Sánchez Korrol note, "The bulk of his writing is constituted by his journalistic essays which, because of their intensily [sic] human interest and anecdotal style, often read more like short stories than mere pieces of social criticism or informative reporting."[24] *A Puerto Rican in New York* was the only book Colón published during his lifetime, comprised of sketches drawn chiefly from his column. The sketches span his childhood in the 1910s, his migration, and his life in New York through the 1950s. He was in the process of writing the second edition of *A Puerto Rican in New York* as well as a new collection of sketches, *The Way It Was*, but neither were completed before his death. *The Way It Was* was published posthumously by Acosta-Belén and Sánchez Korrol to include the sketches he clearly indicated were to be in the collection as well as other sketches that the editors believed spoke to comparable themes.[25] In the late 1960s and early seventies, near the end of Colón's life, youth-driven, grassroots groups arose that were influenced by, but not beholden to, Marxist-Leninist-Maoist thought.[26] One of these was the New York Young Lords. David J. Vázquez claims that Colón's "complex first-person personal narrative portrayals prefigure the growing militancy within Puerto Rican communities in the US,"[27] and indeed, there is a clear continuum from Colón's writing to the Young Lords' writing.[28]

The New York Young Lords emerged from the Young Lords Organization, a Puerto Rican street-gang-turned-activist organization in Chicago, founded in 1968 and strongly influenced by the Black Panther Party (BPP).[29] In 1969, a New York City branch of the YLO was founded in Spanish Harlem.[30] Influenced by the BPP's Rainbow Coalition,[31] the New York Young Lords were comprised of three community organizations working to improve the lives of people in Harlem. One of these groups was named La Sociedad de Albizu Campos, after the Afro–Puerto Rican Nationalist Party president, a mythic figure who had led Puerto Rican nationalist resistance and suffered greatly for the cause until his death in 1965. After becoming a branch of the YLO and then eventually their own political organization, the Young Lords of New York formed a primarily AfroLatino/a Central Committee which became the core leadership. Members holding Central Committee positions at some point included Pablo "Yorúba" Guzmán, Felipe Luciano, Miguel "Mickey" Melendez, Iris Morales, Richie Pérez, Juan "Fi" Ortiz, David Pérez, Denise Oliver, Juan González, and Gloria González. Most of the Young Lords' offensives and accomplishments occurred during the YLO and YLP years (1969–1972). They dissolved in 1976.[32]

Colón influenced the YLP literarily as well as politically, contrary to Juan Flores's claim that late 1960s Nuyorican literature "arose with no direct reference to or evident knowledge of the writings of either earlier period [1917–1945 and 1945–1965]."[33] In their newsletter, also called *Palante*, the YLP imitated Colón's inclusion of biographies about figures outside of Puerto Rico and the history of Latin American and Caribbean countries. Colón used polemical, provocative, sometimes humorous titles, such as "Trujillo's Fair of Blood" and "The Origin of Latin American Dances (According to the

Madison Avenue Boys)."[34] The YLP crafted similarly provocative headlines, such as "Cristo Era un Young Lord [Christ was a Young Lord]" and "Puerto Rican Genocide!" in reference to the mass sterilization of Puerto Rican women.[35] In addition, they linked their work to that of other radical groups, such as the Tupamaros in Uruguay.[36] Their polemics went further, deploying controversial terminology to refer to police officers, politicians, and reformists working in anti-poverty programs ("poverty pimps"), and naming and shaming specific individuals in their "Pig of the Week" column.[37]

The collaborative autobiography *Palante*, written by the Central Committee and other rank-and-file members, is part origin story (or, more accurately, stories), part manifesto and call to action. At the beginning, the authors identify the work as an answer to the question, "How did you begin?"[38] The following "Roots" section tells the readers the origins of five members' radicalism. In the sections "Revolution within the Revolution" and "The Party," every Central Committee member except Melendez and Luciano spell out the YLP's goals and principles. They position themselves as a revolutionary group within an American revolutionary tradition. After a substantial photo-essay, *Palante* ends with "Tengo Puerto Rico en Mi Corazón," an essay about a march in Puerto Rico in which they took part. While the YLP starts in New York, it ends in Puerto Rico, at the beginning of their (ultimately unsuccessful) expansion to the island.

The Afro-Boricua: Challenging Hegemonic Mestizaje and the Jíbaro Myth

Colón's sketches and the YLP's collaborative autobiography represent their life narratives as theorizations and activations of Afro–Puerto Rican socialist identities and futures.[39] Their lives become evidence towards a larger theory of Afro–Puerto Rican socialism, which espouses Puerto Rican self-determination, anti-imperialism, and anti-racism, focused especially on making visible the impact of Puerto Rican Blackness on culture but also on the independence movement. Their politically driven writing was primarily personal, first-person narratives of ordinary people used to tell what Carole Boyce Davies calls a "collective life story" rather than celebrate themselves as exceptions. Collective life stories can be read as individual narratives "or they can be read collectively as one story refracted through multiple lives."[40] In essence, these stories look at individual life narratives as pieces of a puzzle that when put together reflect a larger reality. Colón and the YLP's collective life stories express and embody Afro–Puerto Rican socialism, using familiar life writing conventions but in a distinct way. In the Young Lords' *Palante: Young Lords Party* (1971/2011), the organization incorporates several genres (poetry, essay, photography) and pieces written by at least twelve different members to promote the multiple identities of its members: AfroLatinos/as, anti-racist feminists, light-skinned allies, and anticolonial socialists.[41] Similarly, Colón's sketches focus on his own experiences as well as those of his community.[42] The term "sketch" implies a drawing or painting, and his autobiography *A Puerto Rican in New York* paints a multifaceted collective portrait of the Puerto Rican community. Sketches also tend to be free-form, providing an outline of the thing being drawn, which allows space for error or revision. By framing his autobiography through the "sketch," he refuses to promise a final, unchangeable portrait of Puerto Ricans. Instead, he offers us a growing, changing community, one partially defined by its past but also one that is creating new contours and reworking old ideas of culture and politics.

Colón and the Young Lords believed that if people took the time to observe, they would see that an ideology of racial domination is the source of injustice against Puerto Ricans in the diaspora and on the island.[43] These writer-organizers' work fits Cathy Park Hong's definition of the "literature of minor feelings,"[44] which originates from "the racialized range of emotions that are negative, dysphoric, and therefore untelegenic, built from the sediments of everyday racial experience and the irritant of having one's perception of reality constantly questioned or dismissed."[45] Hong focuses on how distorted perceptions, primarily from white people who do not experience racial traumas, lead to feeling stuck in place. Rather than focusing on individuals overcoming and growing despite racism, "the literature of minor feelings explores the trauma of a racist capitalist system that keeps the individual in place."[46] As a literature of minor feelings, Colón and the YLP's "observe and participate" autobiographies consider the racial dimensions of capitalism and refuse to provide individual capitalist success stories. Their attention to racial discrimination and Afro–Puerto Rican experiences was controversial in the US and Puerto Rico.[47] The "observe and participate" autobiography challenges the long-standing myth of racial harmony among Puerto Ricans. For these writers, this is a matter of representation; they desire to represent fully human portraits of Afro–Puerto Ricans and represent Puerto Ricans (particularly politically active ones) as a people of the African diaspora. In addition, these writer-organizers used their personal accounts to engage with broader narratives of puertorriqueñidad and the simultaneous invisibility and hypervisibility of Black Puerto Ricans, as well as material texts such as sculpture and music. Colón and the YLP's personal narratives challenge nationalist and literary projects that erase Blackness, particularly the hegemonic narrative of mestizaje and the "mythico-historical figure" of the Puerto Rican jíbaro.[48]

Like the Mexican "mestizo" and "peon," the jíbaro provides a working-class, mixed-race archetype that sanitizes the violence of rape, coercion, and discrimination in Puerto Rican culture. As Arlene Dávila argues, "the rural peasant (*jíbaro*) is represented as the embodiment of all three ancestral heritages in a single Puerto Rican culture."[49] While nominally multiracial, Dávila emphasizes that "the *jíbaro* is usually portrayed as a white male whose main influence comes from his Spanish predecessors although he has a tinge of Indian heritage" but never anything indicating African ancestry.[50] Indeed, José Luis González points out that Manuel A. Alonso's *El gíbaro* (1845) is touted by "most Puerto Rican literary historians [. . .] as the first literary expression of [Puerto Rican] national identity" despite the fact that "it in no way reflects the true racial composition of Puerto Rican society."[51] Any representation of the Puerto Rican self must contend with the jíbaro image and its connection to a nationalist concept of mestizaje.[52] While mestizaje implies a sense of racial equality, Arlene Torres and Norman Whitten Jr. argue it also acts as a project of blanqueamiento (whitening), rewarding light skin politically, economically, and socially.[53] Hegemonic mestizaje, in the Puerto Rican context, presents a neat narrative of the mixture of Indigenous and Spanish blood and culture while marginalizing or even ignoring Africanity.

By choosing to represent Black Puerto Rican lives, the life writing of Colón and the Young Lords Party contests this whitened image of the representative Puerto Rican. Colón's depictions of his own life and struggles with anti-Black racism on the mainland and the island challenged who could represent "A Puerto Rican in New York." For the Young Lords Party, AfroLatinidad united a leadership that was negotiating what Juan González in a 2005 interview called a "wide spectrum of differences" that included "the more nationalist wing of the Black liberation movement" (Felipe Luciano), "the Black Panther and its ten-point program" (Pablo Guzmán), Puerto Rican Nationalism (Richie Pérez and Gloria Gonzáles Fontanez), two differently developed "socialist and anti-imperialist perspective[s]" (Juan González and Denise Oliver), and anti-machismo / Third World feminism (Iris Morales and Denise Oliver). *Palante: Young Lords Party* demonstrates how the party finds unity in their ethnoracial identity and experiences of marginalization. They indicated this literarily and politically by opposing the conflation of "Puerto Rican" with "jíbaro" and introducing the Afro-Boricua as a foundational character in the Puerto Rican narrative, as Colón's memoir had done.

Matters of representation are at the core of Colón's *A Puerto Rican in New York*. In his preface, Colón challenges the authority of "official reports" and "the New York press" to represent Puerto Rican lives, since they were attached to the narrative of "The Puerto Rican Problem." The "lurid depictions" of his community and their portrayal as a hypervisible monolith, "the 'unwanted, unassimilable Puerto Ricans,'" concerns Colón.[54] As Sidonie Smith and Julia Watson argue, "Western eyes see the colonized as an amorphous, generalized collectivity," and Colón shows the danger in making a people into a symbol rather than a heterogenous community of individuals.[55] Colón attacks the negative impact of US colonial media representations on society's imagination of who and what Puerto Ricans are and can be. Because the media will not represent Puerto Ricans as individuals with dignity, his collection dares to represent the multiplicity of New York Puerto Ricans. Colón places himself—an Afro–Puerto Rican communist—as a representative authority of the Puerto Rican diaspora when he emphasizes that "through the medium of personal experience" he will "throw a little light on how Puerto Ricans in this city *really* feel, think, work, and live."[56] He uses a phrase of visibility ("throw a little light"), because he wants to determine the terms under which the Puerto Rican lives he illuminates are made visible. Colón's primary literary tool in this endeavor is the juxtaposition of societal narratives, which he uses to make readers question entrenched beliefs about race and racism. In doing so, Colón brings the material world, which he navigates, observes, and participates in as an Afro–Puerto Rican man, into his reflections on otherwise abstract concepts.

His life writing contends that anti-Black racism deforms individual and societal interaction and distorts how people see each other. Several of Colón's sketches emphasize Afro–Puerto Ricans' liminal space in the US and Puerto Rican racial imaginary.[57] Colón sometimes explores this ambiguity through the voices of young people, positioning the reader as a student on issues of race. Children are known for their curiosity and willingness to question "the normal" in society. Adults regularly share stories about children asking uncomfortable questions, often at inconvenient times.[58] For example, in the brief sketch "A Bright Child Asks a Question," Colón foregrounds the Latin American and Caribbean myth of mestizaje so that he can reject US society's Black/white binary and the continued use of that binary in the rhetoric of the US Civil Rights Movement. Colón's first two paragraphs describe the four hundred years after the encounter with Columbus. Like the mestizaje myth frequently does, Colón masks the violence of mestizaje by using the terms "mixing and marrying" and "disappeared" rather than rape or genocide.[59] The sketch's broad historical overview of mestizaje then abruptly cuts to a new setting: present-day Spanish Harlem. Moving from the broad strokes of history, the sketch narrows quickly to focus on a "Puerto Rican progressive mother" in the 1950s teaching her daughter the gospel protest song "We Shall Overcome." When she reaches the lyric "black and white together," the child asks, "'Mother, what am I, black or white?'"[60] In doing so, the daughter questions the erasure of Brownness and particularly of Puerto Rican struggles within the US Civil Rights Movement. Colón refuses to answer the girl's question, ending the sketch.

By leaving the question dangling for the reader, he invites the reader into the sketch. Rather than "teaching us a lesson," the open-ended question that structures the sketch asks the reader to think about how they would answer the girl and, in doing so, asks them to reflect on the visibility of race in Puerto Rican discourse and how they define whiteness, Blackness, and Puerto Ricans' place in the hegemonic Black/white binary in the US. The sketch exemplifies Colón's intertextual writing style. He puts the lyrics of "We Shall Overcome" in conversation with the historical "text" of Puerto Rican postcontact history. The song imagines a world of "black and white together," but this child comes from a culture which supposedly accepts and encourages race-mixing and in which "brown" is the default color.[61] If Puerto Rican history post-1510 (after Spanish contact and the violent transportation of enslaved Africans) is the answer to what a world of "black and white together" looks like, then should the US endeavor to be like Puerto Rico? By placing the text of Puerto Rican history in conversation with this racial justice song, Colón warns against utopic visions of race mixture. Discrimination and exploitation, as his sketches show, still exist in mixed-race societies, and race-mixing itself does not guarantee an egalitarian social order. Colón's sketch implores US racial justice organizers to engage narratives of Brownness and Afro–Puerto Ricanness alongside narratives of mestizaje and the US Civil Rights Movement.[62]

Colón also critiques Puerto Rico's mythologized idea of race mixture. In "Angels in My Hometown Church," a sketch from *The Way It Was*, he contests the common assertion that racism is a US import to Latin America and the Caribbean. Showcasing the tangible harms of the jíbaro myth, he demonstrates pointedly that anti-Black racism and Black hypervisibility were part of Puerto Rican culture even before the US invasion. To do so, Colón presents himself as a child. Thus, he becomes both the observer of and the child character who suffers from anti-Black racism in Puerto Rico. Through the life narrative and his adult perspective, he wishes to question and highlight these experiences of anti-Black racism. He demonstrates the harmful ways in which Puerto Rican and US conceptions of race and racism combine, particularly through the tourism industry, to create even more destructive racist practices. Colón does not romanticize the island as a place where racial harmony has always reigned. By providing two experiences, one from his childhood and the other from his most recent visit to Puerto Rico, Colón shows that Puerto Rico has historically practiced anti-Black racism and in doing so has refused to truly "see" Black Puerto Ricans as worthy of respect. In addition, the growth of the tourism industry has led to the erasure of the few community spaces that held positive conceptions of racial difference.

Colón represents a church from his childhood in Cayey as an anti-racist sanctuary, a place where as a child he escaped experiences of racial discrimination. Each time the mother of a friend would shout racist comments, a young Colón would run into the church and take comfort in the multiracial angels, symbolic of the humanity and divinity of people of all colors. However, when he returns to Cayey in 1965, he notices that the Brown and Black angels have been cemented over. He talks to an older Puerto Rican woman in the church, who provides different excuses. At first, she offers color-blind reasons: "the church had to be painted and remodeled," the painting was "deteriorated by some rain water infusing the church roof," and "those parts [the Black and Brown angels] became very grimy."[63] Nonetheless, the racialized reasons behind the change become clear when the older woman admits, "You know, Puerto Rico is becoming a great tourist center. Many, many Americans are visiting our hometown and our church every year . . . You have been living in the United States for a very long time . . . Don Ramón Frade [the painter], the pride, not only of our hometown but of Puerto Rico, had very queer ideas . . ."[64] In the woman's reply, Colón uses several ellipses, particularly when she talks about the impact of segregationist racism on Puerto Rican spaces. These ellipses create pregnant pauses in the text, depicting racist attitudes that can be read "between the lines." Colón, and the reader, see the ways in which racism can be communicated by capitalist concerns for aesthetics (e.g., the remodeling of the church and covering up grimy art) and, ultimately, not offending the racist sensibilities of US tourists.

However, Colón's childhood experience of racist taunting disputes the idea that these racist erasures and this whitewashing of private and public spaces are entirely tourist-driven. In another instance of intertextual conversation, Colón places two works by Puerto Rican artist Ramón Frade in conversation. Frade is primarily known for his painting *El pan nuestro de cada día* (Our daily bread) (1905), an iconic representation of the campesino/jíbaro figure in Puerto Rico named after the "Our Father" prayer. Based in artistic realism, the painting focuses on an older, light-skinned farmer, his formerly dark hair whitened from age and a life of hard labor. He wears a straw hat and no shoes as he treks on mountainous terrain. Colón places this realist portrait alongside the angels, a more idealistic artwork imagining the perfect beings of the afterlife and, in doing so, highlights the striking differences between the two. Recognizing the diversity of Frade's work is symbolic: if one can recognize and celebrate the diversity of an artist's oeuvre, one can do the same for the diversity of Puerto Rico. The multiracial angels contest the myth of racial harmony and embrace the multifacetedness of Puerto Rican identity itself.[65] Rather than accept the idea that Frade's art upholds the jíbaro myth, Colón uses the story of Frade's angels to argue that the painter's work had literally and figuratively been whitewashed. Instead of being a keeper of the status quo, Frade becomes an artist with "queer ideas" about racial equality, an influential artist who celebrated the island's racial diversity. Frade's art represents the good and bad of the island: its history of racial diversity *and* racial discrimination. The whitewashing of Frade's artistic legacy, and the older Puerto Rican woman's justification of the erasure of these multiracial angels, demonstrates that anti-Black racism is a historical fact on the island, exacerbated by US influence. While US colonialism adds new dimensions to anti-Black racism on the island, it builds on a solid foundation represented by the racist taunts of Colón's past "ricocheting from the church's thick walls that through time and space refused to die."[66]

Like Colón, the New York Young Lords challenge the jíbaro narrative through the first-person tales of multiple Afro-Boricua voices in a diverse range of media. The structure of the Young Lords' collaborative projects highlights their investment in centering and providing a nuanced portrayal of Afro-Boricua people and concerns. The 1971 edition of *Palante* begins with Afro–Puerto Rican poet Pedro Pietri's renowned poem "Puerto Rican Obituary," and the Newsreel film *El pueblo se levanta* is bookended by Pietri's reading of the poem during the YLP's First Church Offensive.[67] In the bilingual article "Entre todo el pueblo se escribe un poema / Pedro's Poetry," the YLP praises the socialist aesthetics of Pietri's poems: "the enemy is always the same—the owner of the factory, the landlord, the owner of the jails. The victim is always the Puerto Rican—the worker, the jíbara, the Afro-boricua."[68] The wording of this second sentence reveals the racial and gender politics of the Lords' adoption of Pietri's poem. The Lords use "jíbara" rather than the masculine construction ending in "-o," contesting the erasure of women that Dávila has also identified in the jíbaro myth.[69] Central Committee member and Last Poets performer Felipe Luciano's spoken-word poem, "Jíbaro, My Pretty Nigger" (1968), also reclaims the foundational Blackness of the jíbaro. In a 2003 performance of the poem on Mos Def's *Def Poetry Jam* (2002–2007), Luciano prefaced his recitation by denouncing those who "would have us believe there is a separate gulf between two nations: Black and Latino," but, he went on to say, "there is no difference between Beaufort, South Carolina and Ponce, Puerto Rico." Poetry like "Puerto Rican Obituary" and "Jíbaro" highlights the racialized class struggle that has historically determined Puerto Rican lives.[70]

Like Colón, the Young Lords also look to Puerto Rico's past, but in addition to unearthing the anti-Blackness within Puerto Rican culture, they also identify the significant historical role of Afro-descendent people in Puerto Rico. *Palante: Young Lords Party* and the biographies in the YLP's newsletter (also titled *Palante*) recharacterized key Puerto Rican figures as Afro–Puerto Rican and, in doing so, revised the history of Puerto Rico and the biography of Puerto Rico's character, reclaiming the Africanity of Boricua identity. They tied Afro-Boricua identity to the act of political participation itself. For example, Juan González's opening essay in the section of *Palante: Young Lords Party* entitled "The Party" establishes the Yoruba of Africa and the Taíno Indians as foundational to "the Puerto Rican [. . .] as a cultural personality."[71] For González, "this personality wasn't really expressed until 1868, when we [Puerto Ricans] had the first major uprising on the island. [. . .] it was led by a Black Puerto Rican, Ramón Emeterio Betances."[72] That is, Puerto Rico's "cultural personality" is Black and Taíno, and those roots motivate Puerto Rico's radical politics and nationalist spirit. Using biographies, the YLP cites Afro–Puerto Ricans as the protagonists of Puerto Rican radical history. For instance, in a May 1971 editorial in *Palante* called "History of Boriken 7," the YLP amends Pedro Albizu Campos's biography so that his Blackness and anti-colonial activism are central to his story. Carlos Aponte describes Albizu Campos as follows: "During 'the war to make the world safe for democracy,' in 1917, a young harvard law graduate entered the draft, and being a dark-skinned Puerto Rican, transferred to Puerto Rico in the hope that he would not be segregated. But he was assigned to an all black regiment. He made lieutenant. After the war, the brother began a journalism career exposing the u.s. as an imperialist power."[73] Since he is called a "brother" and the focus is on his experience of racial discrimination in the military, Albizu Campos's political history becomes tied to a political construction of Black identity. This biography and others in the YLP's publications, such as the biographies of Sojourner Truth and Malcolm X, fill historical silences that white America and the colonial Puerto Rican government created. They also provide models of people who moved from bystanders in their own lives to agents of individual and, more importantly, communal change.

The YLP's life writing refuses the mainstream depiction of Puerto Ricans as docile jíbaros (an image explored first in René Marqués's "El puertorriqueño dócil" [1967]) or light-skinned revolutionaries. These biographical writings are representative of "black narrative modes" that Arlene Torres and Norman Whitten Jr. describe as "enlightened and insightful black representation of the entwined histories, presents, and futures of conquest, domination, and self-liberation."[74] The YLP recentered AfroLatino leadership and recast Afro-descendent resistance as foundational to Puerto Rico, though like Arturo Schomburg, this AfroLatino leadership was almost exclusively male. The framing of *Palante: Young Lords Party* places the YLP and their life writing in an American revolutionary tradition just as much as an Afro–Puerto Rican one. In the American tradition, life writing has venerated the "uses of great men" (e.g., Emerson in 1850). The YLP reappropriates this notion of greatness, pointing towards the contributions of AfroLatinos, who have often been seen as at the bottom of the power hierarchy, and recasts these figures as revolutionary models to whom we should look, whose value comes from their experiences of and subsequent resistance against exploitation and discrimination.

Rather than being written about, the Young Lords shape the narratives of their own African diasporic and Puerto Rican history. In particular, the YLP links their organization's origins to Pablo Guzmán's nickname: Yorúba. The story of Yorúba's name symbolizes the struggle of negotiating Black, Puerto Rican, and migrant identities, a formative struggle for the organization. Growing up, Yorúba "was related more closely to the struggle of Black People in Amerikkka than to that of Puerto Ricans," but when he "returned to the States from a stay in Mexico, which was part of his schooling," he reclaimed his Latino roots.[75] However, Yorúba's struggle to reconcile his Blackness and Puerto Ricanness was based in anti-Black racism within the Puerto Rican community, rather than his own resistance. The disconnect "was because his dark skin and Afro hair made it difficult for Puerto Ricans to relate to him, especially light-skinned ones."[76] The structure of the sentence emphasizes that the distance Yorúba felt from his Puerto Rican roots was based in "light-skinned" Puerto Ricans' discomfort about his existence at the intersection of Blackness and puertorriqueñidad. When seeing his Blackness, they wanted to turn away, because to see and accept him as a Black Puerto Rican would be to accept the Blackness of Latinidad. The fact that Yorúba did not connect fully with "his Latin roots" until his trip to Mexico suggests that Afro–Puerto Rican identities had been previously unimaginable in the Barrio. The accent over the "u" in Yorúba, a term describing a Western African people, visually symbolizes the connection that the Young Lords see between Africanity and Puerto Ricanness.

In the photo-essay portion of *Palante*, the New York Young Lords also work to connect island history with the present-day conditions that Puerto Ricans live in Puerto Rico and as part of the diaspora in New York. The use of photography is also a claim to visibility; the YLP takes control of their own visibility and the visibility of the island. They write, "In most history books Puerto Rican history stops in 1898. Everybody talks about how the Americans raised our standard of living."[77] By presenting a current photograph, *(December 1970)*, the YLP asserts that this narrative of US improvement contradicts their own experiences and makes visible the lie of US imperialism.[78] In fact, the YLP argues that the fanguito (slum) best represents *post*-1898 Puerto Rico, not its imagined "backward" past. Directly following this photograph, the Young Lords present two pictures, one over the other. In the upper photograph, there are two older Puerto Ricans, one ebony-skinned and the other lighter but still dark-skinned. They reside in San Juan in front of a shack made of rusted, corrugated metal. In the bottom photograph, there is a picture of a lighter-skinned woman in an apartment on Cauldwell Avenue in the Bronx.[79] The apartment is in disrepair, the (presumably lead) paint peeling directly over the kitchen area. The woman appears to be pregnant and much younger than the first couple. By asking the reader to view the images side by side, the Young Lords show the subpar living conditions on the island and in New York City. In addition, they draw attention to the cycle of poverty that Puerto Ricans experience. We see the older couple, living the end of their lives in poverty. And we see the young woman, about to give birth to another Puerto Rican life in a New York tenement. Thus, the YLP points to the inescapability of deprivation and hardship in Puerto Rico and the United States due to Puerto Ricans' experiences as colonized peoples. The YLP connects the history and present-day experiences of Puerto Ricans on the island and in the diaspora visually. These photographs force the reader to confront the poverty that creates and perpetuates Puerto Rican migration and diaspora. In addition, the representation of darker- and lighter-skinned Puerto Ricans, men and women, attempts to show a diverse picture of the Puerto Rican community.

The Young Lords hope that these pictures will work in conjunction with the other sections of *Palante* that discuss the life narratives of Afro–Puerto Rican men and women. By drawing comparisons to the common experiences of Puerto Ricans suffering everywhere, the Young Lords develop a visual expression of the "divided nation" ideology, which worked to see Puerto Ricans and Nuyoricans as one people with common cause.[80] As Anne

Garland Mahler argues, this call to the divided nation also aspires to "the Tricontinentalist project of generating a new transnational political subject held together through affective attachment."[81] These images inspire a feeling of linked fate among Afro–Puerto Ricans on the island and in the diaspora. In addition, these images disrupt the visual representation of Puerto Rico and Puerto Ricans. By providing a photo-essay in which Afro–Puerto Ricans are heavily represented, the Young Lords' life writing, like Colón's, disrupts the racial myth that has marginalized Afro–Puerto Ricans on the island and in the continental United States.

"Observe and participate" autobiographies' contestations of the jíbaro were not always successful. The New York Young Lords in particular sometimes muddled their assertion that to be Puerto Rican was to be Black. As Torres argues, "as [Puerto Ricans seen by others as black] celebrate their black identity, they draw upon contradictory and complementary paradigms that emphasize their cultural autonomy."[82] Two contradictions arise at times in the YLP's writing. First, some YLP leaders and those promoting the Blackness of puertorriqueñidad might not be seen by others as Afro-Boricua. Are Mickey Melendez, Juan González, and Pedro Pietri, for example, too light-skinned to be Afro–Puerto Ricans? Is this what Omaris Zamora has noted as "non-Black Latinos/as/xs laying claims to Blackness or AfroLatinidad [as] only another way of reinscribing mestizaje and White supremacy by failing to name Whiteness and usurping Blackness"?[83] Secondly, the New York Young Lords still employed the language of the jíbaro in its 13 Point Plan and other documents of the time.[84] While it would have made sense to think of the jíbaro as similar to the Guatemalan ladino, in that both ladino and jíbaro are identities that depend on proximity to whiteness and deny the influence of the African diaspora to the nation and Latin American more generally, the Young Lords do not indicate the problems of such identities. Rather, they sometimes develop the idea of the Afro-Boricua alongside the jíbaro rather than attempting to supplant it. Despite these moments of unclarity, the "observe and participate" model of life writing engages its reader in discussions of race and ethnicity, hoping to change the reader's views and, more importantly, to encourage them to join the struggle for liberation.

The "Observer Becomes Participant" Plot: Race, Gender, and Third World Feminism

The "observer becomes participant" plot is a political conversion narrative.[85] The content revolves around a protagonist—sometimes the writer, sometimes a friend or relative of the narrator—who starts as a passive character. Events happen *to* these characters, not because of them; they accept the status quo. The narrative action revolves around their conversion from passive recipients of life's happenings to active participants in their own lives and a larger community. Colón and the Young Lords' life writing work as what Sidonie Smith calls "autobiographical manifestos." Their life narratives "always foreground the relationship of identities to power. It insists on new interpretations, new positionings of the subject as a means of wresting power, resisting universalized repetitions that essentialize, naturalize, totalize the subject. In service to that political cause, the autobiographer issues the call for a new, revolutionary subject."[86] "Observe and participate" autobiographies, through their attention to colonial, capitalist, racist, and sexist power structures, refuse hegemonic identities like the jíbaro. They go further by imagining "revolutionary subjects" who embrace their own agency and use that agency to expand their opportunities and the lives of others. Their life writing, then, dichotomizes the authors and the reader into either passive (status quo) subjects or active (revolutionary) subjects. The life writers tell stories in which they transform their lives and actions to align with socialist, anti-racist practices and, in doing so, present the radical potential of literature. In addition, both Colón and the YLP engage racialized conceptions of gender in their "observe and participate" autobiographies, though the YLP expands that analysis in relation to their commitment to Third World feminism.

Colón articulates the transformational power of literature that guides his Afro–Puerto Rican socialist life writing through his first sketch in *A Puerto Rican in New York*, entitled "A Voice through the Window." Trained as a tabaquero, Colón grew up in a radical Marxist educational environment provided to mostly illiterate workers through the lector, who would read aloud to them as they worked. According to Araceli Tinajero, this culture followed the monastic tradition of reading aloud.[87] The cigar-rolling workshop's quiet design accommodated perfect conditions for the lector as well as the time for thoughtful conversations.[88] Colón details how, as a child, he would listen to the lector read literary giants such as "Zola, Balzac, [and] Hugo" and "working class weeklies or monthlies published or received from abroad."[89] Thus, the workers engaged critically with journalistic nonfiction and literature. Both were meaningful avenues to explore and connect one's own experiences and abstract ideals of justice. In pointing to both highbrow literature and lowbrow journalism as legitimate literary sources, Colón introduces the reader to how he intends to engage with art in his collection. By providing a capacious definition of art, he takes a cultural studies approach, using want ads, sculptures, protest songs, and personal experience as texts that reflect societal beliefs. Analysis of these texts (observation) provides the impetus towards meaningful participation in the world outside the text.[90]

Colón's vignettes, then, are usually structured as observations about the actions and inaction of Puerto Ricans in New York. For example, in "Little Things Are Big," Colón explores the ways in which racialization can determine who is an observer and who is a participant. That is, how we are seen and see others influences our ability to connect and to treat each other with dignity. One of Colón's better-known sketches, the story recalls a time when Colón did not help a mother with children with her packages, due to his fear that she would see him as an aggressor rather than a Good Samaritan. The story underlines the pressures of anti-Black racism and xenophobia and how Colón experiences the hypervisibility of Black Puerto Rican masculinity.

Observations of how Colón and the white woman with children he sees on the subway occupy space dominate the first page of the sketch. Her exhaustion and overwhelmed affect come through as he tries to understand how she is juggling her luggage and children. He characterizes himself as a man with no excuse not to offer a hand, "with no bundles to take care of—not even the customary book under my arm without which I feel that I am not completely dressed."[91] The two disparate characterizations—an overwhelmed white woman and an unburdened dark-skinned man—play two roles. Doing so first arranges a seemingly simple scenario: there is a woman who needs assistance and a man clearly willing and able to help. If they both had the same skin color and same accent[92]—if both could see each other as the same—there would be no conflict, as Colón would help the woman and the day would continue. However, her white womanhood creates a barrier and reinterprets the scene for onlookers.

With no props to legitimize him as a "safe" man of color (like the book he usually carries), he worries the woman and other observers will judge him based on racial animus: "how could I, a Negro and a Puerto Rican approach this white lady who very likely might have preconceived prejudices against Negroes and everybody with foreign accents."[93] He is, figuratively, almost naked, a canvas onto which white people can project their fears. He chooses not to help the woman, but he writes the sketch as a promise to never allow racism to decide when and how he participates in acts of goodwill in the future. "Little Things Are Big" demonstrates the racialization of "participation" and particularly values like "courtesy," which Colón presents as a Puerto Rican value that he fails to uphold.[94] Further, he argues that whiteness is a powerful oppressive force that even makes values like courtesy inaccessible to Afro–Puerto Rican men and other men of color. Colón's Blackness is hypervisible, as is his decision not to help; both paint him as dangerous, with no way to move outside of this image in white people's eyes.

While "Little Things Are Big" is a powerful critique of the assumptions of Black criminality and Latino foreignness on Black Puerto Rican bodies, one might also see the sketch as bemoaning dark-skinned men's inability to engage in chivalry. Indeed, Colón's work has rarely been read as feminist.[95] However, several of Colón's sketches center women's experiences and the ways in which women uniquely struggle with issues of labor as well as religious institutions. Colón's sketches, I argue, do not erase women and, in fact, critique gender discrimination. As a socialist, Colón is clearly most interested in the issue of labor and exploitation. In "My Wife Doesn't Work" ("Mi mujer no trabaja"), written for *Oye, Boricua* but apparently unpublished, he defends the work that Puerto Rican women do in the home.[96] He presents a feminist tract about the tedious, unacknowledged nature of women's work, particularly for the Puerto Rican men who proudly proclaim that their wives do not work. He breaks down the phrase "my wife doesn't work" to reveal to his Puerto Rican audience that this phrase, usually interpreted as a signal of manliness and as a sign that the wife is well cared for, actually works to diminish the work women do every day. For Colón, the phrase "makes a little slave out of the woman, one who serves him twelve to fourteen hours a day without a salary and many times without love."[97] He quantifies the work that "stay-at-home" women do, re-casting this labor as a full-time job. He points out that even the use of the words "mi mujer" emphasizes her objectification and lack of agency, "as if she were a thing."[98] "The average man" (a phrase repeated throughout the sketch), according to Colón, sees himself as his wife's owner. Thus, he positions husbands as a management class, invested in controlling and limiting women's lives. Colón asserts that these men's greatest fear is that working outside of the home would expose their wives "to her rights as a woman and a worker," emphasizing a feminist socialism. In addition, a successful working woman "would be a mortal blow to masculine claims of superiority."[99] While this sketch does not engage race explicitly, Colón shows his awareness of the intersection of socialism and feminism. In doing so, he challenges machista attitudes.

In another sketch, "Carmencita," Colón again writes a woman navigating multiple identities: older woman, Puerto Rican, migrant, and Catholic. Again, the discussion of how race interconnects is less stark (and better explored later by the Young Lords); however, Colón offers an observer-turned-participant often denied autonomy or nuanced depiction in literature: the oft-maligned mother-in-law. "Carmencita" is a nuanced portrait of a Puerto Rican woman's struggle with religion and her desire to see, and create, a just world. The sketch is longer than most of the others in *A Puerto Rican in New York*, which allows Colón to show multiple instances in which Carmencita (or Tita) becomes an observer forced to question her closely held Catholic beliefs and to act upon those doubts. In addition, Colón avoids centering himself in the narrative; Carmencita is not a character that is being used to develop Jesús or support his growth. Her story is her own and is meant to show the multiplicity of Puerto Rican relationships to community, religion, and socialism.

Colón details his mother-in-law's journey from a devout believer who conflates capitalism with Catholicism to a Catholic who sees socialist activism as more compatible with her faith, providing an early model of liberation theology.[100] Carmencita is "the living austere portrait of a medieval Catholic woman," characterized as both firm and caring, "commanding" but also with "a world of sentiment and love for the downtrodden" beneath her "rigid composure and fierce, almost defiant saintliness."[101] Rather than present Carmencita as developing agnostic beliefs, Colón instead shows us her growing participation in defining her own religiosity. She develops her own "theory" of humanitarian worship.[102] Carmencita becomes a more active participant both in a personal sense, as a woman who more clearly understands her relationship to God, as well as in a political sense, making her mark on the world by helping to translate *The Soviet Power* (1939) by the Dean of Canterbury.[103] The sketch ends during the Second World War, and Carmencita has begun to use her spiritual tools to support communism. She spends months reciting "La Oracion de las Once Mil Virgenes" and praying for Stalin's health and success.[104] Ultimately, Colón details both a religious and a political conversion.[105]

Tita's journey to a new understanding of her faith is shown through small acts, such as meaningful and reciprocal conversations and the development of unlikely friendships. For instance, Colón emphasizes a civil exchange in which he listens to Carmencita explain the stories of her saints and then Carmencita listens as he talks about the institutionalized racism that undermines US claims to democracy. He describes how the Rockefellers, who own the Radio City Café, enforced segregated seating and refused to let Diego Rivera paint a mural of a Black man and a white man along with Lenin.[106] He provides numerous conversations and observations that lead Carmencita to question her image of the United States as a democratic, egalitarian space and that show the Catholic Church failing to take care of the poor and downtrodden. Carmencita grows close to Joe Hecht, a Jewish American socialist activist, due to his efforts on behalf of working-class people seeking welfare support and his choice to join the Abraham Lincoln

Brigade and fight fascism during the Spanish Civil War.[107] While Joe dies fighting the Nazis during World War II, her reflection on the kindness, generosity, and bravery of this Jewish American socialist encourages Carmencita to reconsider the relationship between capitalism, fascism, and religion.

Ultimately, the feminism of this sketch comes not only from the time and attention spent on Carmencita's politico-spiritual journey but also from the fact that she moves from a passive observer to an agent of her own religious beliefs and practice. Colón never presents himself as indoctrinating the truth of socialism or molding Tita in his image; Carmencita chooses to investigate and partially adopt socialist beliefs. By the end, Carmencita and Colón continue to have different views, since she derives her belief in socialism from the Catholic mandate "to 'ayudar el caido' (help the downtrodden)" and not Lenin's concept of the proletarian dictatorship.[108] Through the lens of his radical AfroLatinidad, Colón elevates this portrait of what others might see as an ordinary, even stereotypical woman: a devout Catholic Latina. By inviting the reader into her life and her spiritual-political journey, Colón deconstructs this stereotype and makes visible an underrepresented Puerto Rican life. This nuanced portrayal of the spiritual and intellectual journey of an older Puerto Rican woman and recent migrant presents a feminist sensibility and exemplifies Colón's use of the "observe and participate" plot structure.

Similarly, members of the Young Lords Party cast themselves as observers who became participants, in the individual sketches of "Roots" in *Palante: Young Lords Party*. Their observations make visible to the reader, who they hope to engage politically, not only the obstacles that Third World women and people of color face but also their resilience and resistance. As Guzmán asserts, "being a Lord is not about *accepting* life. [. . .] Being a Lord is about saying, 'Now that I know where things are at, I'm equipped to go out there and change the motherfucker.'"[109] Like in Colón's sketches, a passive/active dichotomy dominates how these writers see themselves. Each narrative begins with the authors describing themselves as bystanders, observing and internalizing the racialized, classed, and gendered dynamics of their lives at home, school, and on the Barrio streets. In doing so, they are either invisible or hypervisible, viewed through a distorted lens that disempowers and disadvantages them. Each then offers clarifying moments where they move from observers in their own lives to participants in the Puerto Rican liberation struggle. Several YLP life narratives foreground this journey to show the danger of shunning racial solidarity. They portray the Young Lords as a positive organization, one that builds bonds inaccessible in gangs or through traditional gender roles.

Like Colón, who prioritized accessible language, the YLP valued street vernacular over "standard" English. In addition, former gang members and addicts wrote their own stories about those experiences, so the reader feels that the writers offer an authentic perspective. Formally, Georgie and other YLP members' use of vernacular gives the piece a conversational tone. The oral quality of the narratives retains a testimonial property, as if they were transcribed, a factor that leads Carole Boyce Davies to argue that collaborative life writing is a "crossover genre" that "blur[s] the boundaries between orality and writing."[110] For example, interruptive phrases such as "like" and "you know" maintain conversational structures which create a sense of intimacy with the audience.[111] Street language instills a sense of authenticity, convincing the reader that this is how things really happened.[112] Colloquial speech plays to two audiences: (1) an imagined Barrio audience that distrusts "standard" or formal English but trusts the raw honesty of the street language they know and (2) a sympathetic white audience. Like Piri Thomas's *Down These Mean Streets*, which also appealed to both audiences, the YLP's use of Barrio speech fits within both the linguistic realities of Barrio life and stereotypes of "broken" English that sympathetic white readers may also expect is "authentically" Puerto Rican.

The YLP uses Georgie's first-person narrative about his gang experiences to show how gang organizations exacerbate racial divisions and play to a toxic masculinity. Though gangs are based primarily on location and ethnic or racial affiliation, they aggravate racial tensions and encourage violence between racialized young men. In Georgie's narrative, he argues that the "choice" to join a gang was hardly a choice at all. He begins the narrative by stating what he never would have been or done if he had been born into different circumstances: "If I had been raised up upstate, man, in a good community, I would've never become a gangbuster, I would've never shot nobody, I would never have stabbed nobody."[113] Georgie's potential and the opportunities *not* available to him are laid bare by the double negatives of his statement. His decision to join the Viceroy gang is passive, something decided for him by gang politics. Because he lived in "Viceroy turf" and was friends with Viceroys, the opposing gang had already tried to kill him, so he had to join to survive.[114] Though he joins out of necessity, the connection between the young men seems superficial to Georgie: "We wasn't thinkin' about the other guys being Puerto Ricans. [. . .] if he was your enemy, you kill him."[115] Being Puerto Rican held no meaning to the gang despite being a Puerto Rican gang. For Georgie, the gang encouraged apolitical thinking, which foreclosed any ability for him to see the similarities between him and all Puerto Rican men. Joining the Young Lords fostered a brotherhood with men across former gang memberships.¹¹⁶ The (active) political struggle, rather than (passive) survival struggle, encouraged by the YLP builds a more meaningful connection for Georgie. He replaces one dichotomy (friend/foe) for another (status quo/revolutionary), but agency is restored in this second opposition. While becoming a Viceroy was a passive choice, becoming a revolutionary means questioning the choices that felt outside of his control and taking control of how others see you. In their analysis of the gang narrative, the Young Lords argue that while gangs often brand themselves as organizations that resist "the system," in fact, they perpetuate the cycle of violence enacted on men of color by men of color. Gangs care about loyalty to the gang, not to a cause.

The Young Lords also explore how gender works alongside ethnoracial identity in becoming an agent of change. In Iris Morales's narrative, which opens the "Roots" section, she writes in the first paragraph that her family was not "typical," because "we were not affected by drugs. We were not affected by daughters going out and getting pregnant. Instead, we were affected by daughters going out and doing organizing, getting political."¹¹⁷ By repeating the word "affected," Morales emphasizes that in her neighborhood, it was more common for someone to feel acted upon rather than to be an actor. By asserting that her family is atypical, she implies that most families were victims of the drug epidemic and teenage pregnancy. The paragraph ends by highlighting that the daughters are "doing" political work. The word choice used here, like that used by Georgie, begins by emphasizing the passivity of Puerto Rican families and emphasizing the negatives of the Barrio. The narrative ends viewing the women as actors in their community, though not without resistance from that same community.

Machista violence looms large in Morales's life narrative. She begins the second paragraph by providing biographies of her mother and father and making observations about her family's history and her parents' strained marriage. Though Morales tries to talk first about her parents' nationality and social class, anti-woman violence forces itself into the narrative. When she first introduces her mother to the reader, she writes, "My mother was the oldest of nine children also (an older sister had been killed by a lover)."¹¹⁸ Her mother's status as the oldest depends on erasing the murder of her older sister, a history of domestic violence that Morales restores with the parenthetical statement. The rest of this paragraph characterizes Morales's mother as a woman whose all-encompassing identity is "mother," since "after her parents died she became the one who took care of all the other children, so she never knew any kind of childhood."¹¹⁹ Her parents' traditional relationship taught Morales to distrust men and narratives of women's respectability. Living in a machista environment, she observed that her freedom as an Afro–Puerto Rican woman could not depend on men's goodwill. But she also observed that other women policed her agency, claiming that being a political participant meant "'think[ing] you're a man.'"[120] Women's organizing erased their femininity, making them hypervisible as "not real" women. Morales's observations lead her to conclude that the status quo allows four roles for women: "housewife, prostitute, or drug addict, and then, when the society needed more labor [. . .] a worker." Dependency, whether financial or physical, defines these roles. However, by the end of her account, Morales embraces the revolutionary role precisely because it threatens the coerced passivity of women at the level of the family and the state. The family, like the state, validates only men's experiences and men's access to violence by explicitly and implicitly supporting men's physical, financial, and sexual control over women (e.g., determining whether a woman can work outside the home, as Colón argued). By "getting political," Morales takes action to write a different narrative for the next generation of Afro–Puerto Rican women. Thus, through Georgie's and Morales's accounts, the YLP asserts that race pride and socialist feminism help individuals and their communities move from bystanders to contributors.

In the preface to *Through the Eyes of Rebel Women* (2016), Iris Morales argues that "most accounts of the organization [Young Lords] to date have focused on a few spokesmen ignoring the fact that this was a people's movement profoundly affected by feminist ideals, activism, and contributions."[121] While Colón's sketches discussed gender primarily in relation to labor, poverty, and religion, the Young Lords provided a strong sense of how gender (and to a lesser extent, sexuality) influenced Afro–Puerto Rican communities. Feminism, and anti-machismo in particular, was integrated into the Afro–Puerto Rican socialism of the New York Young Lords, as seen in the life writing within *Palante: Young Lords Party*, Morales's reflections in *Through the Eyes of Rebel Women*,[122] and issues of the *Palante* newsletter.

The Young Lords forward anti-machismo as an organizational priority numerous times in their collaborative autobiography and newsletter, though these documents also show the internal disagreement and struggle to define and implement anti-machista practices. Iris Morales's testimonial writing and collection of women Young Lords' voices in *Through the Eyes of Rebel Women* provide a clear sense of the importance of Third World feminism in the YLP's writing and work. This is something that, Cynthia Young argues, is displayed in the Newsreel film *El pueblo se levanta*: "Morales's feminist consciousness is an attribute the film takes pains to extend to the Young Lords Party itself. In another conscious revision of the conventional Black Panther Party media image, more than half of the testimonials come from female Young Lords. Even male Young Lords reiterate the party's commitment to gender equality."[123] In the YLP origin story, the organization recounts that after a retreat in 1970, they decided that what they needed to "[attack] was *machismo* and male chauvinism" (13). The section "The Revolution within the Revolution" details extensively the ways in which gender oppression (and, to a lesser extent, oppression based in sexuality) inhibits the possibility of a truly revolutionary party. The 13 Point Program and Platform, which was published in every issue of *Palante*, was revised in November 1970 to project a more feminist vision by moving Point 10, "WE WANT EQUALITY FOR WOMEN. MACHISMO MUST BE REVOLUTIONARY AND NOT OPPRESSIVE," to the position of Point 5 and by changing the language of "revolutionary machismo" to "DOWN WITH MACHISMO AND MALE CHAUVINISM." In addition, the description added that "sisters make up over half the revolutionary army."[124] These changes depended on the intellectual labor of theorizing anti-machismo, which fell almost entirely on the women of the Young Lords, who, through the Women's Caucus and their collaboration with other Third World feminist groups, pushed Third World feminist ideas that faced resistance from the YLP leadership and general membership.[125]

The YLP discuss "Latin machismo," as it is most frequently referred to, as a gender ideology that is impacted by racism and white supremacy.[126] Yorúba Guzmán recounts how the women Young Lords presented the racialized nature of womanhood in America. As they put it, "the thing with white women is that they have been put on a pedestal, right; however, with Third World women the problem has been that the white man has put the white woman on the pedestal, and then messed around with Third World women."[127] In this way, the YLP recognizes that white supremacy has not allowed for a homogenous experience of womanhood and, in fact, women of color face even greater violence than white women. For example, Richie Pérez argues that Latin machismo limits the development of women and men. He argues that Third World men die to prove their masculinity, in a system that questions their claims to manhood.[128] Rather than just detail what machismo is, he goes further and offers several concrete ideas for what anti-machista socialism would look like: women in leadership roles, providing women the opportunity to "develop and grow," changing men's explicit and implicit biases against women, eliminating sexist language, talking to women (particularly about sex) honestly.[129] These solutions place much of the burden of change on men, as the oppressor, rather than on women, though this is contradicted in other places within the collaborative autobiography.[130]

By providing an analysis of their own errors—not initially embracing Third World feminism and struggling to apply those principles—the Young Lords also model the "observe and participate" model within their own organization. That is, they show how the observations of women members (as well as gay and lesbian ones) led to change within the organization. Rather than project a "perfect" politics, the YLP indicates that as humans, we all must be open participants in individual and collective change. As Puerto Rican studies scholar Edna Acosta-Belén asserts, the collective autobiography was not only "a full portrait of the origins of the [Puerto Rican] movement" but also "an appealing and effective recruitment tool for an expanding inclusive movement."[131] The life narratives within *Palante* offered readers a community where they could become their best selves. Like Colón, the New York Young Lords presented to their readers concrete ways to educate themselves and to participate in creating stronger communities. They made visible the forces of oppression so that potential solutions could also be brought to light. Particularly in their discussion of machismo and gay liberation, Denise Oliver, Richie Pérez, and Yorúba Guzmán created testimonies about how they confront machista, sexist, and anti-gay views.[132] These strategies move away from abstract thoughts about communism and a new world order and instead present manageable first steps towards larger change. By giving the reader practical strategies to pursue individual and community change, the YLP invites readers to participate in the larger project of liberation. Part of what the YLP recognizes is that vaguely outlined ideas of freedom and oppression are harder to pursue than clear, concrete strategies. In a sense, they made visible the realities of liberatory work. In focusing on their embodied experiences of racism, sexism, and oppression, they recognized that activism must also present embodied solutions; that is, people must be able to *see* the kinds of things they can do. By providing their own experiences of education and personal growth within the Young Lords, they offer the reader a similar opportunity: join us, and you will have a community that does not have all the answers but, together, will strive to do better.

These life narratives by Jesús Colón and the Young Lords Party use an "observe and participate" plot structure to exhibit Afro–Puerto Ricans moving from observers of injustice—of their own struggle, their family's struggle, and the struggle of those fighting for self-determination—to active participants in movements for justice. These plot narratives worked toward a larger goal: to engage the reader as a participant in Afro–Puerto Rican liberation.

Conclusion

The literary-cultural production of Afro–Puerto Rican Communist Jesús Colón and the New York Young Lords Party responded to a crisis of the twentieth century: the continued colonial exploitation of Puerto Rico. The island's status as one of the few remaining colonies in the world begets political and literary challenges that continue into the twenty-first century, as seen in the aftermath of Hurricane María, the #RickyRenuncia protests, the 2020 earthquakes, and the 2021 LUMA Energy protests. By applying a literary lens to Afro–Puerto Rican works that have heretofore been analyzed primarily through the lens of politics, I have detailed the Afro–Puerto Rican socialist aesthetic of "observe and participate" life writing.[133] As Bissau-Guinean and Cape Verdean revolutionary Amilcar Cabral writes, "if imperialist domination has the vital need to practice cultural oppression, national liberation is necessarily an *act of culture*."[134] Colón and the YLP fused the political and cultural through representation and characterization, intertextuality, the juxtaposition of literary narratives and broader narratives of racialization, and open-ended conclusions. These strategies combine to create a life writing tradition that offers an array of Afro–Puerto Rican lived experiences.

Colón and the New York Young Lords' literary contributions continue alongside their political impact. Autobiographers and testimonial writers such as Aurora Levins Morales and the Latina Feminist Group adopted communal life writing structures while developing critiques of cultural nationalism that "repress women's voices by reaffirming heterosexist utopic visions."[135] In popular culture, we have begun more openly discussing the anti-Blackness of the Latina/o/x community, exemplified by Puerto Rican-Dominican-Haitian trans actor Indya Moore's 2019 red carpet statement to *Remezcla* that they no longer identify as Latinx and instead claim an "Afro-Taíno" identity. Puerto Rican scholarship on 2017's Hurricane María embraces journalistic testimonials alongside quantitative studies.[136] In the wake of the January 2020 earthquakes, Puerto Rican self-determination organizations, such as Brigada Solidaria del Oeste and Espicy Nipples y La Sombrilla Cuir (a transfeminist network) rise to the occasion as the US government once again ignores its colony. The power of "observe and participate" life writing and politics continues to empower Puerto Ricans as active combatants against anti-Black racism, wealth inequality rooted in colonialism and capitalism, misogyny, and the silencing of those on the margins of the margins.

CHAPTER 3

AfroLatinidad as Creative Destruction: Piri Thomas's Life Writing as a Theorization of Violence

Introduction

Piri Thomas (1928–2011), Afro–Puerto Rican / Cuban poet and memoirist, challenges the models of AfroLatino biography and life writing that the previous foci of this study—Arturo Schomburg, Jesús Colón, and the Young Lords Party—worked so hard to create. Thomas's published life writing does not so much push the generic boundaries of life writing as challenge what life writing for AfroLatinx people had looked like up until that point. Schomburg had reimagined the genre of biography by recasting Afrodiasporic, and particularly AfroLatino, men as integral to the history of the Americas, reclaiming the importance of Black achievements and the foundational nature of Africanity to the Americas. However, Schomburg embraced the Great (white) Man historical narrative by attempting to incorporate AfroLatino and Afro-Hispanic excellence into the model. Colón's sketches also worked specifically to combat negative stereotypes of Puerto Ricans,[1] and while the Young Lords Party employed the narratives of former gang members and people in recovery, they partly did so in order to distance themselves from the gang roots of the Young Lords Organization in Chicago.

Thomas's three memoirs challenged the tradition of showing Afro–Puerto Rican people only in their best light—as luminaries, trailblazers, and hardworking people who had to work ten times harder to get half of what a white American received. While the impulse to do so was understandable and important in many ways, Thomas's writing dared the reader to see his life as fully human: the good, the bad, and the ugly. As Nicole Fleetwood writes in reference to visual culture studies, "the visible black body is always already troubling" to those viewing it.[2] Thomas's gritty, realistic memoirs lean into that troubling view,[3] as they refuse to paint a pretty portrait of the

AfroLatino experience of boys and men in Spanish Harlem.[4] He does not shy away from showing, warts and all, how he coped with colorism in his family—through misogynistic violence—or how he proved his masculinity—through antiqueer and gang violence. Substantial scholarship has explored the relationship between race and violence against women and queer people that Piri commits in *Down These Mean Streets*, much of which my analysis engages.[5]

This chapter argues that Thomas uses life writing to theorize the connection between violence and identity, through which he comes to define his AfroLatinidad. Violence, when one commits it and when one is its object, is an act of extreme visibility. By becoming the perpetrator or victim of violence, all other aspects of one's identity can be subsumed under the category of "victim" or "criminal." In addition, in the US, violence is often attached to Blackness as a perpetual mindset, thus making Blackness an experience of perpetual visibility. As Saidiya Hartman asserts in regards to images of the Black poor, "to be visible [is] to be targeted for uplift or punishment, confinement or violence."[6] In white supremacist logic, it is assumed that if one watches someone with dark skin long enough, they will commit an act of violence. Thus, Black bodies, particularly Black boys and men, are closely surveilled. Thomas's AfroLatino identity, as portrayed through his memoirs and his archive, is inseparable from his self-identification as a cis-heterosexual man, so his conception of AfroLatinidad is decidedly masculine. His memoirs provide a rich and honest grappling with the intersections of race, ethnicity, masculinity, and sexuality. In negotiating these vectors of his identity, Thomas could not escape the ways in which the use of violence against him, and his own use of violence, shaped his life and his idea of what it means to be an Afro–Puerto Rican man.

He views his AfroLatinidad as an identity of creative destruction, one that decimates assumptions about race, ethnicity, and culture in order to pave a path for the fuller flourishing of AfroLatino men's lives. Creative destruction is not merely an act of analysis; it also depends on the perpetration of violence. It is not only violence as metaphor but violence as action. Thomas's lens of creative destruction, elaborated on in his archival writings, is a theorization of the creative potential of violence and a working-through of how one might turn the violence experienced and perpetrated by Barrio children and adults into a productive tool. The purpose of thinking through the shaping forces of violence and violence as a methodological lens is not to apologize for the prevalence of misogyny and antiqueer violence in Thomas's work.[7] In fact, this facet of his work might limit the application of his theories to AfroLatina and queer AfroLatinx lives.[8] For example, Afro–Puerto

Rican writer Marta Moreno Vega, whose memoir I analyze in chapter 4, covers the same time period (1930s-1950s) as Thomas's *Down These Mean Streets* and yet constructs a very different image of the time period and of how she constructed her AfroLatinidad. Thomas still offers an example of how AfroLatino men have attempted to work through violence as the central shaping force of their life stories.[9]

In fact, I contend that Thomas's trilogy of memoirs, like those of W. E. B. Du Bois, provides "an autobiography of a[n ethno-]race concept": a personal narrative and sociological reflection on AfroLatino masculinity focused particularly on the shaping power of violence.[10] Thomas, through the characterization of himself as Piri, presents creative destruction as an approach to negotiating the hypervisibility and invisibility of Afro–Puerto Ricanness through violence. First, in presenting his perceptions of himself as a child, Thomas contends that contemplation is an embodied experience.[11] That is, while we often think of identity as a mental process, an interior reasoning and justification that leads to a mostly coherent definition of ourselves, in fact, this mental process is inseparable from bodily experiences (such as violence). Then, Thomas presents the reader with the creative destruction inherent in AfroLatino practices of speech, showing how practices like the dozens can destroy assumptions of static racial definitions within communities of color. In addition, these practices also can interrogate the contradiction within mestizaje and Black nationalist narratives.[12] Simultaneously, he points to the violence of academic discourse that prettifies the violence inherent in the process of ethnoracial identification. Through the depiction of Gerald West, he demonstrates how academic conceptions of race can act as a linguistic means of blanqueamiento (whitening the race).

To understand Thomas's varying approaches to AfroLatinidad and how he writes against mestizaje, one must examine Thomas's theorization of the self and its connection to the prevalence of violence in his family, on the streets, and in his relationships. Thomas's trilogy of memoirs examines the centrality of violence to Blackness, puertorriqueñidad, migration, masculinity, and community.

Theorizing Violence and the Self in the Archive

This section illuminates why Thomas, perhaps best known for his poetic performances, would see life writing as the most productive genre through which to present his theorization of violence and AfroLatinidad as creative destruction. In the process of writing his memoirs, Thomas's thought process intertwined with his reflections on the prevalence of violence in his life. To understand Thomas's theory of life writing and his impetus for publishing his trilogy of memoirs, one must understand the personal and sociohistorical context into which he was born.

As a frequent speaker and performer, Piri Thomas's archive holds numerous versions of his biography. In one telling of his origins, Thomas emphasizes his jíbaro and Afro-Cuban roots. He writes, "I was born on September 30th, 1928 in Harlem Hospital New York City—in the black (colored then) part of town—of a Puerto Rican born mother—Dolores Montanez natural of Bayamon—from the mountain people—and a Cuban born father natural from El Oriente del Sur who found his way to Puerto Rico at the age of 16 and then to the United States Nueva York (New York) and passed for Puerto Rican for the rest of his days."[13] This biographical fragment, part of a much larger handwritten document in Thomas's archive, establishes Thomas as an Afro-Caribbean Latino, born of migrant parents in the continental United States.[14] In addition, Thomas's last comment about his father's "pass[ing] for Puerto Rican" reflects the Thomas men's struggle to reconcile their dark skin and Hispanophone Caribbean heritage. Thomas never mentions his father's Cuban origins in his memoirs; however, it informs the negotiation of his identity in writing the memoir.[15] Thomas's father's choice to "pass" for Puerto Rican reflects acts of violence central to AfroLatino identity: the erasure of one's self, the experience of anti-Black prejudice, questions of citizenship and belonging, and internal conflict over one's own worth in relation to lighter-skinned folk. However, in the memoirs, his father's passing is recast as an attempt to pass as Puerto Rican despite his Blackness, which instead shifts Thomas's commentary to consider the false dichotomy created between (US) Blackness and (white) puertorriqueñidad. In the wake of the great migration of Puerto Ricans to the continental US and the racial discourses occurring as the Cold War began, Piri and his father are related by a common conflict around ethnoracial identity.

Thomas grew up during several momentous events in US and Puerto Rican history, and his memoirs cover this period of the late 1930s through the 1950s. He experienced the Great Depression and the influx of jobs that came along with the decision to declare war on the Axis powers after the bombing of Pearl Harbor. He witnessed the growing presence of Puerto Rican islanders moving to New York as an effect of Operation Bootstrap.[16] After serving nearly seven years in prison for the armed robbery of a gay nightclub and attempted murder of a police officer during the commission of that crime, Thomas became a well-known advocate for children and prisoners. He was active in community-based activist organizations for children in the Barrio as well as in prison outreach, specifically leading creative writing workshops with incarcerated men. Thomas was perhaps best known as a poet, a staple of the Nuyorican Poets Café, a performance poetry space which birthed, supported, and continues to cultivate Black, Latinx, and Afro-Caribbean poets, like Tato Laviera, Sandra María Esteves, and Elizabeth Acevedo.

Thomas felt that the impetus for his writing came from the Civil Rights and Black Power Movements. He believed that the perspectives of Afro–Puerto Ricans were missing from writing produced and published in the 1960s. In one fragment of writing found in his archive, he writes: "Today, because of this fantastic Negro social revolution that is exploding throughout the world and is live lights throughout the United States, many Negro writers are finding an open market for their inner sensitivity and escense [sic] of personal involvement. What about the Puerto Rican Negro, whose tongue speaks spanish [sic] and skin shouts Negro?"[17] This visual imagery—"live lights" and the skin whose color "shouts" to be noticed—reflects Thomas's belief in the importance of Black visibility but also indicates that Black Puerto Rican experiences were being erased by mainstream and Black presses. The publication of *Down These Mean Streets* in 1967, then, was meant to highlight a Black Latino story and explore AfroLatinos' shared and distinct political and literary concerns. The memoir's publication coincided with the growth of the Black Arts Movement, the publication of Dr. Martin Luther King Jr.'s *Where Do We Go from Here*, and distrust from younger, more militant Black Power activists no longer convinced that nonviolent resistance was a suitable tool against white supremacist institutions. The next year would see the publication of Eldridge Cleaver's controversial prison essays, *Soul on Ice*. The influence of more militant movements grew, and Black men's voices were at the center of political and literary fields. Much of the Black Power writing that scholars examine from that era is just as supportive of toxic masculinity and patriarchy as it is of racial solidarity and anti-capitalism. *Down These Mean Streets* was exceptional in its centering of an Afro–Puerto Rican author but also shared the focus on hypermasculinity and misogynistic and homophobic violence exhibited by other writing of the era.

The memoir was incredibly successful, compared by reviewers alongside recently released coming-of-age stories by US Black Americans from ghettoized neighborhoods, namely Claude Brown's 1965 *Manchild in the Promised Land*.[18] In fact, *Kirkus Review* entitled their review of *Down These Mean Streets* "Manchild in the Barrio." The two share many similarities, joining a subgenre of life writing about poor racialized men who, after time in prison, become community artists and activists.[19] However, reviewers often ignored

Thomas's AfroLatino identity, focusing primarily on his status as a former offender and his dark skin. For Thomas, the hypervisibility of his masculinity and his Blackness in the home, streets, school, and prison worked to oversimplify his narrative by erasing his Puerto Rican identity, seen in the early reviews of his work as primarily an African American memoir. The major contribution of *Down These Mean Streets* is, first, its unapologetic portrayal of Thomas's life and the barriers he faced in finding acceptance and belonging in the multiple spaces he inhabited and, second, its grappling with the impact of Barrio violence and forced migration due to US colonialism on the development of AfroLatino men.

Down These Mean Streets covers Thomas's childhood, teenage years, and time in prison.[20] After this critically received memoir, Thomas wrote two less commercially successful autobiographies. The second, *Savior, Savior, Hold My Hand*, is about his conversion to Pentecostalism and his work against street violence. In this memoir, he struggles to reconcile his activism with the fatalism and racism of white Christianity, ultimately leading to his rejection of organized Christianity.[21] *Seven Long Times*, his last memoir, presents his experiences during his seven years in prison and offers his observations on the ineffectiveness and inhumanity of the prison system, ultimately advocating for prison reform. *Seven Long Times* was intended to be published as the second in this trilogy of life narratives, but Thomas struggled to write about that traumatic time of his life, as indicated in a 1974 interview.[22]

By taking into consideration earlier drafts of *Down These Mean Streets*, I analyze Thomas's writing process and particularly the ways he thinks through the prevalence of violence—personal, gendered, and institutional—in his life.[23] Thomas's writing and his archive are the basis of his theorizations of violence and life writing.[24] His conception of AfroLatinidad as creative destruction stems from his theorization of the creative potential of violence.[25] This theory of the creative potential of violence allows for the creative destruction with which Thomas breaks down the arguments and assumptions that keep him on the margins of US, Black, and Puerto Rican communities. However, this theory also depends heavily on misogynist and antiqueer violence. Through the lens of Thomas's theorization of life writing, this trilogy of memoirs becomes a means to negotiate the positive and negative power of violence for Thomas.

In the drafting stage of *Down These Mean Streets*, Thomas struggles to explain the prevalence of violence in his life and in El Barrio. Having survived those "mean streets," he is reluctant to disavow the people and practices that helped him survive, even if they also endangered him in other ways. As Monica Brown argues, texts like Thomas's "challenge stereotypical presumptions about Latino/a gang members" so that we can understand "the links between youth violence and systemic, historically based racism" and a litany of other inequitable and debilitating systems that create "the figure of the urban gang member."[26] Thomas does not begin with the presumed deficiencies of the urban gang. Rather, in his archival reflections, he marvels at the creative impulses behind street vernacular and gang formation. In an annotated draft of *Down These Mean Streets*, Thomas writes an author's note not included in the published version of the autobiography but that I see as a guiding principle for his memoirs. In an x-ed out box of text, he writes, "Author's Note: There is a beauty in birth, a national function, a creative expression of God in street talk, the ability to spread seeds and watch them grow into blocks called streets in a place like Harlem and its people. So it is with the gangs, the natural creativeness of the coming into being, of 'It Things' happening."[27] Thomas gently and lovingly describes "street talk," equating it with the divine. While often considered vulgar and lowbrow, Thomas sees the language as generative, literally creating the streets of Harlem and the community. The comparison of "blocks" and their people who have blossomed from seeds evokes the popular quotation of empowerment, "They tried to bury us. They did not know that we were seeds."[28] In validating the suffering of ghettoized Harlemites, Thomas celebrates the culture that has come from their oppression. In fact, he even declares that there is a "national function," meaning a way in which this linguistic practice has built national identities through Black nationalism and Puerto Rican nationalism. This passage also acts as a tribute to gangs, described as "the natural creativeness of coming into being." These organizations are often represented as violent and counterproductive to community uplift, and not without reason. However, for Thomas, the gang becomes a space where the rules of everyday life, the ones that pervade "the worlds of home and school," can be challenged and reformed. Gang life has its own logic and a dynamic culture, in which gang names, signs, and practices are rewritten and practiced differently with each generation. In his autobiographies, Thomas praises these creative impulses in gang life and street talk, integrating them into his own writing.

In another unpublished fragment, Thomas reflects on why his life could best represent the street kid, always gendered male in his writing, believing that he can represent the repressed creativity within each Barrio kid.[29] He writes, "street kids [. . .] see that violence is a universal expression. These kids fight because it is the only way they know to be expressive. [. . .] When I was a kid, I fought like all the rest and didn't really know why. Now I know. My fight was for acceptance, for anything and everything, for pride and stature, for street glory, for understanding and the right to express the positive creative latent talents that were within me."[30] Again, we see violence as a form of expression, the only form of expression available to children not provided alternate outlets.[31] Thomas sees his own violence as a child as both an outlet for repressed creativity but also as a way of making space for himself, for every part of himself—Black, Puerto Rican, boy, and man. He demands an all-encompassing acceptance.

Thomas goes back to the question of recognition and acceptance in the epilogue to his last memoir, *Seven Long Times*. This time, he also places this sentiment in relation to an understanding of systemic racism and classism. He thinks, "*I committed the crime . . . But who's going to stand up and admit it was this country's racial and economic inequalities that forced so many of us to the brink of insanity . . . Racism was my mind and anger was my heart, and I fought in the only way I figured was left open to me.*"[32] Here Thomas indicates the violence done to his mind through racism, particularly the internalization of anti-Black attitudes. The metaphor "anger was my heart" suggests that rage, pumping like blood through his body, was the only feeling he could express. Thomas fought the only way he could against the deeply ingrained forms of injustice in the US. The state treated him almost exclusively through violent means, his father violently punished his Blackness, and the streets taught him that violence, even against other marginalized people, could give him power. Violence was the primary experience for Piri Thomas, so his writings struggle with how to convey the complexity of that violence—the sense of community it created, the simultaneous powerlessness and empowerment, the freedom it created for himself even as he abused and oppressed others.

In writing and theorizing his life writing, Thomas requires the reader to consider the complexity of violence. Like James A. Tyner, I define violence as "a social and spatial practice."[33] Violence, for Thomas, is a lens for analyzing identity formation. In *Unspeakable Violence* (2011), Nicole Guidotti-Hernández asserts that "violence is a central category of analysis in and of itself because it is a process of extreme differentiation."[34] If identity has often come from recognizing difference from a norm, violence, especially who can and cannot wield it with legitimacy, is the ultimate process of determining difference and power. Guidotti-Hernández encourages scholars not to shy away from the hypocrisies and complicities of marginalized communities in committing violence. Viet Thanh Nguyen goes further, arguing that stories about finding oneself are historically acts of violence. He writes, "Literature and violence are, in the end, public acts, and certain genres, like myth and its more prosaic descendants such as the *bildungsroman* or novel of formation, unify both literature and violence."[35] That is, the novel of education and identity formation, commonly at the foundation of the autobiography and memoir, is one necessarily of and about violence. American identity itself, as Nguyen argues, "has a long tradition of deploying violence to define itself."[36] Whether through the violence of chattel slavery, genocide against Indigenous peoples, or brutality against migrants, being American often means laying claim to a history of state-sanctioned violence with little consequence. Similarly, Guidotti-Hernández theorizes "that the pain and suffering that result from violence against the body and the subject are integral to the production of subjectivities."[37] While Guidotti-Hernández and Nguyen speak in the context of Mexican, US, and Indigenous borderlands history and Asian American literature respectively, their call to examine violence not merely as a plot device but as a lens of analysis certainly applies to US, Puerto Rican, and Afro–Puerto Rican history.

Puerto Ricans' status as liminal citizens and colonial subjects—US citizens perpetually viewed as foreigners—comes together with the violence of perpetual othering and foreignness associated with Blackness. As Veena Das and Arthur Kleinman argue, "the pressure to create a different kind of past for oneself is related to how one deals with the violence of memories in the present."[38] That is, the act of life writing forces Thomas to engage with his past violence in two ways, one compliant and the other resistant. First, there are already existing narratives about violence in Afro–Puerto Rican history that hegemonic institutions will forcefully encourage, through the publishing industry, of course, but also through readily accepted and official notions of US violence in the everyday. From media, literature, academia, and the state, hegemonic notions of the colonization of Puerto Rico as well as narratives of Black criminality and Latino foreignness persist. These forces pressure Thomas to present a particular kind of past in line with US imperialist and white supremacist history. However, there is also the pressure that Piri feels to throw off those narratives, and by dissecting that past violence in the present, he can "create a different kind of past"—one that resists the distorting lens of hypervisibility and invisibility that erase his AfroLatino identity and struggles. So, Thomas leans into the violence of his life, and in doing so, it can seem to glorify that violence even as it dismantles the ideologies behind it.

Thomas's first memoir in particular venerates men's violence, though it also reveals the ways in which marginalized men hurt themselves and other marginalized communities. While one could focus solely on acts of state-supported violence, I also examine the deeply *personal* violence that permeates Thomas's work. Interpersonal violence is inseparable from the structural violence of a society,[39] and Thomas uses his life to show how they interact in the lives of everyday people. The use of violence as expression and oppression shapes Thomas's deployment of the life writing genre and provides insight into Thomas's multiple methods of defining himself as an AfroLatino subject. For example, if, as Guidotti-Hernández argues, a subject's citizenship is enacted by "contesting violations of their person,"[40] then Piri's performance of violation appears to him as an act of empowerment, fighting against racialized powerlessness, even as it also perpetuates American assumptions of Black criminality and Latino illegality.[41]

Through this chapter's focus on Thomas's theorization of writing the self and its entanglement with violence, I shift the discussion on Thomas's memoirs, which has focused primarily on place and space, to explore his theorization of violence.[42] As noted by scholars such as Ylce Irizarry and Lyn Di Iorio Sandín, Thomas is certainly concerned with how he navigates space and place in the US.[43] Thomas shows how, rather than this place-based violence destroying him, Piri negotiated this ever-present violence in defining himself as an AfroLatino boy and, eventually, man. He portrays different modes of creative destruction—embodied reflection, physical violence, and speech practices like the dozens—to highlight his differing theorizations of the self and the representation of the self through writing.

Embodied Reflection: Contemplating Violence in *Down These Mean Streets*

Down These Mean Streets (*DTMS*), Thomas's first memoir, begins in his childhood, a time of great vulnerability and exploration. As Aurora Levins Morales notes, "childhood is the one political condition, the one disenfranchised group through which all people pass.... They see clearly what custom has made invisible to us and are outraged by all injustices, no matter how small."[44] By attempting to put himself back into the position of child-Piri, Thomas makes visible the norms around race and masculinity that as adults we no longer notice (or try not to notice). *DTMS* represents one theorization of the purpose of life writing for Thomas: that the genre illuminates the internal struggle to find ourselves and that often, the construction of an AfroLatino identity stems from quiet reflection on quotidian experiences of violent language, violent acts, and dangerous expectations. As M. Jacqui Alexander observes, "so much of how we remember is embodied: the scent of home: of fresh-baked bread; [. . .] Violence can also become embodied, that violation of sex and spirit."[45] By focusing on the interior life of Piri as an AfroLatino boy, Thomas theorizes the self as an act of embodied contemplation.[46] This narrative contemplation allows Piri to question others' categorizations of himself and to think things that he cannot imagine saying aloud.

Quiet acts of reflection allow one to speak forbidden truths: for Piri, this is the uncomfortable reality that his brothers and sisters do not look like him, that they are favored because of that difference, and that this difference is based primarily on skin color. Identification begins by allowing oneself to notice difference and the harmful consequences associated with deviating from unspoken norms. For Piri, the family home is often the place where reflective thought occurs.

While many consider home a static place, the impact of social identities, such as race, ethnicity, and gender, can exert oppressive force on members from inside and outside of the family home. Many critics have used the concepts of "home" and belonging as the driving conflict of *DTMS*.[47] But the home is more than a space. As Carole Boyce Davies asserts, "the writing of home exists narratively," through narrative choices such as "conversations, letters to family, stories passed on to children as family history or to friends as reminiscences. Thus, the rewriting of home becomes a critical link in the articulation of identity."[48] Thus, I argue that "home" in the novel is a narrative space. In *DTMS*, "the house and its specific rooms become metaphors of self and loci of self-identification."[49] The home and its rooms are strategically evoked to explore the obviously visible things that cannot be spoken. Our family home is the first, though not the only, space where we encounter and negotiate narratives of race, ethnicity, gender, and sexuality. These encounters inform our negotiations in the so-called public sphere.

Piri's first reflection on being AfroLatino occurs when he realizes that his family holds colorist ideas, which privilege his lighter-skinned siblings while marking his darker skin as a constant source of trouble.[50] As William Luis argues, "Thomas's identity crisis is centered around what he perceives to be his family's rejection."[51] The realization of his family's colorism is one way that Piri defines AfroLatinidad as a form of creative destruction. Piri's mental construction of himself as a Black Puerto Rican eventually forces his family to confront the presumed whiteness of Latinidad, and at the same time, it provides an opportunity to create a new dynamic in the family. These thoughts are internal but also experienced and embodied. Colorist thought has a physical impact on Piri and creates an internal struggle about his sense of worth and self-definition.

The choice to portray his feelings and fears through scenes in which Piri retreats to the interior serves as an example of Kevin Quashie's theorization of quietude and the interior life of Black people in *The Sovereignty of Quiet* (2012). For Quashie, the line between silence and quiet is thin but distinct, and the scenes in which the reader gets inside child-Piri's mind straddle this line. Quashie asserts, "Silence often denotes something that is suppressed or repressed, and is an interiority that is about withholding, absence, and stillness. Quiet, on the other hand, is presence (one can, for example, describe prose or a sound as quiet) and can encompass fantastic motion."[52] While Piri's thoughts are often ones that he feels are unspeakable in his home, they also act as a way to solve problems and work through issues. Since these moments of reflection help Piri see the impacts of racialization on his own life and his father's, Piri's scenes of thoughtfulness are moments of quietude. Thomas's choice to portray so much of his early life through contemplation itself expands notions of AfroLatino masculinity. As Quashie notes, "historically, the concept of interiority has been constructed as the domain of women, and as a result, it is often women's culture that has labored to make the terms of inner life (domesticity, privacy, vulnerability) meaningful rather than pejorative."[53] Thus, Thomas's choice to reclaim the masculine interior, particularly to think through the love between a father and son, is a narrative choice that combats the notion that this is a novel focused only on action and dominance. In addition, several of Piri's turns to the interior focus on the importance of violence in the domestic sphere as a shaping force for AfroLatino identity.

The family home, particularly in *Down These Mean Streets*, is where Piri first realizes that his ambiguous ethnoracial identity puts his racial loyalty and his national and ethnic pride in question. Piri offers a picture of himself in which visible identity markers play a critical role in his subject formation within the home. He describes his siblings and mother as light-skinned Puerto Ricans, leaving him and his father as the dark-skinned outliers. While Piri does not identify his Blackness within the text of the memoir until his mother calls him "*morenito*" and jokes about his Blackness,[54] he presents his AfroLatino identification in the prologue of *DTMS*. Piri is "a skinny, dark-face, curly-haired, intense Porty-Reecan."[55] Piri's dark skin and lack of the straight hair valued in Latina/o/x culture make him an other in the Latinx mestizo narrative.[56] In addition, he claims Puerto Rican identity, writing it out phonetically in a US accent, thus identifying himself as a diasporic Puerto Rican more comfortable with a Spanglish language politics. He is aware that Puerto Rico is read as "foreign" even though Puerto Ricans are legally US citizens.[57] This prologue is a similar call to acceptance to the one in his archives. He begins the autobiography not through polite language but yelling. Piri talks about how often he went to the "rooftop and yelled out to anybody: 'Hey, World—here I am [. . .] I'm here, and I want recognition, whatever that mudder-fuckin word means."[58] In this first paragraph of the memoir, he repeats "I'm here" three times. This repetition and the description of his body and face are acts of embodied contemplation.

Thomas forces the reader to place themselves on the rooftop. He writes his presence into existence. Piri also compares himself to the shadows, as part of "this warm *amigo* darkness," pointing to his African ancestry as well as the forced invisibility of that heritage within his family.[59] In the beginning, Piri is like a shadow, merely a silhouette of his full self since he is disallowed from recognizing his Blackness. In addition, his dark skin is a like a shadow, following him into every interaction at home, in the streets, at school, and eventually, in prison.

These markers of Africanity connect him to his Afro-Cuban father, and though this connection between father and son has the potential to draw them closer together, Piri spends most of his autobiographies struggling to understand and mend their estranged relationship. Understanding this dynamic is necessary for understanding Thomas's negotiations of race, ethnicity, and gender. Piri's father is a foil to Piri, an example of a man unwilling to claim the fullness of his identity and whose shame manifests itself through violence. By characterizing Piri's father in this way, Thomas indicates that internalizing racism does not lead to an easier life, but rather continues a cycle of light-skinned favoritism, racialized violence, and sexist aggression. The first chapter of *DTMS* ties Piri's complicated relationship with his father to his struggle with identity.[60] In the "boiling" thoughts that the reader first encounters as Piri recounts why he has run away from home, he laments internally, "*I'm his kid, too, just like James, José, Paulie, and Sis. But I'm the one that always gets the blame for everything.*"[61] Piri, in trying to stop his brother José from knocking down "a large jar of black coffee," ends up breaking it himself. As Poppa "looks at the river of black coffee," he, without asking for an explanation, chooses Piri as his target for punishment.[62] The punishment is not merely for breaking the jar. The "black coffee" mirrors his and his father's dark skin. Like the black coffee, their Blackness cannot be contained, creates a mess, overflows, and unsettles the home. Their conspicuous Blackness makes their claims to Puerto Ricanness suspicious. Thus, from the beginning, Piri wonders how his physical features impact his standing in the family and in his community. Lisa Sánchez González reads this first scene, in which Piri runs away and returns home to find out that no one missed him, as "prefigur[ing] his perpetual flight from confusing and contradictory familial and social contexts in the novel."[63] Instead of viewing this scene and the novel as a perpetual attempt at escape, I view it as a means of confrontation. Piri does not run from the contradictions, he thinks deeply on them and what it means to identify one way in theory versus in practice.

The running away scene in chapter 1 is just the first of many scenes in which child-Piri reflects on the subtle and overt ways in which his dark skin sets him apart. For example, as a child taking a bath, Piri reflects on how his father's affection is often tied to racialized characteristics. As Arnaldo Cruz-Malavé notes, the family's bathroom is "where the novel's main gender and racial conflicts are explored and taken to their limit."[64] The bathroom also comes to represent a private space of reflection where the unspoken can be explored. Like his silent reflections after running away, Piri uses the limited privacy of the bathroom to think about the less loving treatment he perceives from his father. He thinks, *"I wonder if it's something I done, or something I am [. . .] Maybe 'cause I'm the biggest, huh? Or maybe it's 'cause I'm the darkest in this family."*[65] Piri wants to know if it is his actions, his physical being, or something outside of himself that causes his father to treat him differently than the other siblings. When Piri begins to list possible reasons, in this case, his size or his skin color, he uses a question mark, a formal signal of uncertainty. Though the last sentence in the quote may be read as a question, due to his use of the word "maybe," Thomas writes it as a declarative statement. As seen in earlier drafts of *Down These Mean Streets*, this punctuation choice was deliberate.[66] Thomas initially used a question mark at the end of "Or maybe it's cuz I'm the darkest in this family?" But he changes it to a period by placing a large circle around the period. This is the only question to be changed to a declarative sentence in this revision process. Thus, Thomas's choice of punctuation signifies a confidence shift. While it remains possible that other factors may be the reason for his poor treatment, Piri seems to assert that he knows for sure his Blackness is a reason for his father's harsh treatment.[67]

In addition to considering these punctuation choices, one must also consider Thomas's use of italics to textualize his thoughts, a consistent formatting choice across all three memoirs. Italics (also known as oblique or slanted) are a text feature generally employed for emphasis and to create narrative distance from the reader. Using italics to indicate interiority may be merely a convenient way for the reader to navigate what occurs in the interior and exterior of Piri's life. However, in a book that also uses italics to mark Spanish-language terms and thus to mark foreignness for a presumed English reader, italics become another way to mark Piri's difference. His thoughts do not often align with how others in his life think. As shown in the examples above, Piri's reflections often question norms or identify difference (racial, national, etc.) that his family or society wants to silence. Dominican American writer Angie Cruz indicates that text features such as quotation marks can harm the reading experience by privileging dialogue over narration or thought.[68] Indeed, Thomas's use of italics is a form of privileging. Typeface without emphasis marks action, speech, and enacted violence throughout the autobiography and is the kind of material often privileged in novels about men of color growing up in ghettoized neighborhoods. Thomas's choice to italicize thoughts privileges the masculine interior while also clearly indicating distance between how Piri views himself and how the world views him. Italics embody, through the text, Piri's feelings and experiences of being marked in his home and in society at large.

Piri's thoughts on his ethnoracial identity coincide with the physical, and mental, exploration of his manhood. Directly after the paragraph in which Piri lists the possible reasons that Poppa loves him less than his siblings, Thomas describes Piri as pulling "absent-mindedly" on his flaccid penis, "like a toy balloon when it's empty."[69] Piri's act of pulling on his penis shows the inextricable tie between his developing sense of masculinity and male embodiment and what it means to be a Black Puerto Rican. Its flaccid state suggests a feeling of being "less than," of missing something. His thoughts then turn to the ways in which Poppa shows his preference for his other, lighter-skinned children, with Piri's sister, Miriam, as the prime example. He notices that Poppa calls her "'honey' and the rest of those sweet names" while Piri rarely gets called these terms of affection. Piri's thoughts turn violent: *"Miriam gets treated like a princess. I'd like to punch her in her straight nose."*[70] Through his reference to "her straight nose" Piri points to Miriam's purported white features, believing that she is "treated like a princess" due to her light-skinned privilege. Rather than wish for more love from his father, he imagines hurting his sister, deforming the "white" nose that his father loves so much. Through this example, the reader sees a link between racial anxiety and sexist aggression that will show up repeatedly in Piri's life. These violent thoughts also represent an example of how, even when Piri recognizes the institutional and systemic origins behind his own experiences of racism, he often places blame for them and projects his anger about these systems on light-skinned women.[71]

One can see the overlap between Piri's quiet reflection on the family's colorism and the process of becoming a man, or as he put it "becoming hombre," in the middle of *Down These Mean Streets*.[72] The ideas about race, culture, and manliness that he gets from his boys in the streets are in constant conflict with those in his home life. In this scene, Piri gets into a verbal and then physical altercation with his brother José after Piri declares that he is "a Negro" and by extension, everyone in the family is also Black.[73] José angrily objects to the idea and repeats the family line that Poppa "has Indian blood in him" rather than African ancestry.[74] Piri seems to hope that by shattering the family's perceived ideas of race—that is, that the family is white except for Piri and Poppa, who are Taíno—he can break the silence around the family's ethnoracial tensions and create a more honest dialogue. José's claim that Poppa and Piri are Indigenous, for example, points out that claiming Indigenous ancestry is often an anti-Black tactic rather than a pro-Indigenous stance. By interrogating his own and his brother José's identity, Piri forces him to face uncomfortable truths about the family's anti-Blackness and brings out into the open the harmful effects of colorism.

Like the contemplative scenes discussed earlier, this scene, too, takes place in the bathroom before spilling out into the living room, much like "the jar of black coffee" from the beginning of the memoir. Arnaldo Cruz-Malavé stresses the symbolism of the fight beginning in the bathroom, asserting that,

> while the streets are the space where ethnic and racial conflict is ostensibly enacted and performed, it is here in this other offstage, palimpsestic, contrapuntal site where the family's repressed colonial history is being negotiated and worked out and a quasibiblical fratricidal climax is being prepared which will erupt placing the disavowed black naked body in the house's most visibly public room amid tears, blood, and urine.[75]

Literally, the family's issues with race begin in a place of semiprivacy: the bathroom, in which people go to complete the most intimate of acts, where shit (literally) gets done, and where we pretend not to hear or know what happens inside. The brothers' fight over identity spilling from that area of socially constructed secrecy to the common, semipublic area of the living room symbolizes the movement of the family's colorist tensions from private to public. The larger question of what it means to be Puerto Rican is brought to the attention of all, not just Piri.

The fight with José begins because young Piri pays careful attention to male genitalia, his own and others. Piri notices that José and his other brother's penises are light-skinned, while "only ones got black peters is Poppa and me, and Poppa acts like his is white, too."[76] By claiming that Poppa "acts like his is white, too," Piri makes a symbolic claim about the kind of manhood that Poppa performs. Piri claims both that his father refuses to accept his Blackness, even when it comes through in the most intimate of spaces, and that Poppa refuses to talk about or consider how race impacts his view of himself as a man. Piri's direct connection between each man's penis and race reinforces the intertwined nature of masculinity and race in Thomas's conception of AfroLatinidad.

The physicality of race and masculinity, and their intertwined nature, also comes through in José's refusal to accept his father's African ancestry and thus his own African ancestry. First, he equates having African ancestry as having distinct physical differences besides skin color. This conflation leads him to base his argument in physical characteristics that have been seen as "Black." He first points to physical features that he sees as white as an act of racialized refusal: "Look at my hair. It's almost blond. My eyes are blue, my nose is straight. My motherfuckin' lips are not like a baboon's ass. My skin is white. White, goddamit!"[77] As José goes through his tirade, he moves from focusing on particular facial features ("my nose is straight") to moving towards racial insults (his lips "are not like a baboon's ass"). Social constructivist conceptions of racial identity, forwarded by scholars such as Michael Omi, Howard Winant, and Eduardo Bonilla-Silva, make it clear that nose shape or hair texture are only social markers of race.[78] However, José reads these features through pseudoscientific racism,[79] the kind that formed the foundation of eugenics and social Darwinism. José claims whiteness to assert that he is not an inferior species of human. He perceives his attempt to recast Piri's and Poppa's Blackness as Indigeneity as an act of love—an acceptance of Piri into the white community. Numerous scholars, such as Omi and Winant, George Lipsitz, and Noel Ignatiev, have pointed to the one-way nature of assimilation into European-descent culture. José refuses to accept assimilation into Blackness, while expecting Piri to be honored by his acceptance by (and into) the white Puerto Rican community.

Thomas, too, in narrating the altercation focuses on his own and his brother's racialized features: José's "white hands," "white, blood-smeared face," and Piri's tender, "flat nose."[80] When the fight spills out of the bathroom and into the living area, Mama, who he always imagined as unaffected by anti-Black racism due to her Puerto Rican upbringing, instinctively screams her concern for José, but not for Piri. "'José, José,' Mama screamed, and I wondered why she didn't scream for me, too. Didn't she know I had gotten hurt the worst?"[81] This is a moment of tragic epiphany. Piri finally realizes that his father is not the only one in the family whose love and affection are mediated through skin color. Through his mother's seemingly instinctive and deeper concern for her light-skinned child, he sees that, despite her claims to the contrary, Mama harbors the same prejudices of colorism. By emphasizing his brother's whiteness in relation to his own dark skin, Piri refuses to be silent any longer about the racialized assumptions built into the family's conception of their identity as Puerto Rican.

Piri understands the abjection of Blackness as a form of emasculation, which leads him to assert a hypermasculine front, even in his own thoughts. During his bathtub ruminations, bathroom battles, and throughout *Down These Mean Streets*, Thomas connects his struggles with masculine identity formation to colorism in Puerto Rican families and communities. Thomas identifies these moments of reflection and conflict in the home to show the ways those thoughts become embodied experience, so the reader can see how they impact his relationship to society at large.

Destructive Language: Verbalizing AfroLatinidad

To this point, I have examined Piri's connection between violence and the shaping of the self through embodied reflection. This section illuminates the creative destruction within language, specifically Thomas's use of culturally grounded practices of dialogic play to explore and claim AfroLatinidad. By placing these discussions in Caribbean and Afro-diasporic oral traditions, Thomas's memoirs make the argument that dialogues about identity must take place among those in Black and Latinx communities, not only among those who feel an easy affiliation with whiteness and especially white American citizenship. In addition, Thomas includes other scenes of dialogue in which he is a background character, observing others grapple with what seeing and accepting AfroLatino difference means for their own conceptions of race and culture. In doing so, he demonstrates that witnessing the identity struggles of others is integral to constructing the self. Lisa D. McGill argues "that *Down These Mean Streets* should be read as a story of the *negotiation of blackness* as Piri tries to find community amid the binary racialization politics of the United States."[82] Thomas shows that this negotiation is not mere metaphor; he literally negotiates what it means to be a Black Puerto Rican, not only within himself but with others, through oral traditions such as the dozens. He speaks to the power of language to make visible the assumptions and exclusion inherent in hegemonic ideas of Blackness and Latinidad as well as in academic jargon. As Sánchez González notes, *DTMS* "disregard[s] the standardization of English in the novel, opting instead to create narrators and characters who speak and signify completely in Boricua and other urban vernaculars."[83] Thomas's privileging of street vernacular is an act of reclaiming the discussion of Blackness and puertorriqueñidad from academic outsiders.

Thomas's most nuanced discussion of race, ethnicity, and community is delivered through a game of the dozens, a tradition of verbal banter in African diasporic communities.[84] Cathy Park Hong describes it as a way "to other English" and "to make audible the imperial power sewn into the language, to slit English open so its dark histories slide out."[85] This verbal practice resists standardization and focuses on the playful and powerful possibilities of language. The dozens is a practice of creative destruction, where, as H. Rap Brown / Jamil Abdullah Al-Amin argues, you "totally destroy somebody else with words."[86] Often imagined as a masculine form of communication, the dozens usually begin by insulting the other man's mother or girlfriend, rather than the person themselves. Brown/Al-Amin identifies attacks on the person themselves as signifying, though both practices focus on insult and humiliation.[87] In addition, the focus is often insults against women (placing them as property or a thing to be protected) and queer people. The dozens flirts with physical violence, daring the speakers to push boundaries but also not to lose control of their tempers. Starting from this practice may, then, appear to be strange, since its focus is verbal violence and some degree of emotional harm. However, Thomas uses the destructive aspects of the dozens to create a space to build something new. The dozens is an entry point for dialogue and discussion, a way for Piri to critically analyze his internalized racism and his idea of how Blackness and puertorriqueñidad relate to US and international ideals of Black unity.

The chapter "Hung Up between Two Sticks" begins with a game of the dozens that explicitly focuses on the difference (if there is one) between race and ethnicity. Piri engages in this dialogic practice with Brew, his Southern Black American friend, initiating the game by playfully insulting Brew for his Blackness, saying, "you sure is an ugly spook."[88] This sentence, meant as a playful insult, closely echoes the supposedly endearing statement by Piri's mother earlier, that she loved him even if he was "*un negrito* and ugly too."[89] By paralleling these two lines in such different contexts, Thomas signals to the reader that these sections are about the same thing: his identity as an Afro–Puerto Rican. In addition, they act in the same capacity: to provoke a conversation about the violence of identity. When Brew responds, he insults Piri for hating his own Blackness: "Dig this Negro calling out 'spook.'"[90] Brew points to Piri's internalized racism, which Piri inadvertently confirms by rejecting Blackness entirely, stating "I'm a Porty Rican."[91] When Brew doubles down that he "only sees another Negro in fron' of [him]," Thomas the narrator introduces us to what is occurring as the dozens, requiring the reader to consider the conversation in that frame. Thomas writes, "This was the 'dozens,' a game of insults. The dozens is a dangerous game even among friends. [. . .] Now I wanted the game to get serious. I didn't know exactly why."[92] Piri wants the game to get serious because he recognizes that he and Brew are bringing to the surface a buried truth about the complexities of race, ethnicity, and colonialism. As two dark-skinned men, they are confronting what, if any, sense of community they should have. So even when Piri ostensibly ends the game soon after, fearing that he has crossed a line and "should get it back on a joke level,"[93] he cannot actually let go of the conversation the game has created and the issue that is now fully visible. Thus, the dozens acts as a gateway to a real dialogue between two dark-skinned men situated in entirely different spaces: an Afro–Puerto Rican born and raised in the Barrio and a Southern Black man who migrated to the North. Thomas establishes the dozens as an acceptable way for men to talk about these deeper aspects of identity and to express vulnerability about Piri's sense of disconnection, and even more, the connections that he wished he did not feel to US Blackness.

Thomas places Piri and Brew on two different sides: Brew argues for the global reality of Blackness and the need for a political coalition around the experience of anti-Black racism, while Piri argues, first, that he is *not* Black and, second, that "global Blackness" is often code for US Blackness. By claiming that "I ain't no damn Negro and I ain't no paddy. I'm Puerto Rican,"[94] Piri denies any racial identity, associating himself only with Puerto Rican ethnonational identity. Brew contests the idea that Blackness and Puerto Ricanness are mutually exclusive. He claims a global Black identity: "Whatta yuh all think? That the only niggers in the world are in this fucked-up country [the US]? They is all over this damn world."[95] To Brew, Piri's claims to nationality and ethnicity are an act of anti-Black racism, made to disconnect from a unified Black political struggle, to deny solidarity, and to cling to language or culture in order to whiten one's identity: "Jus' cause you can rattle off some different kinda language don' change your skin one bit."[96] Politics is at the core of Brew's definition of Blackness. As Ylce Irizarry argues, Piri's relationship with Brew leads him to conclude that "it is his sensitivity to the harsh realities of racism, not his skin color, which makes him Black."[97] But Piri wants to show Brew that the experience of discrimination as a Black man may differ when it is based in having dark skin *as well as* speaking something other than English. Piri forces Brew to consider and respond to a particular hypervisibility that being AfroLatino entails, like their experience of colonialism and xenophobia, and to question the application of US conceptions of Blackness to Afro-Caribbean migrants.

Piri argues that US Black (as well as pan-African) attempts to adopt and forcefully include Puerto Ricans in the Black struggle are misguided and disempowering if they oversimplify and even make invisible the differing struggles of US Black and Afro–Puerto Rican communities. That is, "Puerto Ricans got social problems, too."[98] Piri feels that others identifying him as (US) Black does not expose the common problems of Black and dark-skinned Puerto Rican people but rather ignores Puerto Rico and the distinct forms of oppression that Puerto Ricans face. Thomas implies that US Black struggles refuse to tackle the effects of US colonialism on Puerto Ricans in the continental US and on the island by recasting their problems as solely an effect of anti-Black racism. In fact, Brew confirms Piri's critique when he disqualifies Piri's opinions and experiences of racism. He directly questions Piri's authority to discuss discrimination, since, having never been in the South, Piri has never experienced Jim Crow laws.[99] By establishing US Southern racism as the "truest" form of racism, Brew strangely counters his own claim to a global Black experience and establishes Southern Black Americans as the only ones with "real" knowledge of racism. The exchange ends with Piri wanting to experience the South in order to assuage his own doubts about what he knows about race and to feel more authentically Black. The chapter ends with another deployment of the dozens, this time in the more classic sense of playful insults towards Piri's dad and Brew's mom.

By bookending the chapter with the dozens, Thomas points the reader to the dialogic nature of self- and community identity. In addition, he also privileges street talk and street practices of masculinity. The dozens acts as a catalyst to negotiate Piri's AfroLatinidad, which challenges the dominance of US Blackness. The dozens, despite its basis in insult and verbal destruction, also is an act of creative destruction. The interrogation deepens Piri and Brew's friendship and helps each to consider how the racial codes that structure discussions of Blackness and Latinidad are enacted differently in the North, the South, and the Caribbean.

Missing from this dialogue, however, are women's voices. Thus, the decision to include a six-page discussion between Brew and his girlfriend, Alayce, in which Piri is essentially nonexistent—a completely passive character waiting in the wings—is, I argue, an important example of the ways in which Thomas uses the memoir to do more than uncritically play out an AfroLatino identity based on dominance over women and femme people. While Marta E. Sánchez reads Piri as "a brown voyeur into blackness" in this scene,[100] I propose that the inclusion of this dialogue between a Black man and Black woman, both migrants from the South to New York, demonstrates the memoir's concern not only with Piri's life but with the idea of creating identity that encompasses race, culture, gender, and sexuality, and most centrally, *how violence shapes personal and communal identity*. Like Jesús Colón and the Young Lords, Thomas uses his own narrative in relation to the narratives of others to think about Afro–Puerto Rican identity more broadly. Unlike the previous dialogue, brought on by the dozens in the street, Brew and Alayce's discussion happens in her apartment and depends on intense vulnerability: namely, the disclosure of each as a survivor of attempted and completed sexual assault, respectively. While Brew and Piri focus almost entirely on skin color and politics, Brew and Alayce focus on culture, gender, and the impact of sexual violence on identity and self-worth.

Brew and Alayce begin their conversation by discussing Piri. When Brew explains that Piri wants to go down South to understand "our people," she is skeptical about the conflation of Brew's Southern Blackness with Piri's Afro–Puerto Rican identity.[101] Like Piri earlier, Alayce differentiates Puerto Ricans from Black Americans through culture. Brew again begins with his international conception of Blackness and anti-Black racism: "His skin is dark an' that makes him ju' anudder rock right along wif tha res' of us, and' tha' goes for all the rest of them foreign-talkin' black men all ovah tha' world."[102] Nonetheless, Alayce points towards the difference between Black and Puerto Rican culture—"they got different ways of dancin' an' cookin', like a different culture or something"—as a legitimate way of sorting the two.[103] Alayce recognizes their cultural differences, while Brew is more concerned with their political similarities. Brew would never consider himself an Afro–Puerto Rican, so why must Piri identify as Black? She does not easily dismiss the cultural dimension to ethnoracial identity.

In this discussion, Brew represents masculinist, ethnonationalist definitions of Blackness, which see Blackness as an international, umbrella identity for political solidarity.[104] By asserting her life experience as a Black woman from the South, Alayce represents an intersectional politics, evoking Dr. Anna Julia Cooper and her book, *A Voice from the South by a Black Woman of the South* (1892). The problem with dialogic developments of identity shows itself in Brew's response to Alayce's declaration that being a Black woman is harder than being a Black man.[105] While in the dozens scene, Brew gives Piri the space to talk and explain even hotly contested statements, Alayce's arguments are consistently cut off. For example, after stating her belief that Black women have it harder, she tries to offer a narrative to explain, but Brew will not allow it: "it don't make no fuckin' difference what happened, yuh supposed to be proud of being a Negro."[106] When Alayce questions Brew's own pride, particularly in practicing the respectability politics that his mother taught him, he lashes out physically, smacking Alayce to the ground, so that she slides across the room.[107] By placing Brew and Alayce on opposite sides of the room, Thomas creates the image of a chasm between the experiences and beliefs of Black men and women in the United States. This literal and figurative gap stems directly from Brew's violent act, representing how violence plays a vital role in the distance that Black people feel from US white supremacist society and that Black women like Alayce feel from the rhetoric of Black ethnonationalist pride.

This scene also examines how racialized and sexualized violence shapes both Brew's and Alayce's history. After Brew's violence against Alayce, the tone of the scene changes sharply. Brew becomes emotional and shares the tragic story of how he came to New York. When he was sixteen, two white men demanded that Brew submit to anal sex and tried to rape him when he refused. He tells a horrifying yet heroic tale about how he verbally and physically fought the two men off by strangulating one man to unconsciousness and kicking the other man in the testicles.[108] Being a Black man acting in self-defense in the Jim Crow South led Brew to fear for his life and the well-being of his family, so he fled North. Brew's narrative reveals how integral this experience was to his life. The act was both racially and sexually motivated, and the story again exhibits how heterosexuality and racial identity are intertwined to Brew and Piri.[109] In sharing this terrible story, Brew shows the centrality of violence to his identity as a Black migrant. His narrative also recenters the discussion on himself, further marginalizing Alayce's perspective in the dialogue.

While Alayce (and Thomas as the narrator) gives Brew the time and space to tell his story of attempted sexual violence, Brew, who has already violently interrupted Alayce once, does not provide her the same space or validation. Brew offers his Black male experience of the South, not in the context of educating Piri but rather as a way of diminishing Alayce's claim of Black women's oppression. "Man's got a right to what he feels," Brew says, but what about women?[110] While Brew's story is provided in two and a half pages, Alayce's dialogue about being gang-raped by four white boys, in addition to innumerable attempted rapes and instances of sexual harassment, is only one short paragraph: "Ah guess Ah can't forget the so many times them white boys tried to pull me into the bushes like Ah was one big free-for-all pussy. Ah can't forget the one time they finally did. Ah fought them as hard as Ah could. There were four of them, an' Ah was fifteen, an' they hurt me an' hurt me an'—"[111] Again, Brew cuts her off and prevents her from sharing her whole story. Alayce demonstrates her feeling of just being an object instrumentalized for white male sexual pleasure. While her story is just as much about her physical resistance as Brew's, neither Brew nor Thomas comment on her attempts at self-defense. While Thomas depicts Brew as comforting her—"I'd never seen my boy so gentle"—he also clearly silences her.[112] Ultimately, Brew uses Alayce's story to enforce a familiar Black Power narrative of pride: "there ain't nothin' so bad can happen that'll make one ashamed of what they is, if they's proud enough."[113] Violence plays a key role in Alayce's narrative, but she is not allowed the space to narrate that impact. Instead, Brew tries to pull the attention back to him, more concerned with appearing caring than with supporting Alayce's voice. Brew's focus on race pride shows its flaws: namely, that it prioritizes Black men's experiences.

In this discussion, Piri associates an image of Jesus with Brew and Alayce's examination of the violence at the center of their migration narratives. During this prolonged scene, Piri seems barely present, so most scholars see his character as a passive observer. Indeed, this choice is deliberate, as earlier versions of the book include Piri as a more active speaker, but Thomas deliberately cut those lines out.[114] It is true that Piri mostly observes; his "joke" statement to Brew about "almost los[ing] your cherry" is the only time he engages in the conversation.[115] Even when Brew assaults Alayce, Piri follows the harmful street code that a man does not interfere with another man's right to discipline his girlfriend.[116] His status as an outsider in this section—during the discussion, he is "looking at [a] picture on the wall"—implies to the reader that his current attempt to identify with Blackness as defined by Brew and Alayce is misguided.[117] However, Thomas uses Piri to further emphasize the purpose of their dialogue: to show the centrality of violence to identity in El Barrio and the connection between violence and displacement. He does so by reflecting on a mythical man primarily associated with violence: Jesus Christ. Marta E. Sánchez claims that Piri's looking at the Christ image in Alayce's apartment is a way of embodying the Malinche position: "Piri uses the picture of Christ to mediate between the antinomies of the dominant mode of sexuality his culture has bequeathed to him—his own warrior masculinity—and the fragile femininity he presumes the Christ represents."[118] However, I read Piri's quiet reflection of the image as a rumination on violence and identity.

In the image hanging on the wall, Jesus is light-skinned ("paddy"), "kneeling with his hands clasped together and looking up at the sky with a hangdog look."[119] The invocation of Jesus is heavily symbolic of both Piri's own life and of Christianity's implication in narratives of suffering and oppression. While Jesus would certainly have been a dark-skinned man, the whitewashing of Jesus allowed him to be seen as a Western figure and to use Christian teachings to support racist ideals (e.g., the curse of Ham) and government policies (e.g., segregation and anti-miscegenation laws). Like Piri and his father wish they could do, Jesus went through the process of blanqueamiento (whitening) so that his followers could erase his status as an anti-government activist and revolutionary, thus siding with the power of the state rather than with those fighting oppression. In addition, Jesus is a man inseparable from his father. God, the father, allows violence against his son for what he imagines to be the greater good. Like the image, which is "lopsided" under the weight of "a pair of Alayce's stockings,"[120] the idea of Jesus is weighted down by the feminine imagery of nonviolence, even as he is supposed to be the ultimate example of man, the divine man. Jesus, the son of the Christian God, is celebrated for his nonviolence, turning the other cheek, while he is also the man who destroys the Pharisees' wares in the temple. His gory, painful death—despite the fact that he could choose not to experience it if he desired—is the ultimate act of self-definition. Jesus Christ is *defined through his relationship to violence*, particularly the relationship between violence and nonviolence. Piri sees himself through Jesus and also sees Brew and Alayce's revelations through that lens as well.

Academic Mestizaje and the Violence of Self-Identification

Both the dozens scene and the argument between Alayce and Brew show how Thomas most values culturally based practices for negotiating the realities of identity, rather than academic discourse. Through the character of Gerald West, *Down These Mean Streets* alleges that academia evades the reality of race and other "socially constructed" identities. Thomas demonstrates that the dialogue of the streets, at least for the men whose voices are fully allowed to be heard, more directly engages with the realities of identity. Brew and Piri's conversation with Gerald West in the US South presents two sides of Piri's view on intellectualism. First, he creates a dichotomy between the masculinity of street talk and the femininity of intellectualism. Brew and Piri consistently denigrate Gerald as effeminate. For example, Gerald frequently uses *uh*'s and cuts off his own sentences. His evasive, stop-start way of speaking betrays a lack of courage, an inability to speak his mind. Intellectualized speech, to Piri, is a woman's way of talking. Multiple times during their conversation, Brew and Piri call Gerald "prissy"[121] to his face and describe his movements as "tender."[122] In addition to viewing academic language as effeminate, Piri contends that academic language allows one to avoid the realities of race, ethnicity, gender, violence, and discrimination. Their discussion reveals what we lose when we privilege academic discourse over culturally based practices of dialogue, and the downside of viewing identity as a negotiation. As Marta Caminero-Santangelo contends, "*Mean Streets* suggests that notions of race are radical or conservative depending on the circumstances of their deployment, rather than on their 'inherent' challenge to dominant ideology."[123] Like Caminero-Santangelo, I read Gerald as "an echo of Piri himself," particularly his more conservative impulses of using language to disavow his racialization and distance himself from marginalized communities.[124] Gerald represents a discourse of academic mestizaje.

Academic mestizaje, I argue, is a language that combines ideologies of biological and cultural mixture, race as social construction, and self-identification, obscuring the centrality of anti-Blackness to arguments about racial self-definition. In doing so, this discourse frequently privileges whiteness and provides an avenue for racialized people to claim whiteness. Of course, academia is not the only place where this occurs; as seen in the bathroom fight scene with Piri's brother, this rhetorical move can be used at home and by other institutions. The chapter "Barroom Sociology" puts in conversation three men of African descent who may otherwise be unlikely to meet as they discuss issues of race, culture, violence, and social change. As noted earlier, Brew is a Black migrant from the US South to New York, while Piri is born and raised in Harlem of Caribbean migrant parents. Both consider themselves dark-skinned. Gerald West, on the other hand, is a light-skinned, college-educated Pennsylvanian who prides himself on his ethnoracial ambiguity. Scholars who have examined this barroom conversation, such as Caminero-Santangelo and Sánchez, point out the parallels between Gerald and another Northern-raised and -educated Black man: W. E. B. Du Bois. Like Du Bois, Gerald comes to the US South to write "a book on the Negro situation."[125] However, unlike Du Bois, Gerald believes that he can engage in work on race and ethnicity without engaging in the reality of violence baked into that discussion.

Gerald presents his own narrative of Blackness in opposition to a narrative of violence. He says, "I'm not seeking violence but rather the warmth and harmony of the southern Negro."[126] Thomas puts Gerald's lens of investigation in direct opposition to his own, seeing Gerald the scholar as avoiding the conflict and violence of identity. While one might see his desire to focus on "the richness of [Black] poverty and their belief in living" as an attempt to look at Blackness in a way that does not pathologize it, Gerald does so to talk *around* the reality of racist and resistant violence. He minimizes racist violence by white people, saying that "white men have been cruel and violent toward the Negro, but only an ignorant and small minority."[127] When Gerald states boldly that Black southerners are "marshaling [their] dignity and preparing [themselves] for a great social revolution," Brew pushes him to reveal what *his* place will be in that revolution.[128] Gerald sees his role as purely intellectual. While some Black people might fight and die "in looking for a solution to this problem,"[129] Gerald believes that "by writing, I will be fighting."[130] Thomas would not disagree with this stance, as he was very aware of the power of words. In an interview transcript with Fay Turner, he affirms the creative and destructive potential of writing: "They have this myth that 'sticks and stones will break your bones, but words will never harm you,' and that's bullshit. Words do harm you, words have power, decibels are poisons, tonations [sic] have power. You mesmerize, you can heal."¹³¹ Thomas's reflections show the power and potential in language. For Piri, the passivity of Gerald's writing, in both style and content, is the issue. Gerald's passive constructions of sentences and his frustrating vagueness around terms—what is "the Negro situation" or "this problem"?¹³²—means that he talks around the concrete challenges facing racialized people.

Gerald must perform mental gymnastics to tie together both the social construction of race with a "scientific" approach to race. When Gerald is pressed to describe how he views himself, he admits, "I feel that the racial instincts that are the strongest in a person enjoying this rich mixture are the ones that—uh—should be followed."¹³³ This declaration depends simultaneously on biological and self-identification models of racial identity. He argues that one should decide based on their feelings (an individual choice), while at the same time following their "racial instincts," a phrase that represents primal desires outside of an individual's control.¹³⁴ Gerald's choice to identify as a white man is presented as a Cartesian syllogism: "I feel white, Mr. Johnson [Brew]; I look white; I think white; therefore I *am* white."¹³⁵ While Gerald attempts to couch his struggle with identity in academic terms, in reality, his identity, too, is shaped by his relationship to violence and anger. In the paragraph in which Gerald makes this syllogism, he uses "feel" or one of its variations six times. Because he does not understand nor feel the "special kind of anger" of the Black man and could build friendships with white boys, he does not see himself as Black. By viewing his life through the lens of emotional lack—that he has not experienced unrelenting racist violence and does not feel anger towards whiteness—Gerald can imagine himself as white. And like a white man, he can ignore the violence that shapes Black bodies.

While the parallels between Du Bois and Gerald may seem obvious, Piri should also be viewed in relation to Du Bois. Sánchez and Caminero-Santangelo rightly point towards Piri's reflection on his similarity to Gerald, in which he states that "Gerald had problems something like mine. Except that he was a Negro trying to make Puerto Rican and I was a Puerto Rican trying to make Negro."¹³⁶ However, Thomas also portrays Piri as a modern-day Du Bois, using his own memoir (and eventually a trilogy of memoirs, like Du Bois) to provide "an autobiography of a[n ethno-]race concept," offering the reader a text that is a personal-narrative-cum-sociological-reflection on AfroLatino masculinity.¹³⁷ Thomas sees himself in this tradition, because while scholars like Gerald may prettify the language of anti-Blackness, scholars like Du Bois clearly described the terror inflicted on Black bodies and how that unceasing violence shaped their communities and their individual lives.¹³⁸ Simultaneously, Thomas is aware of the ways in which writing creates distance; thus, he recognizes his attempts to represent the AfroLatino man coming into his own on the streets, as well as what is lost in attempting to create a treatise about this experience.

Conclusion

Piri Thomas's memoirs and archive construct an AfroLatino masculine identity founded in violence. His work uses violence as the primary lens through which to consider his own life and the lives of men in El Barrio. While focused primarily on men, with women and queer people as a means through which to enforce certain strictures of manhood, Blackness, and puertorriqueñidad, Thomas's theorization of violence and identity shows up in contemporary AfroLatinx memoirs as well (as we will see in chapter 5). Thomas's conception of creative destruction was a means of recognizing the promise and limitations of the "mean streets." While his AfroLatinidad depends on misogynist and antiqueer violence, his memoir also invites critiques of this violence. In addition, Thomas's choice to represent the interior life of an AfroLatino boy reclaims the masculine interior as an embodied space of thoughtfulness and critical examination.

While chapters 1 through 3 have focused discussion on AfroLatino writers and masculinist AfroLatinidades, the barriers to examining Afro-Latina voices in the early twentieth century (through the example of Pura Belpré), and Third World feminism, the remaining chapters focus squarely on life writing by AfroLatinas and queer AfroLatinx women, which construct AfroLatinidades that emphasize spirituality, sexuality, secrecy, and domesticity. However, I want to reiterate the importance of thinking of the influence of gendered norms, woman-of-color feminism, misogyny, and antiqueer violence as essential topics of AfroLatinx life writing across the last century, especially in the writing of AfroLatinos. Even when the authors themselves may not have consciously analyzed gender and sexuality, their constructions of AfroLatinidad highlight gendered realities for AfroLatino men even as they often erased AfroLatina women and queer AfroLatinxs. The following chapters present examples of speaking against the masculinism of AfroLatinidades that dominated the twentieth century. In chapter 4, we examine the life writing of Marta Moreno Vega, who, while writing about the exact same time period as Piri Thomas, crafted an entirely different image of El Barrio and AfroLatinidad.

CHAPTER 4

Call-and-Response AfroLatinidad: Spirituality, Race, and Gender in Marta Moreno Vega's and Lourdes Casal's Life Writing

Introduction

While the previous chapters in this book have primarily focused on Afro–Puerto Rican men's life writing, this chapter shifts to AfroLatina negotiations of visibility rooted in the politico-cultural influence of Afro-diasporic religions.[1] For the AfroLatina spiritual practitioners of Lucumi whose work I discuss, life writing and feminist spirituality are necessarily entangled. As Phillis Isabella Sheppard argues, "we are tethered to the diversity of black women's lives in examining black women's experience of religion and spirituality. The way into their stories is by giving black women's voices a new and in-depth hearing and by facing both the obvious and the concealed that is revealed."[2] Sheppard points towards the necessity of truly hearing Black women, but also the need to attend to the secrets beneath the obvious. While Lucumi is not a womanist Christian theology, this Yoruba-based religion shares a woman-of-color feminist outlook with the AfroLatina life narratives discussed in this chapter. Unlike several of the masculinist AfroLatinidades in the first part of this monograph, secrecy and weaponized invisibility are valued over visibility, due to the history of santería within Latin America and the Caribbean. This chapter examines the spiritual theorization and life writing of Afro–Puerto Rican Lucumi santera (practitioner or priestess of santería) and scholar Marta Moreno Vega. I begin by framing the conception of AfroLatinidad that Moreno Vega posits through a short life narrative by queer Afro-Cuban-Chinese scholar and santera, Lourdes Casal (1938–1981). By constructing woman-centered AfroLatinidades based on spiritual practices outside of the vertical power structures of Christianity, Casal and Moreno Vega construct an AfroLatina spiritual feminism.

Casal and Moreno Vega's AfroLatinidad employs spirituality as a politico-cultural act of empowerment based on controlling the terms of their visibility. They navigate AfroLatina hypervisibility and invisibility within the structures and strictures of family and religion. As outlined in the introduction, AfroLatinx life writers construct "AfroLatinidades" as social, cultural, and political constructions based in the embodied experiences of Black Latinxs. AfroLatinidades call attention to the realities of living in a Black body, particularly in relation to the anti-Blackness of mestizaje narratives. Thus, to construct an AfroLatinidad is to point out how US narratives of Blackness dominate and erase other forms of diaspora Blackness[3] *and* how white and light-skinned Latinxs dominate and erase other forms of Latinidad. As they negotiate their invisibility, visibility, and hypervisibility, these AfroLatina writers construct an AfroLatinidad that brings to light the distortions and erasures that they struggle against and, at times, adapt and reappropriate.

Moreno Vega's and Casal's life writing connects music, mysticism, espiritismo (spiritism, or communication with ancestors, orisha spirits, or both), and ancestry to create what I term a "call-and-response AfroLatinidad." Call and response, like "the dozens" discussed in chapter 3, is rooted in West African cultural expressions adapted and transformed by Afro-diasporic peoples in the Americas, expressed popularly in Black church sermons and music. As the leader or storyteller calls, the community responds. The Afro-diasporic tradition of call and response is thus a practice of transformation, representing the negotiation of an individual with the community.[4] The call and response of AfroLatina life writing combats masculinist ideas that dominate earlier AfroLatinx literary history,[5] such as the forced separation between culture and politics, the erasure of voices based in the domestic realm, and the rejection of religion as a space for liberation.[6] Call-and-response AfroLatinidad places US Blackness, AfroLatinx religions, and Caribbean conceptions of Latinidad in dynamic conversation rather than in a struggle for hegemony. Call-and-response AfroLatinidad refuses Latin American and Caribbean narratives of hegemonic mestizaje, as well as US claims to defining authentic Blackness.[7] This socioformal conception of AfroLatinidad also demonstrates how the structure of AfroLatina life writing itself calls and responds to the AfroLatina feminist spiritual practices and questions contained in the text. For Moreno Vega, this call and response can be seen in the use of Lucumi patakís (parables) and a textual espiritismo that embodies the connection between human and divine. In doing so, these memoirs center the influence of Africanity in Afro–Puerto Rican and Afro-Cuban religions.

Writing against Mestizaje and Reclaiming the Spiritual: Santería Foundations of Moreno Vega's and Casal's Life Writing

The African diasporic history of Afro-Caribbean religions invites discussion of mestizaje narratives. In Lourdes Casal's "Memories of a Black Cuban Childhood,"[8] the images that document the racial and immigrant backgrounds of her family are the seeds of Casal's interest in the Cuban mestizaje myth.[9] Her mother's choice to initiate Casal into Lucumi starting at the age of seven mediates Casal's sense of self as an Afro-Cuban-Chinese woman. The essay begins with a few paragraphs in Spanish focused on Casal's origins; though only "una cuestión de curiosidad y fantasía y no un problema [a question of curiosity and fantasy and not a problem]" in Cuba, when she came to the United States, "mi color me define más que mi cultura [my color defines me more than my culture]."[10] A portrait of Casal's very proper and Catholic grandmother is the focal point, with the text wrapping around the image. While the essay's first three paragraphs are presented in italicized Spanish, the rest of the essay is in unitalicized English. The essay's focal image, Spanish paragraphs, and English introduction center two portraits, visual and textual, that make visible and authoritative Casal's Chinese and Black ancestry, while also suggesting that in the United States and Cuba those images are interpreted differently. These portraits provide Casal with her origins and the origin of her life narrative. She writes, "My very early preoccupation with my roots can be traced to the puzzling portraits which so intensely stimulated my childhood curiosity and fantasies."[11] These portraits spoke against a history of Spanish and Indigenous mixture in Casal's family and in Cuba. The curiosity they stimulate leads to a lifelong questioning of the place of race in Cuban communities.

Casal's immigration to the United States led her to interrogate both Cuban mestizaje and US conceptions of ethno-race. Born and raised in Cuba, Casal moved to the United States as an adult in early 1961.[12] Movements for civil rights and cultural nationalism led her to reexamine her Blackness: "I had become accustomed to considering myself *una mulata* in a mulatto country, in a quintessentially mulatto culture. The US was a shock. Here I had to learn to assert my Blackness somehow—even or particularly as a Hispanic Black—in a country where Black and white were defined in opposition to one another and where any attempt to avoid the dichotomy seemed to be some kind of betrayal," she writes.[13] Casal's statement reflects a recurring narrative in which Latin American and Caribbean immigrants come to the United States and realize that racialization frequently revolves around US

Black/white dichotomies.[14] However, many of those immigrant stories detail the shock of becoming raced, or of no longer being able to claim whiteness; instead, Casal struggles with what it means to assert her Afro-Cuban experiences in a country in which only US Blackness (not "Hispanic Black[ness]") is legible. As Laura Lomas argues, "Casal's autobiographical writing illustrates the evolution of Casal's self-identification from simplistic criollo nationalist discourses to a complex transnational, multilingual, multigenerational, and heterogeneous understanding of the Cuban diaspora, as it intersects with the histories of the African and Asian diasporas."[15] Casal's Black Cuban-Chinese girlhood as a Lucumi santera and her immigration to the United States call and respond to each other. Her Afro-diasporic religious practice converses with US hegemonic notions of race in ways that force her to interrogate both US and Cuban conceptions of AfroLatinidad.[16]

Both Marta Moreno Vega and Casal mediate the spirits and their ancestral roots without glorifying mestizaje rhetorics. Hegemonic mestizaje in the Caribbean presents a neat narrative of the mixture of Indigenous and Spanish blood and culture while marginalizing or even ignoring Africanity.[17] As Lourdes Martínez-Echazábal writes, hegemonic mestizaje "is not the recognition and proclamation of ethnic difference or of a heterogeneous identity but the Eurocentric glorification of a cultural sameness, of similarity in identity."[18] The AfroLatino authors of the earlier chapters rarely discussed religion or, due to political commitments, were weary of it. However, mestizaje narratives also have spiritual implications for Lucumi writer-practitioners. For example, rather than paying attention to the African presence, many scholars have considered Lucumi a "syncretic" religion, just a mixture of Catholicism and Yoruba practices.[19] However, Moreno Vega rejects the "syncretic" moniker in her Yoruba religious philosophy and in her memoirs, which depend not on a vague sense of spiritual mixture but rather on a very specific Yoruba-based, Afro-Cuban Lucumi spirituality. By rejecting the metaphor of mixing for a dynamic act of playfulness, Moreno Vega and Casal reject the racial mythology that erases them and their families from the collective histories of Puerto Rico and Cuba.

Marta Moreno Vega's life has been a testament to the influence of Yoruba spirituality and culture across the Americas. Her two memoirs and documentary center on Lucumi, a Cuban Afrodiasporic religion. Moreno Vega (1942-present) was born and raised in New York City's El Barrio and is an accomplished Afro–Puerto Rican scholar, writer, and "transnational cultural worker" advancing the liberation of people of color globally.[20] Moreno Vega served as the second director of El Museo del Barrio and established the museum's physical presence in Spanish Harlem. She founded the Caribbean

Cultural Center in 1976, later renamed the Caribbean Cultural Center African Diaspora Institute (CCCADI). CCCADI is housed in East Harlem and focuses on marginalized African diaspora histories, art forms, and cultural expressions. The institute is also concerned with social and cultural activism and community advancement. She continues to be an influential presence through her work connecting practitioners of Yoruba-based religions in the US, Cuba, Brazil, Nigeria, and Benin.[21]

Like Jesús Colón in *A Puerto Rican in New York* and other Afro–Puerto Ricans before her, Moreno Vega uses her first memoir to fight mainstream stereotypes, including the view perpetuated by US and Caribbean media and institutions that Lucumi is demonic or dark magic.[22] In 1981, Moreno Vega was initiated into the Lucumi religion in Cuba.[23] Her first memoir, *The Altar of My Soul: The Living Traditions of Santería*, details Marta's journey to become an initiated santera and provides an overview of her childhood, marriage, divorce, and familial estrangement.[24] In her second memoir, *When the Spirits Dance Mambo: Growing Up Nuyorican in El Barrio*,[25] Moreno Vega looks back through the character of Marta/Cotito/Coty in El Barrio during the 1940s and 1950s. She demonstrates how the spirits of her ancestors, the orisha, and African-based practices of spirituality shaped her childhood even before she become an adherent.[26] While *When the Spirits* takes place in the same historical time period as Piri Thomas's more well-known *Down These Mean Streets*, her portrayal of AfroLatina identity and visibility demonstrates a substantially different conception of AfroLatinidad. Moreno Vega's memoirs center the influence and experiences of AfroLatina women at home and in the realm of cultural maintenance and revitalization.[27]

Unlike the masculinist AfroLatinidades discussed in earlier chapters, such as those of the New York Young Lords, who often separated the political from the cultural, AfroLatina feminist spirituality views the cultural and spiritual as necessarily political. In fact, Moreno Vega begins her 1995 dissertation on Yoruba spirituality with a quotation from the Bissau-Guinean and Cape Verdean revolutionary, Amilcar Cabral: "If imperialist domination has the vital need to practice cultural oppression, national liberation is necessarily an *act of culture*."[28] For Cabral and Moreno Vega, culture *is* an act of resistance and liberation. While the Young Lords cautioned against cultural nationalism,[29] AfroLatina feminist spirituality embraces the primacy of culture. As a speaker declares in Moreno Vega's documentary, *Cuando los espíritús bailan mambo* (2002; When the spirits dance mambo), "Ninguna política es más fuerte que la cultura [No political system is stronger than culture]."[30] Thus, it is fitting that Moreno Vega's memoirs examine and commemorate women's cultural work. In *The Altar of My Soul*, Moreno Vega appears to provide the impetus for *When the Spirits Dance Mambo*. She was inspired by a life-changing encounter with her mother's spirit: "My mother's presence triggered memories and emotions that had long been buried, forcing me to recall my childhood encounters with the spirits. My mother's instructions were clear—it was time to face my past so that I could step into the future."[31] Moreno Vega had to radically rethink her past to include the spiritual side of her childhood that she had forgotten or repressed.

Her memoir and its origins align with the Latina Feminist Group's conception of *papelitos guardados* in *Telling to Live* (2001). The term has multiple meanings, including: "protected documents, guarded roles, stored papers, conserved roles, safe papers, secret roles, hidden papers, safe roles, preserved documents, protected roles."[32] It can describe the relationship of hiding one's self, one's story, and its documentation until the right eyes can read, understand, and engage it. One facet of papelitos guardados, then, is controlling visibility and understanding how secrets, strategic invisibility, and forced invisibility can influence how we see ourselves within our families, communities, and nations. By examining Moreno Vega's memoirs as papelitos guardados, one can examine the roles the memoirs play as an archive of AfroLatina women's lives, a reflection on the many roles expected of wives, daughters, sisters, abuelas, and nietas in the domestic space.[33] In addition, Moreno Vega's papelitos guardados emphasize spirituality and ritual as spaces of safety, secrecy, and growth. By seeing *When the Spirits Dance Mambo* as un papelito guardado unlocked by spiritual reconnection and vulnerability, Moreno Vega reveals the hidden parts of her life and the sacredness of AfroLatina lives in the 1940s and 1950s. She also renders visible the ways that gendered racialization can create very different ideas of AfroLatinidad, even within the same sociohistorical context.

As a santera, medium, and scholar of santería, Moreno Vega's own scholarship on Yoruba philosophy is the primary lens through which to engage her focus on Lucumi in her memoirs. In "Certified Organic Intellectual," Aurora Levins Morales writes, "The intellectual traditions I come from create theory out of shared lives instead of sending away for it."[34] Thus, in providing background on Lucumi, santería, espiritismo, and Afro-diasporic religions generally, I depend primarily on Moreno Vega herself, namely her 1995 dissertation on Yoruba philosophy, her life writing, as well as the practitioners and scholars who influenced her work, like Mary Ann Clark. Moreno Vega adopts Clark's view of "Santería as a female-identified religious tradition [. . .] that valorizes rather than denigrates women's roles and activities."[35] Moreno Vega identifies the defining aspect of African-based religions: the coexistence of the human and divine. That coexistence allows for continual access to ancestral wisdom and guidance and emphasizes the importance of mindful rituals to maintain individual and communal balance, which encourages devotees to create a morally grounded reality rather than look towards the afterlife for justice and peace. As Moreno Vega explains, "Santería is a religion that holds you accountable for your actions on Earth, here and now."[36] Practitioners, then, represent Yoruba orisha worship as part of the political-cultural resistance of the African diaspora in which feminine orishas and women have played defining roles.

For Moreno Vega, African-based religions dispose of the arbitrary divide between the human and divine realms. Thus, Lucumi and African religions oppose blind obedience to a distant god; rather, the routine rituals of our lives, such as caring for altars to the eguns (ancestor spirits) and orisha,[37] create and maintain the gods and the divine realm.[38] Lucumi fosters "the ability to function within two realms of reality [which] is critical to the Yorubas in the Americas and Africa . . . The ability to balance, exist in and 'see' two worlds provides a repertoire of information unique to our African-based experiences."[39] That is, African-based religions have allowed African-descended peoples, who Moreno Vega characterizes as "the Yorubas in the Americas and Africa," to navigate widely divergent realities and to see how the physical and spiritual worlds overlap and influence each other. In addition, the adaptation of Yoruba spirituality by enslaved people in the Caribbean provided a space where community could be built. While Christianity was forced on enslaved Black people to increase their economic value and ensure their obedience by promising a better life after death,[40] Yoruba-based religions did not require dreams of freedom, love, and flourishing to be deferred.

The importance of natural and divine imagery in the stories of santería makes change and transformation central to its belief system. Moreno Vega praises Lucumi's adaptability, asserting that "the centrality of the forces of nature, ancestors and spirits in the Yoruba traditional belief provides the ability to adapt, transform, incorporate and eliminate aspects which are not relevant to its practitioners."[41] For a religion that has been attacked by Christianity and colonizers, survival requires both tenacity and a willingness to adjust. That adaptability makes it available as a tool of resistance. Like Piri Thomas, who valorizes the oft-maligned street practices of survival in El Barrio as I argued in chapter 3, Moreno Vega celebrates Lucumi's "creative ways of circumventing authority."[42] For example, in *The Altar* when Marta goes to Cuba to fully initiate in 1981, she encounters much stricter regulations by the Castro government against santería and foreigner initiation. She connects santería's history of colonial resistance, often through weaponized invisibility, to the clever ways that practitioners thwart current-day restrictions.

In prefacing my analysis of Moreno Vega's writing, I stress that I am not a santería devotee; by considering how Lucumi impacts the form of Moreno Vega's life writing, I do not wish to cast Lucumi-santería as merely a metaphor or a generic convention of religious life writing. In fact, Lucumi-santería is so integral to the AfroLatina feminist spiritual life writing represented by Casal and Moreno Vega that its influence is visible not only in the text's content but also in its form. In an effort to honor the influence of Lucumi-santería in their life writing, I argue that santería is the primary lens through which Moreno Vega views her girlhood. History that challenges the official story becomes a medicine, a means to heal communities and her sense of self in a marginalized community. Moreno Vega becomes what Levins Morales calls "a curandera historian."[43] Curandera historians are not themselves always curanderas, or healers in Latin American and Latinx communities who depend on traditional and folk remedies. In this case, curandera historians create histories that visibilize the absence of AfroLatina women's life narratives, "tracing the outlines of a woman-shaped hole in the record" and emphasizing the agency of Afro-diasporic subjects, particularly AfroLatina women's resistance to mistreatment and control.[44] Moreno Vega's memoirs are "medicinal histories" that provide the space for childhood Marta to heal and recover an AfroLatina spirituality that was awakened after her initiation into Lucumi.[45]

The organization of Moreno Vega's memoirs replicates certain ritual practices and storytelling techniques from Lucumi-santería. For instance, *The Altar of My Soul* employs the pataki (a parable or "teaching tale").[46] While both memoirs also feature the presence and invocation of several orisha, my reading is not focused on interpreting the use of particular orisha as representatives of larger ideals,[47] but rather as characters that Moreno Vega uses to make certain arguments. These parables and orishas allow her to navigate her Afro–Puerto Rican identity as a girl growing up in El Barrio and, later, as an initiate and practitioner who has the power to initiate new devotees.

Pataki

Moreno Vega uses the *pataki* in conjunction with her experience of initiate ceremonies in *The Altar of My Soul* so she can tie together the cultural and political underpinnings of African diasporic religion. Each chapter of *The

Altar is comprised of the following sections: the patakí; Marta preparing for the ceremony that allows her to initiate future santeras; a portion of Marta's autobiography; and "A Message from My Elders" or "A Message from My Godparents." In this way, the memoir and each chapter within it adopt rituals of Lucumi. For example, she narrates a weekly misa (mass or prayer) with her godchildren, which begins with a story about Ellegua, the orisha of the crossroads.[48] All ceremonies begin and end by honoring Ellegua, so Moreno Vega's memoir does so, too. Using Ellegua also introduces the crossroads of Yoruba Africanity and AfroLatinidad and begins from the intersection of those identities. The pataki that begins each chapter educates the reader about orisha mythology—such as the creation myth and birth of orishas that open chapter 1—and provides an entry point into Moreno Vega's own narrative. The pataki serve more than an educational purpose, however. They also reflect a Yoruba spiritual and diasporic worldview that writes against mestizaje. In using the pataki, Moreno Vega grounds us in this religious tradition and offers a perspective of AfroLatina identity that valorizes the multifaceted self. Through these pataki, she makes visible Black girls and women as essential actors in African diasporic spirituality and mythology.

The myth of Yemayá, which begins the second chapter of *The Altar of My Soul*, foregrounds the ritual and cultural importance of feminine power and imagines a femininity based in curiosity and experimentation. In this pataki, we learn that Yemayá, the female creator god and orisha of the ocean, is "the female head of the Santería religion."[49] One day, she grows tired of life in Ile Ife and decides to journey west. With her she carries a potion to use in case she is in terrible danger.[50] When her absence is noted, the king of the orisha, Obatalá, sends his army to bring her back. She escapes by using her magic bottle and creating "an enormous river that safely drew her out to sea."[51] Instead of violently confronting the orisha's army—a patriarchal force wishing to constrain her movement—she uses nonviolent magic to maintain her freedom of mobility. Yemayá's characterization as a determined traveler who follows her own desires challenges stereotypes of Black womanhood. Yemayá is not the steadfast rock who must care for her orisha family or sacrifice her desires for the greater good. She creates a potion to produce a river in order to remain independent and establish herself—and Yoruba-based religions— outside of her home. Moreno Vega follows the pataki with another legend that claims that Yemayá is an equal to Olodumare, the masculine creator god, since "it was upon her home, the ocean, that Earth was formed."[52] Quite literally, femininity is the foundation of the Earth. In addition, Yemayá's domain represents a body of water that cannot be contained, that is constantly changing and roiling. Yemayá, like the ocean and the women she represents and empowers, is dynamic and multifaceted. The legend represents Yemayá as a figure for celebration and adulation. The tale praises her as an inquisitive and powerful woman rather than cautioning against feminine curiosity, in contrast to the Greek myth of Pandora or the biblical Eve.

The story of Yemayá also explains the widespread practice of Yoruba-influenced religions. She personifies the dispersion of Yoruba beliefs as a way of recognizing women's central role in maintaining the religion. Through the story, Moreno Vega explains that the existence of Africanity outside of Africa is not solely because of white imperialism and the enslavement of Africans, suggesting that the divine will of Yemayá also played a role in the dispersal of Africa's religions and its people. The story ends without the orisha returning to Ile Ife, suggesting that she continued her travels west, eventually leaving the African continent. In implying that Yemayá is a vector through which Afro-diasporic spirituality spread to the New World, Moreno Vega restores a degree of agency to the dispersal of African-centered religions. Moreno Vega offers readers an African spiritual force that influences the world, rather than assigning all the agency to European colonialism and enslavement. In doing so, Moreno Vega places herself in a larger conversation about where the foundations and commitments of Blackness lie: the West or Africa.[53] Through the story of Yemayá, Moreno Vega underscores African agency, and particularly Afro-diasporic women's agency, in the global circulation of Africanity. She also argues for the primacy of the "Afro" in AfroLatina, demonstrating that AfroLatinx culture and communities draw from different philosophical and spiritual traditions than the culture and communities of white Latinxs.

In line with her depiction of Yemayá, Moreno Vega uses pataki to make political claims about the sexist world in which we live. While *The Altar of My Soul* avoids in-depth discussion of issues of sexism and gender segregation by Lucumi practitioners and Lucumi practice in general,[54] Moreno Vega uses pataki to emphasize that Yoruba-based spirituality condemns patriarchal oppression. For example, chapter 5 begins with a pataki about Ochun.[55] Moreno Vega prefaces the story by telling the reader that her godmother first shared it with her to show how Lucumi "address[es] the resiliency and power of women to struggle and thrive against all odds."[56] Ochun, the orisha of sweet water, fertility, and love, has been taken up in pop culture and scholarship as a feminist icon. For example, in "Hold Up" from superstar singer Beyoncé's visual album *Lemonade* (2016), Twitter users, bloggers, and traditional scholars read Beyoncé, in a bright yellow dress, walking out of a flooded doorway with a baseball bat, as a representation of Ochun.[57] Certainly Beyoncé is beautiful but not powerless, and her beauty is not conveyed as power—or else she would not need the baseball bat. While some falsely paint Ochun as an African Aphrodite, the patakí that Moreno Vega shares highlights feminine power and the global harm done when women are ignored and marginalized from political participation. In Moreno Vega's telling, Ochun is not invited to a secret, all-male orisha meeting and is turned away once she tries to attend. Enraged, she "made all the women barren and turned the affairs of the world into chaos."[58] Olodumare explains to the male orishas that "without women and children, the world could not function. Without Ochun, the world would always be in a state of confusion."[59] The anti-machista lesson of the story easily applies to the earthly realm of politics and family, illustrating that when we erase the perspectives of Afro-diasporic women and girls, the world cannot be just or equitable.[60] The story rejects paternalistic narratives in which men argue that they represent the interests of the entire family or that a small subsection of men can represent the full diversity of experiences and opinions of all people. In addition, she rejects narratives of paternalistic protection—that men know best and can do what's best for women without their input. Ochun teaches us that one person cannot speak for others but must actively seek, amplify, and support the voices on the margins.

Although I use the terms "female" and "male" orisha as Moreno Vega does in *The Altar of My Soul*, gender is not strictly binary for spirits. There are many caminos (ways or roads) for each orisha, representing their multifaceted identities. While each orisha is primarily male or female, some male orishas have feminine caminos and some female orishas have masculine caminos.[61] In Moreno Vega's memoirs, a full portrait of womanhood is one in which Yoruba and Hispanophone Caribbean conceptions of femininity coincide. In the last pataki of *The Altar of My Soul*, Moreno Vega emphasizes her fluid conception of AfroLatinidad. By considering the core parts of her identity in terms of the Lucumi concept of orisha caminos, she forwards a spiritually grounded conception of the "multiplicity" of identity.[62] When the orisha Obatalá "claims her head" and becomes her guardian orisha,[63] Moreno Vega discusses the various caminos of the orishas. The caminos of the orishas represent the dynamism of call-and-response AfroLatinidad that writes against mestizaje. Similar to the concept of intersectionality, the caminos highlight how we are many things all at once and more than the sum of our parts. That is, AfroLatina womanhood is not the product of a mixture but rather a responsive dialogue among one's papelitos guardados. Who we are is always in response to the world around us, our internal doubts, our external questioning, our societal and relational roles, and our constantly changing sense of self through physical, mental, and spiritual shifts. By ending with a patakí that emphasizes the multiple caminos of Lucumi deities, Moreno Vega brings together the mosaic-like structure of her first memoir.[64] Her experiences and memories, presented through her straightforward autobiographical sections, the lessons embedded in Lucumi pataki, and her elders' messages, are a montage that reflect her identities as AfroLatina, santera, madrina (godmother), daughter, mother, scholar, teacher, and cultural activist. In addition, her representation of the pataki and the orishas pushes back against masculinist constructions of identity and spirituality. Rather than depending on hierarchical, patriarchal power structures and rigid binaries of gender and power, the parables of the orisha showcase the multiplicity of deities and people. By conceptualizing her own spiritual growth and changes alongside the tales of female orishas, she makes visible the centrality of Afro-diasporic womanhood to santería's view of what determines the world's spiritual and political well-being.

Textual Incarnations of Espiritismo

A key moment in *The Altar of My Soul* is the prophecy that Moreno Vega will become an espiritista (a medium for spirits) like her Abuela.[65] Unlike other prophecies in the memoir, such as the one that she would become a madrina (a godmother who initiates santeras) with many godchildren, Moreno Vega does not affirm that the prediction came true. However, I read Moreno Vega's life writing as a way of fulfilling that prophecy. Her life writing channels her egun, particularly women like her mother and sister, who continue to struggle with the constraints they navigated in their lives. By examining *The Altar of My Soul* as "theory in the flesh"[66] and an example of Folasade Hunsu's "Oloto theory" in the African diaspora,[67] we can see how dispersal and adaptation influence the structure and content of *When the Spirits Dance Mambo*. In *The Altar of My Soul*, Marta's Lucumi godmother comments, "'Life does not follow sequential chapters like a book. Sometimes you have to arrange the chapters in a way that works specifically for you. Santería is a learning process that guides you and helps you create a sacred space that works for you."[68] Thus, Moreno Vega restructures the memory of her own life inspired by the epiphanies brought on by her religious conversion. That restructuring, and the impact of her female ancestors in bringing memories from the shadows that make her rethink the entirety of her life, drives the organization of her life writing. The conditions under which Moreno Vega can unlock her narrative and share the shaping forces of her AfroLatina girlhood include open and vulnerable dialogue between women and the lessons of Lucumi. Moreno Vega's writing is a textual incarnation of espiritismo, providing a space for her ancestors to speak. Identifying herself as a medium, Moreno Vega's writing mediates the voices of women ancestors who have not had access to tell their stories.

Lucumi and santería are orisha-based religions, adapted from the religious traditions of Yoruba African peoples, while espiritismo is a western European creation of the nineteenth century. Also known as the Kardec movement, led by Allan Kardec (born H. Leon Denizard Rivail, 1804–1869), the espiritismo tradition is detailed in five works, known as the Codification. According to Margarite Fernández Olmos and Lizabeth Paravisini-Gebert, "spiritism was a moral philosophy rather than a religion, incorporating the ideas of Romanticism and the scientific revolution to bridge the gap between the material and spiritual worlds."[69] Two of the primary spiritist contributions to Regla de Ocha and espiritismo are the focus on spiritual evolution (being able to purify one's own spirit and the spirits of one's ancestors) and the perspective on protector spirits, to whom one has a responsibility to tend through altars and ablutions.[70] Espiritistas act as mediums, sometimes for the orishas themselves and other times for ancestral spirits. They act as a speaking vessel but also take on the personality and mannerisms associated with the orisha or ancestor. As M. Jacqui Alexander notes, communing with the Sacred rejects definitions of visibility made in secular terms: "In the realm of the secular, the material is conceived of as a tangible while the spiritual is either nonexistent or invisible. In the realm of the Sacred, however, the invisible constitutes its presence by a provocation of sorts, by provoking our attention. [. . .] We do not see Wind, but we can see the vortex it creates in a tornado."[71] Within the memoirs, there are scenes of mediumship, but the memoirs themselves also provide a vessel through which Moreno Vega's girlhood self and her female ancestors can tell their previously hidden or distorted stories. The effects, in essence, are just as visible as the causes and can be traced not only in the story but in the memoir's narrative choices.

Moreno Vega's and Casal's memoirs both use espiritismo to drive the plot, to embrace the coexistence of the past and present, and as a ritual for invoking call-and-response AfroLatinidad. In *Altar* particularly, espiritista experiences are the means through which we learn about Moreno Vega's family and her past.[72] The narrator describes several different visitations from women, like her mother and sister, who facilitate her journey to becoming a santera. In *When the Spirits Dance Mambo*, espiritismo is a frame showing the reader the coexistence of the past and present, the living and spirits. In particular, music acts as a medium for the egun and the orishas, facilitating spiritual and cultural possessions within the book. In this way, espiritismo centers AfroLatina voices and establishes AfroLatinidad as a playful engagement between race and culture, embodiment and the intangible.

According to Mary Ann Clark, the contemporary practice of spirit possession in Puerto Rico and the Caribbean is based both on the earlier Yoruba practice of Egungun—in which masked dancers channel the spirits of the community's ancestors—and the Kardec or Spiritist movement. In this iteration, individual ancestor spirits became generalized into categories such as the Gypsy, the Kongo, and the Madam, figures that appear in Moreno Vega's life writing.[73] Some people, like Marta's grandmother Abuela Luisa, are mediums who can speak to certain spirits.[74] In the documentary *Cuando los espíritus bailan mambo*, José Millet describes at least ten different versions of espiritismo, some of which allow people to act as mediums for the orishas such as Changó and Ochun, others that allow people to act as mediums for the dead, and still others that allow a specific spirit to speak through the medium for the purpose of mutual spiritual elevation.[75] For example, Abuela Luisa, in *When the Spirits Dance Mambo*, can channel one of her guardian spirits, Juango, who is also the Kongo (or fugitive from slavery) figurine on her bóveda (espiritista altar),[76] and an abused woman, Alma, channels the orisha Ochun in a botánica.[77] In *The Altar of My Soul*, Marta's contact with Abuela and Mami through mediumship advance her spiritual journey, providing a woman-centered and woman-led spirituality that ties together both African and Caribbean influences. By engaging with feminine spirits and woman ancestors at several different points in the initiation process, Moreno Vega demonstrates that Lucumi "is an essentially feminine religion that valorizes female attitudes and practice," placing women at its heart.[78] Moreno Vega's spiritual-cultural conception of AfroLatinidad reveals the individual experiences of AfroLatina women and their struggle to assert a coherent, respected identity and generate a positive definition of AfroLatina femininity not based in weakness and lack.

When the Spirits Dance Mambo responds to Solimar Otero's question in *Archives of Conjure*: "What does it mean if we take AfroLatinx dialogic practices with the dead, like spirit mediumship, divination, and sacred art-making, as the central components to creating ethnographic reciprocity?"[79] Moreno Vega's initiation made her reevaluate her childhood, particularly her relationship with her Abuela and the spiritual and domestic dimensions of her life. In fact, the book implies that her mother's visitation during an espiritista, or medium session, is the reason *When the Spirits Dance Mambo* exists. Through that encounter, Marta learns about her mother's regrets: being unable to follow her dream of becoming a nurse, her choice not to combat the machismo in her own home and to provide her daughters with the opportunities that their brother received, and refusing to accept her destiny to be a medium as indicated to her by the orishas. Speaking through the espiritista, Marta's mother, believing that the family's multigenerational refusal to follow the orishas' desires had torn them apart, tells Marta that her journey to santería will restore the family. Moreno Vega's attempt to break the cycle is by accepting her espiritista calling. To do so, she must make visible how entangled Lucumi, AfroLatina womanhood, and secrecy have been in her family's history.

Moreno Vega examines secrecy to present the history of Lucumi as a wrongfully persecuted religion and to correlate that history with the secrecy that surrounds discussions of AfroLatina womanhood and femininity. While she grew up in the same time period and facing similar issues as Piri Thomas, including the heroin epidemic of the 1950s and the post–World War II struggle for civil rights, Moreno Vega's *When the Spirits Dance Mambo* contrasts starkly with Thomas's representation of the time period. Most of Moreno Vega's autobiography takes place in her family's or Abuela Luisa's apartments, as ideas of purity and virginity drive her parents' decisions about the opportunities available to the girls in the family. Since Afro-diasporic religions and AfroLatinas' lives in the domestic realms are often presented through distorted lenses by both white people and Black Latino men, Moreno Vega's memoir combats those distortions and reclaims the power of domestic spaces and domestic stories. AfroLatina girls and women have often been restricted to the home by husbands, societal expectations, and religion. Within those homes, women have laughed, schemed, cried, lost themselves, and found themselves. Thus, domestic space is also politico-cultural; Moreno Vega's memoirs are set in girls' bedrooms, the kitchen, or her grandmother's apartment while she completes her ritual sweeping and ablutions. As Yomaira Figueroa argues, "the kitchen table is a place of politics, poetics, kinship, and sustenance. Likewise, we know that this hallowed quotidian space is also a site of violence, revelation, and revolt."[80] To expand on Figueroa's conception of "kitchen table histories," I examine the kitchen table politics of Moreno Vega's memoirs. This politics argues that representations of the love, laughter, work, and anger that happens at the kitchen table are a call to AfroLatina girls and women to situate their lives within a longer history of the work carried out by AfroLatina women to maintain and revitalize Black Latinx communities.

The family's connection to santería goes back to Moreno Vega's Abuela Luisa. By beginning with Abuela's story in Puerto Rico, Moreno Vega ties her own story to the island and to santería's African roots. In addition, she explores the relationship between AfroLatina womanhood, racism, and secrecy in Puerto Rico to provide context for AfroLatina experiences in the United States. In the beginning of *When the Spirits Dance Mambo*, an older Marta narrates her Abuela Luisa's life in Puerto Rico before she came to the mainland. Abuela's own grandmother, María de la O, had been born into slavery and had raised Abuela Luisa because she had been abandoned by her light-skinned mother, an expression of colorism on the island.[81] Abuela Luisa had been a practitioner of santería her whole life, and it put her body in physical danger, Moreno Vega explains. She identifies the continuing conflation of Blackness and labor in the wake of the abolition of slavery, the sexual abuse of dark-skinned women, and the persecution of santería. She writes, "Even after slavery was abolished in 1873, racism and discrimination continued [. . .]. A single black woman was prey to the roving eyes of her bosses. If she refused the advances of her white employer, she could be brought to court and accused of being *una bruja*, a witch."[82] Abuela's Afro–Puerto Rican female body and her African diasporic spiritual practices are used by criollos (white descendants of Spanish colonists) and those in power to further oppress her in Puerto Rico. In fact, any resistant act by a Black Puerto Rican woman is automatically equated with witchcraft. In a sense, then, her santería can never truly be secret, unless she complies with an invisibilizing idea of Blackness that rewards passivity and blind obedience to white authority. Her migration is the only way to escape the anti-Black racism in Puerto Rico, but she maintains the secrecy of her status as a Lucumi practitioner because of the state-sanctioned persecution of her religion.

Secrecy as a form of protection is prevalent in Lucumi, and Moreno Vega shows how that concept continues even in intimate family practices. Darlene Clark Hine argues that "Black women, as a rule, developed and adhered to a cult of secrecy, a culture of dissemblance, to protect the sanctity of inner aspects of their lives. [. . .] Only with secrecy, thus achieving a self-imposed invisibility, could ordinary Black women accrue the psychic space and harness the resources needed to hold their own in the often one-sided and mismatched resistance struggle."[83] The kinds of secrecy that can be deployed exist along a spectrum. One might stringently guard a secret, never allowing others even a hint of the truth, or a secret may be open, a known fact that everyone knows but does not discuss.[84] For example, although it is a common tradition in Latinx families, using nicknames in *When the Spirits Dance Mambo* also reflects santería beliefs in the power of words and naming. Marta is called Cotito or Coty, her sister Socorro is called Chachita, and her brother Alberto is called Chachito. Coty's mother suggests that she has two names for two realms: the birth certificate name that faces towards institutions, like school and the government, and the nicknames for their identity at home.[85] Cotito thinks of the multiple names as "some kind of game" similar to "our Catholic saints whose names disguised the ancient gods of Africa."[86] In comparing her own neighborhood's nicknaming practice to those of Lucumi, Coty suggests that the nicknames also have a spiritual valence that is part of a tradition of protection, from the colonial institutions that tried to annihilate santería practices, to present-day institutions like schools that also practice cultural oppression. The use of multiple names in the memoir nods to the roots of santería while also invoking a crucial shared experience among AfroLatina devotees: the double-edged sword of secrecy.

While secrecy has been used ritually in the religion to protect practitioners and resist cultural oppression, for individual AfroLatina women, secrecy can also be a tool of patriarchal and anti-Black oppression. Chachita's secret relationship shows that while secrecy can be used by AfroLatina women to pursue their own desires, it also provides a tacit acceptance of the status quo. The woman chooses to pretend as if she is following patriarchal rules but can flout them as long as no one knows (or no one talks about it). For example, Chachita's experience dating a US Black man in secret shows the proscribed way in which secrecy works for AfroLatina women. Chachita hopes to use the secret relationship to defy the control that her parents have over her body, though ultimately to no avail. Chachita reveals her secret relationship to Marta, who eventually gives up her sister's secret to their parents. Chachita knows that it is a risk to bring others in on a secret, but she tells her sister out of a desire to find validation and someone to support her in her choice.

For Chachita, the secret allows her to maintain the image of the good woman that her parents so desperately want, while being able to experience the freedom that Afro–Puerto Rican men, like her brother, Chachito, take for granted. Chachita recognizes that her boyfriend's identity as a US Black American would not be accepted by her parents, due both to their anti-Black racism and their concern for her virginity. She herself even justifies the relationship using anti-Black logic: "'He's *un negro*, but light,' acknowledging without even thinking about it our [Puerto Rican] culture's ingrained prejudice against dark skin."[87] Marta recounts the emphasis that her parents put on "'*adelantar la raza*.' 'Advancing the race' by marrying someone with a lighter complexion."[88] However, Marta notes that this unwritten rule was not followed by her own mother, who had married a dark-skinned man "and had two children that were the color of rich brown cinnamon."[89] That observation suggests that perhaps "advancing the race" is only a priority for dark-skinned Afro–Puerto Ricans due to their lower status in Puerto Rican communities. At one point, Chachita rationalizes away Joe's Blackness entirely, pointing out "He's the same color as I am."[90] By sharing this clandestine desire and rebellion against the strictures of Afro–Puerto Rican womanhood, Chachita builds a sisterly bond, a tenuous support system that must replace the support Chachita should be getting from her mother and father. The shame attached to female sexuality, particularly Black Puerto Rican sexuality, as well as the anti-Black attitudes she has witnessed and internalized, forces her to embrace secrecy. This secrecy is a resistant response to anti-Black patriarchal oppression but also a means of protecting herself from that same force. Through Chachita's story, Moreno Vega shows that claiming an AfroLatina identity as an individual is radical, rejecting Afro–Puerto Rican traditions that erase AfroLatina autonomy. For many, the attempt to claim an independent identity ends in failure.

Moreno Vega's memoir reflects the tension between the resistant deployment of secrecy and the resistant "making public" of AfroLatina lives that have been hidden "behind closed doors." Moreno Vega makes public the private pain of AfroLatina women constrained by anti-Black notions of puertorriqueñidad. The real-life sister who Chachita represents died young, after years of drug abuse and estrangement from Moreno Vega's family. While ostensibly about her own life, Moreno Vega's *When the Spirits Dance Mambo* provides deeper characterization of her sister to show the forces that act upon AfroLatina women, making them fade into the background of their community's history. In particular, Chachita's choice to defy the norms imposed on her becomes a choice to forfeit the few protections that AfroLatina girls have.[91] As Marta debates whether to tell Mami about the secret boyfriend, she asserts that by having a clandestine relationship, "my sister had violated my parents' authority as protectors."[92] When Mami finds out Chachita's secret, she paints her daughter as "defiant, [. . .] *una atrevida* [a bold girl]" who "in her sneaky way, [. . .] tries to get what she wants."[93] In this quote, Mami condemns Chachita for having individual desires and acting independently to attain them, something she would never say about their brother, Chachito, due to the double standards of gender. As the son, Chachito's movement is never constrained, and he dates openly, without judgment. To be a boy is to have your independence encouraged, while—as Chachita's story shows—to be a girl is to have that autonomy discouraged. Chachito can pursue relationships publicly, while Chachita must do so in the shadows. Chachita's independence is viewed as a defect, rather than a facet, of her femininity.

When Marta reveals to Chachita that she divulged her secret, Chachita responds with quiet submission, not anger. She says, "'Sooner or later, I would have had to confront the situation. I'm tired of being a prisoner in my own house because I'm not trusted. [. . .] Mami and Papi have already determined my future,' she went on, 'It doesn't matter what I think or want.'"[94] By describing herself as a prisoner, Chachita shatters the image of benevolence that her mother constructs as justification for the family's controlling behavior. As Marta and her mother help her tend to her wounds (her father beats her when he finds out about the relationship), Marta is scared of touching her bleeding and bruised face. The fear of Chachita's blood mirrors the anxiety that surrounds women's menstrual blood in both the Moreno household and African diasporic spiritual beliefs. While Clark writes that menstrual blood is feared in blood sacrifices since it represents the failure of life,[95] I read Chachita's blood in this instance as a bold assertion of life. The blood, in demanding a full experience of life and love, represents the powerful truth of women's oppression in her Afro–Puerto Rican household and El Barrio in general. In the patriarchal conception of Afro–Puerto Rican femininity, secrecy and desire are no different from deception and betrayal. The blood of Chachita's suffering is a powerful reminder of the prison of feminine gender expectations. The story of Chachita's secret illuminates the multifaceted way in which secrecy shapes AfroLatina women's lives—as shame, an act of defiance, or a means of support or protection. Abuela Luisa's clandestine spiritual practices and Chachita's own attempt at wielding secrecy for her own desires demonstrate a spectrum of secrecy and its impact on AfroLatina lives.

"When the spirits dance mambo, I know that our memories live": Music as Spiritual Transportation

In addition to providing a means for the reader to see Marta's negotiation of her Afro–Puerto Rican womanhood in the context of secrecy and her papelitos guardados, Moreno Vega's memoirs textually facilitate her ancestors' spirits by overlapping the past and present and posing music as a means of spiritual transportation. In *When the Spirits Dance Mambo*, Moreno Vega's "memories take [her] on a spiritual, musical voyage to El Barrio."[96] Moreno Vega highlights the coexistence of the past and the present and the incorporation of santería practices and beliefs in the popular culture of both the historically Latino and historically Black sections of Harlem.[97] As Heredia writes, "the fluidity of the physical borders between the Puerto Rican Spanish (East) Harlem and African American (West) Harlem in New York City speaks to the conviviality of people sharing musical tastes."[98] By providing espiritismo as a framing structure for the memoir, Moreno Vega highlights the way that the ancestors and the spirits speak through literature and music, portraying AfroLatinidad as an identity formed through a call-and-response relationship between Africanity and Latinidad. Moreno Vega mediates the spirits and her ancestral roots without glorifying mestizaje rhetorics. By rejecting the metaphor of mixing for a dynamic act of playfulness, she rejects the racial mythology that erases her and her family from the collective histories of Puerto Rico, Cuba, and the United States.

In an essay in *The Afro-Latin@ Reader* (2010), Moreno Vega traces the connection between the arrival of santería in New York and its influence on important jazz and mambo musicians:

> The presence of Cuban musicians such as "Machito" Grillo and Mario Bauzá, founder of the Afro-Cubans Orchestra, influenced Afro-American jazz as well as Latin music. Bauzá's introduction of the master Afro-Cuban drummer Chano Pozo to Dizzy Gillespie, and the incorporation of Chano Pozo—an initiate of Afro-Cuban religions—into Dizzy's orchestra, opened new musical horizons in African American jazz.[99]

In fact, she argues that Gillespie "further [. . .] popularize[d] traditional Afro-Cuban music" and "throughout his career" included "the music of Santería."[100] In 1956, Tito Puente "introduced Yoruba chants for the first time in contemporary commercial recordings in New York City."[101] Nowhere is the continuing influence of Yoruba spirituality more visible, for Moreno Vega, than in the Harlem music scene. AfroLatinidad is infused in the music created by US Black and Afro-Caribbean artists in Harlem.

The first words of *When the Spirits Dance Mambo* are commands, directed towards the reader, insisting that they let the AfroLatinx music of her childhood invade their body and soul.[102] She uses second-person commands to evoke the rhythmic feeling of an espiritista ritual, complete with heartbeat-like drumming ("the *ta-ta-ta, ta-ta* of the *clave*").[103] While she identifies the music as mambo, the description parallels the batá drum ceremonies that she describes in *The Altar of My Soul*. Marta talks about "the mind-altering power of music in African-based religions in the New World."[104] Casal, in "Memories of a Black Cuban Childhood," similarly situates the batá drums as sacred tools that blur the lines between mind, body, and spirit. She reflects:

> In my most rational and materialist moments, I tried to find logical explanations for the phenomena I was witnessing. But other times I simply let myself be carried away by the peculiar beauty of it all, by the drums and the chants, by the dance and the prayers, by the gripping power of ritual

and a language that took my head by assault and threw it back to the primeval forest, to the sacred forest of my ancestors."[105]

In both Casal's and Moreno Vega's life narratives, the batá drums hypnotize the listener, leading them through time and space, allowing them to bring the past and the present together. Casal points to the contradiction that appears to exist in focusing on material circumstances and rationality while also living as a santera. She is "carried away" and taken back to a "primeval" time and place. In describing the "sacred *batá* drums" played during drumming ceremonies, Moreno Vega describes how "the drums' piercing beats echo the rhythmic patterns of the heart."[106] While Moreno Vega notes that the drums can only be played by men according to Lucumi tradition, she uses them metaphorically several times in *When the Spirits Dance Mambo*, particularly in moments that center women. By tying together drumbeats and heartbeats, the memoir's "spiritual, musical voyage to El Barrio" blurs the line between the body and the spirit, a line that does not exist in Lucumi and espiritismo. An older version of Marta narrates that through mambo, "my body recalls my childhood."[107] Similarly, to begin the second chapter, the elder Marta recounts, "There are occurrences from my childhood in El Barrio that echo throughout my body as if they happened yesterday."[108] By using espiritismo as a frame, Moreno Vega represents literarily her multiple identities and the Yoruba-based conception of time that allows six-year-old Marta and fifty-year-old Marta to coexist alongside other humans, the orisha, and the dead. Rather than thinking about her Africanity and Latinidad as intersecting ideas, she views them as overlapping, each constitutive of the other.

The elder Marta frames *When the Spirits* by using music as a catalyst. She asserts, "Memories are the musical notes that form the composition of our souls. Feelings churned by memory connect us to the past, help us treasure the present, and can even reveal to us our future."[109] Each chapter is cast as a note in a song, beginning with the lyrics of famous Afro-Caribbean music. The inclusion of the lyrics revises music history, "subtly tracing a transnational history of mambo" that, Juanita Heredia argues, restores the place of AfroLatinas in that male-dominated account.[110] Through descriptions of Afro-Caribbean music and imagery of thunder, the sea, and the orishas Yemayá and Changó, Marta evokes the memories of her family, particularly her Abuela's weekly ritual cleansing of the bóveda.[111] The bóveda is a shrine "used by espiritistas to pray and meditate in an effort to maintain connections with their spirit guides."[112] Their maintenance supports the evolution of spirits. For Abuela Luisa and Marta, the upkeep of the bóveda maintains relationships with their guardian spirits, Juango (Kongo), La Gitana (Gypsy), and Rosario del Sol (Madama / "young mulatta").[113] Abuela tells Cotito that "the right music calls the spirits."[114] While performing her ritual cleaning, Abuela plays the AfroLatinx music of Tito Puente, Machito, Graciela, and others. The older Marta recounts how "Celia Cruz brought Africa to our home," emphasizing how Africanity influenced her experiences with family and the way she experienced her music-saturated world.[115] In remembering her childhood ritual of assisting her Abuela, the feelings of the older Marta, writing in the 2000s, mix with her six-year-old self's feelings, unaware of the spiritual meaning behind the weekly cleansing of the bóveda. Just as Celia Cruz takes the elder Marta back to the 1940s and her African ancestry, music can transport Abuela "back to Puerto Rico to relive important moments with family members no longer with us."[116] Abuela uses music to transport herself physically and spiritually to the island and the family she left behind. This musical transportation brings to light the connections between santería spirituality and the events of Marta's childhood.

Moreno Vega shows how music can be deeply personal, as it connects her and her Abuela with their African and Puerto Rican ancestors, but it is also essential to public ceremonies in Cuba and El Barrio that bring together the spirits of the living, the dead, and the orisha. These scenes in Cuba and Harlem reflect the call-and-response conception of AfroLatinidad. In a key scene, Moreno Vega uses spirit possession to frame an Afro-Caribbean music concert that Marta-Cotito attends with her brother. The concert, as performed by the mambo greats of Spanish Harlem at the Apollo Theater of historically Black West Harlem, shares similarities to the batá drum ceremonies that call the spirits. The ceremony entices the orishas "to come down to Earth and take over the consciousness" of espiritistas and also "draws practitioners into the spirit world," emphasizing the commingling of the visible and invisible realms.[117] At the concert, Moreno Vega's writing evokes the same electricity, spiritual presence, and communal connection that she witnessed at the drum ceremonies she attended in Cuba. There, AfroLatina singers such as Graciela and Celia Cruz, sing and dance for aché (spiritual energy) and the orisha.[118] The AfroLatinx musicians at the concert become "gods and goddesses,"[119] playing in a space where Blackness and Latinidad mingle and weave together seamlessly. The women singing at the concert appear to be physical representations of Abuela and Cotito's guardian spirits. For instance, Cotito compares the Afro-Cuban Cruz to "the figurine of the Spanish dancer that graced [her] Abuela's altar" and imagines her as "my *gitana*, my gypsy spirit."[120] Cotito compares the effect of Cruz's music to possession and calls her "the high priestess of song."[121] She claims that "the hypnotic live music infused and took over my body."[122] As Cruz continues her mesmerizing dance and song, the drums begin to play "a low, reverent African rhythm [. . .] replicating the sound of my heart."[123] Cruz honors the warrior gods, Elégua and Ogun, and Marta describes the Yoruba divinities as "warrior spirits that had traveled from Africa to Harlem," implying that the deities now reside with the children of the African diaspora in the Americas.[124]

Moreno Vega repeatedly uses the language of possession to describe her experience at the concert. She uses words such as "enthralled," "possessed," "entrancing," and "paralyzed" to describe how she, her brother, and the audience react to the performers.[125] The scene continuously employs the image of thunder and "rhythmic pounding" to describe the musical environment, paralleling the santería drum ceremonies.[126] Using the traditional call-and-response method of espiritista drum ceremonies, the crowd responds to Celia Cruz's question, *"De qué color son tus bembas?* [What color are your lips?]," with an answer that "roared through the Apollo like rolling thunder."[127] This popular song, "Bemba Colorá," boldly calls to racialized markers as a proud claim to Black beauty, defying the use of the question, which is often used to call someone Black (and thus, imagining Blackness as a bad trait). In the batá drum rituals, "voices chant and escalate, causing the steps of the dancers to quicken,"[128] and the same occurs at the Apollo when Graciela and Machito play their song "Tanga," "pushing the crowd to a state of sublime ecstasy. Pulled by an invisible force, the audience became part of the show."[129] Moreno Vega's description of the spiritual elevation created through these mambo greats shows how African diasporic music, based in rhythmic drumming and call and response, creates a space for the celebration of AfroLatinx identity.

Conclusion

For Moreno Vega, mambo embodies a positive definition of AfroLatinidad and rejects the idea that being AfroLatina means trying to solve an unsolvable ethnoracial puzzle. While speaking from her perspective as a Catholic theologian, M. Shawn Copeland identifies the body as a site of divine revelation, arguing: "In theology, the body is a contested site—ambiguous and sacred, wounded and creative, malleable and resistant—disclosing and mediating 'more.'"[130] In Moreno Vega's memoirs, the bodies of the concertgoers and of the women in her life embrace the body's creativity and malleability.

The call-and-response AfroLatinidad takes the individual experiences of Moreno Vega and Casal and "ensure[s] that the[ir] art will be meaningful or functional to the community."[131] Through call-and-response methods used by the musicians and Moreno Vega's recollections, mambo and memoir become meaningful ways to reaffirm the AfroLatinx community. Through the celebration of spiritual-cultural practices—Afro-Caribbean music and Lucumi drum ceremonies—Moreno Vega portrays the harmony of Africanity and Latinidad, in which Africanity does not strive to join with white Latinidad. Rather, Africa and the Americas call to each other. The rhythm of Yoruba batá drums brought to the Americas, pulsing like a heartbeat, call across the Atlantic to their origins in Yorubaland but reflect their own rhythm, one that evolved in response to Spanish colonialism and the survival practice of protective secrecy.

CHAPTER 5

Queer AfroLatinidades: Monstrosity and Reclaiming Black Latinx Girlhood in Jaquira Díaz's *Ordinary Girls* and Ariana Brown's Verse Memoirs

Introduction

Queer Afro-Boricua writer Jaquira Díaz, in interviews and essays, has often framed her writing in terms of visibility. Her 2019 interview in the *Los Angeles Review of Books* is entitled "Either Hyper-Visible or Invisible," pulling the title from a quotation in the conversation.[1] In "You Do Not Belong Here," she admits to almost leaving the *Kenyon Review* because

> in Ohio, I am invisible. In Ohio, I am hypervisible. Both of these statements are true. It's also true that I considered leaving, but stayed. Every day I leave. Every day I stayed.[2]

Like all the life writers in *Invisibility and Influence*, Díaz speaks to the navigation of visibility that AfroLatinx writers and communities face. Rather than find a space on the spectrum, she lays claim to both extremes. To be AfroLatinx is to be extreme, to be on the edge of what society can see or ignore. Díaz similarly maintains both her absence and presence in Ohio, creating the image of a torn body, attempting to leave but forced (by willpower or perhaps other coercion) to stay. Like a ghost, she haunts and is haunted. It is no surprise then, that her memoir, *Ordinary Girls* (2019) fixates on monsters of the supernatural and criminal varieties.

Monstrosity can itself be invisible or invisibilized. Behind closed doors, cruelty is enacted and tacitly accepted. The fact that others did not "see" it happen is then used as an excuse to accuse the victim of exaggeration or mendaciousness. Monstrosity can also be hypervisible. When mass murders occur or media show us the gruesome and horrible things humans are capable of, those actions often overtake every other facet of a person. For people of color, and especially queer people of color, one act of monstrosity can come to define whole communities as monsters. For example, Christina Sharpe in *Monstrous Intimacies* demonstrates how acts of monstrosity committed against Black subjects were (and are) hidden, their horrific effects denied, and even twisted "to make manifest, measurable, and readable an essential black inferiority and black monstrosity, not the monstrosity of slavery and slavery's complicated black performances."[3] Similarly, the historical criminalization of queerness, both as sexual acts and as gender performance, as well as its description as a form of deviance has made gay, lesbian, trans, and queer people and communities into criminals, demons, and monsters.[4] The grisly, violent, and terrifying scenes that populate *Ordinary Girls* reclaim monstrosity, but not in order to redeem or excuse it. Like Viet Thanh Nguyen argues in his conception of "just memory," the coexistence of the inhuman in the human is often elided, ignored, or erased in order to encapsulate a person, group, or nation as either monster or prey, hero or victim.[5]

This chapter examines Díaz's memoir *Ordinary Girls* alongside queer Afro–Mexican American poet Ariana Brown's verse memoirs, as I term them. Brown's poetry similarly explores the ways in which Blackness has been invisibilized and marginalized in Mexico and the Southwest United States in which she grew up. She attempts to construct a "just memory" of Blackness in Latin American and Latinidad, moving beyond celebratory narratives of historical reclamation. Both Díaz and Brown navigate the invisibility and hypervisibility of AfroLatinidad though through very different means. Recall that *Invisibility and Influence* uses "AfroLatinidades" to refer to social, cultural, and political constructions based in the embodied experiences of Black Latinxs. AfroLatinidades call attention to the realities of living in a Black body and contest the equation of "Black" with "US Black." In addition, AfroLatinidades call attention to the anti-Blackness of mestizaje narratives. Thus, AfroLatinidades arise from the negotiation of invisibility, visibility, and hypervisibility. That is, AfroLatinx writers construct an AfroLatinidad by bringing to light the distortions and erasures they must navigate within themselves and in the world around them that both invisibilize and hypervisibilize their presence.

These twenty-first-century, queer AfroLatinx writers—Jaquira Díaz and Ariana Brown—navigate the spectrum of visibility through an exploration of the monstrosity of colonialism and anti-Blackness. In the memoirs I examine, queer AfroLatinidades emerge from a reckoning with monstrosity, a concept frequently used against queer communities of color. Adopting Saidiya Hartman's concept of "waywardness" as well as monster theory, I illuminate Díaz's conception of queer AfroLatinidad in relation to the legend of La Llorona, true crime stories, and a reclamation of Black Latinx girlhood.[6] While Brown's verse memoirs, *Sana Sana* (2020) and *We Are Owed.* (2021), depend on sociohistorical grounding, critical fabulation (per Hartman), and a call for a postnationalist AfroLatinidad, she too ultimately calls for Black Latinx girls to find love with one another. Both writers—through Díaz's centering of Afro-Boricua Jaqui and the stories of other girls of color and through Brown's numerous poems centering a six-year-old Ariana—use the life writing genre to argue for the authority and necessity of queer Black Latinx girls' stories. As Leigh Gilmore and Elizabeth Marshall argue in *Witnessing Girlhood*, memoirs that center girls' voices imbue those life narratives with the "values associated with autobiography—truth telling, the authority of experience, and credibility."[7] In doing so, these life narratives demand love and acceptance for Black and Black Latinx girls in a world that distrusts and demonizes them.

Neither Díaz's nor Brown's works present themselves as queer coming-out narratives; however, they fit into this category in their claim to be visible on their own terms and for their own purposes. Each writer claims queerness by demanding the love often withheld from Black girls. The approach to "coming out" in Díaz's and Brown's memoirs aligns with Trinh T. Minh-ha's concept of "speaking near-by." When an artist speaks near-by, they do not approach a subject bluntly or directly; rather than pretend to know where they want to end up, these writers write around, in circles, and in the parentheticals to avoid "the comforting illusion that one knows where one goes."[8] Neither Brown nor Díaz depict coming-out scenes for their reader; however, the importance of queer love within friendships, romantic relationships, and even with historical figures we admire shines through. In this way, these queer AfroLatinx writers claim space within an AfroLatinx literary present, while also calling (and responding) to its past.

In exploring these twenty-first century texts' deployments and definitions of queer AfroLatinidades, one must consider what it means to combine these two terms. The term *queer* as noun, adjective, and verb has many definitions. In the wake of bell hooks's death in 2021, one popular definition circulated on social media comes from a panel entitled, "Are You Still a Slave? Liberating the Black Female Body," in which hooks asserts that we reframe our approach to queerness "as being about the self that is at odds with everything around it and has to invent and create and find a place to speak and to thrive and to live."[9] In other words, queerness is not a unidimensional identity based solely on sexual practice (though disconnecting the term from sexuality entirely is suspect). Queerness, for hooks, is about how we construct our sense of self against normative claims steeped in racism, sexism, classism, xenophobia, etcetera. This definition aligns with Juana María Rodríguez's exploration of identity in *Queer Latinidad*. For Rodríguez, "identity is about situatedness in motion: embodiment and spatiality. It is about a self that is constituted through and against other selves in contexts that serve to establish the relationship between the self and the other."[10] In analyzing identity, we must move away from pure questions of definition and move further to its application: "'What is identity?' becomes transformed into 'What is identity for?' Under what circumstances is it constructed and whose interests does it serve?"[11] Black Caribbean lesbian writers like Jewelle Gomez and Audre Lorde have both argued that their queerness alongside their ethnoracial heritage, class, and other facets of identity have been important frames to their writing and politics. We must name difference and allow difference to coexist, without hierarchies, to be fully ourselves and to serve others well, according to Lorde and Gomez.[12] Though this may appear to oppose Rodríguez's approach to identity, in fact, they all gesture to how José Esteban Muñoz defines "queers of color," which collectively he calls an "identity-in-difference," whose "emergence is predicated on their ability to disidentify with the mass public and instead, through this disidentification, contribute to the function of a counterpublic sphere."[13] To disidentify is a Foucauldian act in which the queer of color is aware that the act of creating identity is an act against and in conversation with, as well as in service of, power.[14] As Muñoz notes, queer people of color, and I argue queer AfroLatinxs, "identify with ethnos or queerness despite the phobic charges in both fields."[15] That is, queer AfroLatinxs must navigate the fact that in the straight world, their queerness makes them monsters; and in the (white) queer world, their skin color makes them monsters. In this model, queerness is an action-based concept, a means to resist and adapt. As Muñoz posits, queers of color do more than "[crack] open the code of the majority," they "use this code as raw material for representing a disempowered politics or positionality that has been rendered unthinkable by the dominant culture."[16] Jaquira Díaz molds this raw material to find beauty in the violence of 1990s Miami; Ariana Brown imagines the queer, postnationalist possibilities in the historical gaps of Afro-Mexican history.

In both Díaz's and Brown's work, visibility is not always freeing,[17] but it charts a different path, rejecting narratives of respectability or attempts to fit into hegemonic notions of US Blackness or white Latinidades. The negotiation of queer AfroLatinidades also highlights the eroticization and sexual dimension of Black Latinidad. As Rodríguez asserts, "Our [Latinx and women of color's] racialized excess is already read as queer, outside the norms of what is useful or productive."[18] This excess comes forth through the aesthetics of Black Latinx life, as Jillian Hernández argues. Like Muñoz, Hernández in *Aesthetics of Excess* embraces the nuance of making queerness in a homophobic and racist world and emphasizes it as an act of willful hypervisibility, though not in service to respectability or representational politics.[19] While Díaz's and Brown's work feels and reads as two distinct and almost incomparable pieces, I put them in conversation because both explore the excess and perceived monstrosity of queer AfroLatinidad and in doing so, reclaim Black Latinx girlhood in the process. These memoirs revisit, validate, and love on the Black Latinx girls of these writers' past as a way of claiming queer love and joy in the present.[20]

Monstrous AfroLatinidades in Jaquira Díaz's *Ordinary Girls*

I start my analysis of *Ordinary Girls* with a confession: when I read the memoir the first time, I did not think I should write about it. Despite having so many parallels to Piri Thomas's *Down These Mean Streets* in its literary strategies and consistent reflection on the shaping power of violence by and against the subject of the memoir, I did not know how to feel. During my second reading, and having recently finished Cathy Park Hong's *Minor Feelings*, the memoir brought me back to Hong's discomfort with the methods and forms available for "writing about personal racial trauma."[21] I worried that it was a trauma porn memoir, feeding into a disturbing desire for women of color's pain.[22] Trauma porn dehumanizes and makes one-dimensional the experience of immigrants, women of color, or victims of abuse. Examples of trauma porn are easy to find; consider Jeanine Cummins's *American Dirt* or Kathryn Stockett's *The Help*, though writers of color can also traffic in these stereotypical stories that play to the ego of white and other privileged readers. However, I realized that I had not read trauma porn; I'd read a memoir driven by monsters and ghost stories.

Díaz parallels her own life, her origin story, and the violence of girlhood to ghost, monster, and true-crime stories. Díaz's memoir reads as a descendent to Thomas's *Down These Mean Streets*, but she puts a queer Afro-Boricua woman at its center. She refuses to protect the reader from the totality of violence and (self-)destruction that shaped Jaqui and the "ordinary girls" that begin and end her memoir. In *Ordinary Girls*, violence and monstrosity is ordinary; monsters (real and folkloric) are at the center of the story. In particular, La Llorona and true crime cases such as the Baby Lollipops case and the Casey Anthony trial, show the racialization and homophobia of monstrosity. Díaz shows that for society, being queer and being AfroLatinx is monstrous. In line with monster theory, I define monsters as social constructions that foreground the borders of normativity in US and Latin American culture. Díaz recognizes queerness and AfroLatinidades as what Jeffrey Cohen calls "monster[s] of prohibition." Such monsters "exist to demarcate the bonds that hold together that system of relations we call culture, to call horrid attention to the borders that cannot—*must not*—be crossed."[23] In crossing the borders of heteropatriarchy and of white supremacist hierarchies, queer AfroLatinidades are monstrous.

Díaz presents her life narrative as an "anti-memoir / literary journalism,"[24] structuring her narrative away from a telegenic story of growth and overcoming. Jaqui's story is not primarily a coming-out narrative, nor a story of redemption. Díaz's conception of the anti-memoir dovetails with Hong's definition of the literature of "minor feelings," defined as "the racialized range of emotions that are negative, dysphoric, and therefore untelegenic, built from the sediments of everyday racial experience and the irritant of having one's perception of reality constantly questioned or dismissed."[25] As Hong writes, "rather than using racial trauma as a dramatic stage for individual *growth*, the literature of minor feelings explores the trauma of a racist capitalist system that keeps the individual *in place*."[26] Jaqui in *Ordinary Girls* exemplifies this sense of staying in place, as the memoir refuses to provide a sense of victory and instead makes the reader linger in the stuckness that racial capitalism forces on Black Latinx girls and women. Instead of striving to overcome, the girls in Díaz's memoir enact what Hartman calls "waywardness,"[27] an impulse towards creative, resistant destruction that is skeptical of visibility's liberatory potential.[28] Visibility is rarely a form of recognition for Black women in the US; rather it is the prequel to violence. To be visible is not inherently freeing because in the US and other white supremacist societies, there is little to no space for a healthy visibility. To be visible is to be a target. Thus, to be wayward, in Hartman's words, is "to claim the right to opacity."[29] Waywardness resides in Black women's "whimsical girlish tones," in their "loud laughter," and as "a will to unsettle, destroy, and remake that is so forceful it takes the breath away."[30] Countering the delinquent and unrespectable connotations of waywardness, Hartman, like Hernández does with her theory of the aesthetics of excess, instead celebrates the ways Black girls' bodies move, dress, and challenge a world that withholds its love and care. Similarly, Díaz presents Jaqui and her friends as always trying to duck visibility to those with power, whether in the classroom or in the street, while also looking for recognition from each other, through bold fashion choices, loud laughter, and acts of strength. No matter what they do, others will see them as monsters and delinquents, but they at least can find community together in that monstrosity.

Like all monsters, Jaqui (the name used to represent Díaz's "narrated I" in the memoir) begins with an origin story, quite literally through the title of her first chapter, "Origin Story." Throughout part 1, Jaqui outlines her monstrous origins through the violent experiences she witnessed and experienced as a girl and the monstrous acts of her parents. Jaqui was born and raised in El Caserío (the public housing projects) of Puerto Rico until age ten. Caseríos have been traditionally "profiled as a place of urban blackness, drugs, violence, and crime"[31] and are frequently visible in the media as a space of Black criminality.[32] During this time, she describes numerous acts of violence, but also of children playing together and neighbors who know and look out for one another. She and her friends throw rocks at a Vietnam veteran who snaps and chases them with a machete; soon after, he is found dead.[33] A stranger exposes himself to young Jaqui, who blames herself and thus keeps this act of sexual violence a secret from her family.[34] Jaqui's parents and their respective whiteness and Blackness is introduced to the reader by a description of their differing hair texture. Mami has "cropped, blond waves blowing in the wind" and when she smokes, she looks like "Marilyn Monroe" or "Michelle Pfeiffer in *Scarface*."[35] Papi is "quiet, stern-faced, his picked-out Afro shining in the sun."[36] Their racialized identities frame the reader's approach. We learn that Mami's mother, Mercy, acts in horrifically anti-Black ways, and Jaqui's own hair is a constant source of attack, identified as "bad hair."[37] On the other hand, Abuela, Papi's mother, "was unapologetically Boricua, unapologetically Black." Her Afro, since she "refused to perm her hair or use a hot comb," signals her pro-Black household.[38] However, despite the clear differences between the outwardly anti-Black and pro-Black attitudes prevalent in each grandmother's home, their unconditional and often unjustly apologetic defensiveness of Jaqui's white-passing Puerto Rican brother, Anthony, reveals the foundations of anti-Black monstrosity within both Black and white Puerto Rican families. Both Abuela and Mercy have grown up with Puerto Rican anti-Blackness, and its influence permeates their interactions.

Díaz's attempt to make visible the things society wishes we did not see is an act of "monstrous intimacy." *Ordinary Girls* demands that the reader consider the resounding power that invisibility and hypervisibility have in the life of a queer Black Latinx girl. According to Sharpe, "monstrous intimacies, [are] defined as a set of known and unknown performances and inhabited horrors, desires and positions produced, reproduced, circulated, and transmitted, that are breathed in like air and often unacknowledged to be monstrous."[39] In our daily proximity to these monstrous acts—as well as histories of denial in how we talk about or teach topics like chattel slavery, sexual and domestic violence, and racist policies—horrific beliefs and actions are considered normal.[40] Díaz calls attention to these monstrous intimacies and the heavy loads that queer Black Latinx girls carry, as a way of naming the forces that make them supposedly monstrous. For instance, while sexual violence against Black Latinx women and girls is "breathed like air," we do not pay attention to those breaths. *Ordinary Girls* makes us linger in the monstrous intimacies of anti-Blackness and antiqueerness. Simultaneously, Jaqui revels in her monstrous status as a queer Black Latinx. Through a focus on monsters, real and folkloric, Díaz shows both the suffering and joy of queer AfroLatinidades.

A panoply of folkloric and true-crime monsters appears in *Ordinary Girls*, though the first one she names explicitly is La Llorona. In her landmark study of the Llorona figure in Chicana/o and Greater Mexican folklore and popular culture, Domino Renee Perez writes, "La Llorona's story is an ideal vehicle for creating intercultural dialogue because she does not recognize any border, and similar figures appear across cultures."[41] While Perez's study clearly indicates her focus on Chican@ deployments of the Llorona legend, I employ her work because it explores such a broad array of usages (including queer revisions),[42] and I am not aware of any substantial studies of Puerto Rican uses of the Llorona figure. As Perez notes, "La Llorona is alternately, and sometimes simultaneously, a person, legend, ghost, goddess, metaphor, story, and/or symbol."[43] Conventional and traditional representations of La Llorona are based in misogyny, representing the woman as "despairing," "selfish, vain, vengeful, whorish, and worst of all, a bad mother, while excusing or ignoring the behavior of the man," according to Perez.[44] As a monster, La Llorona reveals "a double narrative, two living stories: one that describes how the monster came to be and another, its testimony, detailing what cultural use the monster serves."[45] This claim by Jeffrey Cohen allows us to consider how the story of a monster's origin is also a story of how a culture defines the normative. Monsters, like La Llorona, "serve as secondary bodies through which the possibilities of other genders, other sexual practices, and other social customs can be explored,"[46] though always with a healthy dose of fear and rejection. We are not supposed to *want* to be La Llorona, but if we allow ourselves to be fascinated by the grotesque acts she committed, we can revel in the possibilities available to wives and mothers if they were to reject the norm of heteropatriarchy.

While only discussed substantially in Díaz's chapter "Monster Story," I argue that La Llorona is the monster that frames all of *Ordinary Girls*. Díaz first introduces La Llorona alongside Jaqui's disclosure that she "was obsessed with monsters." And not just any monsters, but the violent and vengeful sort, from "witches who came back from the dead to kill the townspeople who'd burned them at the stake" to "zombies, werewolves, Frankenstein's monster, [and] Dracula," as well as urban legends like "the possibility of killer alligators living in the sewers."[47] Jaqui's obsession with monsters reflects her desire to be allowed to rage against the people and institutions that marginalize her. Thus, La Llorona, as a female Puerto Rican monster, intrigues her. Jaqui's first mention of La Llorona focuses on her supposed appearance; she is "sometimes a pumpkin-headed demon in a tattered wedding dress, sometimes a woman with a goat's head."[48] The first description is not particularly scary, sounding more like a cheap Halloween costume, while the second imagines her in the tradition of the human-animal hybrid, a tradition frequently tied to racialist thought.[49] As "a bogeywoman,"[50] La Llorona is a threat wrapped in a bedtime story to ensure children's compliance. Díaz writes, "If you were a troublemaker, if you got into fights, if you didn't eat what your abuela made for dinner, if you refused to sleep come bedtime, La Llorona rose from the darkness to make you hers."[51] Jaqui, of course, consistently does all of these things, especially fighting and troublemaking. Thus, both Jaqui and La Llorona, by being "transgressive, too sexual, perversely erotic, a lawbreaker" are both monsters who challenge the norms of their Puerto Rican and Puerto Rican diasporic communities.[52]

The story of La Llorona and her crimes, as narrated to young Jaqui, is not shared until ten pages into the chapter, "Monster Story." Díaz writes,

> The stories say that La Llorona killed her children—one boy, one girl—whose names I didn't know.
> The stories say that La Llorona killed her children after being rejected by a lover. She had taken her two babies from their beds one night, had walked with them through the woods down to the river, held their bodies underwater until they both drowned. Then, when she realized what she'd done, with their lifeless bodies in her arms, she walked into the river and let it take her, too.[53]

This account, which aligns with several Chicanx tellings of the tale,[54] is told with an unemotional, matter-of-fact tone. La Llorona is a mother, though not a wife, who drowns her two children as a reaction to romantic rejection and then gives herself the same fate as punishment. The tale itself appears to have no opening for resistance: this woman failed as a mother and took her own life, but her suicide provides her no relief, as now she "wails in the dead of night, haunting rivers and beaches and lakes [. . .] calling out for her ghost children."55 However, in Jaqui's account, the gender of the lover is not revealed, nor is it clear if the two children were shared by La Llorona and her lover. La Llorona could have been rejected by a female lover or because she had more than one; no reason is provided for her rejection. This Llorona is a mother, but her sexuality is in question, providing a space to push against the normative in the story. While Jaqui has told us what makes the Wailing Woman "a cultural villain," she also opens up the possibility, as Perez asserts, "to read La Llorona as a figure of liberation."56

Monstrosity and haunting are both reckonings with visibility. While ghosts and monsters may seem to be invisible forces, in fact, they are willful acts of visibility.57 For Avery Gordon, "these specters or ghosts appear when the trouble they represent and symptomize [sic] is no longer being contained or repressed or blocked from view."58 Ghosts force us to face the trauma created by oppressive systems and cultures. They refuse to sweep injustice under the rug. La Llorona haunts "Monster Story" and parallels Mami's (Jaqui's mom) story in Miami. "Monster Story" begins with a brief summary of what led Jaqui's family to migrate to Miami, which was Mami's transformation after a significant trauma. Mami's mental illness was triggered by a horrifying experience in which the family was robbed at gunpoint in their home. Her mental health steadily worsens, and she is eventually diagnosed with schizophrenia alongside her worsening addiction to drugs. Mami and Papi divorce, and all three kids are living with Papi. The story then becomes eerily similar to the Llorona tale. Mami comes in the middle of the night, takes the two daughters from their beds without telling their father, and kidnaps them.59 Jaqui and her sister attempt to run away. They "ran towards the beach" but their mother hears them and gives chase. As they run, Jaqui wonders, "We're supposed to love our mothers. We're supposed to trust them and need them and miss them when they're gone. But what if that same person, the one who's supposed to love you more than anyone else in the world, the one who's supposed to protect you, is also the one who hurts you the most?"60 Mami becomes La Llorona, the mother who betrays her children, chasing them and catching them at the beach. While she does not literally kill them, she destroys their trust, becoming a villain in their story. Just like in Díaz's description of the Wailing Woman "hunting" children,61 Mami takes on La Llorona's animalistic, hunter mentality: "That morning on the beach, when our [Jaqui's and Mami's] eyes met, I knew that Mami would catch us. I saw it in her face. She knew it, too. And she would never let us go."62 Jaqui depicts Mami as possessed, a hunter obsessed with catching its prey. Drawn to water, her hunting grounds are Miami Beach.63 In a secondary sense, Mami is possessed by the spirit of La Llorona, whose monstrous love destroys her children and herself.

As a monstrous mother, La Llorona represents different maternal fears, one of which is the fear that one failure will forever label a mother as "bad." While La Llorona's act is horrific, it also erases the rest of her life and identity. As Perez notes, when "La Llorona is only remembered for what she became after she murdered her children, then her previous role as a life-giving, loving nurturer is erased."[64] Díaz does not pull punches in describing the horrific acts that Mami commits, but she also provides moments that evoke sympathy and make visible the inner turmoil that simmers underneath her "blonde bombshell" veneer. For example, during their kidnapping, Mami talks to the man that haunts her during a schizophrenic episode. She explodes, "'I've given you everything!' she said, 'Everything! And now I have nothing left!'"[65] Mami's constant muttering and verbal explosions, symptoms of her schizophrenia, are again made to align her with La Llorona and her wailings. One can imagine La Llorona's own feelings of not being enough, of bitterness towards a culture that celebrates self-sacrifice but never rewards it.

Díaz's characterization of Mami as a real-life Llorona exists alongside the true-crime monster story of the Baby Lollipops case. The details of the Baby Lollipops case are truly grotesque, so I will spare the reader the details, though *Ordinary Girls* does not. A surprising amount of the memoir discusses the Miami case, in which Afro-Cuban mother Ana María Cardona and her girlfriend Olivia González tortured, starved, and eventually left Cardona's baby son Lázaro to die in a bush.[66] Along with Mami and Cardona, Díaz also adds Mami's mother, Mercy, as another Llorona iteration. None of these women are perfect victims (not even close): Mami neglects her children for her addiction and rarely takes her medicine, Mercy's virulent anti-Black racism harms her grandchildren, Cardona's defense that her girlfriend committed most if not all the abuse against Lázaro begs the question, "why didn't you stop her?" These women, all La Llorona in some way, are "presented as a 'wounded' figure, a woman who endures great suffering as a consequence of her actions, a figure worthy of reconsideration."[67] The wailing of La Llorona, Díaz suggests, is a cry for help, a cry to be seen, a refusal to silently suffer.

By exploring Cardona's story in more depth, Díaz makes visible the racial and sexual dimensions that haunt her case. Ana María Cardona was part of the Mariel boatlift, an event that shifted how the United States regarded Cuban exiles. As Hernández explains, "the Castro government framed the refugees as trans and homosexual perverts and/or deviant criminals, and many were treated as such when they arrived on US shores. The lower socioeconomic positionalities, queerness, and phenotypical Blackness of the marielitos also spurred their rejection by established, white-identifying Cuban American communities."[68] While Díaz does not explicitly mention Cardona's Afro-Cuban identity in *Ordinary Girls*, she makes this explicit in other writing on Cardona.[69] In *Ordinary Girls*, she relates that Cardona "came to the US in 1980 during the Mariel boatlift, she says, alone and pregnant, and got into sex work out of desperation."[70] By naming her a Marielito, Díaz attaches the racialized identity associated with this group of refugees. Her Blackness, alongside her sex work, marks her as deviant. Cardona is further portrayed as a monster due to her lesbianism and the fact that in the days after abandoning her child, she went to Disneyworld with González, as if she were celebrating. This act elicits disgust, abhorrence, but perhaps also some jealousy, that Cardona found a way to free herself of the weight of motherhood.[71] Cardona is not the only character in the memoir who abandoned her child; Mami's mother, Mercy, also gave up her own kids to be raised by others.[72] Jaqui's mother, through her neglect, physical abuse, and untreated mental illness, basically leaves Jaqui and her sister to raise themselves as well. Like La Llorona, Mami hurts them endlessly, physically and emotionally, but also refuses to let them go. However, while she refuses to let them live with their father, their father does nothing to fight for them. In fact, the ending of Mami's La Llorona story of kidnapping, when Jaqui and her sister return to Papi's apartment, lingers on Papi's own coldness and apathy. Jaqui laments,

> When Papi came back inside our apartment, he didn't wrap his arms around us or pick us up or twirl us in the middle of the living room like I'd imagined he would. He just went to the bathroom to get ready for work. I wanted to shake him and shake him. Did he know how scared we'd been? How many times Mami had threatened to take us away, to keep us from him? Why hadn't he tried to find us? [. . .] I realized then that if my mother wanted to take me and Alaina, she could have us, and there's nothing my father would do about it.[73]

Jaqui refuses to suppress or leave unanswered the question of the man's role in this Llorona tale.[74] She does not submerge Papi's complicity in their kidnapping, which is perhaps due to his own selfish desire to take care of just his (white) son rather than his darker-skinned daughters. In this Llorona tale, if these children are to be taken or even to die, it is because the father would let them. And in fact, Mami does return to take Jaqui and her sister (but not her brother) and "Papi just stood there."⁷⁵ The other parent who haunts the Llorona tale is made visible. He watches the monster take the children; he lets her take them and convinces himself not to see the truth: that he is a monster, too.

The Llorona legend, however, comments on sexuality as much as motherhood, as the tale enforces obedience and discourages sexual exploration.⁷⁶ Díaz's decision to frame the memoir through La Llorona, then, points to the mythic figure's double monstrosity: she was a bad mother and she had strong sexual desires. The first description of Jaqui's queerness comes in directly after a page describing Mami's liberated (hetero)sexuality. Mami "loved and enjoyed her body" and thought bodies of all sizes were beautiful. She even taught Jaqui and her sister "about masturbation, giving us detailed instructions about how to achieve orgasm." Sexual desire and expecting sexual fulfillment were "perfectly normal. Nothing to be ashamed of."⁷⁷ While nominally more acceptable than Jaqui's queerness, Mami's embrace of sexual pleasure also goes against heteropatriarchal expectations of women. As Mami's mental health deteriorates and she falls into addiction, her sexuality is demonized. Jaqui sees her mother's sexuality as a crude tool to get things from men and does not want her mom walking her to school, since "'You look like a prostitute.'"⁷⁸ Though she immediately regrets what she said, as it goes against her mother's sex-positive teachings, this scene also shows the fine line that women walk when it comes to sexual expression. When she was married and young, Mami's Marilyn Monroe and Madonna styles were acceptable deviances, but at twenty-seven and divorced, with an addiction and mental illness to boot, to dress "like a teenager, flaunting her curves, using her body to get what she wanted from men" becomes less tolerable. Her seemingly excessive sexuality makes her an unfit mother. However, while Mami's sexuality is discussed as inappropriate, Jaqui presents her own queerness as a monstrous secret, one that is not even allowed the same space on the page. Jaqui discloses her first kiss, shared with an older girl, through a long parenthetical paragraph. She quite literally shows how queerness is unspeakable, something hidden in the margins.⁷⁹

Unlike Mami's flaunted sexuality, which confirms for some that women's pleasure is a form of deviance and acts as a cautionary tale to confirm heteropatriarchal norms, Jaqui's secretive sexuality haunts the texts. As noted above, Ana María Cardona, the mother of Lázaro (Baby Lollipops), was sentenced alongside her girlfriend Olivia González (a white Latina) for the baby's torture and murder.⁸⁰ The media and the people in Jaqui's life identify Cardona's lesbianism as a warning sign or contributing factor to her ability to torture and kill her son. After listening to neighbors call the women homophobic slurs and argue, "'That baby would still be alive, [. . .] if only they'd kept him away from those lesbians,'" Jaqui notices that "it seemed as though being a lesbian was part of the crime, something a mother could also be charged with."[81] Through this example, Díaz points to the long history of criminalizing lesbianism and representing lesbians as inherently violent and delinquent.[82] Cardona's lesbianism is a crime in itself, at least in the people's court, and it suggests that her character is deviant and lacking. Jaqui herself then is made to wonder if, through her own queerness, she is capable of horrific acts. In fact, the chapter "Monster Story" ends with Jaqui's incarceration in a juvenile detention center after stabbing her brother with a knife (after her brother tries to strangle her). In the escalation to the fight, Anthony uses Jaqui's diary as a sign of her monstrosity. He holds up the pages as "hard evidence of the monster [she] was" and asks, "What kind of a girl are you?"[83] This question haunts Jaqui. Her violent reactions to the beatings her mother and her brother put on her make her, officially, a juvenile delinquent and even make others question if she even really is a "girl." As an adult, when she believes she has found a new home in the US Army, her status as the right kind of woman for the military is similarly attacked. Already having to work harder than others due to her color and sex, when her fellow soldiers find out that she is queer and having a relationship with another woman, they taunt her with the name "Don't Ask, Don't Tell," leading her to go AWOL and be dishonorably discharged.[84] The nickname itself, drawn from the Clinton-era policy that allowed queer soldiers to serve as long as they were closeted, is a statement on the forced invisibility of queerness. In marking herself as visibly queer, particularly alongside her racialized identity, she is no longer the right kind of soldier, just like she was not the right kind of girl.

If to be queer is to be nonnormative, then AfroLatinidad itself can be seen as inherently queer. As Cohen writes, "this refusal to participate in the classificatory 'order of things' is true of monsters generally: they are disturbing hybrids whose externally incoherent bodies resist attempts to include them in any systematic structuration."[85] To be queer and to be AfroLatinx is to transgress the borders of ethnoracial, sexual, and gendered normativity.[86] AfroLatinidad is demonized in Jaqui's family, especially by her grandmother Mercy, who views Blackness as an invasive, corrosive aspect of Latinidad. This view aligns with ideas of monstrosity derived from racialist ideas of hybridity. In white supremacist–aligned sciences, Black humans were viewed as not fully human; thus interracial sex would lead to a hybrid subhuman.[87] Other social mythologies of ethno-race, such as Latinidades, especially through celebrations of mestizaje, admit to a degree of Blackness. This lineage of Blackness, however, has often been viewed as a cultural deficiency.

Historically, this viewpoint has even led to policies (like those in Argentina) that encouraged European immigration that was perceived as whitening the population and offsetting the supposed inferiority of Black and Indigenous "mixing."[88] Mercy's anti-Blackness exemplifies this fear of white dilution. In addition, Mercy's anti-Black racism against Papi, Abuela, and other Afro–Puerto Ricans manifests itself through associations with the demonic. For example, Mercy "made up stories about how she [Abuela] was doing voodoo in her kitchen to ruin my mother's life," and when her daughter Xiomara marries a Black man, she also accuses his mother of leaving "a voodoo hex outside Xiomara's door."[89] Similarly, Mercy melds ghost and alien stories into her racist ideals,[90] connecting to a long history of crediting aliens instead of people for building the Pyramids or the Nazca lines. These conspiracy theories diminish Black and Indigenous peoples and the accomplishments of those civilizations before colonization. Mercy's constant accusations of Afro–Puerto Rican "black magic" exemplify the anti-Blackness that equates Blackness with monstrosity and alienness.

Afro–Puerto Rican queerness does more than refuse racial and sexual classifications; I argue that queer AfroLatinidad rejects the idea of hybridity itself. AfroLatinidad is more than a mix of Blackness and Latinidad, and *Ordinary Girls* avoids dividing out what is Black and Puerto Rican about her family. In fact, this rejection of classifications and binaries manifests itself in Jaqui's depiction of her queerness. Jaqui never labels her sexual identity. While she talks about the many boys, girls, men, and women to whom she was attracted, she does not call herself a lesbian or even bisexual.[91] Jaqui may desire to avoid labeling her bisexuality to avoid biphobia, which commonly stereotypes bisexuals as confused, inauthentic, and impossible to trust (in straight and queer communities alike). However, she may also want to avoid the hybrid definition inherent in the label, which seems to say that it is a mix of straightness and lesbianism or gayness. Just as Jaqui's ethnoracial identity is not a mix of (US) Blackness and (Latinx) whiteness, her sexuality is not a combination of straightness and gayness.

Ultimately, *Ordinary Girls* embraces the monstrous by celebrating Black Latinx girlhood. While the memoir begins and ends with an ode to ordinary girls, when Jaqui dresses up as herself, as "teenage me," for Halloween eighteen years after the Baby Lollipops murder, she claims the title of monster. She describes her costume as follows:

> I was wearing baggy jeans, a baggy white T-shirt, high-top Jordans, a gold chain around my neck, my hair in cornrows. I put in my seventeen piercings, fake gold doorknockers, tiny gold hoops. I'm wearing penciled-on

dark brown lip liner, brown lipstick, thick black winged eyeliner, lord knows how many coats of mascara. I painted on a fake black eye, put fake blood under my nose, on my knuckles. I stuffed my pockets with Charms Blow Pops and Ring Pops.[92]

Jaqui's costume relies on representing two facets of her girl self: the use of what Jillian Hernández calls "chonga body politics" and aesthetics of excess, and the violence of her childhood. The term "chonga," as Hernández describes it, is a Miami Latinx term for "so-called low-class, slutty, tough, and crass young women," which has been often presented by media and cultural institutions "as an undesirable and deviant mode of embodiment."[93] Black and Latinx women who take on chonga body politics embrace this deviance and "embody ethnic pride, sexual autonomy, and indifference toward assimilating to whiteness."[94] While respectability politics laments these women of color who wear "too much" makeup, whose hoops are "too big," who wear clothes with prints that are "too loud," and who take up "too much" space, Jaqui's costume revels in this excess through her "lord knows how many coats of mascara," her double-digit piercings, and her corn rows, which call attention to her Black Latinidad. In addition to this embrace of extraness, Jaqui adds as part of this costume the violence that shaped her. Fake blood for Halloween evokes monsters like horror-movie killers, and Jaqui uses the "fake black eye" and "fake blood" for a similarly monstrous effect, portraying herself as dangerous. But she is also a fighter, as the blood on her nose and knuckles demonstrates her willingness to defend herself and her girls, though she does not come out unscathed. While a girl who fights may be seen as deviant or delinquent, she wears the violence she committed and that was done against her visibly as a badge of honor. Doing so is an embrace of the ordinary girls for whom she wrote this memoir.

The memoir is bookended by two short chapters, "Girl Hood" and "Ordinary Girls." The title "Girl Hood," evokes both the state of being a girl or "girlhood" but also a space or a "hood" that belongs to the ordinary girls. Díaz considers how time and place can coincide, much like the AfroLatina spiritual feminism of Lourdes Casal and Marta Moreno Vega. To fully consider what it means to be an AfroLatinx girl, Díaz must consider both age and space but also how the feeling of girlhood can linger on, even as we transition to womanhood. In this opening chapter, Díaz describes the girls in her neighborhood, her home girls, and the girls she was, imagining herself at different moments as different girls. In doing so, she does not allow a particular moment in her life, like when she was "homeless and on the run," to subsume her full identity.[95] She establishes herself as girl who loved other girls from the start but also refuses to cast those girls as merely love interests. They struggle like her, rarely having the support systems they need to thrive. However, she commemorates these girls as fonts of wisdom and support: "Hood girls, who were strong and vulnerable, who taught me about love and friendship and hope."[96] In addition, she centers "girls who were black and brown and poor and queer. Girls who loved each other."[97] In doing so, her work is an act of writing from the margins, since she embraces the people in the margins for more than their lack and suffering. As bell hooks writes, marginality is not only something that "one wishes to lose—to give up or surrender as part of moving into the centre—but rather as a site one stays in, clings to even because it nourishes one's capacity to resist. It offers to one the possibility of radical perspective from alternatives, new worlds."[98] Importantly for hooks, this was not a symbolic marginality but an embodied one. For Díaz, this "space of radical possibility" allows queer AfroLatinx girls like herself to confront and even love what is monstrous,[99] as well as to mourn the childhoods made inaccessible through racism, homophobia, and the hypervisibility/invisibility spectrum.

Thus, the end of *Ordinary Girls* begins as it ends: dedicating itself to the girls who are invisible or whose lives and bodies are distorted by hypervisibility. She concludes:

> This is who I write about and who I write for. For the girls they were, for the girl I was, for girls everywhere who are just like we used to be. For the black and brown girls. For the girls on the merry-go-round making the world spin. For the wild girls and the party girls, the loudmouths and troublemakers. For the girls who are angry and lost. For the girls who never saw themselves in books. For the girls who love other girls, sometimes in secret. For the girls who believe in monsters. For the girls on the edge who are ready to fly. For the ordinary girls. For all the girls who broke my heart. And their mothers. And their daughters. And if I could reach back through time and space to that girl I was, to all my girls, I would tell you to take care, to love each other, fight less, dance dance dance until you're breathless. And goddamn, girl. Live.[100]

Again, Díaz calls to the fullness of girlhood, its sadness and delight. She also expands this "girl hood" not only to Jaqui, Flaca, China, and others but also the past girls that their mothers and grandmothers were. While the memoir itself provides a litany of monsters and monster stories, the memoir is also a ghost story. As Avery Gordon writes, "ghost stories [are] stories that not only repair representational mistakes, but also strive to understand the conditions under which a memory was produced in the first place, toward a countermemory for the future."¹⁰¹ In presenting her life story, Díaz attempts to understand why society saw her queer AfroLatinidad as monstrosity and to forward a counterdefinition. If queer AfroLatinidad is feared and cast as monster because of its challenge to the norms of racial, ethnic, sexual, and gendered identities, *Ordinary Girls* instead argues for the ordinariness of violence against women. The memoir also argues that these girls' anger, defiant laughter, and deepest depression are sensible responses to the violence committed against them and to society's fear and denigration of queer pleasure. The memoir does not merely reverse the roles, calling society the true monster while queer AfroLatinxs are the heroes or epitome of humanity. Díaz encourages queer AfroLatinxs, and all readers, to embrace the monsters that reside in us, because to do so is to truly become human.

Ariana Brown's Verse Memoirs: Postnationalist AfroLatinidad and Blackness in the Gaps

Ariana Brown's 2021 poetry collection declares *We Are Owed*. The title has the period included at the end—inserted, like a confident punto, emphatic and conversation-ending. There is no argument to be had in this title. But who is the "we" who are owed?[102] And what are they owed? Brown, "a queer Black Mexican American poet," as she describes herself,[103] has made it clear in her Twitter presence and her poetry that her first commitment is not to Latinidad or mestizaje but to Black people.[104] She has been weary of those who would see her as representing AfroLatinidad and has challenged the utility and inclusivity of key Latinx studies scholars and concepts, most prominently and infamously, Gloria Anzaldúa's *Borderlands / La Frontera: The New Mestiza* (1987).[105] *We Are Owed*. in fact, begins by asking readers to move beyond *Borderlands*. In "At the End of the Borderlands," Brown begins, "We need new origins" and ends with the questions that would determine what those new origins would be: "who are you without your country   what would you give   would you fight for those you don't love   to whom you are indebted."[106] Brown's poetry, like Díaz's memoir, explores the monstrosities that haunt queer AfroLatinidad, focusing on the monstrosity of anti-Blackness and colonialism.

While poet Ariana Brown's life writing takes on a different form from that of Díaz's monstrous reflections, she also reclaims Black Latinx girlhood and the possibilities inherent in queering love in her collections *Sana Sana* and *We Are Owed*. Brown's poetry collections, I argue, are "verse memoirs." I adapt this term from Anna Jackson's conception of the "verse biography."[107]

According to Jackson, these biographies focus especially on brevity, as "the line breaks, stanza breaks, and spaces on the pages make the works shorter still, at once moving the narrative more rapidly on, and demanding a different sort of attention from the reader that may slow the reading down."[108] Verse memoirs, in my definition, write against the need for copious archival evidence. This poetry inhabits the gaps and silences of history. As Alice Oswald contends, "one of the differences between poetry and prose is that poetry is beyond words. Poetry is only there to frame the silence."[109] By engaging poetic form, verse memoirs highlight the role of poetry in framing historical and autobiographical silences. While a verse biography tells the life story of a historical figure, Ariana Brown's AfroLatinx verse memoir communicates the poet's own life narrative and contextualizes it within the larger history of Blackness in Mexico and the Southwest. Brown depends on the strategies outlined by Jackson and Oswald: pacing, space, and silence.

While historically, professors may teach students to separate the poet from the speaker of the poem, verse memoirs recognize that most poets cannot so easily claim this supposed separation.[110] In fact, in one of the last poems of *We Are Owed.*, "Introductions," Brown calls herself ("ariana") into the collection: "child of méxico, africa, usa—/ i have someone else's name. / i was born in a cemetery."[111] By claiming space within her poetry collection as the subject of this memoir and introducing herself into the text, Brown asserts the poetry collection as a life narrative. Her staccato lines punctuate her claims to ancestry and to loss, while the complete lack of capitalization gives equal weight to all the factors that shape her as a Black Mexican American, whether it be Fredrick Douglass, the US–Mexico War and 1848 Treaty of Guadalupe Hidalgo, or her father, who died during an Air Force training exercise before she was born. Further, she describes her life narrative as one shaped by conquest ("i've been conquered."), history, and the dead who preceded her (by being born in "a cemetery").[112] Through this introduction, the poet names the sociohistorical, cultural, ancestral, and colonial influences that stretch back centuries but also continue to affect her present. In inserting herself and rejecting the idea of a separate, disconnected "speaker" of the poetry collection, Brown's AfroLatinx verse memoirs challenge what is generally accepted, or the "mythical norm" in poetry,[113] such as the line between poet and speaker or the meaning of blank space.

Twenty-first-century Black Caribbean and Black Latina verse memoirs radically reconsider the purpose of white space in poetry. White space is more than an aesthetic consideration; it is also a racial one. For example, one can see the power of space, and particularly white space, in Claudia Rankine's *Just Us: An American Conversation* (2020).[114] Rankine uses photo-quality, glossy white paper that adds to the heft of the book and thus physically represents the weight of whiteness. Further, the highly reflective quality of the paper used to publish Rankine's verse memoir causes the white space to be blinding. Considering that the book is a meditation and conversation about whiteness, the glaring pallor of the pages also points to the discomfort that comes from shining a light on the injustice of racializing discourse and its impact on narratives of desirability and security. Lastly, Rankine's choice to highlight whiteness through what we often call "blank space," alongside her paper choice, also forces the reader to "see" whiteness, since the harm that whiteness causes often comes from its weaponized invisibility. To claim whiteness is to claim to be non-raced; whiteness invisibilizes itself in order to shroud its power in everyday society and institutions in the United States, Latin America, and the Caribbean.[115] However, while reading *Just Us*, I also realized that this pristine white paper is easy to mess up, to crease, to wrinkle. Only the perfect, untouched page can perfectly reflect the light and blind us entirely. Once we touch whiteness, turn it around in our hands, we reveal and can reject the illusion that whiteness is an absence of race. I offer this reading of Rankine's verse memoir as a preface to a close reading of Brown's life writing, to highlight the power of white space in Brown's AfroLatinx verse memoirs.

Like Rankine, Brown's use of white space also calls to mind the way she navigates spaces that are white Mexican American, white Latin American, and non-Latinx white. For example, in *We Are Owed.*, Brown begins with "At the End of the Borderlands," a prose poem that takes up one-third of the page, leaving a gaping white space followed by a blank white page and then another nearly empty page, with an Alice Walker quotation, "We will not be forced away from what is ours,"[116] centered and bolded in black on the page. All this space forces the reader to take their time through the book, establishing the pace for the reader, demanding a different kind of attention to time. "At the End of the Borderlands," while written as a prose poem, uses multiple spaces to create gaps rather than writing in a prose structure that uses periods and single-spacing. The poem's block of text appears to have holes, like gaps between teeth. These white gaps protract the reading process. In my experience reading the poem aloud (as I did for the entire verse memoir), the reader is forced to breath in those gaps, to let each line linger and resonate in the white space. Empty spaces, entirely white pages, and pages that include only a few lines or a symbol continue throughout the book, such as in the six-page poem about her father's death, "Quick Story."[117] Despite the page length of the poem, it has only thirty-five lines; the first page contains only three. The poem is then followed by substantial blank space, with the next poem coming on page 27. Like the Walker quote indicates, Brown will not let us glide through her verse memoir easily. She will not be forced to make her experience small or to be efficient with her tale. As a queer Black Mexican American poet, she allows her poetry, and herself, to spread out and take up space, because it is what she (and other AfroLatinxs) are owed.[118]

Brown also uses gaps and white space as a method of exploration. She looks for the gaps and silences, creating narratives for those whose stories were deemed unworthy of preservation by the archive and its producers. These AfroLatinx stories are ruins that have lived on despite neglect. Cathy Park Hong suggests, "The lyric as ruin is an optimal form to explore the racial condition, because our unspeakable losses can be captured through the silences built into the lyric fragment."[119] Ruins can be preserved, or they can be what remains despite lack of care. They are the fragments and traces from which archaeologists and historians attempt to draw conclusions. Brown's poems examine the ruins of Blackness in Latin America—ruins that had not been tended by those in power but only those individuals in community with Black cimarrones (maroons) and resisters throughout history. In *We Are Owed.*, Brown applies Saidiya Hartman's method of "critical fabulation" to historical figures with traces in the historical record.[120] For instance, as Alán Pelaez López writes in their foreword to the 2021 verse memoir, Brown rejects the only institutional representation of Gaspar Yanga, an enslaved West African for whom a town in Veracruz, México, is named.[121] Through a reading of Yanga's gaps—the figurative gaps in the historical record and the literal tooth gap that she imagines in the letter she writes to him—she delineates the postnationalist potential of the Black Americas.

In Brown's arc of poems focused on Yanga in *We Are Owed.*,[122] she imagines Yanga as a father figure, a font of knowledge about freedom. She writes the first two poems in the arc in Yanga's voice, marked through the use of italics. In the first, he sings Ariana a lullaby which features his palenque (a free town for cimarrones), and in the second, he explains why he is leaving her, though he promises, *"I'll be back. / I want to know you looked for me. / Mijita, never stop looking."*[123] The voice then shifts in the third poem, "Letter to Yanga, from Six-Year-Old Ariana," to embody Ariana as a little girl. Whether as a form of time travel or as a manifestation of Brown's inner child, the voice recurs in the Yanga arc, as well as in other poems in her verse memoirs. In this letter to Yanga, young Ariana asks about his physical appearance, hobbies, and favorite fruit.[124] In doing so, she remakes his Afro–Latin American body beyond labor and the monstrous dehumanization created by enslavement. In "Yanga Builds Me a Panga," his laboring body reappears but he works at his own pace. As Brown writes, "Yanga has one rule: don't ask when he'll be done."[125] Beyond the rule, the speaker also "ain't never been one to rush somethin' love makes."[126] Like in the poem "Superpower" in her other verse memoir, *Sana Sana*, Brown calls to the power of Black Latinx love and to the slow, measured pace of love. For a formerly enslaved person, the ability to go at one's own pace, to labor out of love and not merely as an exploited actor, is itself a form of freedom.

These poems are critical fabulations that fill in representational gaps but not solely as political machination. That is, through her poems, Brown fleshes out the historical Yanga beyond his actions as a liberator. Rather, her poems imagine Yanga outside of the political sphere, in the domestic space, sitting on a porch as in "Letter to Yanga" or building a fishing boat (panga). Fishing can be a labor-intensive activity necessary to support a family or an industry, or it can be a leisurely one, where two people sit meditatively in the open water listening to the silence or sharing stories. The panga that Yanga builds in the poem appears to be for travel, though where he will take Ariana is another thing that cannot be asked: "Don't ask where we'll go, either. Places it's safest to be don't exist on a map."[127] Both Ariana and the reader are not allowed to view Yanga's travel plans, and most importantly, the kind of places that he wants to go are those not visible to those with the power to draw borders and maps. Thus, Yanga also represents the mediation of invisibility and hypervisibility as a negotiation of safety. Considering the history of palenques, which often needed to hide themselves from Spanish authorities in order to remain a safe haven from slavery, Brown also argues for the safety inherent in being shrouded from sight or unmappable.

The Yanga cycle of poems resides in the gaps of Afro–Latin American and AfroLatinx history. In "Why I Want to Know What Yanga Looked Like," the gap is literally the speaker's imagining of Yanga as a gap-toothed man.[128] Brown uses em dashes strategically to describe the small gap between the two teeth, physically manifesting what she imagines for Yanga. The gap is described lovingly, as a unique aspect of his appearance, "the crack in a bell that makes the song sweeter—".[129] The gap, rather than seen as a physical flaw, is a beautiful detail, one that brings sweetness, joy, and a unique tinge to his voice. As the vibrations of the bell are influenced by a crack, Yanga's voice, and his smile too, are affected by this playful gap. The gap also manifests both a dark shroud and a beam of light, existing as both an invisible and revealing border space, "where everything goes black for a minute and then the lights come on and somehow what you are seeing is more beautiful because of the interruption."[130]

The image of the gap represents the negotiation of AfroLatinx invisibility and hypervisibility, reflected in Yanga's Afro-diasporic identity and Ariana's experiences as a Black Mexican American in Mexico. That negotiation is visualized on the page in the poem that follows, entitled "Field Notes." In this poem, which moves away from the prose poems that dominate the rest of the arc, Brown explores the distorted visibility she encounters as an Afro-Mexican American woman and the monstrosity of racism.[131] Brown weaves her own experiences of racist aggressions in Mexico City with the historical facts of Yanga's life. In addition to the difference in how they are printed (neutral versus italics), each stanza of racialized experience and historical fact is separated by a line of white space. Again, Brown forces the reader to sit with each stanza but also to bridge the gaps we see, by connecting this long-dead historical figure to the anti-Black racism that Brown experiences in the present moment. As the poem ends, Ariana laments the lack of images of Yanga. The poet tries to fill the absence of visual representation with her own body: "i can't find an image of yanga online. instead, i / try harder to love my own face, nose, lips, hair."[132]

While the Yanga poems have, up until the end of the cycle, been purely celebratory and warm, Brown ends with an interrogation of Yanga. In doing so, she refuses to idealize or flatten Yanga, nor to allow him to speak as the only voice of AfroLatinidad. In fact, she questions the possibility of his monstrosity. In the final poem of the cycle, "Yanga," the poet addresses the historical figure by asking,

> did you really agree to turn in runaways
>   in exchange for freedom
>
>   your people's freedom?
>
> were you a patriarch?[133]

These two questions ask about the price that Yanga was willing to pay for his own and his people's freedom, the possibility that he would engage with the monstrosity of slavery. What would it mean to be free if that freedom is obtained by reenslaving others? The second question considers another dimension of freedom: that of gender and sexual expression. These symbolic, historical, and physical gaps in Brown's poetry explore AfroLatinx visibility, freedom, and unfreedom through the lens of ethno-race and queerness. The poet leaves open the possibility that he was a heterosexual patriarch but also that he could have had a queer family structure or queer relationships. She asks,

> were you a man
>
> or something freer?[134]

The question yearns to find in Yanga the possibility of a masculinity that does not attempt to reign supreme over other genders, or even a person whose gender identity centered freedom over constraint. The poem itself, while textually sparse, extends itself across the pages. The blank space vertically and historically makes the speaker read as if she hesitates to ask these questions. In some lines, I imagine Ariana making a claim or asking a half-question, closing her mouth and looking up at the sky, and then completing the thought or the question. Like someone dipping her toe in freezing water, she is asking the questions that celebratory narratives of AfroLatinidad elide or do not wish to face. In the last third of the poem, the speaker shifts from questions to requests and promises. She entreats,

> teach me to be a person without a nation
>
> on the other side of enslavement[135]

These lines return us to her desire in "At the End of the Borderlands" and "A Quick Story" for a rejection of nationalism because "Countries will kill everyone you love / & everyone else too—foreign & domestic."[136] These three poems embody the postnationalist AfroLatinidad that Brown advances. She wants to believe that models of this postnationalist AfroLatinidad already exist for communities to build from, and also wants to be an ancestor that other AfroLatinxs can look to in the future, one that can help them imagine what seems unimaginable.[137]

By exploring the ruins of Latin American Blackness and living in the gaps, Brown posits a postnationalist concept of AfroLatinidad beyond the Anzaldúan borderlands. Brown's postnationalist AfroLatinidad questions the embrace of Anzaldúan borderlands as a liberatory space for Black Latinxs, even those from Texas. Pelaez López speaks to Brown's anti-nationalism in his foreword. Her poetry is postnationalist because it looks after and beyond, not merely against. Pelaez López encapsulates my own take on Brown's concept when they write, "A 'new origin,' then, is a transnational and hemispheric approach to braiding Black life in this continent together which immediately opposes the formation of nation-states and empires."[138] Brown's attempt to locate her origins "at the end of" Anzaldúa's *Borderlands / La Frontera* parallels Lorgia García-Peña's theorization of "El Nié," a term she adopts from artist Josefina Báez. García-Peña's theorization pushes against spatial definitions of the borderlands.[139] While Báez herself claims "the Anzaldúa from *Light in the Dark*, [. . .] the militant Anzaldúa" as the source of her concept of El Nié,[140] her concept imagines "border as a place of being."[141] Similarly, Brown wants to move beyond borders and nationalist identity or belonging. While Brown's poems delve into the experience of embodying Black Latinidad, spirituality and healing ceremonies are also at the core of her work, placing her in conversation with the life writing of Lourdes Casal, Marta Moreno Vega, and Raquel Cepeda.[142]

Brown's conception of a queer, postnationalist AfroLatinidad is also an act of reclaiming her Black Latinx girlhood, as Jaquira Díaz does in *Ordinary Girls*. In addition to claiming the queer possibilities of Gaspar Yanga, the free-verse poem "Myself, First" from *Sana Sana* returns to the importance of Black Latinx love. Originally published as a prose poem in the 2017 chapbook *Messy Girl* (made available to Patreon supporters digitally in 2021),[143] Brown prefaces this poem with an italicized statement about her choice not to revise these poems, which were originally written in 2014, despite the valorization of machismo and self-sacrificing love that many espoused.[144] This contextualizing text ends with a coming-out statement, which reads: "*I now identify as queer. I date people of different genders. I am interested in unselfish reciprocity. I am not interested in sacrificing this much of myself, to anyone, again. I hope that sharing this work, in its bareness, offers some kind of affirmation to you.*"[145] Like in "Letter to Yanga," the poem "Myself, First" calls back to six-year-old Ariana. Brown's claim to queerness is tied to a validation of her Black girlhood self. The poet writes, "The first time I loved a Black girl I learned / to love myself. I say *girl* / 'cause it's what we're not allowed to be, / except around each other."[146] Brown's first relationship with another Black woman is a way of loving Black girls and her own inner child. Because conceptions of childhood innocence are racialized as white and imagined as straight, queer Black Latinx girls are often denied girlhood. In this queer Black girl love, rather than sacrifice one's self, that love is given and received simultaneously: "I whisk my six-year-old self / to a tender present, offer / the grace I was denied—/ a gentle hand at the back of the neck, / a lesson in commitment."[147] Time runs together and overlaps in this queer relationship. As Ruth Nicole Brown writes, "the making of space to celebrate Black girlhood exists out of time and order."[148] That is, when the poet talks about her six-year-old self, she conflates that little girl with the "I" of the poem's present, offering not only that little girl of the past but the Ariana of the present the "grace denied." Queer love, as explored through both the cimarrón Yanga and Brown's first relationship with a Black woman, is crucial to an AfroLatinidad beyond borders, beyond borderlands, which imagines freedom as an act of community and communal healing.[149]

Conclusion

Ariana Brown and Jaquira Díaz provide two conceptions of queer AfroLatinidad by engaging directly with the forces that attempt to marginalize and deny their presence today, tomorrow, and in the US and Latin America's past.[150] Through challenging conventional narratives and employing legendary figures, such as La Llorona and Gaspar Yanga, these writers make themselves visible on their own terms. Díaz and Brown approach monstrosity differently in terms of form and content. While Díaz employs two monsters, La Llorona and Ana Cardona, to complicate and even reclaim a queer monstrosity, Brown considers historical erasure and racist imperialism as monstrous powers that continue to impact her sense of self and community in the present day. Both authors go beyond a desire for recognition but rather act out of love and healing for young Jaqui and Ariana, as well as other queer Black Latinx girls, as they navigate the ordinary experiences that cast them as monsters lurking in the shadows. Brown and Díaz tell these girls about the dangers inherent in leaving the shadows, the joy that can be found in the shadows and gaps, and the delight that is possible in embracing the monstrous.

As very recent works, *Ordinary Girls* and *We Are Owed.* provide a sense of the possibilities of AfroLatinx life writing in the twenty-first century, particularly the use of "verse memoirs" and queer AfroLatinx life narratives. They respond to what are now AfroLatinx classics, like *Down These Mean Streets*, but do so in ways that highlight what those classics missed since they focused primarily on AfroLatino male protagonists; they also allow us to see a wider range of AfroLatinx responses (not limited to Puerto Rican responses) to the classic Puerto Rican life writing of Thomas, Colón, and Schomburg. In revising narratives of monstrosity to fill in the gaps by looking backward both personally (to girlhood) and culturally (the stories of La Llorona and Yanga), the two texts also look forward, to new forms of AfroLatinidades that carve out room for the monstrous. In the epilogue to this book, I will examine another memoir that similarly looks backward in order to look forward, although in potentially troubling ways.

Epilogue: Science, Spirituality, and Changing Notions of Ancestry in AfroLatinx Narratives

In *Invisibility and Influence*, I have traced constructions of what it means to be AfroLatino/a/x from the early twentieth century through 2021. These "AfroLatinidades" are social, cultural, and political constructions based in the embodied experiences of Black Latinxs, which attend to the realities of living in a Black body which contests the hegemony of "US Blackness" as well as the mestizaje rhetoric of white or Brown Latinidades. From Arturo Schomburg's auto/biographical writings to Ariana Brown's verse memoirs, AfroLatinx life writers call attention to and write against the anti-Blackness of mestizaje narratives. These life narratives of AfroLatinidad negotiate a spectrum of invisibility, visibility, and hypervisibility. That is, AfroLatinx writers construct an AfroLatinidad by bringing to light the distortions and erasures they must navigate within themselves and in the world around them that simultaneously invisibilize and hypervisibilize their presence.

While the life writing in the first half of the book centered Afro–Puerto Ricans (and primarily men), the second half examined life writing by Afro-Cuban and Afro-Mexican women writers alongside Afro–Puerto Rican women's memoirs. The introduction began with an analysis of Afro-Panamanian life writer Veronica Chambers, to position my entry point into AfroLatinx studies as a white Guatemalan American woman. As discussed in the introduction, though the body of this book examines AfroLatinx life writing that writes against mestizaje, the memoir I have chosen to conclude with considers the growing role of what I call "genomic life writing." As narratives about race and racialization increasingly return to roots in racialist science,[1] DNA ancestry tests may have increasing sway and lead back to troubling narratives of mixture. In this epilogue, I examine Afro-Dominican writer, journalist, and documentarian Raquel Cepeda to posit questions about how the increasing claims of commercial DNA ancestry tests complicate the future of AfroLatinx studies. While narratives about these tests are potentially promising, I argue, they have an equal potential to imagine ancestry that feeds into mestizaje narratives that erase AfroLatinidades.[2]

As discussed in chapter 4, the dynamic, spiritual, and historically grounded AfroLatinidades posited by Casal and Moreno Vega imagine ancestry as a narrative, one rooted in Yoruba-based religious philosophies and practices as well as the stories of Black Caribbean women and girls. These ancestral narratives possess the plot of Moreno Vega's memoir. Women, living and dead, commune with the spirits through espiritismo, secrecy, and music. While these older life narratives call to ancestry as a sacred, cultural practice, Raquel Cepeda's *Bird of Paradise: How I Became Latina* (2013), her documentary sequel *Some Girls* (2017), and the proliferation of YouTube and social media videos in which AfroLatinxs reveal their DNA ancestry test results suggest a tension between past conceptions of ancestry and genealogy. Pivoting from definitions based in storytelling, oral and paper archives, and spiritual practice, 23andMe genealogists look to science to validate and even replace the stories handed down by ancestors, living and dead. This turn to what we might call "scientific spirituality" brings promise and peril.

The peril of genetic genealogy in AfroLatina narratives is the calcification of stereotypes and repackaging of racialist science as liberating tools for AfroLatinx people unsure of their heritage. Several sections of the memoir *Bird of Paradise* exemplify these dangers. Half traditional memoir and half travel narrative based on her DNA ancestry results, Cepeda's *Bird of Paradise* shows that spiritualist approaches to AfroLatinidad are not inherently feminist or pro-Black. Though Cepeda's memoir points to hip-hop and Black art as the key to her survival in a dysfunctional family, she presents DNA ancestry tests as a curative to her struggle with identity, a means to grow closer to her father, who rejects his own Dominicanness after his migration to the US, and a contextualization of her own life experiences. While promising a collaboration of the scientific and the spiritual, Cepeda depends on problematic notions of what Stephan Palmié calls "racecraft,"[3] or the idea that DNA provides true insight into your "invisible essences," not available through supposedly unscientific means, such as family stories.[4] Cepeda turns to DNA tests partially because of the historical distortions and erasures of Afro-Dominicans in traditional archives and family narratives. Stephan Palmié similarly asserts that genetic ancestry tests have been a way to employ "the prestige of genomic technologies of knowledge production" to cause "the retrospective realignment of 'official historiography' with previously disqualified forms of historical knowledge that have long circulated in the U.S. black community."[5] While Cepeda offers her reader genomic testing as a lifeline to familial healing and spiritual connection, Palmié concludes that genomic technologies "systemically reproduce fundamentally racist modes and models of sociality."[6] That is, the tests are more often used to double down on anti-Black attitudes and racial ideologies.

DNA ancestry tests appear to some as a disruptive and empowering model of identity, playing a role in racial reconciliation projects or being offered as new sources of data for communities who have been otherwise erased from documentation of their roots.[7] However, Cepeda's memoir shows how easily ancestry tests can be used to reinscribe anti-Black and orientalist conceptions of hegemonic mestizaje and racial essentialism.[8] Cepeda, in fact, provides examples of people "with obvious mixed ancestry" she met who used their ancestry tests to increase their claims to whiteness or to try to distance themselves from the violent history of whiteness, aligning more with colorist and mestizaje rhetorics than with liberatory ones.[9] However, she offers no meaningful discussion of how these examples, which revel in proximity to whiteness, should be confronted, nor does she reflect on the possibility that she may be doing the same.[10] While Cepeda takes a surprising amount of time attempting to explain these DNA tests in layperson's terms, she does not point to all the things these tests cannot tell you, nor does she engage critiques of their accuracy.[11] The DNA ancestry tests become no more than "racial folklore" that tells the same tale but with different tools.[12]

Cepeda expects a lot from genetic ancestry tests, believing they provide a true sense of Dominican history. In doing so, she falls into troubling conceptions of rediscovering Indigenous identity.[13] For example, Cepeda's call to Taíno identity depends on colonial notions of racial purity and forecloses Indigenous agency. She writes, "Taínos [. . .] left a genetic imprint, a footnote that reads: 'We may not be living in huts or dressing in the traditional garbs of our ancestors but we're here, albeit in fragments."[14] In viewing Taíno culture as "fragments," shards of a shattered whole, Indigenous cultures are defined solely by colonialism. Indigeneity is not allowed to adapt, evolve, or change on its own. Further, it suggests that Indigenous identity today can never be authentic; it is always a shadow of its former, truer self. In her documentary *Some Girls*, Cepeda's close reading of the Columbus statue in Santo Domingo similarly represents Indigeneity in troubling ways. She laments the Indigenous woman, who she indicates is likely the cacique Anacaona, for being at the base, forced to etch Columbus into the stone of history, rather than writing her own name or her own Indigenous history. While she laments the erasure of Indigenous history, she does not mention how the statue erases African diasporic history.[15] The statue is a mestizaje narrative—one in which

Europeans are at the top, Indigenous people are at the bottom, and Africanity is not to be seen, and Cepeda does not challenge that African erasure.

Similarly, Cepeda's description of physical difference at times aligns with troubling, orientalist stereotypes. According to Edward Said, "orientalism" is a theory and set of practices that imagines the Orient (East) and Occident (West) as two foundationally different mindsets, races, and epistemologies. This dichotomy is constructed by the West and thus also presents Europe and the West as superior and the East as inferior.[16] In *Bird of Paradise*, orientalism manifests in taking up stereotypes of Middle Eastern / North African / Far Eastern racialization by physical difference. For instance, at one point Raquel attributes the slant of a Dominican family member's eyes to Asiatic origins: "Their eyes moored into a slant that evoked an alleged maternal ancestor who made the impossible trip to the island from a place called Indochina, *di'que*."[17] Eye shape becomes physical proof of a family story about an ancestor coming from modern-day Vietnam.[18]

Cepeda also does not question the ideological and economic investments inherent in these tests. She presents ancestry tests, in the memoir and through explicit marketing, as objective evidence towards the subjective work of identity. However, she never analyzes the commercial nature of genomic testing (as these are private companies). In fact, Cepeda's memoir itself becomes a source of advertising, as she includes a 10-percent-off coupon for Family Tree DNA in the back of the book.[19] Cepeda obscures the subjective nature of DNA tests, despite the fact that much of the book, even after the DNA results are presented, depends on conversations and traditional research. This was the case before DNA tests, as genealogical work comprised archival research and oral histories, and despite the memoir's claims, DNA tests have not much changed that aspect of genealogy. Family histories are interpretations, subject to bias. But so are DNA tests, despite their marketing.[20] For example, as Daniel Strand and Anna Källén observe, "leveraged by the general confidence in DNA as a source of truth, images of 'the Viking' that were once created for political, cultural or commercial purposes are revived in new embodied forms and can start to circulate in new social and political contexts, where they, by association, appear to be confirmed by genetic science."[21] In short, the danger of associating more truth value to DNA tests is that they appear to confirm socially constructed notions of "the Viking" or, in Cepeda's case, Latinidad. In fact, while this memoir frequently mentions Cepeda's desire to have her parents recognize their Black roots,[22] she does not explicitly identify as Afro-Dominican in the memoir.[23]

The promise of DNA ancestry tests, as posited by *Bird of Paradise*, lies in their power to make visible Latinx connections to Africa and emphasize feelings of spiritual connection while also interrogating harmful ones, such as the erasure of Africanity within conceptions of Latinidad. For example, like Lourdes Casal in her visit to Nigeria,[24] Cepeda finds connection in the music of the Islamic Sufis, which sounds just like the santería practitioners praising Yemayá on Rockaway Beach in New York.[25] The spiritual trances she sees the practitioners enter and the rhythmic drumming bring together the transnational practices of the African diaspora in New York, the Caribbean, and North Africa. In addition, she sees modern examples of Afro-diaspora cultural travel in the graffiti art and "hip-hop of Morocco."[26] This discussion of music relates back to Cepeda's argument that science and spirituality can "jive holistically."[27] Cepeda calls science, specifically DNA testing, "logos," and spirituality "mythos." She writes, "My spiritual self still identifies with the *mythos*, the transcendent qualities found in Jewish Kaballah, Sufi Islam, Indigenous and West African mysticism and religion. My rational self is drawn by the potential of ancestral DNA testing—the *logos*—to work in tandem with the incorporeal to help us make sense of our whole selves."[28] She asserts that the spiritual advisors she talked with during her journey see science as a way to illustrate that "there's one fundamental force in the universe." One rabbi of Kaballah and Jewish spirituality, for instance, "believes that the union of the scientific and the mythos is a messianic vision."[29] In her preface, she ties together the rabbi with "a seer in Fez, and a santero in Queens" to show the connection between these spiritual philosophies.[30] These statements offered at the end of the memoir provide an optimistic view of how DNA ancestry tests can influence one's conception of identity formation as well as notions of the divine.[31]

Another major promise for genomic testing, according to Cepeda's memoir, is the ability to validate and interrogate family narratives. Despite her claim to the centrality of DNA testing to the second part of her memoir, the tests themselves are often only a jumping-off point, since their specificity is limited.[32] They lead her to fly to Morocco and Dominican Republic and to speak with historians, tour guides, and spiritual leaders and followers. The tests often provide more questions than answers. While *Bird of Paradise* often talks around this fact, these tests should be embraced for the connections they make possible. In the past, grounding one's self ancestrally was to ask one's mothers, abuelitas, and abuelos about family history. Yet families can be invested in anti-Black histories or a "possessive investment in whiteness."[33] Since Cepeda's ancestry results rarely offer more than a broad geographic area, the memoir offers broad strokes of Caribbean, Spanish, North African, and Sub-Saharan African history as well as her conversations with family members with whom she reconnects or meets for the first time due to her DNA journey. In fact, all the detailed, meaningful information she learns about her family history comes from those oral histories. While she argues that "discovering and connecting to my Indigenous and African roots is just one area in which ancestral DNA testing succeeds where genealogy cannot,"[34] the primary methods by which she learns "how she became Latina" are traditional forms of genealogical research: family narratives and documentation. Rather than view these test results as an endpoint, they should be seen as one possible starting point for ancestral histories.

However, Cepeda also celebrates that DNA ancestry tests can provide information without close family relationships. For example, Raquel never asks her biological mother to send in a testing kit and debates if she even wants to share the results with her.[35] As she notes, her parents are "two reasons why I prefer ancestral DNA testing over genealogy—history is easier to digest than people who consistently challenge you."[36] Haplogroups on a screen do not allow for pushback or interrogation the way that family stories do. Cepeda does not need her mother to discover intimate biological information about her. On one hand, this fact allows Cepeda to explore her roots without reconnecting with a person who harmed her, as she details extensively in part 1 of *Bird of Paradise* (though her father's abusive acts are similarly horrific, yet she forgives him).[37] On the other hand, ancestry tests may promise to provide information that perhaps cannot otherwise be known. AfroLatina writer Nelly Rosario encapsulates how, through genomic memoirs like *Bird of Paradise*, "writers can offer a counterforce against the potential scientific conquest of our DNA." She imagines writers like Cepeda as "translators/transcribers of the human experience," who take on the role of biological units like RNA.[38] In this optimistic take on genomic life narratives, Rosario emphasizes the role of translation and interpretation that the writer can take on in this genomic life writing. However, I fear that the *subjectivity* of this knowledge is undermined in memoirs like *Bird of Paradise*. As life narratives, both in traditional and digital media, become more inflected by genomic thinking, we must be cautious not to reinscribe white supremacist narratives and racialist science.

Ultimately, AfroLatina life writing that attempts to combine science and spirituality must consider the potential power these stories have on the construction of individual and communal identity. The impact of genomic testing on art and culture has only increased. Afro-Cuban artist Juana Valdés's 2019 art installation "Terrestrial Bodies" uses the results of her mother's 23andMe ancestry test.[39] The YouTube channel Pero Like has uploaded ancestry DNA reveal videos with AfroLatinxs, and many individuals upload reaction videos to their test results on Twitter, TikTok, and other social media. In one Pero Like video, Alexis, an Afro–Puerto Rican woman, exemplifies the promise of what Aurora Levins Morales and the Latina Feminist Group call "genealogies of empowerment."[40] Alexis says, "I'm excited to take this test in particular because I want to know more about my African ancestors and these spirits that I know are still with me."[41] The way she chooses to enter the test reflects an awareness of how "the complicated structures of inheritance and identity formation, legacies of colonial and patriarchal subordination influence our lives."[42] In doing so, she does not promise to throw out the knowledge passed on to her by her ancestors through oral and spiritualist traditions but hopes this scientific knowledge will empower her to think critically about the complicated inheritances of AfroLatina womanhood. Genomic life writing, whether in traditional memoirs or social media, provides both a new way to think about identity and a possible return to the old (and troubling) ways.

Through *Invisibility and Influence*, I have attempted to show how a range of visibility narratives in the United States, Central America, Puerto Rico, Cuba, Mexico, and Dominican Republic has continued to influence how AfroLatinxs imagine themselves. I have argued for the importance of the life writing genre to a century's constructions of AfroLatinidades. In the twentieth and twenty-first centuries, these AfroLatinidades have negotiated the distorted images from media and history books, the hypervisibility of Blackness, and acts intended to forcibly erase Black Latinx narratives. These AfroLatinx memoirs demonstrate a long history of literary production by AfroLatinx communities in conversation with US Black, US Latinx, Latin American, Caribbean, and hemispheric American communities. Because of their need to navigate ethnoracial and sociohistorical expectations alongside their own particularized situations, AfroLatinx writers have presented their lives in a variety of forms: traditional memoirs, monster stories, collective autobiographies, verse memoirs, and biographical narratives that blur the personal and communal. While life writing is often seen as a quintessentially individualistic genre, AfroLatinxs have employed it primarily to make claims about community and belonging.

In this book, I have provided a sense of the wide range of AfroLatinidades these writers have created that intentionally complicate monolithic conceptions of AfroLatinidad and contest the erasure of AfroLatinidad through mestizaje. The life writing of these authors—whose lived experiences are an important source of expertise—forces us to radically reconsider the utility and the implications of mestizaje rhetorics in AfroLatinx lives and for AfroLatinx communities.

Notes

Introduction

1. As Ifeoma Nwankwo states, "the beginning of the text is set in the girl's world, the world she shares with her 'girls,' the world of double-dutch girls. The beginning pronounces the value of the girls' worlds, and the girls' knowledge at the same time [*sic*] subtly calls for the equal valuation of girls' and boys' worlds and knowledge" (Nwankwo, "Veronica Chambers," 25–26).
2. Chambers, *Mama's Girl*, 1.
3. Chambers, 1.
4. Chambers, 2.
5. Chambers, 2.
6. Chambers, 2.
7. Chambers, 2.
8. Chambers, 7.
9. Or, as Bertram Ashe calls it, "blaxporation." Ashe, "Theorizing the Post-soul Aesthetic," 615.
10. In her memoir, Chambers describes her father being born in Dominican Republic (*Mama's Girl*, 12), but in other places, she notes that her father's parents were from "Costa Rica and Jamaica" ("Secret Latina at Large," 21).
11. For a recent exploration of Black Panamanians in Panamá and the US, see Corinealdi, *Panama in Black*.
12. Lorde, qtd. in Chambers, *Mama's Girl*, epigraph, frontmatter.
13. In line with Arturo Arias's examination of Central Americans as "silenced and invisible from their very conformation as an 'improper' social group, an unnameable, undefined otherness that remains 'unrepresentable' in the oligarchic vision of what the West is supposed to mean." Arias, "Central American–Americans," 181.
14. Chambers also describes the struggle of not being claimed as Latina in "Secret Latina at Large." A version of this piece was also published in *Essence*.
15. In recent years, there have been a few Afro–Central American writers with published works. One can turn to contributions in Moreno Vega, Alba, and

Modestin, *Women Warriors*. Afro-Honduran publisher Saraciea J. Fennell recently edited an anthology that includes other Black Central American voices in Fennell, *Wild Tongues Can't Be Tamed*. See also the writing of Vanessa Martír, who has published short memoir pieces such as her Writing the Mother Wound series at *Longreads*, but not a full-length memoir (yet).

16. Chambers covers her life from the age of seven through the mid-1990s, where she was one of only two Black editors at the *New York Times*. Shorter memoirs from Afro–Central American writers are included in collections such as *The Afro-Latin@ Reader* and *Women Warriors of the Afro-Latina Diaspora*. See Hoy, "Negotiating among Invisibilities," and Moreno Vega, Alba, and Modestin, eds., *Women Warriors of the Afro-Latina Diaspora*.
17. Wyatt, "Patricia Hill Collins's Black Sexual Politics"; Nwankwo, "Veronica Chambers"; and Springer, "Third Wave Black Feminism?"
18. Like the other life writers in this book, Chambers's memoir is sometimes framed as an act of visibility. See, for example, Garrison, "When the Seen."
19. Masiki's "Post-soul Latinidad" is the first peer-reviewed article to do so, though he argues that the book ultimately claims a post-soul African American feminist identity rather than an AfroLatina one.
20. When talking generally about people of Latin American and Hispanophone Caribbean descent, I use the term *Latinx*. My use of the *-x* ending rather than the *-a/o* or *@* ending, is not only because of its gender inclusivity but because it aligns with Claudia Milian, Ricardo L. Ortiz, and Alán Pelaez López's definitions of the *x* as both a term that embraces the history of *x* as an unknown (Milian) or simultaneous act of futurity and "critical dig into the complicated now" (Ortiz, "Critical Futurities," 201), but also because it represents "the wound" of anti-Blackness (Pelaez López). However, when I believe that a writer speaks in a specifically gendered way, I will indicate that use through the *-o* or *-a* endings. See Milian, *LatinX*; Ortiz, "Critical Futurities"; Pelaez López, "The X in Latinx." Ortiz also offers a comprehensive list of publications discussing Latinidad and the *x* through 2018 (*Latinx Literature Now*, 9–10n3).

    I define the term *AfroLatinx* as describing a person of African and Latin American / Hispanophone Caribbean descent who lives in a Black body. That is, I do not count those who claim heritage in Africa but that do not navigate the world or find community in Black Latinxness. For another definition, see Jiménez Román and Flores, *Afro-Latin@ Reader*, 1–15.
21. Hoy, "Negotiating among Invisibilities," 429.
22. Unless italicized within a text, I do not mark Spanish or other non-English words with italics, as I do not see them as foreign to the US, Latin America, or the Caribbean.
23. In Guatemala, "ladino" is an identity that rejects Indigenous culture and embraces Spanishness and Europeanness more broadly. As anthropologist Charles Hale asserts, "people who identify as ladino generally have absorbed an ideology of racial superiority in relation to Indians: viewing themselves as closer to an ideal of progress, decency, and all things modern, in contrast to Indians, who are regrettably and almost irredeemably backward." Hale, *Más que un Indio*, 9.

24. "Overall, more enslaved Africans permanently entered the Spanish Americas than the whole British Caribbean, making Spanish America the most important political entity in the Americas after Brazil to receive slaves." Borucki, Eltis, and Wheat, "Atlantic History," 434. For one of the earliest and few overviews of Black history in Latin America, see Rout, *African Experience in Spanish America*.
25. There is an ever-growing body of work examining Afro–Central American and Black Indigenous Central American identities, by Black, Indigenous, Black Central American, and Garifuna scholars, such as Hooker, *Race*; Mays, *Afro-Indigenous History*; López Oro, "Love Letter to Indigenous Blackness," "Garifunizando ambas Américas," and "Refashioning Afro-Latinidad"; Artiaga, "Garífuna Voices"; and White, "Afro-Nicaraguan Diasporas." See also Cosgrove et al., *Surviving the Americas*. These scholars make visible the impact of stories being told through oral histories, social media, solidarity movements, and other methods outside of traditional publishing outlets. Other Central American scholars, such as Maritza E. Cárdenas and Claudia Milian, have also engaged with Central Americanness, Blackness, and Indigeneity. See Cárdenas, *Constituting Central American–Americans*; and Milian, "Latinos and the Like" and *Latining America*. See also the edited collection by Wolfe and Gudmundson, *Blacks and Blackness in Central America*. This scholarship alongside recent US Afro–Central American life writing, like that by Saraciea J. Fennell and Yvette Modestin, emphasizes that Blackness in Central America has a long historical legacy, giving us a glimpse into the literary possibilities that will come from the exploration of US–Central American Afrolatinidades.
26. Chow, "These Afro-Latino Actors"; and Otero, "Afro-Latinos and Black History Month."
27. Take, for example, the 2016 controversy over Dominican American congressman Adriano Espaillat requesting to be part of both the Congressional Black Caucus (CBC) and Congressional Hispanic Caucus (CHC). At the time of this book's publication, Espaillat represents Harlem, famous for its contributions to and construction of US Black culture, but also an area with a historically strong AfroLatinx population. Accordingly, he also considered becoming the first member of both the CBC and CHC. Espaillat was readily accepted by the CHC, but he faced a surprising amount of resistance from the CBC (Caygle, "Black Caucus"). Of course, Espaillat would not have been the first AfroLatino in the CBC. There had been others in the past—including Espaillat's predecessor and the man who cofounded the CBC, Black Puerto Rican Charles Rangel. Just as Espaillat did in 2017, in 2020, gay AfroLatino congressman Ritchie Torres also asked the CBC and CHC in the lead-up to his election if he could join both caucuses. The CBC's response to *Politico* on this question was nearly identical to their response nearly four years prior: the Black Caucus had never faced that issue in the past and would have to figure out their policy (Barrón-López and Caygle, "CBC Head"). Did the CBC forget that they faced the same question in regard to Espaillat? Why this cycle of discovery and then amnesia?
28. Flores and Jiménez Román, "Triple-Consciousness?," 321.

29. For an overview of "life writing" and life writing studies, see Howes, "Life Writing—Genre, Practice, Environment." I expand on how I engage life writing studies later in the introduction.
30. Zamora, "Transnational Renderings," 94.
31. Like Antonio López, I argue that AfroLatinx life writers are writing in conversation with, and oftentimes against, US and Latin American conceptions of white supremacy. López writes, "Central to Afro-Latinidad is the social difference that blackness makes in the United States: how an Anglo white supremacy determines the life chances of Afro-Latinas/os hailed as black and how a Latino white supremacy reproduces the colonial and postcolonial Latin American privileging of blanco over negro and mulato (mixed-race) identities" (López, *Unbecoming Blackness*, 4–5). As Omaris Zamora asserts, the "Afro" in AfroLatinidad should not be "another way of reinscribing mestizaje and White supremacy by failing to name Whiteness and usurping Blackness as part of [non-Black Latinxs'] own racially mixed identity politics" (Zamora, "Transnational Renderings," 95).
32. In this way, I subscribe to Lorgia García-Peña's definition of "hegemonic blackness." García-Peña, *Translating Blackness*, 4.
33. In Black studies, see Lorde "Transformation of Silence," 42; and Fleetwood, *Troubling Vision*, 6. Discourses of invisibilization have also been prevalent in US–Central American Studies, most recently in Padilla, *From Threatening Guerrillas to Forever Illegals*, but starting in Arias, "Central American–Americans." See also Milian, *Latining America*.
34. For my influences in discussing mestizaje and racial democracy and inclusion in a Latin American context specifically, see Martínez-Echazábal, "Mestizaje"; Hooker, "Hybrid Subjectivities"; Godreau, *Scripts of Blackness*; and Alberto and Hoffnung-Garskof, "'Racial Democracy' and Racial Inclusion."
35. Jones, "Afro-Latinos," 571.
36. Jennifer A. Jones offers this definition: "The concept of *Afro-Latinidad* seeks, in part, to examine how comparable conceptual meanings and experiences of blackness move and take root in various parts of the Americas. It also offers a critical analysis of the forces that sustain anti-blackness throughout the region, despite what many consider dramatically different national discourses about race" (Jones, "Afro-Latinos," 570–571). Vanessa K. Valdés defines her concept of "Afro-Latinx subjectivity" as "constructed in response to shifting circumstances that influence whether one's blackness *and* one's *latinidad*, both, concurrently, are decipherable to members of the surrounding communities" (Valdés, *Diasporic Blackness*, 18–19).
37. Puerto Rico's technical status is as a commonwealth and unincorporated territory, though writers in this book, such as Jesús Colón, the Young Lords, and Jaquira Díaz explicitly argue that PR is a US colony.
38. My colleague Trent Masiki will publish *The Afro-Latino Memoir* (UNC Press) in late 2023.
39. Davis, *Lectures on Liberation*, 4. Indeed, in Davis's original outline of her lectures, she had intended to end with a discussion of Black Cuban poet Nicolás Guillén's work.

40. Lao-Montes, "Afro-Latinidades and the Diasporic Imaginary"; and Arroyo, *Writing Secrecy*.
41. Noel, *In Visible Movement*, 22.
42. Noel, xvi.
43. Consider, for instance, how María Elena Martínez engages pura sangre (blood purity) as a colonial system. Martínez, *Genealogical Fictions*.
44. Hoy, "Negotiating among Invisibilities," 426.
45. The most important literary studies scholarship in this area is Rafael Pérez-Torres's *Mestizaje: Critical Uses of Race in Chicano Culture* (2005). More recently, we might consider Marco A. Cervantes's 2010 dissertation, "Afromestizaje." Both, however, focus on Chicano conceptions of mestizaje. For a literary perspective focused on Latin America, see Juan E. de Castro, *Mestizo Nations*. Social scientific and legal perspectives against mestizaje can be found in Hernández, *Racial Innocence*; Hooker, "Hybrid Subjectivities"; and Dinzey-Flores, *Locked In, Locked Out*. See Flores, "'Latinidad Is Cancelled'" for a recent art history perspective.
46. Feracho, *Linking the Americas*, 1–2. Feracho masterfully engages life writing studies with Latin American literary studies.
47. Ramírez, *Colonial Phantoms*, 4.
48. Lao-Montes, "Afro-Latinidades"; and Lao-Montes and Buggs, "Translocal Space of Afro-Latinidad."
49. Figueroa is not "enticed by merely being seen or by tropes of representation." Rather, she petitions, "let us instead be faithful witnesses to the intimate folds of Afro-Latina becomings and take on the labor of seeing, knowing, and feeling the aches and beauties of Blackness for ourselves and with one another" ("Your Lips," 6). Saidiya Hartman also subverts the perceived goodness of visibility, when she reflects on her desire to blend in and "experience[e] the intimacy and anonymity of the crowd" (Hartman, *Lose Your Mother*, 57).
50. Lorde, "Transformation of Silence," 42.
51. Fleetwood, *Troubling Vision*, 6.
52. Milian, *Latining America*, 149. This quote draws from a discussion of the Garifuna in Central America and thus itself makes connections between Africanity in Central America and Central Americans in the US.
53. Arias, "Central American–Americans," 168.
54. Alejandro de la Fuente, for example, argues for the utility of mestizaje narratives, using the example of the fight for a Cuban nation (de la Fuente, "Myths of Racial Democracy").
55. Arrizón, "Mestizaje," 134.
56. Vasconcelos, *Cosmic Race*. As Arrizón notes, Vasconcelos even imagines Blackness fading away entirely. Arrizón, "Mestizaje," 135. See also Hooker, "Hybrid Subjectivities"; and Hooker, *Theorizing Race in the Americas*.
57. See, for example, González, *Puerto Rico*. One of his arguments focuses on Spanish brutality and oppression, another on considering the lens of class and capitalism in the analysis of Puerto Rico.
58. For helpful histories of both the hegemonic power and contestation of the mestizaje or racial democracy narrative, see Alberto and Hoffnung-Garskof,

"'Racial Democracy' and Racial Inclusion." For discussion of US Chicano/a deployments of mestizaje, see Pérez-Torres, *Mestizaje*, 3–50.
59. While mulataje has been substantially developed (e.g., see the work of José Buscaglia-Salgado), particularly in the Caribbean, the term doesn't have much purchase in US Latinx and Chicanx communities.
60. Anzaldúa, *Borderlands / La Frontera*, chapter 7. For later thoughts on mestizaje, see Anzaldúa, *Light in the Dark / Luz en lo oscuro*, 140–141. See also Delgadillo, *Spiritual Mestizaje*.
61. Latinidad, in my definition, can be more broadly defined as the practices, politics, or experiences that define what it means to be Latinx. Unless otherwise noted, I do not equate Latinidad with mestizaje and instead use the above definition. Debates regarding definitions of Latinidad often focus on how static or dynamic the term is. As can be seen in my usage of *AfroLatinidad*, I tend toward Ricardo Ortiz's sense that "a US-based *latinidad* continues [. . .] to emerge as a shifting, heterogeneous, and evanescent formation" (*Latinx Literature Now*, 8).
62. Delgadillo, *Spiritual Mestizaje*, 13.
63. Muñoz, "Feeling Brown," 676.
64. Pérez-Torres, *Mestizaje*, xiii.
65. Pérez-Torres, *Mestizaje*, xiii.
66. Jiménez Román, "Looking at That Middle Ground," 67.
67. Hernández, *Racial Innocence*; Zamora, "Transnational Renderings"; and Jones, "Afro-Latinos."
68. Martínez-Echazábal, "Mestizaje," 37.
69. Nelson, *A Finger in the Wound*.
70. Pérez-Torres, *Mestizaje*, 195.
71. Telles and PERLA, eds., *Pigmentocracies*; Hooker, "Hybrid Subjectivities," 189; and Twine, *Racism in a Racial Democracy*, 65–86 and 135–153. Nancy Mirabal similarly elucidates the concept of "diasporic blanqueamiento" as essential to Cuban exile communities (Mirabal, *Suspect Freedoms*, 15).
72. Trouillot, *Silencing the Past*, xxiii.
73. Foundational scholarship on testimonio includes Beverley, *Against Literature*; Beverley, *Testimonio*; Beverley and Zimmerman, *Literature and Politics in the Central American Revolutions*; Cantú, "Memoir, Autobiography, Testimonio"; and Harlow, *Resistance Literature*.
74. Smith and Watson, *Reading Autobiography*, 282.
75. Beverley, "Margin at the Center," 93. Beverley also recognizes the testimonio as a genre with a longer history within the influential crónica and essay genres in Latin American history. Today, however, many people equate testimonio to Latin American freedom fighters or political prisoners telling their stories to white academics who translate and edit the story for US and European audiences.
76. Gordon, *Ghostly Matters*, 19.
77. Latina Feminist Group, *Telling to Live*, 8, 11–12, 19.
78. Latina Feminist Group, 20.
79. Howes, "Life Writing"; and Kadar, "Coming to Terms," 197.
80. Broughton and Anderson, *Women's Lives / Women's Times*.
81. Smith and Watson, *Reading Autobiography*, 4.

82. See Mohanty, "'Under Western Eyes' Revisited," 519; and Perkins, *Locating Life Stories*. Maíz and Peña also wrote in 1988 of the nearly nonexistent work on "Spanish American" autobiography (Maíz and Peña, "Between Lines").
83. Braxton, *Black Women Writing Autobiography*; Moody, *History of African American Autobiography*; and Portillo, *Sovereign Stories and Blood Memories*. See also Perreault, *Writing Selves*; and Smith and Watson, *De/colonizing the Subject*.
84. Homans, "'Women of Color' Writers and Feminist Theory," 75. As Boyce Davies notes, "we have to admit that many scholars in the academy participate in the devaluing of Black women who are writers and theorists by not recognizing them or engaging their ideas" (*Black Women*, 55).
85. Lorde, "Age, Race, Class, and Sex," 122.
86. For example, Craig Howes's *Oxford Bibliographies* entry, "Life Writing—Genre, Practice, Environment," provides little commentary on women-of-color feminist life writing studies nor from women-of-color scholars writing in this field. While providing an international perspective rather than a narrow US-centric one, most of the scholars Howes mentions are white Americans, Scandinavians, or other Europeans, and the entry lacks substantial discussion of Caribbean, Latin American, or African life writing studies beyond testimonio, which is discussed outside of its Latin American roots. While he mentions special issues as examples of African American life writing, South Asian life writing, and African life writing, among others, Howes does not clearly claim their centrality to developing the theoretical foundations of life writing studies. Positionality is identified as a newer innovation, and scholars like Carole Boyce Davies, bell hooks, Saidiya Hartman, and Gloria Anzaldúa are not mentioned at all. There has been some recent work that attempts to take an intersectional life writing studies approach, such as Gilmore and Marshall, *Witnessing Girlhood*. For an example of earlier scholarship that attempted to bring together life writing and Chicano history, see García, *Literature as History*.
87. Gusdorf, "Conditions," 28.
88. An American example of this strain of biographical writing can be seen in Emerson, *Representative Men*. The Great Man theory of history and leadership is usually ascribed to Thomas Carlyle, *On Heroes, Hero-Worship, and the Heroic in History*. In chapter 1 of *Invisibility and Influence*, I discuss the US Black tradition that similarly focused on Great Men (and sometimes women).
89. Gusdorf, "Conditions," 28.
90. See the twenty-first-century examples provided in Perkins, "Never the Twain," 2–3.
91. Pitts, Ortega, and Medina, *Theories of the Flesh*.
92. Moraga and Anzaldúa, "Entering the Lives of Others," 19.
93. Most definitions of autohistoria and autohistoria-teoría come from footnotes or appendices in posthumously released collections of Anzaldúa's work or in interviews. For example, Keating's introduction in the *Gloria Anzaldúa Reader*, 9, 319. I use the definition offered by Anzaldúa in the following interview: Lara, "Daughter of Coatlicue," 52.
94. An example of this is Theresa Delgadillo's examination of Afro–Puerto Rican Marta Moreno Vega's *When the Spirits Dance Mambo*. The framework of spiritual mestizaje that Delgadillo uses, which she developed in her 2011 book,

appears at first to be useful, since it offers a framework that rejects the spirit/body split. Instead "body + mind + psyche + spirit denotes the fullness of being in the body." However, Delgadillo also argues that spiritual mestizaje is particularly useful as a lens for Moreno Vega because it "does not designate a particular practice or belief, but instead represents a critical mobility through which religious change occurs and one acquires a new consciousness." That is, Delgadillo is more interested in santería as a religion of mixture rather than its Yoruba-based and Caribbean-bred specificity (Delgadillo, "African, Latina, Feminist, and Decolonial," 164).
95. Anzaldúa, *Borderlands / La Frontera*, 108. Other brief mentions of Africanity appear: 85, 102, 106. There has been some use of Anzaldúa's mestiza consciousness (usually in combination with other ideas from Black Thought), such as Falcón, "Mestiza Double Consciousness."
96. Anzaldúa, "La Prieta," 198. This essay has a long revision history and was part of what was supposed to be a longer memoir. See Camp, "Radical Rhetoric."
97. Neyra, "Question of Ethics."
98. See also Trevino, *Brazilian Is Not a Race*. Carole Boyce Davies cautioned against the uncritical use of Anzaldúa's mestiza-centered theory for Black and Afro-diasporic writing as well (*Black Women*, 16). M. Jacqui Alexander scolds those who uncritically celebrated the pain of the borderlands, as a form of appropriation (*Pedagogies of Crossing*, 285).
99. Trinh T. Minh-ha attests to the power of art "where the borderline between theoretical and non-theoretical writings is blurred and questioned, so that theory and poetry necessarily mesh" (Minh-ha, *Woman, Native, Other*, 46). Rosamond King advocates for "radical interdisciplinarity," or "the use of methodologies that combine traditional scholarship with that which is not traditionally considered either scholarship or even part of an academic discipline—specifically poetry and other creative arts" to uncover the marginalized voices of Afro-Trinidadian women in the archive (King, "Radical Interdisciplinarity," 445). Similarly, Boyce Davies's concept of critical relationality "asserts the specificity of the other, but works together and from each other in a generalized purpose of resistance to domination" and "becomes a way in in which other theoretical positions interact relationally in one's critical consciousness" (Boyce Davies, *Black Women*, 56).
100. Latina Feminist Group, *Telling to Live*, 1.
101. bell hooks, "Choosing the Margin."
102. Rodriguez, *Latinx Literature Unbound*.
103. Moya, *Social Imperative*, 10.
104. Christian, "Race for Theory," 68.
105. I draw this argument from Bryant, *Rivers of Gold*, 3.
106. Matory, "Many Who Dance in Me," 243.

Chapter 1: Arturo Schomburg, Pura Belpré, and the "Racial Integrity" of Auto/biography

1. Kadar, "Coming to Terms," 202. Brackets are included in original quotation.
2. In particular, the 2021 special issue on Schomburg in *African American Review*.

3. For Schomburg's Masonic work, see Arroyo, *Writing Secrecy in Caribbean Freemasonry*. For his importance as a historian and bibliophile, see Hoffnung-Garskof, "The Migrations of Arturo Schomburg"; and Holton, "Decolonizing History."
4. García-Peña, "Non-essential Knowledge"; Sánchez González, *Boricua Literature*; and Valdés, *Diasporic Blackness*.
5. Sánchez González, "Decolonizing Schomburg."
6. Valdés, *Diasporic Blackness*, 72.
7. Valdés, 71–90. I am aware of only one recent essay that takes a primarily literary studies approach: Holton, "Arturo Alfonso Schomburg's Archival Encounters."
8. The masculinist focus of Schomburg's work has been discussed in Sánchez González, "Decolonizing Schomburg," 135; and Valdés, "Afterlives of Arturo Alfonso Schomburg," 148.
9. Sánchez González, *Boricua Literature*, 78.
10. Belpré, *Stories I Read*, 247.
11. Another angle of gendered analysis regarding Schomburg is the influence of his mother and Black women on his life. See Asukile, "Arthur Alfonso Schomburg"; Laurent-Perrault, "Arturo Alfonso Schomburg"; and Negrón-Muntaner, "'Here Is the Evidence.'"
12. I do not believe that Sánchez González judges or condemns Belpré's husband or her choice to marry and leave the workforce but rather that she points to the gendered expectations of women and to Belpré's own religious beliefs, which may have led to this twenty-year period outside of the New York Public Library with little published writing. Sánchez González, "Pura Belpré," 48–49.
13. Sánchez González, "Pura Belpré," 45.
14. Sánchez González, ix.
15. Refer to Sánchez González's annotations of Belpré's archival pieces in *The Stories I Tell to Children*.
16. I was unable to view Belpré's papers during my time at El Centro as a summer dissertation fellow. The COVID-19 pandemic prevented a planned second trip meant to allow time to examine her papers.
17. Another argument for studying Schomburg and Belpré together can be seen in Núñez, "Remembering."
18. Jiménez García, *Side by Side*, 71.
19. Sánchez González declares that Belpré's own biography and the fact that "she knew Arturo Schomburg, she knew Piri Thomas, and she was very active in the 1960s and 1970s in New York City during the apogee of the Young Lords Party and the Nuyorican poetry movement" might make it seem like she would have been part of this larger legacy of reclaiming Afro–Puerto Rican history. "Yet," Sánchez González notes, "she did not choose to explore African diasporic identity per se, nor the blackness intrinsic to Puerto Rican culture, in her writing and public intellectual work of that period" (19). See Sánchez González, "Pura Belpré," 19–22.
20. Sánchez González, *Boricua Literature*, 98.
21. Sánchez González, "Pura Belpré," 65–73.
22. Sánchez González, "Pura Belpré," 28; Sánchez González has vacillated about how to describe Belpré's identity. She clearly identifies her as Afro-Boricua in

Boricua Literature but hedges on this identification in the 2013 collection of Belpré's work. While earlier in her biographical introduction, Sánchez González claims that Belpré crossed with ease the color lines drawn in North America ("Pura Belpré," 21), she later indicates that she clearly would have suffered racial discrimination (28).
23. Jiménez García, *Side by Side*, 79.
24. In "I Wished to Be Like Johnny Appleseed," Belpré writes that Puerto Rico is "a beautiful island with a culture enriched by old, old stories gained from many people." Belpré, *Stories I Read*, 258.
25. Belpré, 205. Sánchez González identifies the piece as undated, possibly from 1977. Belpré, *Stories I Read*, 268n1. For more on the treatment of African presence in the Iberian peninsula, see deGuzmán, *Spain's Long Shadow*.
26. Belpré, *Stories I Read*, 205.
27. Belpré, 209.
28. Belpré, 262.
29. Recall from the introduction that I define "AfroLatinidades" as social, cultural, and political constructions based in the embodied experiences of Black Latinxs. AfroLatinidades arise from the negotiation of invisibility, visibility, and hypervisibility. That is, AfroLatinx writers construct an AfroLatinidad by bringing to light the distortions and erasures they must navigate within themselves and in the world around them that both invisibilize and hypervisibilize their presence.
30. We might also consider the hegemonic Latin American autobiographical tradition that Lawrence La Fountain-Stokes discusses (La Fountain-Stokes, *Queer Ricans*, 23).
31. Casper, *Constructing American Lives*, 1.
32. Casper points out that in the latter half of the 1800s, people were already questioning the "archaic, romantic emphasis on great men" that ignored the "larger forces" that determined history more than individual men (Casper, *Constructing American Lives*, 5). However, the influence of this tradition certainly had not wavered in either Black or white American biographical writing in the first half of the twentieth century.
33. Qtd. in Valdés, *Diasporic Blackness*, 74.
34. Valdés, 85.
35. Valdés, 87. Casper also discusses the differentiation that began in the 1850s between "literary biography" and the popular biographies that most people actually read (Casper, *Constructing American Lives*, 6).
36. Hong, *Minor Feelings*, 64. Emphasis original.
37. Flores and Jiménez Román, "Triple-Consciousness?"
38. Hong, *Minor Feelings*, 9.
39. Hong, 64.
40. Casper, *Constructing American Lives*, 10–11.
41. Casper, 6, emphasis original.
42. Howes, "Life Writing."
43. Casper, *Constructing American Lives*, 11.
44. Kadar, "Coming to Terms," 202.

45. Howard Dodson claims that Schomburg was born in Cangrejos (also called Santurce) ("Introduction," 8), but Sinnette, Ortiz, and Valdés all assert that he was born in San Juan but grew up in Cangrejos (respectively: Sinnette, *Arthur Alfonso Schomburg*, 7; Ortiz, "Arthur A. Schomburg," 19; Valdés, *Diasporic Blackness*, 3).
46. For more comprehensive biographies of Schomburg, refer to Ortiz, "Arthur A. Schomburg"; Sinnette, *Arthur Alfonso Schomburg*; Salgado, "Archive"; and Valdés, *Diasporic Blackness*.
47. Valdés notes that Schomburg was particularly influenced by Ramón Emeterio Betances. She writes, "with Betances [. . .], an AfroLatino who was deeply invested in the liberation and union of black peoples throughout the Caribbean, Schomburg found an exemplar of African diasporic thought" (*Diasporic Blackness*, 37). Ortiz claims that Schomburg "probably met" Betances, since he was in exile in the Virgin Islands at a time that likely overlapped with Schomburg's stay in St. Thomas ("Arthur A. Schomburg," 25). However, Valdés and Sánchez González are skeptical of the evidence produced by Sinnette and Ortiz that Schomburg was ever in St. Thomas (Valdés, *Diasporic Blackness*, 33; Sánchez González, "Arturo Alfonso Schomburg," 142).
48. For more on the Antillean Independence movement in New York, see Mirabal, *Suspect Freedoms*.
49. Svirsky and Bignall, *Agamben and Colonialism*, 7.
50. Ortiz points to a 1903 letter to the editor Schomburg wrote to the *New York Times* ("Arthur A. Schomburg," 35, 115nn18–20).
51. Sinnette, *Arthur Alfonso Schomburg*, 55.
52. Sinnette, 41–42.
53. Holton, "Decolonizing History," 219. Schomburg is also credited as a member of the advisory board for Du Bois and Johnson's *Encyclopedia of the Negro* (Holton, "Decolonizing History," 216). Furthermore, according to Sinnette, Schomburg was working with Du Bois on an *Encyclopedia Africana* (Sinnette, *Arthur Alfonso Schomburg*, 34, 207n46).
54. In addition to curating the 135th Street collection for several years, he was also the curator specializing in African diasporic materials at Fisk University for a year (1931–1932). Ortiz records that Fisk's collection increased "by at least 4,000 volumes" during his brief tenure (Ortiz, "Arthur A. Schomburg," 97). See also Valdés, *Diasporic Blackness*, 101–103.
55. For example, Sinnette quotes a 1973 interview with Jesús Colón saying, "something happened whereby Arturo shifted his interest away from the Puerto Rican liberation movement and put all his energy into the [Black] movement" (Sinnette, *Arthur Alfonso Schomburg*, 23). See also Ortiz, "Arthur A. Schomburg," 41.
56. Valdés, *Diasporic Blackness*, 6.
57. Sinnette, *Arthur Alfonso Schomburg*, 68. Sinnette quotes from a letter written by Bruce.
58. James, *Holding Aloft*, 197.
59. Jorge, "Black Puerto Rican Woman," 187.
60. César Salgado, for instance, outlines the scholarly debate that has occurred regarding claims to Schomburg as part of a US Black or decolonial Caribbean tradition, as well as a third AfroLatinx legacy. See Salgado, "Archive."

61. Holton, "Arturo Alfonso Schomburg," 32.
62. Caine, *Biography and History*, 71.
63. Sánchez González, "Arturo Alfonso Schomburg," 148.
64. While Valdés makes a strong case for labeling these narratives as crónicas—journalistic pieces that explore the travels of a writer, which are part of Latin American literary tradition—Schomburg's auto/biographical writing, published and unpublished, was almost entirely in English. His essays were published in US Black venues and not in the Caribbean or Latin America. One important exception to this is his writing in Spanish for José Martí's *Patria*, though these writings were about the Puerto Rican independence movement and were not history or biographies.
65. Castromán Soto, "Schomburg's Black Archival Turn," 73.
66. Castromán Soto, 73–74.
67. Schomburg, "Racial Integrity," 5.
68. Schomburg, "Racial Integrity," 6.
69. Schomburg, "Negro Digs," 231.
70. I agree with Valdés that "Schomburg historiography, which for this writer includes Schomburg's own publications, is decidedly male-centered (that is, there is a notable absence of women, seemingly in his professional life and work)" (*Diasporic Blackness*, 36). Castromán Soto argues that women play a larger role in this work, as presented in "Racial Integrity" ("Schomburg's Black Archival Turn," 80).
71. Schomburg, "Racial Integrity," 6.
72. Schomburg, 6.
73. Schomburg, 7.
74. Schomburg, 18.
75. Schomburg, 19.
76. Valdés, *Diasporic Blackness*, 71.
77. See Anzaldúa, *Interviews/Entrevistas*, 157; and Lorde, "Age, Race, Class, and Sex," 122.
78. "Cyrille Charles Auguste Bissette," Arturo Alfonso Schomburg Papers, Reel 10, Box 12, Folder 8.2, Manuscripts and Archives Division at the New York Public Library. When I indicate that a text was unpublished, I mean to say that this text was found in the Arturo Alfonso Schomburg Papers at the SCRBC and is not indicated as published in any venue in the bibliographies of Schomburg's work compiled by the SCRBC (1986) and Sinnette (1989), which were based on Kaplan Gubert and Newman, *Nine Decades of Scholarship*, 64–71.
79. For a discussion and contextualization of this unpublished cookbook, see Rafia Zafar, "Negro Cooks." For a similar piece with images from the archives, see Zafar, "Arturo Schomburg's Gastronomica."
80. An example of what it might look like to blend biography and cookbook, see Diaz, *Coconuts and Collards* (2018).
81. Schomburg Papers, Reel 10, Box 12, Folder 8.2, 3.
82. Piñeiro de Rivera, *Arthur A. Schomburg*, 11.
83. Schomburg, "Racial Integrity," 5.
84. For example, see Patricia Hill Collins, *Black Feminist Thought*, 24.
85. Schomburg, "Racial Integrity," 12.

86. Schomburg, 12.
87. For a recent archival-poetical view of Wheatley, see Honorée Fanone Jeffers's *The Age of Phillis* (2020). For recent scholarship reading Wheatley against master narratives, see Ford, "Difficult Miracle."
88. Sinnette, *Arthur Alfonso Schomburg*, 89.
89. Morrison, *Playing in the Dark*, 6.
90. Morrison, 6–7, 80–81. Morrison also comments that immigrant literature contextualizes the Americanness of immigrants in relation to Black Americans, which is something to consider for Black immigrant subjects like Schomburg (47).
91. Morrison, *Playing in the Dark*, 37, 51.
92. Schomburg, "An Appreciation," in Piñeiro de Rivera, 96.
93. Schomburg, 97.
94. Schomburg, 98.
95. An earlier draft of his article, entitled only "Crispus Attucks," was found in the Arturo Alfonso Schomburg Papers, Reel 10, Box 12, Folder 8. How much earlier it was created is unclear, though the fact that he signed his name as "Arturo A. Schomburg" rather than "Arthur A. Schomburg," suggests it was one of his later writings, since he returned to using "Arturo" later in life (Valdés, *Diasporic Blackness*, 5). It was through Mitch Kachun's *First Martyr of Liberty* that I found out that this piece had been published: "In May 1935 the *Chicago Defender* published a full-page essay telling the story of Crispus Attucks and his heroism at the Boston Massacre. Arthur A. Schomburg published a similar lengthy piece on Attucks a few months later for the *New York Amsterdam News*" (Kachun, *First Martyr*, 107). My reading considers both the earlier draft and the published version.
96. The King Institute claims that in the 1940s, the newspaper boosted a circulation of over a hundred thousand (King Institute, "New York Amsterdam News").
97. Schomburg, "Crispus Attucks," 6A.
98. Dred Scott v. John F. A. Sanford, 60 US 393 (1856).
99. Schomburg, "Crispus Attucks," 6A.
100. Schomburg, 6A.
101. Schomburg, "Free Negroes," Schomburg Papers, Reel 10, Box 12, Folder 8. I could not determine when the piece was written.
102. Frederick Douglass had also argued that the US Constitution was not inherently white supremacist. See Ives, "Frederick Douglass's Reform Textualism."
103. Schomburg, "Free Negroes," 3.
104. Schomburg, 3.
105. Schomburg, 3.
106. Schomburg, "Crispus Attucks," 6A.
107. Schomburg, 6A.
108. Presented at the 1915 convention of the American Negro Academy. For an analysis of this essay, see Valdés, *Diasporic Blackness*, 81–83.
109. Schomburg Papers, Reel 10, Box 12, Folder 8, 1.
110. *Oxford English Dictionary Online*, s.v. "providence."
111. Schomburg, "Crispus Attucks," 6A.
112. Schomburg could also be referencing the *Elizabeth*, nicknamed "the *Mayflower* of Liberia," which carried the first African American people to the Sierra Leone

region in 1820 through the American Colonization Society (ACS), a white philanthropic organization.
113. Schomburg, "Crispus Attucks," 6A. However, in the earlier draft, he writes "Black Pilgrims," capitalizing the "B" to indicate people of the African diaspora, rather than just people with dark skin color. This is a choice to identify a culture, rather than a color. However, using a lowercase "b" was common in newspaper publications and thus the lower-case "b" is likely a style change made by the publisher. Schomburg Papers, Reel 10, Box 12, Folder 8.
114. What the *Mayflower* was used for after departing New England is unclear, since there were many ships named the *Mayflower*. Rendell Harris attempts to trace the ship's history, debunking certain claims, and ultimately arguing that it most likely acted as a whaling ship (Harris, *Last of the* "Mayflower," 46). The argument is traced out in chapter 4, "The '*Mayflower*' as Whaling Ship." I could not find any other sources that attempted to trace the *Mayflower* in the years after the pilgrims' arrival to New England.
115. For a detailed history of the connection between the enslavement of Indigenous and African peoples to the development of New England and the Caribbean, see Wendy Warren, *New England Bound*. She states that "the first documented shipment of enslaved Africans arrived [to New England] in 1638, eighteen years after the *Mayflower*'s journey" (7). For an examination by Black writers of the juxtaposition of the *Mayflower* and the ship that brought enslaved Africans to Jamestown in 1619, see Kenyon Gradert, "The *Mayflower* and the Slave Ship."
116. The essay was tentatively titled, "Some Notable Colored Men from the West Indies," in the Schomburg Papers, Reel 10, Box 12, Folder 8, 1–2.
117. Schomburg, "Negro Digs," 231.
118. Schomburg also wrote several essays on Haiti and Haitian contributions to hemispheric American and global developments, such as "Military Services Rendered by the Haitians in the North and South American Wars for Independence" (*AME Church Review*) and "Henri Christophe, King of Haiti" (May 1935 and June 1935, *Looking Forward*). Clearly, Schomburg saw Haitian history as an integral part of AfroLatino history.
119. Emerson, *Representative Men*, 4.
120. Schomburg, "General Antonio Maceo," in Piñeiro de Rivera, 175.
121. Holton argues that this essay also acts to move back to the center the role of Afro-Cubans in the Cuban fight for independence (Holton, "Arturo Alfonso Schomburg," 45).
122. bell hooks, "Choosing the Margin," 20.
123. Schomburg, "General Antonio Maceo," in Piñeiro de Rivera, 175.
124. Schomburg, 180.
125. Published in *Mission Fields at Home*, a Catholic publication of the Sisters of the Blessed Sacrament for Indians and Colored People in Cornwells Heights, Pennsylvania. This probably explains the amount of time spent discussing Campeche's devoutness. Schomburg quotes at length a Bishop's eulogy given upon Campeche's death (207).
126. See Valdés, *Diasporic Blackness* (1–3), for her reading of the Campeche sketch as emblematic of Schomburg's recovery project.
127. Schomburg, "José Campeche," in Piñeiro de Rivera, 201.

128. Schomburg, 201.
129. Schomburg, 206.
130. Schomburg, 208.
131. For a detailed examination of Schomburg as a visual arts collector, see Negrón-Muntaner, "Here Is the Evidence."
132. There are other examples as well, such as his 1909 essay on Plácido, the Afro-Cuban poet. See Piñeiro de Rivera, *Arthur A. Schomburg*, 61.
133. Schomburg, "In Quest of Juan de Pareja," in Piñeiro de Rivera, 140.
134. Schomburg, 140.
135. In fact, Vanessa K. Valdés and David Pullins cocurated an exhibit on Juan de Pareja that ran at the New York Metropolitan Museum of Art from April 3 to June 16, 2023. Framed by Schomburg's writing, the cocurators also produced the catalogue, *Juan de Pareja, Afro-Hispanic Painter in the Age of Velázquez* (2023).
136. Schomburg, "In Quest of Juan de Pareja," in Piñeiro de Rivera, 143.
137. Schomburg, 142.
138. I refer to quietude in chapter 3, as well, and find the concept useful across AfroLatinx literary production, as can be seen in Mills, "Beyond Resistance."
139. Quashie, *Sovereignty of Quiet*, 21–22.
140. Holton, "Arturo Alfonso Schomburg," 43.
141. Schomburg, "Notes on Panamá," in Piñeiro de Rivera, 161.
142. Schomburg cites "Historia de Panamá. J. E. Sosa and E. J. Aver. Panama p. 164" as his source for this claim. He is likely referring to Juan B. Sosa and Enrique J. Arce's *Compendio de historia de Panamá* (1911).
143. Schomburg, "Notes on Panamá," in Piñeiro de Rivera, 161.
144. Schomburg, 162.
145. Schomburg, 162.
146. Holton, "Arturo Alfonso Schomburg," 34. While this brotherhood is no longer composed of Black people, it was a Black cofradía (confraternity) for centuries, starting in the 1300s. See Moreno, *La Antigua Hermandad de los Negros de Sevilla*.
147. Schomburg, "Negro Brotherhood," in Piñeiro de Rivera, 150.
148. Schomburg, "Negroes," in Piñeiro de Rivera, 154.
149. See my earlier section "Revising America's Beginnings" for more on Schomburg's invocation of the Taney opinion in *Scott v. Sanford*.
150. Schomburg, "General Evaristo Estenoz," in Piñeiro de Rivera, 74.
151. See Valdés, *Diasporic Blackness* (75–79), for contextualization of Amendment 17 and the Race War of 1912.
152. Schomburg, in Piñeiro de Rivera, 74–75.
153. Valdés, *Diasporic Blackness*, 78.
154. Irizarry Rodríguez, "Evolving Identities," 32.
155. Schomburg, "Negro Brotherhood," in Piñeiro de Rivera, 145.
156. Schomburg, 148.
157. Schomburg also begins with the story of Estevanico in "My Trip to Cuba in Quest of Negro Books," establishing him alongside the first white Spaniards (in Piñeiro de Rivera, 181). Very little documentation is left about Estevanico. For a fictional history of Estevanico's life, see Lalami, *Moor's Account*.
158. Schomburg, "The Negro Brotherhood," in Piñeiro de Rivera, 148–149.

159. Schomburg spells his name "Xavier" rather than the more common "Javier." I have maintained his spelling.
160. Schomburg, "Notes on Panamá," in Piñeiro de Rivera, 164.
161. Schomburg, 165. On the same page Schomburg says that it was "a very rare and precious privilege, indeed, to hold these documents."
162. Schomburg, 164.
163. Schomburg, 166.

Chapter 2: Jesús Colón, the New York Young Lords, and "Observe and Participate" Autobiography

1. See Flores, who saw "Puerto Rican literature produced in the United States" as part of a "'new' American literary history" since this literature "straddle[s] two national literatures and hemispheric perspectives" (Flores, "Puerto Rican," 143).
2. While there are debates over what to call Puerto Rico (colony, free associated state, commonwealth, etc.), Colón and the Young Lords clearly see Puerto Rico as a US colony. For more on the political, economic, and social history of Puerto Rico and the diaspora, see Acosta-Belén and Sánchez Korrol, "World of Jesús Colón"; Duany, *Puerto Rican Nation*; Sánchez Korrol, *From Colonia to Community*; and Wagenheim, *Puerto Rico*.
3. See Kanellos, "Sotero Figueroa."
4. For more on Marín, see Lomas, *Translating Empire*; Flores, "Puerto Rican"; and Jiménez Román and Flores, *The Afro-Latin@ Reader*.
5. Lomas, "Migration," 157.
6. I use the terms "New York Young Lords" or "Young Lords Party" (YLP) to refer to the organization. Because most of the Young Lords' activism and writing occurred between 1969 and 1972, I focus exclusively on this period of the organization, though I encourage future scholars to examine the period between 1972 and 1976.
7. José Luis González sees periodicals as "virtually the cradle of our [Puerto Rican] literature" (González, *Puerto Rico*, 40).
8. Acosta-Belén, "Notes," 183–184.
9. I draw this argument from Sherwin Bryant's *Rivers of Gold, Lives of Bondage* (2014). For Bryant, slavery is inseparable from colonialism. Slavery is a colonial tool that legitimates Eurocentrism and European control of borders and land—that is, of the ability to govern. Bryant writes:

> Slavery was not merely a labor system, nor was it a separate institution. Rather, it was one of the chief governing practices and juridical claims that constituted Castile's colonial relation to New World territories, subject peoples, and natural resources. In short, it was one of the chief European technologies used to exercise dominion over the Indies. (3)

In other words, Blackness is an identity of sovereignlessness created through slavery, naturaleza, and casta. To be white is to be able to govern; to be Black was to be governed and controlled.

10. In this way, Afro–Puerto Rican socialism reflected the work of later Black Latin American radicals, such as Afro-Nicaraguan June Beer's revolutionary art and poetry. As Frank Guridy and Juliet Hooker state, "In a country where blackness had long been denied or relegated to the marginalized Caribbean coast, Beer's art presciently suggested that racism could be an Achilles heel of the [Sandinista] revolutionary project." Guridy and Hooker, "Currents," 212.
11. Guzmán ("Pablo," 14–15; YLP, 70), and "Untitled," Richie Pérez Papers, Series VIII: Audiovisual (1979–2004), Box 41, Item 1B, Centro Library and Archives (CLA).
12. Sánchez González, *Boricua Literature*, 79.
13. Jorgensen, *Principles*, 2.
14. Jorgensen, 3, 12–13; DeWalt and DeWalt, *Participant Observation*, 15.
15. The Young Lords allowed Michael Abramson (a photographer) to embed himself within the organization for an extended period of time, another form of the participant-observer method.
16. The term, which invokes the Taíno foundations of the island, also resists colonized identity.
17. The increased presence of the YLP in academic scholarship is thanks to Johanna Fernández, Darrel Wanzer-Serrano, Frances Negrón-Muntaner, and Anne Garland Mahler. See Fernández, "Between Social Service Reform"; Fernández, "Denise Oliver"; Fernández, *Young Lords*; Enck-Wanzer, *Young Lords*; Wanzer-Serrano, *New York Young Lords*; Negrón-Muntaner, "Look of Sovereignty"; and Mahler, *From the Tricontinental*. Lisa Sánchez González (*Boricua Literature*, 2001) also provided the first literary and intellectual history of Boricua, though she focuses on writers beside Colón and the Young Lords.
18. We can even see this pro-independence or at least, anti-statehood and anti-colonial view expressed by Pura Belpré (Belpré, *Stories I Read*, 260–261). She was "the first Boricua and AfroLatina librarian in the NYPL [New York Public Library] system" (Sánchez González, *Boricua Literature*, 74). Belpré is discussed further in chapter 1.
19. As president of the Cervantes Fraternal Society—the Latino arm of the International Workers Organization (IWO)—Colón was an active and influential member of the CPUSA (Communist Party USA) until his death in 1974, even running for New York City Comptroller on the Communist party ticket in 1969. Colón was an important member of the CPUSA at a national level, as evidenced in his archive by a 1945 invitation to a high-level CPUSA event as part of "a small, but representative meeting of leading Party members." See Invitation from CPUSA national office dated August 23, 1945. Jesús Colón Papers, Reel 2, Box 3, Folder 2, CLA. While the CPUSA was only lukewarmly supportive of Puerto Rican independence, Colón's own commitment to the CPUSA did not interfere with his support for Puerto Rican sovereignty, as can be seen by the many materials supporting the Movimiento Pro Independencia (MPI) in his archive.
20. Acosta-Belén and Santiago, *Puerto Ricans*, 23.
21. See Colón's sketch "Stowaway" in *A Puerto Rican in New York*. Though Colón leveraged this claim in several letters and attempts to sell *A Puerto Rican in New York* to schools and libraries, it is doubtful that this stowaway story is true.

Colón's identification card, held by the Center for Puerto Rican Studies, suggests he came to the continental US under less exciting, safer circumstances. For more of Colón's biography, see Acosta-Belén and Sánchez Korrol, "World of Jesús Colón," and Flores's foreword to *A Puerto Rican in New York*.
22. In 1952, Puerto Rico gained limited autonomy as a commonwealth, what Juan Flores calls "lite-colonialism" (Flores, *From Bomba*, 36–37), or a more indirect form of colonial control with perfunctory forms of autonomy. Indeed, while Puerto Ricans are technically US citizens, they cannot practice any of the fundamental democratic practices of the United States while remaining residents of the island. That is, they have no meaningful voice in the US government and limited influence within the colony, usually related only to cultural and linguistic issues, such as the administration of education. To vote, Puerto Ricans must move to the continental United States.
23. Troublingly, we have no record that Colón ever denounced the Stalin regime; rather, he makes his support for Stalin clear in several sketches in *A Puerto Rican in New York* (for example, "Carmencita") and through his use of Stalin's writings to teach about nationalism while a lecturer at the Jefferson School of Social Science, run by the CPUSA. See Jesús Colón Papers, Reel 7, Box 10, Folder 4, CLA. See also Shaffer (*Black Flag Boricuas*, 176), where he discusses Colón's disapproval of anarchism based squarely in "uncritical" summaries of Stalin's writings. Dave Vázquez argues that the "critical inattention" to Colón's work comes from his refusal to break with the Party (Vázquez, *Triangulations*, 52). However, his life writing provides one of only a few opportunities to see the experiences of Afro–Puerto Ricans in the first half of the twentieth century.
24. Acosta-Belén and Sánchez Korrol, "World of Jesús Colón," 21.
25. Colón, *Way It Was*, 7–8.
26. For Afro–Puerto Rican socialists, this strand of Marxism mattered most because of its attention to capitalist-driven colonialism.
27. Vázquez, *Triangulations*, 59.
28. Without a doubt, Jesús Colón also politically influenced the New York Young Lords Party. Colón and the YLP were writers and organizers invested in their Puerto Rican and barrio communities, fighting for a socialist future in which Puerto Rico would no longer be an exploited US colony. Former Young Lord Iris Morales, in *Through the Eyes of Rebel Women*, affirms that a major influence on her life and activism was Colón's *A Puerto Rican in New York*, which she "read and reread. [She] related to his account of Puerto Rican working people making their way in the city" (xiv). Morales also indicates that because most Lords couldn't read Spanish, his work was one of only a few Puerto Rican writing influences accessible to them (Morales, *Through the Eyes*, 25). Richie Pérez, another former Young Lord, uses the sketch "Because He Spoke Spanish" from *A Puerto Rican in New York*, on the race-motivated murder of Bernabe Nuñez, as a historical source for a timeline of Puerto Rican political history. See draft of "We Didn't Drop from the Sky," Richie Pérez Papers, Box 34, Folder 5, CLA.
29. See Wanzer-Serrano, *New York Young Lords*; and Morales, *Through the Eyes*, for a more detailed biography of the New York Young Lords.
30. YLP, *Palante*, 10–11.

31. This was a coalition made up of the YLO, the BPP, and the Young Patriots, a radical, socialist Appalachian organization.
32. For details on these offenses, see Wanzer-Serrano, *New York Young Lords*; Hinojosa, *Apostles of Change*; and Fernández, *Young Lords*. Fernández details their dissolution.
33. Flores, "Puerto Rican," 150.
34. Colón, *Puerto Rican*.
35. See cover of *Palante* vol. 2, no. 1 (1969), and Iris Morales Luciano, "Puerto Rican Genocide!" in *Palante* vol. 2, no. 2 (1969), A La Izquierda Collection, CLA. When citing issues of *Palante*, I generally cite either *The Young Lords: A Reader* or *Through the Eyes of Rebel Women*, unless otherwise noted.
36. See Juan González, "Latin American Vanguard," A La Izquierda Collection, CLA.
37. Fernández, *Young Lords*, 282.
38. YLP, *Palante*, 10.
39. See the introduction for more on the life writing scholarship that grounds this work.
40. Boyce Davies, "Collaboration," 4.
41. The YLP's work is not the only collaborative piece of life writing from that year. The Black Panther 21's "collective autobiography," *Look for Me in the Whirlwind* (1971), may have influenced *Palante: Young Lords Party*, as the Black Panther 21 were offered the opportunity to write their book when they were imprisoned in 1969 (Om, "Look for Yourselves," 2).
42. For another discussion of the importance of the term "sketch" for Colón, see Rúa and Ramos-Zayas, "Introduction."
43. Adalaine Holton makes a similar argument about the writing of Jesús Colón. She categorizes Colón's writing as crónicas and does so in the service of expanding ideas of Black radicalism. She writes, "Colón demonstrates that through the events of everyday life we can most clearly witness power structures at work, and he also suggests that the ordinary can be an opportunity for social transformation" (Holton, "'Little Things Are Big,'" 7).
44. Hong, *Minor Feelings*, 56.
45. Hong, 55.
46. Hong, 56.
47. See the discussion of the resistance to Afro-Boricua identity in Denise Oliver, "Yanquis Own Puerto Rico," 148–149. Originally published in Palante 2, no. 17 (December 11, 1970). An original copy can be found in the A La Izquierda Collection, Reel 8, CLA.
48. Torres, "La Gran Familia," 289.
49. Dávila, *Sponsored Identities*, 71. Pura Belpré's deployment and discussion of the folklore character Juan Bobo, a representative of the jíbaro image, similarly focuses on the jíbaro as a mestizo peasant. Belpré, *Stories I Read*, 204. For more discussion of scholarship on mestizaje beyond Puerto Rico, see the introduction.
50. Dávila, *Sponsored Identities*, 71–72. As Arlene Torres and Norman Whitten, Jr., note, "although, in many areas, *jíbaros* vary in phenotype from brown to black, there is little if any 'national' emphasis on the African component of Puerto Rican heritage" (Torres and Whitten, "General Introduction," 1:14).

51. González, *Puerto Rico*, 41.
52. Another way of thinking about mestizaje in Puerto Rico is the idea of "la gran familia," which "presented Puerto Rico as a racial paradise that overcame its racial divisions, even as anti-black stereotypes and stigmatization were, and are, common" (Jones, "Afro-Latinos," 589). See also Duany, *Puerto Rican Nation*; and Rivera-Rideau, *Remixing Reggaetón*. For a discussion of "la gran familia" with an added attention to gender and patriarchy, see Moreno, *Family Matters*, 61–74.
53. Torres and Whitten, "General Introduction," 1:14.
54. Colón, *Puerto Rican*, 9.
55. Smith and Watson, "Introduction," xvii.
56. Colón, *Puerto Rican*, 10. Emphasis original.
57. See Stanchich, "Insular Interventions," for a list of Colón's English and Spanish writings on Puerto Rican relationships with the concept of race.
58. See also "The Mother, the Daughter, Myself, and All of Us" (Colón, *Puerto Rican*, 118).
59. Colón, *Way It Was*, 46. This portion of the essay is similar to the beginning of Pura Belpré's essay "I Wished to Be Like Johnny Appleseed," which similarly elides the colonial violence inherent in mestizaje (Belpré, *Stories I Read*, 258). Yet, Colón interrogates this narrative with his ending, while Belpré does not.
60. Colón, *Way It Was*, 46.
61. Colón, 46.
62. For another example of a sketch on race that ends with an open-ended conclusion, see "The Mother, the Daughter, Myself, and All of Us" (Colón, *Puerto Rican*, 118). This very short sketch discusses the time that a little girl in a diner called Colón the N-word and no one (including him) said anything.
63. Colón, 54.
64. Colón, 54.
65. I have not yet found the piece to which Colón refers; however, there is a Church of Our Lady of Assumption in Cayey, whose "pews were designed by the renowned Puerto Rican painter Ramón Frade and which houses a sculpture called *Virgen Taína*, by Tomás Batista-Encarnación" (Grupo Editorial EPRL).
66. Colón, *Way It Was*, 54.
67. The 2011 edition of *Palante* does not include this poem. For one of the few in-depth analyses of *El pueblo se levanta*, see Young, *Soul Power*, 100–144.
68. YLP, *Palante* (newsletter), vol. 3, no. 13: 16.
69. Dávila, *Sponsored Identities*, 71. For additional analysis of Pietri's work, see Dalleo and Machado Sáez, *The Latino/a Canon* (chapter 1); and Noel, "'Geography of Their Complexion.'"
70. Mahler reads "Puerto Rican Obituary" for its connection to the Young Lords and Nuyorican tricontinental literature (Mahler, *From the Tricontinental*, 150–153).
71. YLP, *Palante*, 54.
72. YLP, 54.
73. Aponte, "Albizu Campos," 95. Reprinted in Enck-Wanzer, *Young Lords*. Originally published in *Palante* 2, no. 14 (October 30, 1970). This history likely comes from Federico Ribes Tovar's biography of Albizu Campos. He writes, "Since he inherited his mother's dark skin, he was personally exposed, in his youth, to the

effects of American discrimination, and the deep scars that humiliation burned into his spirit were indelible" (Tovar, *Albizu Campos*, 17).
74. Torres and Whitten, "General Introduction," 1:27.
75. YLP, *Palante*, 10.
76. YLP, 10.
77. YLP, 81.
78. YLP, 80.
79. YLP, 82.
80. For more on the YLP's rhetoric of the "divided nation," see Morales, *Through the Eyes*.
81. Mahler, *From the Tricontinental*, 109.
82. Torres, "La Gran Familia Puertorriqueña," 2:288.
83. Zamora, "Trasnational Renderings," 95.
84. In particular, attempts to differentiate the jíbaro and the Afro-Boricua were based in the supposed logic of the mestizaje myth. Take, for example, the definitions of "jíbaro" and "Afro-Boricua" delineated in the pamphlet *The Ideology of the Young Lords Party*, developed in 1971 and distributed in 1972. See Enck-Wanzer, *Young Lords*, 17.
85. See Durán, "Latina/o Life Writing" (171–172), for a discussion of the prevalence of Latinx conversion narratives.
86. Smith, "Autobiographical Manifesto," 195.
87. Tinajero, *El Lector*, particularly part 2 on Puerto Rico and the US.
88. Tinajero, 9, 19.
89. Colón, 11. See also Vega, *Memoirs of Bernardo Vega*, 19–26.
90. See also Holton's reading of "A Voice through the Window," which further supports my argument ("'Little Things Are Big,'" 8–9).
91. Colón, *Puerto Rican*, 115.
92. Colón emphasizes the woman's whiteness throughout the short sketch, consistently referring to the woman as a "white lady" with her "white children" (Colón, 115, 116).
93. Colón, 116.
94. Colón, 117.
95. Edwin Murillo argues, through a close reading of some of Colón's earlier sketches in Spanish published in the late 1920s and early 1930s, that Colón holds anti-Latina attitudes (Murillo, "Hostile Anxieties").
96. Publication history and translation from Spanish to English provided by Acosta-Belén and Sánchez Korrol. *The Way It Was*, 67n1.
97. Colón, *Way It Was*, 68.
98. Colón, 68.
99. Colón, 68.
100. See Gutierrez, *Teología de la liberación* (translated into English in 1973).
101. Colón, *Puerto Rican*, 103.
102. Colón, 109.
103. Originally published as *The Socialist Sixth of the World*, the book paints a rosy picture of Stalin's Soviet Union in the 1930s and was later discovered to have taken many sections word-for-word from Soviet propaganda. See Butler, *Red Dean*.

104. Colón, *Puerto Rican*, 110.
105. The YLP also appealed to the rhetoric of Christianity, particularly in their famous occupation of the First Spanish United Methodist Church, which they renamed the "People's Church." In the documentary, *El pueblo se levanta*, one spokesman showcases his knowledge of scripture to prove his commitment to Christian ethics (Newsreel). He provides several scriptures that characterize the Young Lords as being more Christ-like than the middle-class parishioners who no longer live in or serve the communities in which they were raised. By highlighting the YLP's commitment to community service and the example of "Jesus who walked among the poor," the YLP ties socialism with spirituality, much like Carmencita. For more on the YLP's appeals to Christian ethics, see Hinojosa, *Apostles of Change*. For another religion-based reading that considers the structure of "Carmencita" as a novena, see García, "Master of the Rosary."
106. Colón, *Puerto Rican*, 103–104.
107. Colón, 106.
108. Colón, 108.
109. YLP, *Palante*, 51. Emphasis original.
110. Boyce Davies, "Collaboration," 7.
111. YLP, *Palante*, 28, 45.
112. Jesús Colón's early Spanish-language writing under the pseudonym Miquis Tiquis used a similar style: "La prosa y el verso de Miquis Tiquis eran portadores de un estilo que simulaba la oralidad con abundancia de giros coloquiales, anglicismos, jibarismos o una jerga popular puertarriqueña sólo para entendidos. [. . .] Hay en sus columnas abundancia de signos de puntuación [. . .] los cuales intentaban aprisionar en la letra escrita lo que solamente podía existir en la oralidad. [Miquis Tiquis's prose and verse were carriers of a style that simulated orality with its abundance of colloquial turns, anglicisms, 'jibarisms' or popular Puerto Rican slang only for those in the know. [. . .] In his columns there is an abundance of punctuation marks [. . .] which tried to solidify in the written word what can only exist in orality.]" (Padilla Aponte, *Lo que*, xxi-xxii. Translation is my own.)
113. YLP, *Palante*, 28.
114. YLP, 29.
115. YLP, 29.
116. YLP, 30.
117. YLP, 18.
118. YLP, 18.
119. YLP, 18.
120. YLP, 21.
121. Morales, *Through the Eyes*, xxii.
122. While the first section of *Through the Eyes of Rebel Women* is primarily academic, it also provides Morales a space to reflect on the experiences she shared with other women in the YLP. The book also provides the transcripts of interviews completed in the 1990s during the making of Morales's documentary *¡Palante, Siempre Palante!* She also recently released another book, *Revisiting Herstories: The Young Lords Party* (2023), which I was unable to read and incorporate before submitting this book, but I imagine will add substantially to our understanding of Third World feminism and the Young Lords.

123. Young, *Soul Power*, 131.
124. Morales, *Through the Eyes*, 67; Enck-Wanzer, *Young Lords*, 9–13 (for both versions of the 13 Point Program and Platform).
125. Refer to Morales's chapter "Women Organizing Women" in *Through the Eyes of Rebel Women* for a detailed description of this struggle. Morales notes that the women Young Lords read the work of Jesús Colón's second wife, Clara Colón, particularly *Entering Fighting: Today's Woman, A Marxist-Leninist View* (1970), which Colón advertises in "The *Fanguito* Is Still There," published in *The Way It Was and Other Writings* (Morales, *Through the Eyes*, 26).
126. For example, see YLP, *Palante*, 18, 42, 47.
127. YLP, 40.
128. YLP, 48.
129. YLP, 48–49.
130. A representative example of this is the YLP's initial claim to a "revolutionary machismo." Morales discusses how the Young Lord women had no idea what "revolutionary machismo" meant and saw it as a contradiction in terms. According to Morales, "an African American woman" in the party said, "It's like saying revolutionary racism. It just doesn't make sense." Morales goes on to argue that, collectively, the women realized that the inclusion of the modifier "revolutionary" really "reflected an ambivalence about the equality of women. It preserved a gendered hierarchy that kept men in power without any commitment to the radical societal and personal transformation needed to make the liberation of women a reality and not just flowery rhetoric" (Morales, *Through the Eyes*, 49). The masculinist orientation of nationalist rhetoric has been well theorized by woman-of-color feminists: "The scripting of nation, as M. Jacquie Alexander, Hazel Carby, Carol Boyce Davies, Ginetta Candelario, Maylei Blackwell, Michelle Mitchell, April Mayes, and Michelle Stephens have so well argued, is a masculinist act that expunges female bodies from a nationalist rhetoric embedded in patriarchal discourses on nation and power" (Mirabal, *Suspect Freedoms*, 12).
131. Acosta-Belén, "Introduction: Unveiling," 3.
132. YLP, *Palante*, 41, 42, 46, 50.
133. Colón's writing has received some attention for the literary quality of his journalistic pieces and letters. See Irizarry Rodríguez, "Evolving Identities"; and Coss Aquino, "Jesús y Concha Colón."
134. Cabral, *Unity and Struggle*, 143. Emphasis original.
135. Latina Feminist Group, *Telling to Live*, 3.
136. See Bonilla and LeBrón, *Aftershocks of Disaster*.

Chapter 3: AfroLatinidad as Creative Destruction

1. While it's clear that Colón's work-in-progress, *The Way It Was*, was intended to show a more complete view of Puerto Rican people's humanity, Colón explicitly stated in *A Puerto Rican in New York and Other Sketches* that he meant to fight the overwhelmingly negative media portrayal of the community and thus often sidestepped less praiseworthy characterizations (Colón, *Puerto Rican*, 9–10).

2. Fleetwood, *Troubling Vision*, 6. Urayoán Noel, in his examination of Nuyorican poetry, "examines how such poets [including Piri Thomas] develop poetics strategically positioned against both institutional invisibility and abject hypervisibility" (Noel, *In Visible Movement*, 2).
3. Noel also notes, "The struggle with a problematic visibility already haunts Piri Thomas's autobiographical novel *Down These Mean Streets* (1967)" (*In Visible Movement*, 2).
4. I use AfroLatino here, as I have in previous chapters, to indicate that Thomas's conception is concerned with masculinity above all.
5. See, for example: Brown, *Gang Nation*; Caminero-Santangelo, "'Puerto Rican Negro'"; Cruz-Malavé, "Antifoundational Foundational Fiction"; Di Iorio Sandín, "Melancholic Allegorists"; Luis, "Black Latinos Speak"; McGill, "How to Be a Negro"; and Sánchez, "La Malinche" and *"Shakin' Up."*
6. Hartman, *Wayward Lives*, 21.
7. As Felice Blake puts it, "although unresolved in the narrative, the novel figures Piri's alignment with patriarchal masculinity as tenuous and problematic rather than as a final solution to racist exclusion" (Blake, "What Does It Mean," 101).
8. The complicated relationship between queer Nuyoricans (and queer AfroLatinx artists in general) and Piri Thomas can be seen in how queer artists evoke him now, as Noel argues in *In Visible Movement* (162).
9. Though, as chapter 5 argues, violence is not exclusive to AfroLatino identity formation, as exemplified in contemporary queer AfroLatinx narratives like Jaquira Díaz's *Ordinary Girls*.
10. For a breakdown of "the autobiographical example" in Du Bois's work, see Chandler, *X*; and Saunders, "Fugitive Dreams."
11. In this way, my work connects with Stephanie Fetta, *Shaming into Brown*, and her exploration of the connection between soma and shame.
12. Blake argues that *Down These Mean Streets* "stages a contestation between Latin American visions of mestizaje and U.S. anxieties about miscegenation" (Blake, "What Does It Mean," 97).
13. Piri Thomas Papers, Box 3, Folder 11, Manuscripts and Archives Division, Schomburg Center for Research in Black Culture (SCRBC).
14. While many people differentiate between Puerto Ricans on "the island" versus "the mainland," I avoid the use of the word "mainland," which privileges the space of the continental United States.
15. As noted by David Vázquez and Yolanda Martínez–San Miguel, the family's heritage is simplified in Thomas's memoirs (see Vázquez, *Triangulations*). Martínez–San Miguel notes, "The narrative is constructed from a series of key erasures, but one of the most important ones is the simplification of the family romance, since Piri represents his parents as a biracial Puerto Rican couple, instead of a binational and biracial couple (his father was black and Cuban and his mother was Puerto Rican and white)" (Martínez–San Miguel, "Ethnic Specularities," 361). For a biographical account of Thomas's father, see López, *Unbecoming Blackness*.
16. Operation Bootstrap was a policy set forth in the 1940s to industrialize Puerto Rico's economy, eliminating agricultural jobs with the unmet promise of

replacing them with manufacturing jobs. During this period of time, Puerto Rican migration from the island to the continental US soared.
17. Piri Thomas Papers, Box 1, Folder 1.
18. See Kandiyoti (*Migrant Sites*, 167) for her analysis of this comparison.
19. See Rudolph, *Embodying Latino Masculinities*.
20. Thomas does not offer many date markers in *Down These Mean Streets*, so pinning down when certain events occurred is difficult. According to *Seven Long Times*, Thomas is released from prison on parole in 1955 (the same year as the 1955 Comstock prison riot he does not participate in). So, as the reader, we can assume that *Down These Mean Streets* ends in 1956, since the court appearance that decides he will not serve more time occurs on November 28 of the same year he was released; Piri also details several months of actions after the court date. *Savior, Savior, Hold My Hand* covers the period after his release from prison (with the occasional prison flashback) to a few years past the birth of his son Ricky. For a more detailed attempt at trying to match Thomas's recollection to archival documents and specific time periods, see Luis, "Black Latinos Speak."
21. *Savior* was also intended to speak, in its fourth section, about his time in Puerto Rico working to implement a peer-support drug rehabilitation program (recovering addicts supporting other recovering addicts) and its attendant issues, as indicated in correspondence from an editor at Alfred A. Knopf on November 22, 1966. According to several of Thomas's bios, that program was called "La Nueva Raza." See Piri Thomas Papers, Box 3, Folder 14, and Box 1, Folder 1.
22. Interview by Diane Green and Bill Thompson in *Metrópoli: East Harlem Arts Review*, found in the Piri Thomas Papers, Box 1, Folder 2.
23. Thomas also discusses spiritual violence in the form of Christian racism, though that is beyond the scope of this chapter.
24. Michael Hames-García views Thomas's memoirs as "a theorization of imprisonment," and his argument, like mine, depends on Thomas's dependence on violence. He contends that Thomas's representation of the penal system disproves Foucault's argument that prisons moved away from physical violence to "noncorporal" modes of punishment. He writes, "Thomas suggests that bodily violence is a central disciplinary technique of the penal system" (Hames-García, *Fugitive Thought*, 148).
25. In fact, scholars sometimes characterize Thomas's exploration of AfroLatinidad in violent terms. For example, Lisa D. McGill writes that, in *Down These Mean Streets*, Thomas "battles with *multiple* communities," "battles with African America," "battles with a white American society," and "battles with the self" (McGill, "How to Be a Negro," 163).
26. Brown, *Gang Nation*, xiv.
27. Piri Thomas Papers, Box 3, Folder 10, 106.
28. While often called a Mexican dicho (proverb) and often used as a message of hope and empowerment among Latin American and Latinx activists, the origins of this quotation appear to be a 1978 couplet from the Greek poet Dinos Christianopoulos. The lines are "what didn't you do to bury me / but you forgot that I was a seed." See Boutopoulou, "On the Origins."
29. Indeed, many scholars in the field have categorized Thomas as an outlaw figure whose experiences in the street constitute a resistant archetype based

in hypermasculinity. Reid-Pharr argues that Thomas's world "is so consistently and insistently masculine and homosocial" (Reid-Pharr, "Tearing the Goat's Flesh," 356). Vázquez makes a similar claim about Piri as an "urban outlaw" and "black gangster" (Vázquez, *Triangulations*, 62–63). Luis also identifies Piri as "the quintessential outlaw" (Luis, "Black Latinos," 33).

30. Piri Thomas Papers, Box 3, Folder 11.
31. James Diego Vigil similarly analyzes youth violence and gang activity in chapters 4 and 5 of *The Projects: Gang and Non-Gang Families in East Los Angeles*.
32. Thomas, *Seven Long Times*, 175. Throughout *Down These Mean Streets*, Thomas uses italics to indicate Piri's thoughts. I maintain his use of italics when I quote these sections, so the reader should keep in mind that the emphasis is always Thomas's.
33. Tyner, *Space, Place, and Violence*, ix.
34. Guidotti-Hernández, *Unspeakable Violence*, 29.
35. Nguyen, "Remasculinization," 133.
36. Nguyen, 130.
37. Guidotti-Hernández, *Unspeakable Violence*, 7.
38. Das and Kleinman, "Introduction," 13.
39. Tyner, *Space, Place, and Violence*, ix.
40. Guidotti-Hernández, *Unspeakable Violence*, 7.
41. See Rosaldo, who argues that "whether or not [Latinos] belong in this country is always in question" (Rosaldo, "Cultural Citizenship," 31).
42. See Cruz-Malavé, "Antifoundational Foundational Fiction"; Irizarry, "Because Place Still Matters"; McGill, "How to Be a Negro"; Di Iorio Sandín, "Melancholic Allegorists"; and Sánchez, "La Malinche."
43. And, in his unpublished writings, how he navigated space and his identity in and with Puerto Rico, though less so with Cuba. I am currently working on an article about Thomas's unpublished writings on Puerto Rico based on papers in the Schomburg Center for Research in Black Culture.
44. Levins Morales, *Medicine Stories*, 104.
45. Alexander, *Pedagogies of Crossing*, 277.
46. One might connect Thomas's writing of a memoir significantly focused on boyhood to Gilmore and Marshall, *Witnessing Girlhood*.
47. Jill Toliver Richardson emphasizes the importance of "home" in AfroLatinx literature, and Thomas's work in particular. She argues that AfroLatina/o writers "employ three concepts of home" as a way to "challenge hegemonic discourse of the nation" (Richardson, *Afro-Latin@ Experience*, 13). Monica Brown makes a similar connection between home and nation in her chapter on Puerto Rican gang narratives, in what she calls "the concept of home(land)/nation" (Brown, *Gang Nation*, 1, 6).
48. Boyce Davies, *Black Women*, 115.
49. Boyce Davies, 126.
50. Alice Walker first used "colorism" to describe "prejudicial or preferential treatment of same-race people based solely on their color" (Walker, *In Search*, 290). For more on colorism in a Chicanx/Latinx context, see also Irizarry's *Chicana/o and Latina/o Fiction*, particularly chapter 3.
51. Luis, "Black Latinos," 33.

52. Quashie, *Sovereignty of Quiet*, 22.
53. Quashie, 131.
54. Thomas, *DTMS*, 18. "Morenito" (or "negrito," since the two terms are often used interchangeably) can be translated as "little black one" or "little dark one" and has two disparate uses in Latinx and Latin American families. The term designates the child with the darkest skin or most stereotypically African features and is used, controversially, both as a term of endearment and a means of expressing anti-Black sentiment.
55. Thomas, x.
56. Curly or kinky hair is often described as pelo malo (bad hair) in Latin American and Hispanophone Caribbean contexts. For a detailed examination of the place of hair in racialization, particularly in a Dominican and Dominican diaspora context, see Candelario, *Black behind the Ears*.
57. See Santiago-Díaz and Rodríguez, "Writing Race," on the connection between the Spanish language and discourses of race in *Down These Mean Streets*.
58. Thomas, *DTMS*, ix.
59. Thomas, ix.
60. See also Hames-García's commentary on the father-son relationship (Hames-García, *Fugitive Thought*, 144–145).
61. Thomas, *DTMS*, 3.
62. Thomas, 3–4.
63. Sánchez González, *Boricua Literature*, 108.
64. Cruz-Malavé, "Antifoundational Foundational Fiction," 10.
65. Thomas, *DTMS*, 22.
66. Piri Thomas Papers, Box 3, Folder 9.
67. Like Piri, Eduardo Bonilla-Silva notes that "very early in my life I noticed that I received less affection from my immediate and extended family than did my siblings" (Bonilla-Silva, "Reflections," 445).
68. At a panel at the 2019 Texas Book Festival, Angie Cruz said, "I feel quotations create a hierarchy between what is said and what is thought" (Cruz and Marlantes, "Born to Tell").
69. Thomas, *DTMS*, 22.
70. Thomas, 22.
71. For an analysis of a central example, Piri's relationship with Trina in *Down These Mean Streets*, see Mills, "Latinx Coming-of-Age Memoirs, 1961–2022."
72. This scene is also adapted in Piri Thomas's *Every Child Is Born a Poet* (2003, dir. Johnathon Robinson), a mixture of documentary and performance art created when Thomas was seventy-five years old.
73. Thomas, *DTMS*, 143.
74. Thomas, 144.
75. Cruz-Malavé, "Antifoundational Foundational Fiction," 13.
76. Thomas, *DTMS*, 142.
77. Thomas, 144.
78. See Omi and Winant, *Racial Formation*; as well as Bonilla-Silva, *Racism without Racists*.
79. Seen most prominently in current discourse that uses the racialist work of Charles Murray.

80. Thomas, *DTMS*, 146.
81. Thomas, 147.
82. McGill, "How to Be a Negro," 164.
83. Sánchez González, *Boricua Literature*, 107.
84. See Gates, *Signifying Monkey*. While Gates argues from a specifically US perspective, despite his intensive knowledge of Black diasporic figures from Juan Latino and the orishas of Afro-Caribbean and Afro-Brazilian worship, he does suggest in his introduction that signifyin' and Black vernacular can appear in similar ways in texts by those outside of the US Black community he constructs (people of African descent who were forcibly relocated through slavery).
85. Hong, *Minor Feelings*, 97.
86. Brown, *Die*, 30.
87. Brown, 31.
88. Thomas, *DTMS*, 121. Brew is a key character in *Down These Mean Streets* who is present in most of the important scenes (outside of the home) where Piri encounters differing ideas on race, identification, and belonging. However, Brew disappears from the story quite abruptly (he does not return to the Merchant Marines ship during one of their stops in the Deep South) and is never encountered again. In earlier drafts of *DTMS* and in drafts of *Savior*, one can see annotations in the margins wherein Thomas wonders what happened to the real-life Brew. See Piri Thomas Papers, Box 3, Folder 6, as well as Box 5, Folder 11.
89. Thomas, *DTMS*, 19.
90. Thomas, 121.
91. Thomas, 121.
92. Thomas, 121.
93. Thomas, 122.
94. Thomas, 123.
95. Thomas, 124.
96. Thomas, 124.
97. Irizarry, "Because Place Still Matters," 158.
98. Thomas, *DTMS*, 124.
99. Thomas, 126.
100. Sánchez, "*Shakin' Up*," 55.
101. Thomas, *DTMS*, 158.
102. Thomas, 159.
103. Thomas, 159.
104. Marta E. Sánchez writes that "Brew sometimes adopts the bravura of an angry black nationalist of the 1960s" (Sánchez, "*Shakin' Up*," 41), but it's more than bravura; Brew represents several prominent arguments within that ideology.
105. Thomas, *DTMS*, 159.
106. Thomas, 160.
107. Thomas, 160.
108. Thomas, 161.
109. For queer of color critiques of Thomas's memoir, see Cruz-Malavé, "'What a Tangled Web!'"; and Reid-Pharr, "Tearing the Goat's Flesh."
110. Thomas, *DTMS*, 163.

111. Thomas, 163.
112. Thomas, 163.
113. Thomas, 163.
114. In addition, Thomas also cut out more of Alayce's lines, in which she talks about language and dialect and its impact (or lack thereof) on experiencing anti-Black racism. Piri Thomas Papers, Box 3, Folder 6.
115. Thomas, *DTMS*, 162.
116. Thomas, 160.
117. Thomas, 161.
118. Sánchez, "*Shakin' Up*," 57.
119. Thomas, *DTMS*, 160.
120. Thomas, 160.
121. Thomas, 172, 173.
122. Thomas, 177. In earlier drafts, anti-gay slurs were hurled even more frequently at Gerald and were more explicitly linked to his failure as a Black man, as in this line in which a drunk Brew says, "'Ah hates prissy niggers'—'I hates prissy niggers' 'Thems the kin' tha is negros caus' they cant do bitchen thing bout' it'" (240, original spelling intact). See Piri Thomas Papers, Box 3, Folder 6.
123. Caminero-Santangelo, "'Puerto Rican Negro,'" 54.
124. Caminero-Santangelo, 54. Caminero-Santangelo similarly argues that Gerald uses academic discourse to work towards whiteness: "Gerald's understanding of race once again challenges dominant ideology in the form of the one-drop rule and its implicit reliance on the illusion of biological definitions of race; further, it opposes the concept of social construction, in which the dominant society holds the power to define race, with the possibility of self-definition" ("'Puerto Rican Negro,'" 64).
125. The parallels to Du Bois are clear. Du Bois spent time in Pennsylvania as a sociology research assistant, which led to his writing of *The Philadelphia Negro* (1899). He attended college at Fisk in Tennessee and Harvard, was a professor at Atlanta University, and wrote some of his most widely read works based on his time and research in the South, such as *The Souls of Black Folks* (1903) and *Black Reconstruction in America* (1935). See Lewis, *W. E. B. Du Bois*, and Alexander, *W. E. B. Du Bois*. Indeed, Du Bois is a foundational figure in the creation of the field of sociology, as argued in Morris, *Scholar Denied*.
126. Thomas, *DTMS*, 170.
127. Thomas, 171.
128. Thomas, 171.
129. Thomas, 171.
130. Thomas, 172.
131. Piri Thomas Papers, Box 1, Folder 2.
132. Thomas, *DTMS*, 170, 171.
133. Thomas, 174.
134. Gerald's discussion of genealogy (Thomas, *DTMS*, 173) in this chapter closely mirrors some of Raquel Cepeda's own problematic usage of genealogy in *Bird of Paradise*, discussed in the epilogue.
135. Thomas, *DTMS*, 177. Emphasis original.

136. Thomas, 177.
137. This is a play off the subtitle of Du Bois's *Dusk of Dawn: An Essay toward an Autobiography of a Race Concept* (1940).
138. See, for example, "Jesus Christ in Texas" in Du Bois's first autobiography, *Darkwater: Voices from within the Veil* (1920). Du Bois's other autobiographies were *Dusk of Dawn* and the posthumously released *The Autobiography of W. E. B. Du Bois: A Soliloquy on Viewing My Life from the Last Decade of Its First Century* (1968), which he began writing in 1958 (Huggins, *W. E. B. Du Bois*, 1304).

Chapter 4: Call-and-Response AfroLatinidad

1. For two important works focused on Puerto Rican women's writing, see Moreno, *Family Matters*; and Rivera, *Kissing the Mango Tree*.
2. Sheppard, "Black Women's Experience," 23. For another source that connects life writing and womanist theology, see Floyd-Thomas and Gillman, "'The Whole Story.'"
3. In this way, I subscribe to Lorgia García-Peña's definition of "hegemonic blackness" (*Translating Blackness*, 4).
4. See Callahan, *In the African-American Grain*, 16; and Gates, *Signifying Monkey*, 21. Gates does not use "call-and-response" as a term separate from "signifying." Connections are also made to "the dozens," discussed in chapter 3. For other earlier scholarship on the place of call and response in US Black literature, see Byerman, *Fingering the Jagged Grain*.
5. See for example, the analysis in the first three chapters of this monograph.
6. With the exception of Colón's "Carmencita" (discussed in chapter 2), religion and spirituality are either not discussed or viewed negatively, particularly by the AfroLatino writers of the twentieth century. However, many of the Afro-Latina and queer AfroLatinx writers of the last few decades have engaged religion and spirituality more thoughtfully.
7. For more work that explores how US definitions of Blackness have often been used to marginalize other definitions and experiences of Blackness in Latin America and the Caribbean, see Figueroa-Vásquez, *Decolonizing Diasporas*; and Masiki and Mills, "Post-soul Afro-Latinidades."
8. The essay was published in a 1978 issue of *Nuestro: The Magazine for Latinos*, which launched in 1977, billed as one of the first primarily English-language magazines for Latinos. Feature pieces had brief Spanish-language synopses, which may be why Casal's essay begins with this Spanish preface. See Magaña, "Marketing *Latinidad*," 28.
9. Nancy Mirabal further explores mestizaje in Cuba and what she terms "*diasporic blanqueamiento*" in the Cuban diaspora. Mirabal, *Suspect Freedoms*, 15.
10. Casal, "Memories," 61. Translation my own.
11. Casal, 61.
12. For a detailed history of Casal, her creative writing, and her sociological scholarship, see Lomas, "Casal, Lourdes"; Herrera, "Lourdes Casal," 274–275; and Lomas, "On the 'Shock' of Diaspora." See also all the articles in the 2018

special issue of *Cuban Studies* on Lourdes Casal. Lomas has also published a recent piece on Casal in the context of AfroLatinidad (Lomas, "Afro-Latina Disidentification").
13. Casal, "Memories," 62.
14. For a fantastic examination of the relationship between Afro-Cubans and African Americans in the first half of the twentieth century, see Guridy, *Forging Diaspora*.
15. Lomas, "Casal, Lourdes."
16. For an Afro-Cuban American man's memoir, see Grillo, *Black Cuban, Black American*.
17. See introduction for a longer examination of dominant mestizaje narratives.
18. Martínez-Echazábal, "Mestizaje," 23.
19. For example, while Theresa Delgadillo offers a nuanced reading of how the sonic and the sacred connect in Moreno Vega's *When the Spirits Dance Mambo*, her framing of the book through a lens of spiritual mestizaje runs the risk of vacating the Africanity of her life story (Delgadillo, "African, Latina, Feminist, and Decolonial"). Critics who have labeled santería and other African religions "syncretic," such as the early Western santería scholar Melville J. Herskovits and community health scholar George Brandon, argue that the religions are comprised of the teaching and rituals of two different belief systems (Herskovits, "African Gods"; and Brandon, *Santeria from Africa to the New World*). Moreno Vega, however, sees the adoption of Catholic saints and practices into Lucumi as a strategic move. For more on the debates occurring in Moreno Vega's time on syncretism, see Apter, "Herskovits's Heritage."
20. Heredia, "Afro-Latina Lives Matter."
21. Moreno Vega discusses this transnational work in Moreno Vega, *Altar of My Soul*.
22. Moreno Vega, 4.
23. I use "Lucumi," "Regla de Ocha," and "santería" interchangeably since these are the terms used by Moreno Vega and Casal and are common names for African diasporic orisha worship in Cuba and Puerto Rico. While "santería" is viewed by some scholars and practitioners as a pejorative term for religions of orisha worship, Mary Ann Clark indicates that the term was actually meant to replace the earlier pejorative, *brujería* (witchcraft). Thus, I continue to use the term, which is better recognized by the average reader, in rotation with the others listed above. In addition, I will occasionally use "the religion," which is often used in discussions with noninitiates, reflecting the fact that devotees have historically felt compelled to keep their religion secret due to racial animus and societal discrimination. Clark, *Santería*, 3. Moreno Vega at times spells Lucumi with a "k," and in those cases, I maintain her spelling.
24. Moreno Vega, *Altar*.
25. The first half of the title corresponds with Moreno Vega's documentary, which examines the history of Yoruba-based religions and their travels from West Africa to Cuba. Moreno Vega and Shepard, *Cuando los espíritus bailan mambo*.
26. In *Altar*, I refer to the protagonist as Marta. In *When the Spirits Dance Mambo*, I refer to the protagonist as Marta, Cotito, or Coty, the latter two being her childhood nicknames.

27. Similarly, Theresa Delgadillo argues, "Her memoir reveals a unique form of Latina feminisms that emerges from the experiences of AfroLatinas" (Delgadillo, "African, Latina, Feminist, and Decolonial," 158).
28. Cabral, *Unity and Struggle*, 143. Emphasis original.
29. According to the Young Lords, cultural nationalists' "sole purpose in life is to revive the culture of the Puerto Rican nation and keep it alive, . . . but that pride alone is not gonna free us" (YLP, *Palante*, 62).
30. Moreno Vega and Shepard, *Cuando*, 33:05.
31. Moreno Vega, *Altar*, 111.
32. Latina Feminist Group, *Telling to Live*, 1.
33. While Moreno Vega's work is not discussed in *Family Matters*, Marisel C. Moreno provides substantial commentary on the idea of "la gran familia" and domesticity.
34. Levins Morales, *Medicine Stories*, 120.
35. Clark, *Where Men Are Wives*, 119.
36. Moreno Vega, "Yoruba Philosophy," 171.
37. The names of African diasporic orishas are spelled in a variety of ways. I use the spellings that Moreno Vega provides in her memoirs, though the spellings between *Altar* and *When the Spirits* sometimes differ.
38. Moreno Vega, 210–211.
39. Moreno Vega, 216–217.
40. Moreno Vega, *Altar*, 131; Moreno Vega, "Yoruba Philosophy," 210–211.
41. Moreno Vega, "Yoruba Philosophy," 169.
42. Moreno Vega, *Altar*, 218.
43. Levins Morales, *Medicine Stories*, 71.
44. Levins Morales, 74, 77–78.
45. Levins Morales, 73.
46. Moreno Vega, *Altar*, 12.
47. For this approach, see Valdés, *Oshun's Daughters*. She examines the use of Oshun, often considered the pinnacle of femininity, in US, Caribbean, and South American women's literature.
48. Moreno Vega, *Altar*, 12.
49. Moreno Vega, *Altar*, 23.
50. Moreno Vega, 23.
51. Moreno Vega, 23.
52. Moreno Vega, 23.
53. See, for example, Kelley, "Foreword," xix. He writes about the tension between Gilroy's conception of Blackness as a product of modernity versus Cedric Robinson's belief that since Black people in the Americas were African first, that worldview shaped transatlantic Blackness.
54. For example, a santera named Chela shares a pataki about a feud between Orula (a male orisha) and Yemayá (a female orisha) regarding the ability to divine. Olodumare creates a compromise in which each orisha has its own realm of divination, in effect preventing Yemayá from practicing all the forms of divination that she knows. Moreno Vega interprets the parable as proof that Lucumi does not "replicate the machismo common in the Latino community" (Moreno Vega, *Altar*, 155). However, a compromise that tells a feminine being

she is not allowed to act within the realm of a masculine one seems to focus on maintaining a man's fragile ego. In fact, Chela casts the story as one in which Yemayá continues to hold the power to divine through all forms but perhaps uses it secretly or subtly, a lesson that is similar to the one we teach women about their ability to influence men covertly, with their sexuality or trickery, so as not to reveal who is really in power. This parable is told in Moreno Vega, *Altar*, 153–155. In addition, the pataki that begins chapter 7 of *The Altar of My Soul* begins with the rape of a female orisha by her son. There is no commentary about the fact that orisha are capable of the kind of gender-based violence perpetrated in the human realm. Moreno Vega, *Altar*, 127.

55. Moreno Vega, *Altar*, 89.
56. Moreno Vega, 89.
57. Knowles-Carter and Kahil, *Lemonade*. For recent scholarly work on Beyoncé's *Lemonade*, see Benbow, "Lemonade Syllabus"; Maner, "'Where Do You Go'"; Tinsley, *Beyoncé in Formation*; and Brooks and Martin, eds., *Lemonade Reader*.
58. Moreno Vega, *Altar*, 89.
59. Moreno Vega, 89.
60. Moreno Vega's invocation of Ochun as the perennial fighter for women and children recurs in *When the Spirits Dance Mambo*, when Alma, a woman in an abusive relationship, acts as a medium for Ochun in a botánica, a shop that sells herbs and plants used in spiritual rituals and for health. Ochun demands that Alma leave her philandering husband for her own sake and for her children (Moreno Vega, *When the Spirits*, 54). Moreno Vega's characterization of Ochun in both memoirs focuses on her rejection of patriarchal structures of male control and on feminine agency.
61. Moreno Vega says that Olodumare, the creator, is both male and female in its primary form. Moreno Vega, *Altar*, 268. For some initiates, having their head claimed by an orisha whose gender does not match their own causes them to struggle with feelings about their gender and sexuality, often revealing homophobic and sexist sentiment. See Carr, *A Year in White*, 153–155.
62. Hames-García, *Identity Complex*.
63. Moreno Vega, *Altar*, 268.
64. Similar to Anzaldúa's description of her own autohistoria as mosaic. Anzaldúa, *Borderlands / La Frontera*, 134.
65. Moreno Vega, *Altar*, 184–185.
66. Cherríe Moraga and Gloria Anzaldúa, "Entering the Lives of Others," 19.
67. Based on a Yoruba proverb, Hunsu positions the Oloto as a woman who is "still part of the community but an autonomous entity with a mind of her own and someone who selectively aligns with collective traditions and values" (Hunsu, "Engendering," 175).
68. Moreno Vega, *Altar*, 113.
69. Fernández Olmos and Paravisini-Gebert, *Creole Religions*, 204.
70. Fernández Olmos and Paravisini-Gebert, *Creole Religions*, 69–70, 207.
71. Alexander, *Pedagogies of Crossing*, 307.
72. Indeed, Moreno Vega suggests that her mother's visitation is the reason for *When the Spirits Dance Mambo*, since it "forc[ed] her to recall [her] childhood encounters with spirits" (Moreno Vega, *Altar*, 111).

73. Clark, *Santería*, 85–86. The term "gypsy" is considered a slur for Roma people; my use reflects practitioners' use, much like the use of other problematic terms like "morenito" or "negrito." It appears that "gypsy" is invoked to represent the wandering and diasporic nature of santería.
74. Moreno Vega, *Altar*, 84.
75. Moreno Vega and Shepard, *Cuando*, 24:20.
76. Moreno Vega, *When the Spirits*, 190.
77. Moreno Vega, 53.
78. Clark, *Where Men Are Wives*, 145.
79. Otero, *Archives of Conjure*, 9. M. Jacqui Alexander similarly calls to the power of the dead to speak through the bodies of Afro-diasporic religious practitioners as vessels to tell untold and silenced stories (Alexander, *Pedagogies of Crossing*).
80. Figueroa, "Your Lips," 4. Figueroa draws her own work from Barbara Smith's reflections on the work she did with Kitchen Table Press (Smith, "Press of Our Own").
81. Moreno Vega, *When the Spirits*, 21. Refer to my discussion of colorism in chapter 3. While Thomas demonstrates the reality of light-skinned privilege in his US-based family, Moreno Vega shows that colorism is a transnational experience.
82. Moreno Vega, 22.
83. Moreno Vega, 22.
84. The kind of secret that elicits tacit acceptance may connect to a family's reaction to perceived queerness. See Decena, *Tacit Subjects*.
85. Moreno Vega, *When the Spirits*, 37. Juanita Heredia reads the "dual forms of appellation" as a representation of a "bicultural identity" (Heredia, "Marta Moreno Vega's," 68).
86. Moreno Vega, *When the Spirits*, 37.
87. Moreno Vega, 131.
88. Moreno Vega, 131.
89. Moreno Vega, 132.
90. Moreno Vega, 131.
91. Heredia reads the aftermath of Chachita's lie, the beating and her forced marriage to Joe, as less about losing her status as a woman worth protecting and more defined by the culture of "el qué dirán / what will others say" but also suggests that the parents see Chachita as "a *traitor* to the family" due to her independence-seeking and her awareness about the fraternization between Black and Puerto Rican residents. Heredia, "Marta Moreno Vega's," 72.
92. Moreno Vega, *When the Spirits*, 150.
93. Moreno Vega, 153.
94. Moreno Vega, 160–161.
95. Clark, *Where Men Are Wives*, 116–119.
96. Moreno Vega, *When the Spirits*, 2.
97. Heredia also examines the relationship between "an alternative non-Western religion *and* popular music in the representation of an AfroLatina identity" (Heredia, "Marta Moreno Vega's," 63). Heredia argues that the influence of Abuela Luisa's spiritual practices and musical tastes pave the way for Cotito to "[mature] into a confident young woman of color or AfroLatina in the United States" (Heredia, "Marta Moreno Vega's," 65).
98. Heredia, 76.
99. Moreno Vega, "Yoruba Orisha Tradition," 246.

100. Moreno Vega, 246.
101. Moreno Vega, 247.
102. Recent scholarship comments on the connection and collaboration among US Black and Afro-Caribbean musicians. See Moreno Vega, "Yoruba Orisha Tradition"; Abreu, *Rhythms of Race*; Heredia, "Latin Jazz"; Diouf and Nwankwo, *Rhythms*; and García, "'We Both Speak African,'" for more on AfroLatinx influences on the Harlem music scene in the 1940s and fifties.
103. Moreno Vega, *When the Spirits*, 1.
104. Moreno Vega, 75.
105. Casal, "Memories," 62.
106. Casal, 62.
107. Moreno Vega, *When the Spirits*, 2.
108. Moreno Vega, 25.
109. Moreno Vega, 2.
110. Heredia, "Marta Moreno Vega's," 74, 75.
111. Moreno Vega, *When the Spirits*, 2.
112. Clark, *Santería*, 89.
113. Moreno Vega, 190, 193, 262–263.
114. Moreno Vega, 8.
115. Moreno Vega, 2.
116. Moreno Vega, 11.
117. Moreno Vega, *Altar*, 75.
118. Moreno Vega, *When the Spirits*, 246.
119. Moreno Vega, 247.
120. Moreno Vega, 247.
121. Moreno Vega, 241, 242.
122. Moreno Vega, 243.
123. Moreno Vega, 242.
124. While the Africanity of these Latin beats is heavily emphasized, Moreno Vega does, at one point, project a certain image of racial harmony reached through this spiritual-musical experience, asserting that "the spirit of mambo" brings people of all races together. Moreno Vega, *When the Spirits*, 244.
125. Moreno Vega, 241–243.
126. Moreno Vega, *Altar*, 75; *When the Spirits*, 241, 242, 244.
127. Moreno Vega, *When the Spirits*, 241.
128. Moreno Vega, *Altar*, 75
129. Moreno Vega, *When the Spirits*, 245–246.
130. Copeland, *Enfleshing Freedom*, 56.
131. Sale, "Call and Response."

Chapter 5: Queer AfroLatinidades

1. Díaz, "'Either Hyper-visible or Invisible.'"
2. Díaz, "You Do Not Belong Here."
3. Christina Elizabeth Sharpe, *Monstrous Intimacies*, 11. Barbara Creed similarly points to the creation of the Black mother as excess fertility in the genre of horror films: Barbara Creed, *Monstrous-Feminine*.

4. See, for example, Mogul, Ritchie, and Whitlock, *Queer (In)justice*. This history has cycled back to become today's news, as book bans against LGBTQ representation, anti-drag legislation, and anti-trans healthcare occur not only in Texas but in many Republican-led state legislatures.
5. Viet Thanh Nguyen, "Just Memory," 18–19.
6. Without claiming to do so, Arnaldo Cruz-Malavé's discussion of queerness in Thomas's *Down These Mean Streets* is very much aligned with monster theory: Cruz-Malavé, "'What a Tangled Web!'"
7. Leigh Gilmore and Elizabeth Marshall, *Witnessing Girlhood*, 10.
8. "Never does one open the discussion by coming right to the heart of the matter. For the heart of the matter is always somewhere else than where it is supposed to be. To allow it to emerge, people approach it indirectly by postponing until it matures, by letting it come when it is ready to come. There is no catching, no pushing, no directing, no breaking through, no need for a linear progression which gives the comforting illusion that one knows where one goes" (Minh-ha, *Woman, Native, Other*, 10). Pages indicate the epub version.
9. hooks et al., "Are You Still a Slave?", 1:55:32.
10. Rodríguez, "Divas, Atrevidas, y Entendidas," 5.
11. Rodríguez, 6. E. Patrick E. Johnson and Ramon H. Rivera-Servera similarly see this theme in Blacktino queer performance, "One of the many themes that emerges across several of these works [. . .] is the disavowal of sexuality as an identity" ("Introduction," 12).
12. For Lorde, embracing the mosaic of the self allows her to act powerfully in service to others through politics and writing ("Age, Race, Class, Sex," 120–121). For Gomez, her sexuality is inseparable from her politics, actions, and desires for the future. She compares the moment in which "theory converged with my reality" to a famous cinematic scene: "Being a Black woman and a lesbian blended unexpectedly for me like that famous scene in Ingmar Bergman's *Persona*. The different faces came together as one, and my desire became part of my heritage, my skin, my perspective, my politics, and my future" (*Forty-Three Septembers*, 12).
13. Muñoz, *Disidentifications*, 7.
14. Muñoz, 19.
15. Muñoz, 11.
16. Muñoz, 31.
17. As Jillian Hernández puts it, "thus, I am not suggesting that aesthetics of excess always presents a liberatory visibility, but that perhaps it could be understood as a dangerous practice of freedom (Pierce 2017). This practice rejects the aesthetics of respectability and instead 'bedazzles the scars' of racialized gendered subjectivity and relations between Black and Latina women and girls (Wallace 2018)" (Hernández, *Aesthetics of Excess*, 54).
18. Rodríguez, *Sexual Futures*, 2. Consider also E. Patrick Johnson and Ramón H. Rivera-Servera's concept of the "blacktino": "queer subjects who configure their identities as both black and brown; queer social exchanges, intimacies, and conflicts between African Americans and Latinas/os; and the historical and contemporary relationships between black and Latina/o queer communities with heteronormative whiteness" (Johnson and Rivera-Servera, "Introduction," 5).

19. She writes, "to present aesthetic excess is to make oneself hypervisible, but not necessarily in an effort to gain legibility or legitimacy" (Hernández, *Aesthetics of Excess*, 11).
20. While I am unaware of a Latina/x girlhood studies tradition, recent Latinx children's and young adult literature scholars as well as Latin Americanist Mary Pat Brady have taken seriously the symbol of the Latinx child. See Jiménez García, *Side by Side*; Rodríguez, "Conocimiento Narratives"; Mills, "Playing at Power and Powerlessness"; and Brady, *Scales of Captivity*. Black girlhood studies has added substantially to the ways scholars think about visibility, innocence and its racialization, and the child as a political and rhetorical object; thus, I draw from this scholarship in my analysis. See Lewis, "Black Girlhood"; Bernstein, *Racial Innocence*; and Wright, *Black Girlhood in the Nineteenth Century*.
21. Hong, *Minor Feelings*, 45.
22. For an accessible and slightly longer definition of trauma porn, see Brittany J., "What Trauma Porn Is."
23. Cohen, "Monster Culture (Seven Theses)," 13.
24. Díaz, "Visible."
25. Hong, *Minor Feelings*, 55 (emphasis mine). To me, "minor feelings" are similar to Hartman's "minor lives," a concept grounded in the early twentieth century, "a placeholder for all the possibilities and the dangers awaiting young black women in the first decades of the twentieth century" (Hartman, *Wayward Lives*, 15–16).
26. Hong, *Minor Feelings*, 56.
27. Gloria Anzaldúa similarly elicits waywardness in her autohistoria-teoría, "La Prieta" (201).
28. In a parenthetical statement, Hartman articulates the relationship of Black visibility and US surveillance policy: "To be visible was to be targeted for uplift or punishment, confinement or violence" (Hartman, *Wayward Lives*, 21).
29. Hartman, 227.
30. Hartman, 348–349.
31. Godreau, *Scripts of Blackness*, 17.
32. "*Mano Dura* thus depicted *caseríos* as sites of abjection, the loci of an urban blackness defined by various 'immoral' characteristics that differentiated them from the presumably more 'respectable' Puerto Rico, all while ignoring the larger structural policies that produced the adverse conditions affecting *caserío* residents" (Rivera-Rideau, *Remixing Reggaeton*, 10–11).
33. Díaz, *Ordinary Girls*, 20–21.
34. Díaz, 12–13.
35. Díaz, 6. Interestingly, both characters reflect two important characteristics of Mami: her broad embrace of a strong female sexuality (Marilyn Monroe) and her addiction to drugs (Elvira Hancock in *Scarface*).
36. Díaz, 5.
37. Díaz, 49.
38. Díaz, 45.
39. Sharpe, *Monstrous Intimacies*, 3.
40. As Ruth Nicole Brown observes, "Black girls living in their bodies know the all-too-familiar expectations of premature and slow death, as they are often

41. Perez, *There Was a Woman*, 9.
42. Perez, 28, 62–65.
43. Perez, 2. For additional discussion of the use of folklore by Latinx writers, see Cotera, "Latino/a Literature and the Uses of Folklore."
44. Perez, 23.
45. Cohen, "Monster Culture (Seven Theses)," 13.
46. Cohen, 18.
47. Díaz, *Ordinary Girls*, 85.
48. Díaz, 85.
49. Jackson, *Becoming Human*; for a brief discussion of monstrosity as hybridization, see Weinstock, *Monster Theory Reader*, 8–11.
50. Díaz, *Ordinary Girls*, 85.
51. Díaz, 86.
52. Cohen, "Monster Culture," 16.
53. Díaz, *Ordinary Girls*, 95–96.
54. See Perez, *There Was a Woman*.
55. Díaz, *Ordinary Girls*, 96.
56. Perez, *There Was a Woman*, 76.
57. As Avery Gordon argues, haunting is "when the people who are meant to be invisible show up without any sign of leaving" (Gordon, *Ghostly Matters*, xvi).
58. Gordon, xvi.
59. Díaz, *Ordinary Girls*, 70–79.
60. Díaz, 74.
61. Díaz, 85.
62. Díaz, 74.
63. Both Mami and Jaqui are continually drawn to water and beaches in *Ordinary Girls*. For just a few of many examples, see Díaz, *Ordinary Girls*, 219, 267, 285, 287.
64. Perez, *There Was a Woman*, 46.
65. Díaz, *Ordinary Girls*, 76.
66. Jaquira Díaz published an article about the case for *Rolling Stone* and also corresponded with Cardona, as she describes in the memoir. Díaz, "Inside Brutal Baby Lollipops Murder Case."
67. Perez, *There Was a Woman*, 45.
68. Hernández, *Aesthetics of Excess*, 44.
69. Díaz directly mentions Cardona's AfroLatinx identity in her *Kenyon Review* piece: "What no one is talking about, what not one person has dared to say—not even the mother [Ana Cardona] herself—is that the woman who was sentenced to death is Afro-Latina. No one involved with this case has talked about sentencing disparity in Miami, or about the criminalization of Afro-Latinxs in a city with a deep and painful history of segregation" (Díaz, "You Do Not Belong Here").
70. Díaz, *Ordinary Girls*, 283.
71. As Cohen writes, "We distrust and loathe the monster at the same time we envy its freedom" (Cohen, "Monster Culture," 17).

72. Díaz, *Ordinary Girls*, 94.
73. Díaz, 79.
74. An example: Díaz implies that her brother's violence towards her aunt Tanisha led to Tanisha's suicide attempt. Díaz refuses to allow men to marginalize their role in a story when it is convenient (87–88).
75. Díaz, 82.
76. Perez, *There Was a Woman*, 28.
77. Díaz, *Ordinary Girls*, 25.
78. Díaz, 70.
79. Díaz, 26.
80. Cardona received the death sentence, while González served jail time and, in fact, was released after seventeen years. Díaz, "Inside Brutal Baby Lollipops Murder Case."
81. Díaz, *Ordinary Girls*, 79, 80.
82. See Chesney-Lind and Eliason, "From Invisible to Incorrigible."
83. Díaz, *Ordinary Girls*, 96.
84. Díaz, 229–231.
85. Cohen, "Monster Culture," 6.
86. As Cohen asserts, "monstrous difference tends to be cultural, political, racial, economic, sexual" (Cohen, "Monster Culture," 7).
87. Jackson, *Becoming Human*, 11.
88. While few Latin American nations were successful in this drive for white European immigration, Argentina is an example of what that "success" looked like.
89. Díaz, *Ordinary Girls*, 94, 256.
90. Díaz, 58.
91. Currently, Jaquira Díaz is married to Lars Horn, a transmaculine writer.
92. Díaz, *Ordinary Girls*, 280.
93. Hernández, *Aesthetics of Excess*, 6, 63–64. Compare also to Muñoz's concept of chusmería, which Deborah Vargas succinctly describes as behavior that refuses to accept that "Latinos should not be too black, too poor, or too sexual, among other characteristics that exceed normativity" (Vargas, "Ruminations on *Lo Sucio*," 715). Vargas is paraphrasing Muñoz's definition (Muñoz, *Disidentifications*, 182).
94. Hernández, *Aesthetics of Excess*, 17.
95. Díaz, *Ordinary Girls*, 1.
96. Díaz, 2.
97. Díaz, 1.
98. hooks, "Choosing the Margin," 20.
99. In fact, we might consider *Ordinary Girls* as part of what Jackson identifies as an Afro-diasporic tradition that "frequently alters the meaning and significance of being (human) and engages in imaginative practices of worlding from the perspective of a history of blackness's bestialization and thingification" (Jackson, *Becoming Human*, 1).
100. Díaz, *Ordinary Girls*, 313.
101. Gordon, *Ghostly Matters*, 22.
102. This title itself seems to converse with the poetry collection by Joshua Bennett, *Owed* (2020).

103. Brown, *We Are Owed.*, 98. This author bio has been consistent for the last several years.
104. See, for example, Brown, "For the Black Kids," in *Sana Sana*, 34–36; and Ariana Brown (@arianathepoet), "Most of My Poems Are Not Actually about Latinidad...," Twitter, March 5, 2021, https://twitter.com/arianathepoet/status/1367986638278832131?s=03. While this original quote is no longer available, the prologue to a recent interview with Brown provides another tweet with a similar message: "I get invited to do a lot of shows in Latinx student orgs/cultural centers, etc. ppl [people] often seem surprised when I show up and talk about Blackness. This is fine: I will not participate in Mexican hegemony, nation-building, and the anti-Black legacy of chicanismo & mestizaje" (Brown, "Gathering What Is Left,'" 86).
105. If you followed the April 2021 posts in the "Society for the Study of Gloria Anzaldúa" Facebook group, you know about this.
106. Brown, *We Are Owed.*, 13.
107. See Jackson, "Verse Biography"; and Anna Jackson, Helen Rickerby, and Angelina Sbroma, eds., *Truth and Beauty: Verse Biography in Canada, Australia and New Zealand*. Wellington, NZ: Victoria University Press, 2014.
108. Jackson, "Verse Biography," vii.
109. Oswald, "Into the Woods."
110. In *Minor Feelings*, Cathy Park Hong argues that while poets will claim that they have no audience or they can rise above their corporeal selves, this assertion is untrue, especially for an Asian American poet or, I would argue, most writers of color, who are constantly being reminded of their bodies. Hong, *Minor Feelings*, 41–42.
111. Brown, *We Are Owed.*, 90.
112. Brown, 90.
113. Lorde, "Age, Race, Class, and Sex," 116.
114. Rankine, *Just Us*. See for example, her discussion of the history of using white walls in art exhibits (178).
115. Here I refer to Trouillot, *Silencing the Past*, xxiii.
116. The quote is from the end of "Coretta King Revisited" in Walker's foundational womanist text, *In Search of Our Mothers' Gardens* (129).
117. Brown, *We Are Owed.*, 16–21.
118. Compare Brown's use of space in *We Are Owed.*, in which white space takes up at least as much space as text, to the text-filled appearance of her previous verse memoir, *Sana Sana*.
119. Hong, *Minor Feelings*, 196–197. Hong is evoking Louise Glück in this quotation.
120. Hartman, "Venus in Two Acts," 11.
121. Pelaez López, "Foreword," 9. For more history of Gaspar Yanga and the town of Yanga, see Rowell, "'El Primer Libertador.'" The entire winter 2008 bilingual issue of *Callaloo* is devoted to Gaspar Yanga and the town of Yanga's history.
122. Brown, *We Are Owed.* The arc of Yanga poems spans pages 62–75.
123. Brown, 64.
124. Brown, 65.
125. Brown, 66.

126. Brown, 66.
127. Brown, 66.
128. Brown, 67.
129. Brown, 67.
130. Brown, 67.
131. For an examination of whiteness and racialization at the US-Mexican border, see Bebout, *Whiteness on the Border.*
132. Brown, 70.
133. Brown, 73. I have attempted to keep her spacing intact.
134. Brown, 74.
135. Brown, 74.
136. Brown, 21. This line is a variation of the second line from the first poem, "At the End of the Borderlands": "countries are killing everyone I love" (Brown, 13).
137. Brown, 75.
138. Pelaez López, "Foreword," 7.
139. On "El Nié," García-Peña writes: "the specificity of Dominican alterity allegorized through Báez's El Nié—which also means, in its most vulgar sense, the 'taint'—queers both the hegemonic narrative of the nation-state(s) and the very location of in-betweenness inhabited by Anzaldúa, [Gustavo] Pérez Firmat and [Luis Rafael] Sánchez. [. . .] El Nié signifies not the border space that the subject inhabits—Anzaldúa's barbwire—but rather the body that carries the violent borders" (García-Peña, *The Borders of Dominicanidad*, 4).
140. Báez, "El Nié."
141. Báez.
142. These authors are discussed in chapter 4 and the epilogue.
143. The earlier version is the ending poem of the chapbook, entitled "epilogue: myself, first": Ariana Brown, *Messy Girl*. The *Sana Sana* version is nearly identical, though with numerous punctuation changes (mostly for words that act as adjectives) and a handful of substantive changes.
144. She also discusses her choice to publish *Messy Girl* in a 2017 interview in *Remezcla* (Reichard, "Ariana Brown").
145. Brown, *Messy Girl.*
146. Brown, *Sana Sana*, 28.
147. Brown, 28.
148. Brown, *Hear Our Truths*, 50.
149. Another important set of poems in *We Are Owed.* for AfroLatinx studies scholars to examine would be the arc on the game of lotería, which dissects the anti-Blackness of specific cards.
150. The many states rolling back gay, lesbian, queer, and trans rights over the last few years make these texts especially important today.

Epilogue

1. For an overview of the revival of biological approaches to "race," see Brubaker, "Return to Biology." See critiques of this return to racialist science in Roberts, *Fatal Invention*; and Tallbear, *Native American DNA*. For a more sanguine view

of ancestry tests, see Nelson, *Social Life of DNA*. C. Christina Lam, for example, takes a more positive approach to Cepeda's use of DNA in *Bird of Paradise* by calling to Nelson. Lam, "Bearing Witness," 30.

2. Indeed, I think this is a good example of what Omaris Zamora has cautioned: "when thinking about negro (Black) and negritud (Blackness) from a transnational Spanish Caribbean context, we should remember that AfroLatinidad, or Black Latinidad, is first and foremost about Black lives, embodied experiences, movement, translatability, and untranslatability. [. . .] What is at stake when we do not do this? We run the risk of reinscribing mestizaje and White supremacy" (Zamora, "Transnational Renderings," 94). Nelly Rosario believes Vasconcelos would see the current treatment of Latino DNA as a gold mine to vindicate his concept of the cosmic race (Rosario, "DNA+Latinx," 104).
3. Karen E. Fields uses the term first in "Witchcraft and Racecraft." Palmié adopts the term in the context of DNA ancestry tests in a 2007 forum of *American Ethnologist* on "Genomics and Racialization."
4. Palmié, "Genomics," 206.
5. Palmié, 207.
6. Palmié, 207.
7. Nelson, *Social Life*; and Roth and Lyon, "Genetic Ancestry Tests and Race."
8. Said, *Orientalism*.
9. Cepeda writes, "It's complicated, though, which roots—African, Indigenous, European, Arabic, and more—we choose to sow. A few days ago I met a young man of obvious mixed ancestry here in the colonial zone. He gushed that his Y-DNA test confirmed his direct paternal ancestors were English. Admittedly, he probably didn't realize how giddy he came across, exalting the European fragments of his self" (Cepeda, *Bird*, 234).
10. One example of a reading that celebrates this narrative as a mestizaje narrative is by Luisa María González Rodríguez, who concludes that Cepeda's DNA journey leads her to "a more comprehensive mestizo, transnational consciousness" (González Rodríguez, "Digging through the Past," 62).
11. For example, Cepeda's Family Tree DNA test results claim ancestry in the country of Guinea-Bissau, a very small country in Africa, and surprisingly and suspiciously specific for genomic tests (Cepeda, *Bird*, 191).
12. Roberts, *Fatal Invention*.
13. Tallbear, *Native American DNA*, 6; An example of this troubling view can be seen in Cepeda, *Bird*, xvi-xvii.
14. Cepeda, *Bird*, 221.
15. Cepeda, *Some Girls*, 24:55. For a foundational discussion of Dominicanidad and its relationship to representations of Indigeneity and Blackness, see Candelario, *Black Behind the Ears*.
16. Said, *Orientalism*, 3.
17. Cepeda, *Bird*, 4.
18. Cepeda also has a strange discussion about mistaking her half-sister for a Chinese boy, while emphasizing her mother Rocío's "Asiatic eyes" (Cepeda, *Bird*, 197).
19. In a 2019 personal interview conducted by C. Christina Lam, Cepeda indicates that she did not receive any money for including the coupon. Quoted in Lam, "Bearing Witness," 30–31.

20. Tallbear, *Native American DNA*; and Palmié, "Genomics." In fact, DNA ancestry tests seem to be more popular and given more weight in the US than in other countries. See Abel, "Of African Descent?".
21. Strand and Källén, "I Am a Viking!", 17.
22. Cepeda, *Bird*, 196.
23. Cepeda, *Bird*, "Author's Note." Cepeda's work would be ripe for analysis through the lens of Dominican Black studies. See Chetty and Rodríguez, "Introduction"; and Torres-Saillant, "Introduction to Dominican Blackness."
24. In this section of her brief memoir, Casal writes of the connection she feels between Lagos and Cuba based on the selling of "oleles" (black-eyed pea cakes) and the Yoruba words she hears that have influenced Cuban Spanish. Casal, "Memories," 62.
25. Cepeda, *Bird*, 180.
26. Cepeda, 183. For further discussion of Cepeda's constuction of Dominicanidad in relation to hip-hop, see Maillo-Pozo, "Reconstructing Dominican Latinidad."
27. Cepeda, 157.
28. Cepeda, 156.
29. Cepeda, 269.
30. Cepeda, xiii.
31. Cepeda's documentary, *Some Girls*, supplements *Bird of Paradise* with its premise that if genetic ancestry tests can provide Cepeda with peace about her identity and heal her relationship with her father, then it can do the same for other Dominican women and girls. The documentary touts ancestry tests as a possible solution to an underdiscussed societal issue: Latina girls' high rates of suicidality. In *Some Girls*, Cepeda partners with the nonprofit organization Life Is Precious (LIP), a suicide prevention program aimed at Latina girls. She suggests that if the girls at LIP can ground themselves and get to know their roots, they will find strength and purpose in life. The results are far more ambivalent than in *Bird of Paradise*, and the documentary's treatment of Blackness and Indigeneity in the Dominican Republic (when the girls travel there with Cepeda) are certainly worth further analysis. Cepeda, *Some Girls*.
32. See Roberts, *Fatal Invention*.
33. Lipsitz, *Possessive Investment in Whiteness*.
34. Cepeda, *Bird*, 255.
35. Cepeda, 204.
36. Cepeda, 240.
37. There are numerous similarities to be drawn between *Bird of Paradise* and Junot Díaz's *The Brief, Wondrous Life of Oscar Wao* (2008). Both have substantial focus on a family fukú (generational curse) and both depict a lot of violence, especially patriarchal violence (like Piri Thomas's and Jaquira Díaz's memoirs). Research on these similarities would be welcome.
38. Rosario, "DNA+Latinx," 112.
39. See Flores, "'Latinidad is Cancelled,'" for a short analysis of the Valdés exhibit (78–79).
40. Latina Feminist Group, *Telling to Live*, 13.
41. Pero Like, *Afro Latinos*, 0:57.
42. Latina Feminist Group, *Telling to Live*, 25.

Bibliography

Abel, Sarah. "Of African Descent? Blackness and the Concept of Origins in Cultural Perspective." *Genealogy* 2, no. 11 (2018). https://doi.org/10.3390/genealogy2010011.

Abreu, Christina. *Rhythms of Race: Cuban Musicians and the Making of Cuban New York City and Miami, 1940–1960*, Chapel Hill: University of North Carolina Press, 2015.

Acosta-Belen, Edna. "Introduction: Unveiling and Preserving a Puerto Rican Historical Memory." In *Through the Eyes of Rebel Women: The Young Lords: 1969–1976*, edited by Iris Morales, 1–11. New York: Red Sugarcane Press, 2016.

Acosta-Belén, Edna. "Notes on the Evolution of the Puerto Rican Novel." *Latin American Literary Review* 8, no. 16 (Spring 1980): 183–195.

Acosta-Belén, Edna, and Virginia Sánchez Korrol. "The World of Jesús Colón." In *The Way It Was, and Other Writings: Historical Vignettes about the New York Puerto Rican Community*, edited by Edna Acosta-Belen and Virginia Sánchez Korrol. Houston, TX: Arte Público Press, 1993.

Acosta-Belén, Edna, and Carlos E. Santiago. *Puerto Ricans in the United States: A Contemporary Portrait*. Boulder, CO: Lynn Rienner Publishers, 2006.

Alberto, Paulina L., and Jesse Hoffnung-Garskof. "'Racial Democracy' and Racial Inclusion: Hemispheric Histories." In *Afro-Latin American Studies: An Introduction*, edited by Alejandro de la Fuente and George Reid Andrews, 264–316. Cambridge: Cambridge University Press, 2018.

Alexander, M. Jacqui. *Pedagogies of Crossing: Meditations on Feminism, Sexual Politics, Memory, and the Sacred*. Durham, NC: Duke University Press, 2005.

Alexander, Shawn Leigh. *W. E. B. Du Bois: An American Intellectual and Activist*. Lanham, MD: Rowman and Littlefield, 2017.

Anderson, Mark. *Black and Indigenous: Garifuna Activism and Consumer Culture in Honduras*. Minneapolis: University of Minnesota Press, 2009.

Anzaldúa, Gloria. *Borderlands / La Frontera: The New Mestiza*. San Francisco, CA: Aunt Lute Books, 1987.

Anzaldúa, Gloria. *Interviews/Entrevistas*. Edited by AnaLouise Keating. New York: Routledge, 2000.

Anzaldúa, Gloria. "La Prieta." In *This Bridge Called My Back: Writings by Radical Women of Color*, edited by Cherríe Moraga and Gloria Anzaldúa, 2nd ed., 198–209. Latham, NY: Kitchen Table: Women of Color Press, 1983.

Anzaldúa, Gloria. *Light in the Dark / Luz en lo Oscuro: Rewriting Identity, Spirituality, Reality.* Edited by AnaLouise Keating. Durham, NC: Duke University Press, 2015.

Aponte, Carlos. "Albizu Campos." In *Young Lords: A Reader*, edited by Darrel Enck-Wanzer, 95–98. New York: New York University Press, 2010.

Apter, Andrew. "Herskovits's Heritage: Rethinking Syncretism in the African Diaspora." *Diaspora: A Journal of Transnational Studies* 1, no. 3 (1991): 235–260. https://doi.org/10.353/dsp.1991.0021.

Arias, Arturo. "Central American–Americans: Invisibility, Power and Representation in the US Latino World." *Latino Studies* 1, no. 1 (March 2003): 168–187. https://doi.org/10.1057/palgrave.lst.8600007.

Arias, Arturo, and Claudia Milian. "US Central Americans: Representations, Agency and Communities." *Latino Studies* 11, no. 2 (June 2013): 131–149.

Arrizón, Alicia. "Mestizaje." In *Keywords for Latina/o Studies*, edited by Deborah R. Vargas, Nancy Raquel Mirabal, and Lawrence La Fountain-Stokes, 133–136. New York: New York University Press, 2017.

Arroyo, Jossianna. "Technologies: Transculturations of Race, Gender and Ethnicity in Arturo A. Schomburg's Masonic Writings." *CENTRO Journal* 17, no. 1 (2005): 5–19.

Arroyo, Jossianna. *Writing Secrecy in Caribbean Freemasonry.* New York: Palgrave Macmillan, 2013.

Artiaga, Scherly Virgill. "The Garífuna Voices of Guatemala's Armed Conflict: Memories of the Civil War in Livingston's Afro-Indigenous Community Excavate an Untold History Long Excluded from the Official Record." *NACLA: Report on the Americas* 52, no. 4 (October 1, 2020): 422–429.

Arturo Alfonso Schomburg Papers. Manuscripts, Archives, and Rare Books Division, Schomburg Center for Research in Black Culture. New York Public Library.

Ashe, Bertram D. "Theorizing the Post-soul Aesthetic: An Introduction." *African American Review* 41, no. 4 (December 1, 2007): 609–623.

Asukile, Thabiti. "Arthur Alfonso Schomburg (1874–1938): Embracing the Black Motherhood Experience in Love of Black People." *Afro-Americans in New York Life and History* 30, no. 2 (July 2006): 69–97.

Báez, Josefina. "El Ni'e: Inhabiting Love, Bliss, and Joy: A Conversation with Josefina Báez." Interview by Joshua Deckman. *Sx salon*, October 2018. http://smallaxe.net/sxsalon/interviews/el-nie-inhabiting-love-bliss-and-joy.

Barrón-López, Laura, and Heather Caygle. "CBC Head: Nothing Is Stopping Afro-Latinos from Joining both Black, Hispanic Caucuses," *Politico*, July 22, 2020, https://www.politico.com/news/2020/07/22/bass-torres-black-hispanic-caucuses-379070.

Bebout, Lee. *Whiteness on the Border: Mapping the US Racial Imagination in Brown and White.* New York: New York University Press, 2016.

Béjar, Eduardo C. "Toward the Nuyorican Condition: The Double Space of Colon and Vega." *Confluencia* 18, no. 1 (2002): 33–43.

Belpré, Pura. *The Stories I Read to the Children: The Life and Writing of Pura Belpré, the Legendary Storyteller, Children's Author, and New York Public Librarian.* Edited by Lisa Sánchez González. New York: Center for Puerto Rican Studies, 2013.

Benbow, Candice. "Lemonade Syllabus." *issuu*, May 7, 2016. https://issuu.com/candicebenbow/docs/lemonade_syllabus_2016.

Bernstein, Robin. *Racial Innocence: Performing American Childhood from Slavery to Civil Rights.* New York: New York University Press, 2011.

Beverley, John. *Against Literature.* Minneapolis: University of Minnesota Press, 1993.

Beverley, John. "The Margin at the Center: On Testimonio (Testimonial Narrative)." In *De/colonizing the Subject: The Politics of Gender in Women's Autobiography*, edited by Sidonie Smith and Julia Watson, 91–114. Minneapolis: University of Minnesota Press, 1992.

Beverley, John. *Testimonio: On the Politics of Truth.* Minneapolis: University of Minnesota Press, 2004.

Beverley, John, and Marc Zimmerman. *Literature and Politics in the Central American Revolutions.* Austin: University of Texas Press, 1990.

Blake, Felice. "What Does It Mean to Be Black?: Gendered Redefinitions of Interethnic Solidarity in Piri Thomas's *Down These Mean Streets*." *African American Review* 51, no. 2 (2018): 95–110.

Bonilla, Yarimar, and Marisol LeBrón, eds. *Aftershocks of Disaster: Puerto Rico before and after the Storm.* Chicago, IL: Haymarket Books, 2019.

Bonilla-Silva, Eduardo. *Racism without Racists: Color-Blind Racism and the Persistence of Racial Inequality in America.* 4th ed. Lanham, MD: Rowman and Littlefield, 2014.

Bonilla-Silva, Eduardo. "Reflections about Race by a Negrito Acomplejao." In *The Afro-Latin@ Reader: History and Culture in the United States*, edited by Miriam Jiménez Román and Juan Flores, 445–452. Durham, NC: Duke University Press, 2010.

Borucki, Alex, David Eltis, and David Wheat. "Atlantic History and the Slave Trade to Spanish America." *American Historical Review* 120, no. 2 (2015): 433–461.

Bost, Suzanne. *Shared Selves: Latinx Memoir and Ethical Alternatives to Humanism.* Urbana: University of Illinois Press, 2019.

Boutopoulou, Alexandra. "On the Origins of 'They Tried to Bury Us, They Didn't Know We Were Seeds.'" Interview by An Xiao. *Hyperallergic*, July 3, 2018. https://hyperallergic.com/449930/on-the-origins-of-they-tried-to-bury-us-they-didnt-know-we-were-seeds.

Boyce Davies, Carole. *Black Women, Writing and Identity: Migrations of the Subject.* London: Routledge, 1994.

Boyce Davies, Carole. "Collaboration and the Ordering Imperative in Life Story Production." In *De/colonizing the Subject: The Politics of Gender in Women's Autobiography*, edited by Sidonie Smith and Julia Watson, 3–19. Minneapolis: University of Minnesota Press, 1992.

Brady, Mary Pat. *Scales of Captivity: Racial Capitalism and the Latinx Child.* Durham, NC: Duke University Press, 2022.

Brandon, George. *Santeria from Africa to the New World: The Dead Sell Memories.* Bloomington: Indiana University Press, 1993.

Braxton, Joanne M. *Black Women Writing Autobiography: A Tradition within a Tradition*. Philadelphia, PA: Temple University Press, 1989.
Brooks, Kinitra D., and Kameelah L. Martin, eds. *The Lemonade Reader*. New York: Routledge, 2019.
Broughton, Trev Lynn, and Linda Anderson, eds. *Women's Lives / Women's Times: New Essays on Auto/biography*. Albany: State University of New York Press, 1997.
Brown, Ariana. "'Gathering What Is Left': A Conversation with Ariana Brown." Interview by Joshua R. Deckman. *Diálogos*, no. 112 (2023): 85–105.
Brown, Ariana. *Messy Girl*. Self-published on Patreon, 2017.
Brown, Ariana. *Sana Sana*. Game Over Books, 2020.
Brown, Ariana. *We Are Owed*. Cleveland, OH: GRVLND, 2021.
Brown, H. Rap. *Die, Nigger, Die!: A Political Autobiography*. New York: Lawrence Hill Books, 1969.
Brown, Monica. *Gang Nation: Delinquent Citizens in Puerto Rican, Chicano, and Chicana Narratives*. Minneapolis: University of Minnesota Press, 2002.
Brown, Ruth Nicole. *Hear Our Truths: The Creative Potential of Black Girlhood*. Urbana: University of Illinois Press, 2013.
Brubaker, Rogers. "The Return to Biology." In *Reconsidering Race: Social Science Perspectives on Racial Categories in the Age of Genomics*, 62–100. New York: Oxford University Press, 2018.
Bryant, Sherwin K. *Rivers of Gold, Lives of Bondage: Governing through Slavery in Colonial Quito*. Chapel Hill: University of North Carolina Press, 2014.
Butler, John R. *The Red Dean of Canterbury: The Public and Private Faces of Hewlett Johnson*. London: Scala Publishers, 2011.
Byerman, Keith. *Fingering the Jagged Grain*. Athens: University of Georgia Press, 1985.
Cabral, Amilcar. *Unity and Struggle: Speeches and Writings of Amilcar Cabral*. New York: Monthly Review Press, 1979.
Caine, Barbara. *Biography and History*. New York: Palgrave Macmillan, 2010.
Callahan, John. *In the African-American Grain: Call-and-Response in Twentieth-Century Black Fiction*. 2nd ed. Middletown, CT: Wesleyan University Press, 1989.
Caminero-Santangelo, Marta. *On Latinidad: U.S. Latino Literature and the Construction of Ethnicity*. Gainesville: University of Florida Press, 2007.
Caminero-Santangelo, Marta. "'Puerto Rican Negro': Defining Race in Piri Thomas's *Down These Mean Streets*." In *On Latinidad: U.S. Latino Literature and the Construction of Ethnicity*, 51–69. Gainesville: University Press of Florida, 2007.
Camp, Jessica Rae. "Radical Rhetoric: Excavating Gloria Anzaldúa's 'La Prieta.'" Master's thesis, Texas Woman's University, 2010.
Candelario, Ginetta E. B. *Black Behind the Ears: Dominican Racial Identity from Museums to Beauty Shops*. Durham, NC: Duke University Press, 2007.
Cantú, Norma E. "Memoir, Autobiography, Testimonio." In *The Routledge Companion to Latino/a Literature*, 310–322. New York: Routledge, 2013.
Cárdenas, Maritza E. *Constituting Central American–Americans: Transnational Identities and the Politics of Dislocation*. New Brunswick, NJ: Rutgers University Press, 2018.
Carr, Lynn C. *A Year in White: Cultural Newcomers to Lukumí and Santería in the United States*. New Brunswick, NJ: Rutgers University Press, 2016.

Casal, Lourdes. "Memories of a Black Cuban Childhood." *Nuestro*, April 1978, 61–62.
Casper, Scott E. *Constructing American Lives: Biography and Culture in Nineteenth Century America*. Chapel Hill: University of North Carolina Press, 1999.
Castro, Juan E. de. *Mestizo Nations: Culture, Race, and Conformity in Latin American Literature*. Tucson: University of Arizona Press, 2002.
Castromán Soto, Margarita M. "Schomburg's Black Archival Turn: 'Racial Integrity' and 'The Negro Digs Up His Past.'" *African American Review* 54, no. 1 (2021): 73–90.
Caygle, Heather. "Black Caucus Chafes at Latino Who Wants to Join." *Politico*, February 3, 2017. http://www.politico.com/story/2017/02/congressional-black-caucus-hispanic-adriano-espaillat-234575.
Cepeda, Raquel. *Bird of Paradise: How I Became Latina*. New York: Atria Books, 2013.
Cervantes, Marco A. "Afromestizaje: Toward a Mapping of Chicana/o Blackness in Tejana/o Literature and Popular Music, 1920–2010." PhD diss., University of Texas, San Antonio, 2010.
Chambers, Veronica. *Mama's Girl*. New York: Riverhead Books, 1996.
Chambers, Veronica. "Secret Latina at Large." In *Becoming American: Personal Essays by First Generation Immigrant Women*, 21–28. Hyperion, 2001.
Chambers, Veronica. "The Secret Latina." *Essence*, July 2000. http://www.veronicachambers.com/#item=secretlatina.
Chandler, Nahum Dimitri. *X—The Problem of the Negro as a Problem for Thought*. New York: Fordham University Press, 2014.
Chesney-Lind, Meda, and Michele Eliason. "From Invisible to Incorrigible: The Demonization of Marginalized Women and Girls." *Crime, Media, Culture: An International Journal* 2, no. 1 (April 1, 2006): 29–47.
Chetty, Raj, and Amaury Rodríguez. "Introduction: The Challenge and Promise of Dominican Black Studies." *The Black Scholar* 45, no. 2 (April 3, 2015): 1–9.
Chow, Andrew R. "These Afro-Latino Actors Are Pushing Back against Erasure in Hollywood." *TIME*, September 17, 2020. https://time.com/5889072/afro-latino-actors-roundtable.
Christian, Barbara. "The Race for Theory." *Feminist Studies* 14, no. 1 (Spring 1988): 67–79.
Ciment, James. *Another America: The Story of Liberia and the Former Slaves Who Ruled It*. New York: Hill and Wang, 2013.
Clark, Mary Ann. "¡No Hay Ningun Santo Aqui! (There Are No Saints Here!): Symbolic Language within Santería." *Journal of the American Academy of Religion* 69, no. 1 (March 2001): 21–41.
Clark, Mary Ann. *Santería: Correcting the Myths and Uncovering the Realities of a Growing Religion*. Santa Barbara, CA: Praeger Books, 2007.
Clark, Mary Ann. *Where Men Are Wives and Mothers Rule: Santería Ritual Practices and Their Gender Implications*. Gainesville: University Press of Florida, 2005.
Cohen, Jeffrey Jerome. "Monster Culture (Seven Theses)." In *Monster Theory: Reading Culture*, edited by Jeffrey Jerome Cohen, 3–25. Minneapolis: University of Minnesota Press, 1996.

Collins, Patricia Hill. *Black Feminist Thought*. New York: Routledge, 1990.
Colón, Jesús. *A Puerto Rican in New York and Other Sketches*. 2nd ed. New York: International Publishers, 1961.
Colón, Jesús. *The Way It Was, and Other Writings: Historical Vignettes about the New York Puerto Rican Community*. Edited by Edna Acosta-Belen and Virginia Sánchez Korrol. Houston, TX: Arte Público Press, 1993.
Cooper, Anna Julia. *A Voice from the South by a Black Woman of the South*. Xenia, OH: The Aldine Printing House, 1892.
Copeland, M. Shawn. *Enfleshing Freedom: Body, Race, and Being*. Minneapolis, MN: Fortress Press, 2010.
Corinealdi, Kaysha. *Panama in Black: Afro-Caribbean World Making in the Twentieth Century*. Durham, NC: Duke University Press, 2022.
Cosgrove, Serena, José Idíaquez, Leonard Joseph Bent, and Andrew Gorvetzian. *Surviving the Americas: Garifuna Resistance from Nicaragua to New York City*. Cincinnati, OH: University of Cincinnati Press, 2021.
Coss Aquino, Melissa. "Jesús y Concha Colón: A Puerto Rican Story of Love, Tradition, Migration and Modernity in Early 20th Century New York." *CENTRO Journal* 29, no. 2 (Summer 2017): 62–87.
Cotera, María Eugenia. "Latino/a Literature and the Uses of Folklore." In *The Routledge Companion to Latina/o Literature*, edited by Suzanne Bost and Frances R. Aparicio, 216–228. New York: Routledge, 2013.
Creed, Barbara. *The Monstrous-Feminine: Film, Feminism, Psychoanalysis*. London: Routledge, 1993.
Cruz, Angie, and Karl Marlantes. "Born to Tell the Story: Fiction Based on Family History." Panel presented at Texas Book Festival, Texas Capitol Building, Austin, TX, October 26, 2019.
Cruz-Malavé, Arnaldo. "The Antifoundational Foundational Fiction of Piri Thomas (1928–2011)." *CENTRO Journal* 24, no. 1 (Spring 2012): 4–19.
Cruz-Malavé, Arnaldo. "'What a Tangled Web!': Masculinity, Abjection, and the Foundations of Puerto Rican Literature in the United States." *Differences: A Journal of Feminist Cultural Studies* 8, no. 1 (1996): 132–151.
Dalleo, Raphael, and Elena Machado Sáez. *The Latino/a Canon and the Emergence of Post-sixties Literature*. New York: Palgrave Macmillan, 2007.
Das, Veena, and Arthur Kleinman. "Introduction." In *Violence and Subjectivity*, edited by Veena Das, Arthur Kleinman, Mamphela Ramphele, and Pamela Reynolds, 1–18. Oakland: University of California Press, 2000.
Dávila, Arlene M. *Sponsored Identities: Cultural Politics in Puerto Rico*. Philadelphia, PA: Temple University Press, 1997.
Davis, Angela. *Lectures on Liberation* (pamphlet). 1970.
Decena, Carlos U. *Tacit Subjects: Belonging and Same-Sex Desire among Dominican Immigrant Men*. Durham, NC: Duke University Press, 2011.
deGuzmán, María. *Spain's Long Shadow: The Black Legend, Off-Whiteness, and Anglo-American Empire*. Minneapolis: University of Minnesota Press, 2005.
Delgadillo, Theresa. "African, Latina, Feminist, and Decolonial: Marta Moreno Vega's Remembrance of Life in El Barrio in the 1950s." In *Theories of the Flesh: Latinx and Latin American Feminisms, Transformation, and Resistance*, edited by

Andrea J. Pitts, Mariana Ortega, and Jose Medina, 157–170. New York: Oxford University Press, 2020.
Delgadillo, Theresa. *Spiritual Mestizaje: Religion, Gender, Race, and Nation in Contemporary Chicana Narrative*. Durham, NC: Duke University Press, 2011.
DeWalt, Kathleen M., and Billie R. DeWalt. *Participant Observation: A Guide for Fieldworkers*. 2nd ed. Lanham, MD: Altamira Press, 2011.
Di Iorio Sandín, Lyn. "Melancholic Allegorists of the Street: Piri Thomas, Junot Díaz, and Yxta Maya Murray." In *Killing Spanish: Literary Essays on Ambivalent U.S. Latino/a Identity*, 101–133. New York: Palgrave, 2004.
Díaz, Jaquira. "Either Hyper-visible or Invisible: An Interview with Jaquira Díaz." Interview by Kavita Das. *Los Angeles Review of Books*, October 29, 2019. https://lareviewofbooks.org/article/either-hyper-visible-or-invisible-an-interview-with-jaquira-diaz.
Díaz, Jaquira. "Inside Brutal Baby Lollipops Murder Case That Shook South Florida." *Rolling Stone*, January 13, 2017. https://www.rollingstone.com/culture/culture-features/inside-brutal-baby-lollipops-murder-case-that-shook-south-florida-113594.
Díaz, Jaquira. *Ordinary Girls*. Chapel Hill, NC: Algonquin Books, 2019.
Díaz, Jaquira. "Visible: Women Writers of Color: Jaquira Díaz." *The Rumpus*, August 17, 2016. https://therumpus.net/2016/08/visible-women-writers-of-color-4-jaquira-diaz.
Díaz, Jaquira. "You Do Not Belong Here." *Kenyon Review Online* (blog), September 2017. https://kenyonreview.org/kr-online-issue/resistance-change-survival/selections/jaquira-diaz-656342.
Diaz, Von. *Coconuts and Collards: Recipes and Stories from Puerto Rico to the Deep South*. Gainesville: University Press of Florida, 2018.
Dinzey-Flores, Zaire Zenit. *Locked In, Locked Out: Gated Communities in a Puerto Rican City*. Philadelphia: University of Pennsylvania Press, 2013.
Diouf, Mamadou, and Ifeoma Kiddoe Nwankwo, eds. *Rhythms of the Afro-Atlantic World: Rituals and Remembrances*. Ann Arbor: University of Michigan Press, 2010.
Dodson, Howard. "Introduction." In *Nine Decades of Scholarship: A Bibliography of the Writings 1892–1983 of the Staff of the Schomburg Center for Research in Black Culture*, 7–15. New York: Schomburg Center for Research in Black Culture, 1986.
Du Bois, W. E. B. *The Gift of Black Folk*. New York: Kraus-Thomson Organization Limited, 1924.
Du Bois, W. E. B., and Guy B. Johnson. *Encyclopedia of the Negro: Prepatory Volume with Reference Lists and Reports*. Walnut Creek, CA: Left Coast Press, 1945.
Duany, Jorge. *The Puerto Rican Nation on the Move: Identities on the Island and in the United States*. Chapel Hill: University of North Carolina Press, 2002.
Durán, Isabel. "Latina/o Life Writing: Autobiography, Memoir, Testimonio." In *The Cambridge Companion to Latina/o American Literature*, edited by John Morán González, 161–177. New York: Cambridge University Press, 2016.
Emerson, Ralph Waldo. *Representative Men: Seven Lectures*. Cambridge, MA: Harvard University Press, 1850.

Enck-Wanzer, Darrel, ed. *The Young Lords: A Reader*. New York: New York University Press, 2010.
Every Child Is Born a Poet: The Life and Work of Piri Thomas. Directed by Jonathan Robinson. When in Doubt Productions, 2003.
Falcón, Sylvanna M. "Mestiza Double Consciousness: The Voices of Afro-Peruvian Women on Gendered Racism." *Gender and Society* 22, no. 5 (October 2008): 660–680.
Feliciano-Santos, Sherina. "Jíbaros and Jibaridades, Ambiguities and Possibilities." In *A Contested Caribbean Indigeneity: Language, Social Practice, and Identity within Puerto Rican Taíno Activism*, 47–74. New Brunswick, NJ: Rutgers University Press, 2021.
"Felipe Luciano Jíbaro, My Pretty Nigger." YouTube Video. Mos Def Poetry Jam, 2003. https://www.youtube.com/watch?time_continue=46&v=LcvKQ4rtKpE.
Fennell, Saraciea J., ed. *Wild Tongues Can't Be Tamed: 15 Voices from the Latinx Diaspora*. New York: Flatiron Books, 2021.
Feracho, Lesley. *Linking the Americas: Race, Hybrid Discourses, and the Reformulation of Feminine Identity*. Albany: State University of New York Press, 2005.
Fernández, Johanna. "Between Social Service Reform and Revolutionary Politics: The Young Lords, Late Sixties Radicalism, and Community Organizing in the New York City." In *Freedom North: Civil Rights Movements outside of the South*, edited by Jeanne Theoharis and Komozi Woodard, 255–285. New York: Palgrave Macmillan, 2003.
Fernández, Johanna. "Denise Oliver and the Young Lords Party: Stretching the Political Boundaries of Black Radical Struggle." In *Want to Start a Revolution? Radical Women in the Black Freedom Struggle*, edited by Dayo F. Gore, Jeanne Theoharis, and Komozi Woodard, 271–293. New York: New York University Press, 2009.
Fernández, Johanna. *The Young Lords: A Radical History*. Chapel Hill: University of North Carolina Press, 2020.
Fernández Olmos, Margarite, and Lizabeth Paravisini-Gebert. *Creole Religions of the Caribbean: An Introduction from Vodou and Santería to Obeah and Espiritismo*. 2nd ed. New York: New York University Press, 2011.
Fernández Olmos, Margarite, and Lizabeth Paravisini-Gebert, eds. *Healing Cultures: Art and Religion as Curative Practices in the Caribbean and Its Diaspora*. New York: Palgrave, 2001.
Fetta, Stephanie. *Shaming into Brown: Somatic Transactions of Race in Latina/o Literature*. Columbus: Ohio State University Press, 2018.
Fields, Karen E. "Witchcraft and Racecraft: Invisible Ontology in Its Sensible Manifestations." In *Witchcraft Dialogues*, edited by George C. Bond and Diane M. Ciekawy, 283–315. Athens: Ohio University Center for International Studies, 2001.
Figueroa, Yomaira. "Your Lips: Mapping Afro-Boricua Feminist Becomings." *Frontiers: A Journal of Women Studies* 41, no. 1 (2020): 1–11.
Figueroa-Vásquez, Yomaira. *Decolonizing Diasporas: Radical Mappings of Afro-Atlantic Literature*. Evanston, IL: Northwestern University Press, 2020.
Fleetwood, Nicole. *Troubling Vision: Performance, Visuality, and Blackness*. Chicago, IL: University of Chicago Press, 2011.

Flores, Juan. *The Diaspora Strikes Back: Caribeño Tales of Learning and Turning*. New York: Routledge, 2009.
Flores, Juan. "Foreword." In *A Puerto Rican in New York and Other Sketches*, ix–xvii. New York: International Publishers, 1982.
Flores, Juan. *From Bomba to Hip-Hop: Puerto Rican Culture and Latino Identity*. New York: Columbia University Press, 2000.
Flores, Juan. "Puerto Rican Literature in the United States: Stages and Perspectives." In *Divided Borders: Essays on Puerto Rican Identity*, 142–153. Houston, TX: Arte Público Press, 1993.
Flores, Juan, and Miriam Jiménez Román. "Triple-Consciousness? Approaches to Afro-Latino Culture in the United States." *Latin American and Caribbean Ethnic Studies* 4, no. 3 (November 2009): 319–328.
Flores, Tatiana. "'Latinidad Is Cancelled': Confronting an Anti-Black Construct." *Latin American and Latinx Visual Culture* 3, no. 3 (July 1, 2021): 58–79.
Floyd-Thomas, Stacey M., and Laura Gillman. "'The Whole Story Is What I'm After': Womanist Revolutions and Liberation Feminist Revelations through Biomythography and Emancipatory Historiography." *Black Theology* 3, no. 2 (July 2005): 176–199.
Ford, James Edward, III. "The Difficult Miracle: Reading Phillis Wheatley against the Master's Discourse." *CR: The New Centennial Review* 18, no. 3 (2018): 181–223.
Frade, Ramón. *El pan nuestro de cada día* [Our daily bread]. 1905. Oil on Canvas, 22" × 12 3/4".
Fuente, Alejandro de la. "Myths of Racial Democracy: Cuba, 1900–1912." *Latin American Research Review* 34, no. 3 (1999): 39–73.
Fusté, José I. "Schomburg's Blackness of a Different Matter: A Historiography of Refusal." *Small Axe: A Caribbean Journal of Criticism* 24, no. 1(61) (March 1, 2020): 120–131.
García, David. "'We Both Speak African': A Dialogic Study of Afro-Cuban Jazz." *Journal of the Society for American Music* 5, no. 2 (May 2011): 195–233.
García, David A. "A Master of the Rosary: Apology and Confession in Selected Writings of Jesús Colón's." *Afro-Hispanic Review* 27, no. 2 (2008): 45–70.
García, Mario T. *Literature as History: Autobiography, Testimonio, and the Novel in the Chicano and Latino Experience*. Tucson: University of Arizona Press, 2016.
García Peña, Lorgia. *Translating Blackness: Latinx Colonialities in Global Perspective*. Durham, NC: Duke University Press, 2022.
García-Peña, Lorgia. *The Borders of Dominicanidad: Race, Nation, and Archives of Contradiction*. Durham, NC: Duke University Press, 2016.
García-Peña, Lorgia. "Non-essential Knowledge: Latinx Studies in Times of Covid-19." *Aster(Ix)*, May 20, 2020. https://asterixjournal.com/non-essential-latinx-studies-covid-19.
García-Peña, Lorgia. "Translating *Blackness*: Dominicans Negotiating Race and Belonging." *The Black Scholar* 45, no. 2 (April 3, 2015): 10–20.
Garrison, Ednie. "When the Seen and Not Heard Start Shouting: Listening to Young Women (Book Review)." *Feminist Collections: A Quarterly of Women's Studies Resources* 18, no. 2 (1997): 1–3.
Gates, Henry Louis. *The Signifying Monkey: A Theory of African-American Literary Criticism*. New York: Oxford University Press, 1988.

Gerke, Amanda Ellen, and Luisa María González Rodríguez, eds. *Latinidad at the Crossroads: Insights into Latinx Identity in the Twenty-First Century*. Boston, MA: Brill, 2021.

Gilmore, Leigh, and Elizabeth Marshall. *Witnessing Girlhood: Toward an Intersectional Tradition of Life Writing*. New York: Fordham University Press, 2019.

Godreau, Isar P. *Scripts of Blackness: Race, Cultural Nationalism, and U.S. Colonialism in Puerto Rico*. Urbana: University of Illinois Press, 2015.

Gomez, Jewelle. *Forty-Three Septembers*. Ithaca, NY: Firebrand Books, 1993.

González, José Luis. *Puerto Rico: The Four-Storeyed Country and Other Essays*. Translated by Gerald Guinness. Princeton, NJ: Markus Wiener, 1980.

González, Juan. "Interview with Juan Gonzalez: His Road to the Young Lords." Interview by Lillian Jiménez. *Centro Voices*, May 2005. https://centropr.hunter.cuny.edu/centrovoices/chronicles/interview-juan-gonzalez-his-road-young-lords.

González, Juan. "Latin American Vanguard: The Tupamaros." *Palante* 2, no. 2 (1970): 12–13. A La Izquierda Collection, Reel 8, Centro Library and Archive.

González Rodríguez, Luisa María. "Digging through the Past to Reconcile Race and Latinx Identity in Dominican-American Women's Memoirs." In *Latinidad at the Crossroads: Insights into Latinx Identity in the Twenty-First Century*, 46–65. Boston, MA: Brill, 2021.

Gordon, Avery F. *Ghostly Matters: Haunting and the Sociological Imagination*. Minneapolis: University of Minnesota Press, 1997.

Gradert, Kenyon. "The *Mayflower* and the Slave Ship: Pilgrim-Puritan Origins in the Antebellum Black Imagination." *MELUS* 44, no. 3 (September 1, 2019): 63–90.

Grillo, Evelio. *Black Cuban, Black American*. Houston, TX: Arte Público Press, 2000.

Grupo Editorial EPRL. "Cayey Municipality." In *Enciclopedia de Puerto Rico*. Old San Juan, PR: Puerto Rico Endowment for the Humanities and the National Endowment for the Humanities. Accessed June 18, 2020. https://enciclopediapr.org/en/encyclopedia/cayey-municipality/.

Guidotti-Hernández, Nicole M. *Unspeakable Violence: Remapping U.S. and Mexican National Imaginaries*. Durham, NC: Duke University Press, 2011.

Guridy, Frank Andre. *Forging Diaspora: Afro-Cubans and African Americans in a World of Empire and Jim Crow*. Chapel Hill: University of North Carolina Press, 2010.

Guridy, Frank A., and Juliet Hooker. "Currents in Afro-Latin American Political and Social Thought." In *Afro-Latin American Studies*, edited by Alejandro de la Fuente and George Reid Andrews, 179–221. New York: Cambridge University Press, 2018.

Gusdorf, Georges. "Conditions and Limits of Autobiography. [1956]." In *Autobiography: Essays Theoretical and Critical*, edited by James Olney, 28–48. Princeton, NJ: Princeton University Press, 1980.

Gutierrez, Gustavo. *Teología de la Liberación: Perspectivas*. Lima, Peru: CEP, 1971.

Guzmán, Pablo [Yorúba]. "Ain't No Party like the One We Got: The Young Lords Party and Palante." In *Voices from the Underground*, edited by Ken Wachsberger, 293–304. Tempe, AZ: Mica's Press, 1991.

Guzmán, Pablo [Yorúba]. "Pablo 'Yoruba' Guzmán on the Young Lords Legacy: A Personal Account." In *Proceedings from the April 8, 1995, IPR Community Forum*, edited by Joseph Luppens. New York: Institute for Puerto Rican Policy, 1995.

Guzmán, Pablo [Yorúba]. "Puerto Rican Barrio Politics in the United States." In *The Puerto Rican Struggle: Essays on Survival in the U.S.*, edited by Clara A. Rodríguez, Virginia Sánchez Korrol, and José Oscar Alers, 121–128. New York: Puerto Rican Migration Research Consortium, 1980.
Hale, Charles R. *Más que un Indio: Racial Ambivalence and Neoliberal Multiculturalism in Guatemala*. Santa Fe, NM: School of American Research, 2006.
Hames-García, Michael. *Fugitive Thought: Prison Movements, Race, and the Meaning of Justice*. Minneapolis: University of Minnesota Press, 2004.
Hames-García, Michael. *Identity Complex: Making the Case for Multiplicity*. Minneapolis: University of Minnesota Press, 2011.
Harlow, Barbara. *Resistance Literature*. New York: Routledge, 1987.
Harris, Rendell. *The Last of the "Mayflower."* Manchester, UK: University Press, 1920.
Hartman, Saidiya. *Lose Your Mother: A Journey along the Atlantic Slave Route*. New York: Farrar, Straus, and Giroux, 2007.
Hartman, Saidiya. "Venus in Two Acts." *Small Axe: A Caribbean Journal of Criticism* 12, no. 2 (June 2008): 1–14.
Hartman, Saidiya. *Wayward Lives, Beautiful Experiments*. New York: Norton, 2019.
Helton, Laura E. "Schomburg's Library and the Price of Black History." *African American Review* 54, no. 1 (2021): 109–127.
Heredia, Juanita. "Afro-Latina Lives Matter: Marta Moreno Vega as Transnational Scholar / Cultural Worker," Latina/o Literary Studies Conference at John Jay College, New York, April 14, 2017.
Heredia, Juanita. "Latin Jazz." In *The Oxford Encyclopedia of Latinos and Latinas of the United States*, edited by Suzanne Oboler and Deena J. González, 478–480. New York: Oxford University Press, 2005.
Heredia, Juanita. "Marta Moreno Vega's *When the Spirits Dance Mambo: Growing Up Nuyorican in El Barrio* (2004): The Diasporic Formation of an Afro-Latina Identity." In *Transnational Latina Narratives in the Twenty-First Century: The Politics of Gender, Race, and Migrations*, 61–84. New York: Palgrave MacMillan, 2009.
Hernández, Jillian. *Aesthetics of Excess: The Art and Politics of Black and Latina Embodiment*. Durham, NC: Duke University Press, 2020.
Hernández, Tanya Katerí. *Racial Innocence: Unmasking Latino Anti-Black Bias and the Struggle for Equality*. Boston, MA: Beacon Press, 2022.
Herskovits, Melville J. "African Gods and Catholic Saints in New World Negro Belief." *American Anthropologist*, no. 39 (1937): 635–643.
Hine, Darlene Clark. "Rape and the Inner Lives of Black Women in the Middle West." *Signs: Journal of Women in Culture and Society* 14, no. 4 (1989): 912–920.
Hinojosa, Felipe. *Apostles of Change: Latino Radical Politics, Church Occupations, and the Fight to Save the Barrio*. Austin: University of Texas Press, 2022.
Hoffnung-Garskof, Jesse. "The Migrations of Arturo Schomburg: On Being Antillano, Negro, and Puerto Rican in New York, 1891–1938." *Journal of American Ethnic History* 21, no. 1 (Fall 2001): 3–49.
Holton, Adalaine. "Arturo Alfonso Schomburg's Archival Encounters in Spain." *African American Review* 54, no. 1 (2021): 31–47.
Holton, Adalaine. "Decolonizing History: Arthur Schomburg's Afrodiasporic Archive." *The Journal of African American History* 92, no. 2 (2007): 218–238.

Holton, Adalaine. "'Little Things Are Big': Race and the Politics of Print Community in the Writings of Jesús Colón." *MELUS: Multi-Ethnic Literature of the United States* 38, no. 2 (June 1, 2013): 5–23.

Homans, Margaret. "'Women of Color' Writers and Feminist Theory." *New Literary History* 25, no. 1 (Winter 1994): 73–94.

Hong, Cathy Park. *Minor Feelings: An Asian American Reckoning.* New York: One World, 2020.

Hooker, Juliet. "Hybrid Subjectivities, Latin American Mestizaje, and Latino Political Thought on Race." *Politics, Groups, and Identities* 2, no. 2 (April 3, 2014): 188–201.

Hooker, Juliet. *Race and the Politics of Solidarity.* New York: Oxford University Press, 2009.

Hooker, Juliet. *Theorizing Race in the Americas: Douglass, Sarmiento, Du Bois, and Vasconcelos.* New York: Oxford University Press, 2017.

hooks, bell. "Choosing the Margin as a Space of Radical Openness." *Framework: The Journal of Cinema and Media*, no. 36 (January 1989): 15–23.

hooks, bell. *Feminist Theory from Margin to Center.* Boston, MA: South End Press, 1984.

hooks, bell, Marci Blackman, Shola Lynch, and Janet Mock. "Are You Still a Slave? Liberating the Black Female Body." Panel discussion, The New School, New York, NY, May 6, 2014. https://www.youtube.com/watch?v=rJk0hNROvzs.

Howes, Craig. "Life Writing." In *Oxford Research Encyclopedia of Literature.* Oxford University Press, 2020. https://doi.org/10.1093/acrefore/9780190201098.013.1146.

Hoy, Vielka Cecilia. "Negotiating among Invisibilities: Tales of Afro-Latinidades in the United States." In *The Afro-Latin@ Reader: History and Culture in the United States*, edited by Miriam Jiménez Román and Juan Flores, 426–430. Durham, NC: Duke University Press, 2010.

Huggins, Nathan. *W. E. B. Du Bois: Writings.* New York: Library of America, 1996.

Hunsu, Folasade. "Engendering an Alternative Approach to Otherness in African Women's Autobiography." *Life Writing* 10, no. 2 (June 2013): 171–185.

Ignatiev, Noel. *How the Irish Became White.* New York: Routledge, 1995.

Irizarry Rodríguez, José M. "Evolving Identities: Early Puerto Rican Writing in the United States and the Search for a New Puertorriqueñidad." In *Writing Off the Hyphen: New Perspectives on the Literature of the Puerto Rican Diaspora*, edited by José L. Torres-Padilla and Carmen Haydée Rivera, 31–51. Seattle: University of Washington Press, 2008.

Irizarry, Ylce. "Because Place Still Matters: Mapping Puertorriqueñidad in *Bodega Dreams*." *CENTRO Journal* 27, no. 1 (Spring 2015): 152–185.

Irizarry, Ylce. *Chicana/o and Latina/o Fiction: The New Memory of Latinidad.* Urbana: University of Illinois Press, 2016.

Ishmael, Hannah J. M. "Reclaiming History: Arthur Schomburg." *Archives and Manuscripts*, January 29, 2019. http://www.tandfonline.com/doi/abs/10.1080/01576895.2018.1559741.

Ives, Anthony Lister. "Frederick Douglass's Reform Textualism: An Alternative Jurisprudence Consistent with the Fundamental Purpose of Law." *Journal of Politics* 80, no. 1 (2018): 88–102.

J., Brittany. "What Trauma Porn Is, and Why It Hurts Black People." *The Mighty*, October 12, 2020. https://themighty.com/2020/10/trauma-porn.

Jackson, Anna. "The Verse Biography: Introduction." *Biography* 39, no. 1 (2016): iii–xvi.

Jackson, Zakiyyah Iman. *Becoming Human: Matter and Meaning in an Anti-Black World*. New York: New York University Press, 2020.

James, Winston. *Holding Aloft the Banner of Ethiopia: Caribbean Radicalism in Early Twentieth-Century America*. London: Verso, 1999.

Jeffers, Honorée Fanone. *The Age of Phillis*. Middletown, CT: Wesleyan University Press, 2020.

Jiménez García, Marilisa. *Side by Side: US Empire, Puerto Rico, and the Roots of American Youth Literature and Culture*. Jackson: University Press of Mississippi, 2021.

Jiménez Román, Miriam. "Looking at That Middle Ground: Racial Mixing as Panacea?" In *A Companion to Latina/o Studies*, edited by Juan Flores and Renato Rosaldo, 325–336. Oxford: Blackwell Publishing, 2007.

Jiménez Román, Miriam, and Juan Flores, eds. *The Afro-Latin@ Reader*. Durham, NC: Duke University Press, 2010.

Johnson, E. Patrick, and Ramón H. Rivera-Servera, eds. "Introduction: Ethnoracial Intimacies in Blacktino Queer Performance." In *Blacktino Queer Performance*, 1–18. Durham, NC: Duke University Press, 2016.

Jones, Jennifer A. "Afro-Latinos: Speaking through Silences and Rethinking the Geographies of Blackness." In *Afro-Latin American Studies: An Introduction*, edited by Alejandro de la Fuente and George Reid Andrews, 569–614. New York: Cambridge University Press, 2018.

Jorge, Angela. "The Black Puerto Rican Woman in Contemporary American Society." In *The Puerto Rican Woman: Perspectives on Culture, History, and Society*, edited by Edna Acosta-Belén, 2nd ed., 180–187. Santa Barbara, CA: Praeger, 1986.

Jorgensen, Danny L. *Principles, Approaches and Issues in Participant Observation*. New York: Routledge, 2020.

Juan Gonzalez Papers, Center for Puerto Rican Studies Library and Archive. Hunter College (City University of New York).

Kachun, Mitch. "Crispus Attucks Meets the New Negro: Black History and Black Heroes between the World Wars." In *First Martyr of Liberty: Crispus Attucks in American Memory*, 97–119. New York: Oxford University Press, 2017.

Kadar, Marlene. "Coming to Terms: Life Writing—from Genre to Critical Practice." In *Theoretical Discussions of Biography: Approaches from History, Microhistory and Life Writing*, edited by Hans Renders and Binne De Haan, revised and augmented edition., 195–205. Leiden: Brill, 2014.

Kandiyoti, Dalia. *Migrant Sites: America, Place, and Diaspora Literatures*. Lebanon, NH: Dartmouth College Press, 2009.

Kanellos, Nicolás. "Sotero Figueroa: Writing Afro-Caribbeans into History in the Late Nineteenth Century." In *The Latino Nineteenth Century: Archival Encounters in American Literary History*, edited by Rodrigo Lazo and Jesse Alemán, 323–340. New York: New York University Press, 2016.

Kaplan Gubert, Betty, and Richard Newman, eds. *Nine Decades of Scholarship: A Bibliography of the Writings 1892–1983 of the Staff of the Schomburg Center for*

Research in Black Culture. New York: Schomburg Center for Research in Black Culture, 1986.
Keating, AnaLouise. *The Gloria Anzaldúa Reader*. Durham, NC: Duke University Press, 2009.
Keating, AnaLouise. *Women Reading Women Writing: Self-Invention in Paula Gunn Allen, Gloria Anzaldúa, and Audre Lorde*. Philadelphia, PA: Temple University Press, 1996.
Kelley, Robin D. G. "Foreword." In *Black Marxism: The Making of the Black Radical Tradition*. Chapel Hill: University of North Carolina Press, 2000.
King, Rosamond S. "Radical Interdisciplinarity: A New Iteration of a Woman of Color Methodology." *Meridians* 18, no. 2 (October 1, 2019): 445–456.
King Institute (Martin Luther King Jr. Research and Education Institute). "New York Amsterdam News." In *King Encyclopedia*. Stanford, CA: The Martin Luther King Jr. Research and Education Institute, Stanford University. https://kinginstitute.stanford.edu/encyclopedia/new-york-amsterdam-news#:~:text=Founded%20in%201909%20by%20James,newspapers%20in%20the%20United%20States.
Knowles-Carter, Beyoncé, and Joseph Kahil. *Lemonade*. DVD. Columbia, 2016.
A La Izquierida Collection. Center for Puerto Rican Studies Library and Archives. Hunter College (City University of New York).
La Fountain-Stokes, Lawrence. *Queer Ricans: Cultures and Sexualities in the Diaspora*. Minneapolis: University of Minnesota Press, 2009.
Lalami, Laila. *The Moor's Account*. New York: Pantheon Books, 2014.
Lam, C. Christina. "Bearing Witness: Alternate Archives of Latinx Identity in Raquel Cepeda's Bird of Paradise: How I Became a Latina." *Studies in American Culture*, 43, no. 1 (June 2020): 26–42.
Lao-Montes, Agustín. "Afro-Latinidades and the Diasporic Imaginary." *Iberoamericana* 5, no. 17 (2005): 117–130.
Lao-Montes, Agustín. "Afro-Latinidades: Bridging Black and Latino Studies." In *Technofuturos: Critical Interventions in Latina/o Studies*, edited by Nancy Raquel Mirabal and Agustin Lao-Montes, 117–140. Lanham, MD: Lexington Books, 2007.
Lao-Montes, Agustin, and Mirangela Buggs. "Translocal Space of Afro-Latinidad: Critical Feminist Visions for Diasporic Bridge-Building." In *Translocalities/Translocalidades: Feminist Politics of Translation in the Latin/a Americas*, edited by Sonia E. Alvarez, Claudia de Lima Costa, Verónica Feliu, Rebecca J. Hester, Norma Klahn, Millie Thayer, and Cruz Caridad Bueno, 381–400. Durham, NC: Duke University Press, 2014.
Lara, Ana-Maurine. "Bodies and Memories: Afro-Latina Identities in Motion." In *Women Warriors of the Afro-Latina Diaspora*, edited by Marta Moreno Vega, Marinieves Alba, and Yvette Modestin, 23–47. Houston, TX: Arte Público Press, 2012.
Lara, Irene. "Daughter of Coatlicue: An Interview with Gloria Anzaldúa." In *EntreMundos/AmongWorlds: New Perspectives on Gloria E. Anzaldúa*, edited by AnaLouise Keating, 41–55. New York: Palgrave Macmillan, 2005.
Latina Feminist Group. *Telling to Live: Latina Feminist Testimonios*. Durham, NC: Duke University Press, 2001.

Laurent-Perrault, Evelyne. "Arturo Alfonso Schomburg, the Quintessential Maroon: Toward an African Diasporic Epistemology." *Small Axe: A Caribbean Journal of Criticism* 24, no. 1(61) (March 1, 2020): 132–141.

Levins Morales, Aurora. *Medicine Stories: Essays for Radicals*. Revised and expanded edition. Durham, NC: Duke University Press, 2019.

Lewis, David Levering. *W. E. B. Du Bois, 1868–1919: Biography of a Race*. New York: Henry Holt and Co, 1993.

Lewis, Shireen K., ed. "Black Girlhood." Special issue, *Black Scholar* 50, no. 4 (Winter 2020).

Lipsitz, George. *The Possessive Investment in Whiteness: How White People Profit from Identity Politics*. Philadelphia, PA: Temple University Press, 2006.

Lomas, Laura. "Afro-Latina Disidentification and Bridging Lourdes Casal's Critical Race Theory." *Meridians* 21, no. 1 (April 2022), 123–154.

Lomas, Laura. "Casal, Lourdes." In *Oxford Research Encyclopedia of Literature*. New York: Oxford University Press, 2019. https://doi.org/10.1093/acrefore/9780190201098.013.406.

Lomas, Laura. "Migration and Decolonial Politics in Two AfroLatino Poets: 'Pachín' Marín and 'Tato' Laviera." *Review: Literature and Arts of the Americas* 47, no. 2 (October 2014): 155–163.

Lomas, Laura. "On the 'Shock' of Diaspora: Lourdes Casal's Critical Interdisciplinarity and Intersectional Feminism." *Cuban Studies* 46 (April 20, 2018): 10–38.

Lomas, Laura. *Translating Empire: José Martí, Migrant Latino Subjects, and American Modernities*. Durham, NC: Duke University Press, 2008.

López, Antonio. *Unbecoming Blackness: The Diaspora Cultures of Afro-Cuban America*. New York: New York University Press, 2012.

López Oro, Paul Joseph. "A Love Letter to Indigenous Blackness." *NACLA: Report on the Americas* 53, no. 3 (November 2021): 248–254.

López Oro, Paul Joseph. "Garifunizando Ambas Américas: Hemispheric Entanglements of Blackness/Indigeneity/AfroLatinidad." *Postmodern Culture: Journal of Interdisciplinary Thought on Contemporary Cultures* 31, no. 1–2 (September 2020–January 2021): 1–29.

López Oro, Paul Joseph. "Refashioning Afro-Latinidad: Garifuna New Yorkers in Diaspora." In *Critical Dialogues in Latinx Studies: A Reader*, edited by Ana Y. Ramos-Zayas and Mérida M. Rúa, 223–238. New York: New York University Press, 2021.

Lorde, Audre. "Age, Race, Class, and Sex: Women Redefining Difference." In *Sister Outsider*, 114–123. New York: Ten Speed Press, 2007.

Lorde, Audre. "The Transformation of Silence into Language and Action." In *Sister Outsider*, 40–44. New York: Ten Speed Press, 2007.

Luis, William. "Black Latinos Speak: The Politics of Race in Piri Thomas's *Down These Mean Streets*." *Indiana Journal of Hispanic Literatures*, no. 12 (1998): 27–49.

Magaña, José. "Marketing *Latinidad*: *La Luz* and *Nuestro*'s Search for a Latino Market in the 1970s." *Perspectives: A Journal of Historical Inquiry*, no. 41 (Winter 2014): 27–52.

Mahler, Anne Garland. *From the Tricontinental to the Global South: Race, Radicalism, and Transnational Solidarity*. Durham, NC: Duke University Press, 2018.

Maillo-Pozo, Sharina. "Reconstructing Dominican Latinidad: Intersections between Gender, Race, and Hip-Hop." *Small Axe: A Caribbean Journal of Criticism* 22, no. 2 (July 1, 2018): 85–98.
Maíz, Magdalena, and Luis H. Peña. "Between Lines: Constructing The Political Self." *A/b: Auto/biography Studies* 3, no. 4 (January 1988): 23–36.
Maner, Sequoia. "'Where Do You Go When You Go Quiet?' Practices of Quietude in the Fictions of Alice Walker, Zora Neale Hurston, and Beyoncé Knowles-Carter." *Meridians* 17, no. 1 (2018): 184–204.
Martínez, María Elena. *Genealogical Fictions: Limpieza de Sangre, Religion, and Gender in Colonial Mexico*. Stanford, CA: Stanford University Press, 2008.
Martínez-Echazábal, Lourdes. "Mestizaje and the Discourse of National/Cultural Identity in Latin America, 1845–1959." *Latin American Perspectives* 25, no. 3 (May 1998): 21–42.
Martínez–San Miguel, Yolanda. "Ethnic Specularities: Exploring the Caribbean and Latino Dimensions of *Down These Mean Streets*." *Latino Studies* 13, no. 3 (Autumn 2015): 358–375.
Masiki, Trent. "Post-soul Latinidad: Black Nationalism in *Mama's Girl* and *Bird of Paradise: How I Became Latina*." *Latino Studies* 20, no. 4 (December 2022): 475–497.
Masiki, Trent, and Regina Marie Mills, eds. "Post-soul AfroLatinidades," special issue of *The Black Scholar* 52, no. 1 (March 2022).
Matory, J. Lorand. "The Many Who Dance in Me: Afro-Atlantic Ontology and the Problem with 'Transnationalism.'" In *Transcendence: Essays on Religion and Globalization*, edited by Thomas J. Csordas, 231–262. Berkeley: University of California Press, 2009.
Mays, Kyle T. *An Afro-Indigenous History of the United States*. Boston, MA: Beacon Press, 2021.
McGill, Lisa D. "'How to Be a Negro without Really Trying': Piri Thomas and the Politics of Nuyorican Identity." In *Constructing Black Selves: Caribbean American Narratives and the Second Generation*, 161–199. New York: New York University Press, 2005.
Milian, Claudia. *Latining America: Black-Brown Passages and the Coloring of Latino/a Studies*. Athens: University of Georgia Press, 2013.
Milian, Claudia. "Latinos and the Like: Reading Mixture and Deracination." In *The Cambridge Companion to Latina/o American Literature*, 195–212. New York: Cambridge University Press, 2016.
Milian, Claudia. *LatinX*. Minneapolis: University of Minnesota Press, 2019.
Mills, Regina Marie. "Beyond Resistance in Dominican American Women's Fiction: Healing and Growth through the Spectrum of Quietude in Angie Cruz's *Soledad* and Naima Coster's *Halsey Street*." *Latino Studies* 19, no. 1 (March 2021): 70–91.
Mills, Regina Marie. "Latinx Coming-of-Age Memoirs, 1961–2022." In *The Routledge Companion to Latinx Life Writing*, edited by Maria Villaseñor and Christine Fernández. New York: Routledge (forthcoming).
Mills, Regina Marie. "Playing at Power and Powerlessness: Agency in *Papo & Yo* and *Life Is Strange 2*." *The Lion and the Unicorn* 48, no. 1 (forthcoming).

Mirabal, Nancy Raquel. *Suspect Freedoms: The Racial and Sexual Politics of Cubanidad in New York, 1823–1957.* New York: New York University Press, 2017.
Mohanty, Chandra Talpade. "'Under Western Eyes' Revisited: Feminist Solidarity through Anticapitalist Struggles." In *The Feminist Theory Reader*, edited by Carole McCann and Seung-kyung Kim, 4th rev. ed., 413–430. New York: Routledge, 2016.
Mogul, Joey L., Andrea J. Ritchie, and Kay Whitlock, eds. *Queer (In)justice: The Criminalization of LGBT People in the United States.* Boston, MA: Beacon Press, 2012.
Moody, Jocelyn K., ed. *A History of African American Autobiography.* New York: Cambridge University Press, 2021.
Moraga, Cherríe. "'Consciencia' Is Not About 'I' but 'We.'" Interview by Marcos Colón. *Latino Book Review*, March 11, 2020. https://www.latinobookreview.com/consciencia-is-not-about-i-but-we---interview-with-cherriacutee-moraga--latino-book-review.html.
Moraga, Cherríe, and Gloria Anzaldúa. "Entering the Lives of Others: Theory in the Flesh." In *This Bridge Called My Back: Writings by Radical Women of Color*, 4th ed. Albany: State University of New York Press, 2015.
Morales, Iris. "¡PALANTE, SIEMPRE PALANTE! The Young Lords." In *The Puerto Rican Movement: Voices from the Diaspora*, edited by Andrés Torres and José E. Velásquez, 210–227. Philadelphia, PA: Temple University Press, 1998.
Morales, Iris, ed. *Through the Eyes of Rebel Women: The Young Lords, 1969–1976.* New York: Red Sugarcane Press, 2016.
Moreno, Isidoro. *La Antigua Hermandad de Los Negros de Sevilla: Etnicidad, Sociedad, y Poder en 600 Años de Historia.* Sevilla: Universidad de Sevilla, 1997.
Moreno, Marisel C. *Family Matters: Puerto Rican Women Authors on the Island and the Mainland.* Charlottesville: University of Virginia Press, 2012.
Moreno Vega, Marta. "Espiritismo in the Puerto Rican Community: A New World Recreation with the Elements of Kongo Ancestor Worship." *Journal of Black Studies* 29, no. 3 (January 1, 1999): 325–353.
Moreno Vega, Marta. "Interlocking African Diaspora Cultures in the Work of Fernando Ortiz." *Journal of Black Studies* 31, no. 1 (September 1, 2000): 39–50.
Moreno Vega, Marta. *The Altar of My Soul: The Living Traditions of Santería.* New York: One World / Ballantine Books, 2000.
Moreno Vega, Marta. "The Ancestral Sacred Creative Impulse of Africa and the African Diaspora: Ase, the Nexus of the Black Global Aesthetic." *Lenox Avenue: A Journal of Interarts Inquiry*, no. 5 (1999): 45–57.
Moreno Vega, Marta. "The Purposeful Underdevelopment of Latino and Other Communities of Color." In *Voices from the Battlefront: Achieving Cultural Equity*, edited by Marta Moreno Vega and Cheryl Y. Greene, 103–108. Trenton, NJ: Africa World Press, 1993.
Moreno Vega, Marta. "The Yoruba Orisha Tradition Comes to New York City." In *The Afro-Latin@ Reader: History and Culture in the United States*, edited by Miriam Jiménez Román and Juan Flores, 245–251. Durham, NC: Duke University Press, 2010.
Moreno Vega, Marta. *When the Spirits Dance Mambo: Growing Up Nuyorican in El Barrio.* New York: Three Rivers Press, 2004.

Moreno Vega, Marta. "Yoruba Philosophy: Multiple Levels of Transformation and Understanding." PhD diss., Temple University, 1995. UMI Dissertation Services.
Moreno Vega, Marta, Marinieves Alba, and Yvette Modestin, eds. *Women Warriors of the Afro-Latina Diaspora*. Houston, TX: Arte Público Press, 2012.
Moreno Vega, Marta, and Robert Shepard. *Cuando los espíritus bailan mambo* [When the spirits dance mambo]. Caribbean Cultural Center African Diaspora Institute, 2002. DVD.
Morris, Aldon D. *The Scholar Denied: W. E. B. Du Bois and the Birth of Modern Sociology*. Oakland: University of California Press, 2015.
Morrison, Toni. *Playing in the Dark: Whiteness in the Literary Imagination*. Cambridge, MA: Harvard University Press, 1992.
Moya, Paula M. L. *The Social Imperative: Race, Close Reading, and Contemporary Literary Criticism*. Stanford, CA: Stanford University Press, 2016.
Muñoz, José Esteban. *Disidentifications: Queers of Color and the Performance of Politics*. Minneapolis: University of Minnesota Press, 1999.
Muñoz, José Esteban. "Feeling Brown, Feeling Down: Latina Affect, the Performativity of Race, and the Depressive Position." *Signs: Journal of Women in Culture and Society* 31, no. 3 (Spring 2006): 675–688.
Murillo, Edwin. "Hostile Anxieties: In-House Prejudices in Latino Literature." *Bilingual Review / Revista Bilingüe* 31, no. 3 (September 2012): 227–241.
Murrell, Nathaniel Samuel. *Afro-Caribbean Religions: An Introduction to Their Historical, Cultural, and Sacred Traditions*. Philadelphia, PA: Temple University Press, 2010.
Negrón-Muntaner, Frances. "'Here Is the Evidence': Arturo Alfonso Schomburg's Black Countervisuality." *African American Review* 54, no. 1 (2021): 49–71.
Negrón-Muntaner, Frances. "The Look of Sovereignty: Style and Politics in the Young Lords." *CENTRO Journal* 27, no. 1 (Spring 2015): 4–33.
Nelson, Alondra. *The Social Life of DNA: Race, Reparations, and Reconciliation after the Genome*. Boston, MA: Beacon Press, 2016.
Nelson, Diane M. *A Finger in the Wound: Body Politics in Quincentennial Guatemala*. Berkeley: University of California Press, 1999.
Neyra, Ren Ellis. "The Question of Ethics in the Semiotics of Brownness." *Sx Salon* (blog), October 2020. http://smallaxe.net/sxsalon/discussions/question-ethics-semiotics-brownness.
Nguyen, Viet Thanh. "Just Memory." In *Nothing Ever Dies: Vietnam and the Memory of War*, 4–19. Cambridge, MA: Harvard University Press, 2016.
Nguyen, Viet Thanh. "The Remasculinization of Chinese America: Race, Violence, and the Novel." *American Literary History* 12, nos. 1/2 (Spring/Summer 2000): 130–157.
Noel, Urayoán. *In Visible Movement: Nuyorican Poetry from the Sixties to Slam*. Iowa City: University of Iowa Press, 2014.
Noel, Urayoán. "'The Geography of Their Complexion': Nuyorican Poetry and Its Legacies." In *The Cambridge History of Latina/o American Literature*, 411–434. New York: Cambridge University Press, 2018.
Núñez, Victoria. "Remembering Pura Belpré's Early Career at the 135th Street New York Public Library: Interracial Cooperation and Puerto Rican Settlement during the Harlem Rennaisance." *CENTRO Journal* 21, no. 1 (2009): 53–77.

Nwankwo, Ifeoma C. K. "Veronica Chambers, *Mama's Girl*." In *Reading U.S. Latina Writers*, edited by Alvina E. Quintana, 25–36. New York: Palgrave Macmillan US, 2003.
Oliver, Denise. "Yanquis Own Puerto Rico." In *Young Lords: A Reader*, edited by Darrel Enck-Wanzer, 146–149. New York: New York University Press, 2010.
Om, Shaba. "Look for Yourselves: An Introduction." In *Look for Me in the Whirlwind: From the Panther 21 to 21st-Century Revolutions*, edited by déqui kionisadiki and Matt Meyer, 1–4. Oakland, CA: PM Press, 1971.
Omi, Michael, and Howard Winant. *Racial Formation in the United States*. 3rd ed. New York: Routledge, 2015.
Ortiz, Ricardo L. "Critical Futurities within Latinx Studies' Disidentifying Present." *Aztlan: A Journal of Chicano Studies* 45, no. 2 (Fall 2020): 201–211.
Ortiz, Ricardo L. *Latinx Literature Now: Between Evanescence and Event*. New York: Palgrave MacMillan, 2019.
Ortiz, Victoria. "Arthur A. Schomburg: A Biographical Essay." In *The Legacy of Arthur A. Schomburg: A Celebration of the Past, A Vision for the Future*, 18–110. New York: New York Public Library (NYPL), 1986. Exhibition catalog.
Oswald, Alice. "Into the Woods." Interview by Kate Kellaway. *The Guardian*, June 18, 2005. https://www.theguardian.com/books/2005/jun/19/poetry.features.
Otero, Anthony. "Afro-Latinos and Black History Month." *HuffPost* (blog), February 1, 2013. https://www.huffpost.com/entry/afrolatinos-and-black-his_b_2600723.
Otero, Solimar. *Archives of Conjure: Stories of the Dead in Afrolatinx Cultures*. New York: Columbia University Press, 2020.
Padilla Aponte, Edwin Karli. "Introduction." In *Lo que el pueblo me dice . . . Crónicas de la colonia puertorriqueña*, edited by Edwin Karli Padilla Aponte. Houston, TX: Arte Público Press, 2001.
Padilla, Yajaira M. *From Threatening Guerrillas to Forever Illegals: US Central Americans and the Cultural Politics of Non-belonging*. Austin: University of Texas Press, 2022.
Palmié, Stephan. "Genomics, Divination, 'Racecraft.'" *American Ethnologist* 34, no. 2 (2007): 205–222.
Pelaez López, Alán. "Foreword." In *We Are Owed.*, 7–10. Cleveland, OH: GRVLND, 2021.
Pelaez López, Alán. "The *X* in Latinx Is a Wound, Not a Trend." *Color Bloq* (blog), September 2018. https://www.colorbloq.org/article/the-x-in-latinx-is-a-wound-not-a-trend.
Perez, Domino Renee. *There Was a Woman: La Llorona from Folklore to Popular Culture*. Austin: University of Texas Press, 2008.
Pérez-Torres, Rafael. *Mestizaje: Critical Uses of Race in Chicano Culture*. Minneapolis: University of Minnesota Press, 2006.
Perkins, Maureen, ed. "Never the Twain: Life Writing's Geographical Contexts." In *Locating Life Stories: Beyond East-West Binaries in (Auto)biographical Studies*, 1–14. Honolulu: Published for the Biographical Research Center by the University of Hawai'i Press, 2012.
Pero Like. *Afro Latinos Get DNA Tested*. YouTube Video. 2018. https://www.youtube.com/watch?v=xsmy3kYNDpI.

Pero Like. *Afro Latinos Get Their African Ancestry Results.* YouTube Video. 2020. https://www.youtube.com/watch?v=Dd_6gQvXUGs.

Perreault, Jeanne. *Writing Selves: Contemporary Feminist Autography.* Minneapolis: University of Minnesota Press, 1995.

Piñeiro de Rivera, Flor. *Arthur A. Schomburg: A Puerto Rican's Quest for His Black Heritage.* Puerto Rico: Centro de Estudios Avanzados de Puerto Rico y el Caribe, 1989.

Piri Thomas Papers. Manuscripts, Archives and Rare Books Division, Schomburg Center for Research in Black Culture. New York Public Library.

Pitts, Andrea J., Mariana Ortega, and José Medina, eds. *Theories of the Flesh: Latinx and Latin American Feminisms, Transformation, and Resistance.* New York: Oxford University Press, 2020.

Portillo, Annette Angela. *Sovereign Stories and Blood Memories: Native American Women's Autobiography.* Albuquerque: University of New Mexico Press, 2017.

Quashie, Kevin. *The Sovereignty of Quiet: Beyond Resistance in Black Culture.* New Brunswick, NJ: Rutgers University Press, 2012.

Ramírez, Dixa. *Colonial Phantoms: Belonging and Refusal in the Dominican Americas, from the 19th Century to the Present.* New York: New York University Press, 2018.

Rankine, Claudia. *Just Us: An American Conversation.* Minneapolis, MN: Graywolf Press, 2020.

Reichard, Raquel. "Ariana Brown Wants Her Poems about Depression to Heal and Empower Black Women." *Remezcla*, October 31, 2017. https://remezcla.com/features/culture/ariana-brown-messy-girl-chapbook.

Reid-Pharr, Robert F. "Tearing the Goat's Flesh: Homosexuality, Abjection, and the Production of a Late-Twentieth-Century Masculinity." In *Novel Gazing: Queer Readings in Fiction*, edited by Eve Kosofsky Sedgwick, 353–376. Durham, NC: Duke University Press, 1997.

Richardson, Jill Toliver. *The Afro-Latin@ Experience in Contemporary American Literature and Culture: Engaging Blackness.* New York: Palgrave Macmillan, 2016.

Richie Pérez Papers. Center for Puerto Rican Studies Library and Archive. Hunter College (City University of New York).

Rivera, Carmen S. *Kissing the Mango Tree: Puerto Rican Women Rewriting American Literature.* Houston, TX: Arte Público Press, 2002.

Rivera-Rideau, Petra. *Remixing Reggaetón: The Cultural Politics of Blackness in Puerto Rico.* Durham, NC: Duke University Press, 2015.

Roberts, Dorothy. *Fatal Invention: How Science, Politics, and Big Business Create Race in the Twenty-First Century.* New York: The New Press, 2011.

Rodríguez, Juana María. "Divas, Atrevidas, y Entendidas: An Introduction to Identities." In *Queer Latinidad: Identity Practices, Discursive Spaces*, 5–36. New York: New York University Press, 2003.

Rodríguez, Juana María. *Sexual Futures, Queer Gestures, and Other Latina Longings.* New York: New York University Press, 2014.

Rodriguez, Ralph E. *Latinx Literature Unbound: Undoing Ethnic Expectation.* New York: Fordham University Press, 2018.

Rodríguez, Richard T. *Next of Kin: The Family in Chicano/a Cultural Politics.* Durham, NC: Duke University Press, 2009.

Rodríguez, Sonia Alejandra. "Conocimiento Narratives: Creative Acts and Healing in Latinx Children's and Young Adult Literature." *Children's Literature*, no. 47 (2019): 9–29.

Rosaldo, Renato. "Cultural Citizenship, Inequality, and Multiculturalism." In *Latino Cultural Citizenship: Claiming Identity, Space, and Rights*, edited by William V. Flores and Rina Benmayor, 27–38. Boston, MA: Beacon Press, 1997.

Rosario, Nelly. "DNA+Latinx: Complicando the Double Helix." In *Critical Dialogues in Latinx Studies: A Reader*, edited by Ana Y. Ramos-Zayas and Mérida M. Rúa, 104–117. New York: New York University Press, 2021.

Roth, Wendy D., and Katherine A. Lyon. "Genetic Ancestry Tests and Race: Who Takes Them, Why, and How Do They Affect Racial Identities?" In *Reconsidering Race: Social Science Perspectives on Racial Categories in the Age of Genomics*, 133–170. New York: Oxford University Press, 2018.

Rout, Leslie B., Jr. *The African Experience in Spanish America*. Princeton, NJ: Markus Wiener, 2003.

Rowell, Charles Henry. "'El Primer Libertador de Las Americas' / The First Liberator of the Americas: The Editor's Notes." *Callaloo* 31, no. 1 (2008): 1–11.

Rúa, Mérida M., and Ana Y. Ramos-Zayas. "Introduction." In *Critical Dialogues in Latinx Studies: A Reader*, 1–11. New York: New York University Press, 2021.

Rudolph, Jennifer Domino. *Embodying Latino Masculinities: Producing Masculatinidad*. New York: Palgrave Macmillan, 2016.

Said, Edward. *Orientalism*. 25th anniv. ed. New York: Vintage Books, 1979.

Sale, Maggie. "Call and Response as Critical Method: African-American Oral Traditions and *Beloved*." *African American Review* 26, no. 1 (1992): 41–50.

Salgado, César A. "The Archive and Afro-Latina/o Field Formation: Arturo Alfonso Schomburg at the Intersection of Puerto Rican and African American Studies and Literatures." In *The Cambridge History of Latina/o American Literature*, edited by John Morán González and Laura Lomas, 371–393. New York: Cambridge University Press, 2018.

Sánchez González, Lisa. "Arturo Alfonso Schomburg: A Transamerican Intellectual." In *African Roots / American Cultures: African in the Creation of the Americas*, 139–152. Lanham, MD: Rowman and Littlefield, 2001.

Sánchez González, Lisa. *Boricua Literature: A Literary History of the Puerto Rican Diaspora*. New York: New York University Press, 2001.

Sánchez González, Lisa. "Decolonizing Schomburg." *African American Review* 54, no. 1 (2021): 129–142.

Sánchez González, Lisa. "Pura Belpré (1899–1982): Her Life and Writing." In *The Stories I Read to the Children: The Life and Writing of Pura Belpré, the Legendary Storyteller, Children's Author, and New York Public Librarian*, 15–61. New York: Center for Puerto Rican Studies, 2013.

Sánchez Korrol, Virginia E. *From Colonia to Community: The History of Puerto Ricans in New York City*. 2nd ed. Oakland: University of California Press, 1994.

Sánchez, Marta E. "La Malinche at the Intersection: Race and Gender in *Down These Mean Streets*." *PMLA* 113, no. 1 (January 1998): 117–128.

Sánchez, Marta E. *"Shakin' Up" Race and Gender: Intercultural Connections in Puerto Rican, African American, and Chicano Narratives and Culture (1965–1995)*. Austin: University of Texas Press, 2005.
Sánchez, Rosaura. *Telling Identities: The Californio Testimonios*. Minneapolis: University of Minnesota Press, 1995.
Santiago-Díaz, Eleuterio, and Ilia Rodríguez. "Writing Race against Literary Whiteness: The Afro-Puerto Rican Outcry of Piri Thomas." *Bilingual Review / La Revista Bilingüe* 31, no. 1 (April 13, 2012): 12–29.
Saunders, Patricia J. "Fugitive Dreams of Diaspora: Conversations with Saidiya Hartman." *Anthurium: A Caribbean Studies Journal* 6, no. 1 (January 1, 2008): Article 7.
Schomburg, Arthur A. "An Appreciation." 1915. Piñeiro de Rivera, 87–98.
Schomburg, Arthur A. "General Antonio Maceo." 1931. Piñeiro de Rivera, 174–180.
Schomburg, Arthur A. "General Evaristo Estenoz." 1912. Piñeiro de Rivera, 73–75.
Schomburg, Arthur A. "José Campeche 1752–1809." 1934. Piñeiro de Rivera, 201–208.
Schomburg, Arthur A. "My Trip to Cuba in Quest of Negro Books." 1933. Piñeiro de Rivera, 181–187.
Schomburg, Arthur A. "The Negro Brotherhood of Sevilla." 1927. Piñeiro de Rivera, 145–151.
Schomburg, Arthur A. "Negroes in Sevilla." 1928. Piñeiro de Rivera, 153–159.
Schomburg, Arthur A. "Notes on Panamá and the Negro." 1928. Piñeiro de Rivera, 161–166.
Schomburg, Arthur A. "In Quest of Juan de Pareja." 1927. Piñeiro de Rivera, 139–143.
Schomburg, Arturo A. "Crispus Attucks—Free Patriot: Sailor's Death Was Factor in Creation of Nation, Schomburg Asserts." *New York Amsterdam News*. August 24, 1935. ProQuest Historical Newspapers.
Schomburg, Arthur A. "The Negro Digs Up His Past." In *The New Negro*, edited by Alain Locke, 231–237. New York: Touchstone, 1925.
Schomburg, Arthur A. *Racial Integrity: A Plea for the Establishment of a Chair of Negro History in Our Schools and Colleges, Etc.* Occasional Paper No. 3, Negro Society for Historical Research. August Valentine Bernier, 1913.
Schomburg Center for Research in Black Culture. *The Legacy of Arthur A. Schomburg: A Celebration of the Past, a Vision for the Future*. New York: New York Public Library, 1986.
Shaffer, Kirwin R. *Black Flag Boricuas: Anarchism, Authoritarianism, and The Left in Puerto Rico, 1897–1921*. Urbana: University of Illinois Press, 2013.
Sharpe, Christina Elizabeth. *Monstrous Intimacies: Making Post-Slavery Subjects*. Durham, NC: Duke University Press, 2010.
Sheppard, Phillis Isabella. "Black Women's Experience of Religion, Race, and Gender." In *Self, Culture, and Others in Womanist Practical Theology*, 23–39. New York: Springer, 2011.
Sinnette, Elinor Des Verney. *Arthur Alfonso Schomburg: Black Bibliophile and Collector*. New York: New York Public Library; Detroit, MI: Wayne State University Press, 1989.
Smith, Barbara. "A Press of Our Own: Kitchen Table: Women of Color Press," *Frontiers* 10, no. 3 (1989): 11–13.

Smith, Sidonie. "The Autobiographical Manifesto: Identities, Temporalities, Politics." *Prose Studies* 14, no. 2 (1991): 186–212.
Smith, Sidonie, and Julia Watson. "Introduction: De/colonization and the Politics of Discourse in Women's Autobiographical Practices." In *De/colonizing the Subject: The Politics of Gender in Women's Autobiography*, xiii–xxxi. Minneapolis: University of Minnesota Press, 1992.
Smith, Sidonie, and Julia Watson. *Reading Autobiography: A Guide for Interpreting Life Narratives*. 2nd ed. Minneapolis: University of Minnesota Press, 2010.
Some Girls. Saboteur Media, 2017. https://somegirlsdoc.com/.
Sosa, Juan B., and Enrique J. Arce. *Compendio de Historia de Panamá*. Panamá: Casa Editorial del *Diario de Panamá* / Morales and Rodríguez, 1911.
Springer, Kimberly. "Third Wave Black Feminism?" *Signs: Journal of Women in Culture and Society* 27, no. 4 (Summer 2002): 1059–1082.
Stanchich, Maritza. "Insular Interventions: Jesús Colón Unmasks Racial Harmonizing and Popular Uplift Discourses in Puerto Rico." In *Hispanic Caribbean Literature of Migration: Narratives of Displacement*, edited by Vanessa Pérez Rosario, 171–187. New York: Palgrave Macmillan, 2010.
Strand, Daniel, and Anna Källén. "I Am a Viking! DNA, Popular Culture and the Construction of Geneticized Identity." *New Genetics and Society* 40, no. 4 (January 31, 2021): 1–21.
Svirsky, Marcelo, and Simone Bignall. *Agamben and Colonialism*. Edinburgh: Edinburgh University Press, 2012.
Tallbear, Kim. *Native American DNA: Tribal Belonging and the False Promise of Genetic Science*. Minneapolis: University of Minnesota Press, 2013.
Telles, Edward, and PERLA, eds. *Pigmentocracies: Ethnicity, Race, and Color in Latin America*. Chapel Hill: University of North Carolina Press, 2014.
Thomas, Piri. *Down These Mean Streets*. 30th anniv. ed. New York: Vintage Books, 1967.
Thomas, Piri. *Savior, Savior, Hold My Hand*. New York: Doubleday, 1972.
Thomas, Piri. *Seven Long Times*. Houston, TX: Arte Público Press, 1974.
Tinajero, Araceli. *El Lector: A History of the Cigar Factory Reader*. Translated by Judith E. Grasberg. Austin: University of Texas Press, 2010.
Tinsley, Omise'eke Natasha. *Beyoncé in Formation: Remixing Black Feminism*. Austin: University of Texas Press, 2018.
Torres, Arlene. "La Gran Familia Puertorriqueña 'Ej Prieta de Beldá' (The Great Puerto Rican Family Is Really Really Black)." In *Blackness in Latin America and the Caribbean*, edited by Arlene Torres and Norman E. Whitten, Jr., 2:285–306. Bloomington: Indiana University Press, 1998.
Torres, Arlene, and Norman E. Whitten, Jr. "General Introduction: To Forge the Future in the Fires of the Past: An Interpretative Essay on Racism, Domination, Resistance, and Liberation." In *Blackness in Latin America and the Caribbean: Social Dynamics and Cultural Transformations*, 3–33. 2 vols. Bloomington: Indiana University Press, 1998.
Torres-Saillant, Silvio. *Introduction to Dominican Blackness*. New York: CUNY Dominican Studies Research Institute, 2010.
Torres-Saillant, Silvio. "The Tribulations of Blackness: Stages in Dominican Racial Identity." *Callaloo* 23, no. 3 (2000): 1086–1111.

Tovar, Federico Ribes. *Albizu Campos: Puerto Rican Revolutionary.* New York: Plus Ultra Educational Publishers, 1971.
Trevino, Wendy. *Brazilian Is Not a Race.* Oakland, CA: Commune Editions, 2016.
Trinh T. Minh-ha. *Woman, Native, Other: Writing Postcoloniality and Feminism.* Bloomington: Indiana University Press, 1989.
Trouillot, Michel-Rolph. *Silencing the Past: Power and the Production of History.* Boston, MA: Beacon Press, 1995.
Twine, France Winddance. *Racism in a Racial Democracy: The Maintenance of White Supremacy in Brazil.* New Brunswick, NJ: Rutgers University Press, 1998.
Tyner, James A. *Space, Place, and Violence: Violence and the Embodied Geographies of Race, Sex, and Gender.* New York: Routledge, 2012.
Valdés, Vanessa K. *Diasporic Blackness: The Life and Times of Arturo Alfonso Schomburg.* Albany: State University of New York Press, 2017.
Valdés, Vanessa K. *Oshun's Daughters: The Search for Womanhood in the Americas.* Albany: State University of New York Press, 2014.
Valdés, Vanessa K. "The Afterlives of Arturo Alfonso Schomburg." *Small Axe: A Caribbean Journal of Criticism* 24, no. 1 (March 1, 2020): 142–151.
Vargas, Deborah R. "Ruminations on Lo Sucio as a Latino Queer Analytic." *American Quarterly* 66, no. 3 (2014): 715–726.
Vasconcelos, José. *The Cosmic Race / La Raza Cósmica.* Translated by Didier T. Jaén. Baltimore, MD: John Hopkins University Press, 1997.
Vázquez, David J. *Triangulations: Narrative Strategies for Navigating Latino Identity.* Minneapolis: University of Minnesota Press, 2011.
Vega, Bernardo. *Memoirs of Bernardo Vega.* Edited by Cesar Andreu Iglesias. Translated by Juan Flores. New York: Monthly Review Press, 1984.
Vigil, James Diego. *The Projects: Gang and Non-gang Families in East Los Angeles.* Austin: University of Texas Press, 2007.
Wagenheim, Kal. *Puerto Rico: A Profile.* New York: Praeger, 1970.
Wailoo, Keith, Alondra Nelson, and Catherine Lee, eds. *Genetics and the Unsettled Past: The Collision of DNA, Race, and History.* New Brunswick, NJ: Rutgers University Press, 2012.
Walker, Alice. *In Search of Our Mothers' Gardens: Womanist Prose.* Orlando, FL: Harvest, 2003.
Wanzer-Serrano, Darrel. *The New York Young Lords and the Struggle for Liberation.* Philadelphia, PA: Temple University Press, 2015.
Warren, Wendy. *New England Bound: Slavery and Colonization in Early America.* New York: Liveright, 2016.
Weinstock, Jeffrey Andrew, ed. *The Monster Theory Reader.* Minneapolis: University of Minnesota Press, 2020.
White, Melanie. "Afro-Nicaraguan Diasporas of Sexual Violence and Visual Art as a Space for Healing." *Caribbean Quarterly* 67, no. 4 (November 2021): 453–472.
Wolfe, Justin, and Lowell Gudmundson, eds. *Blacks and Blackness in Central America: Between Race and Place.* Durham, NC: Duke University Press, 2010.
Woodson, Carter G. *The Negro in Our History.* Washington, DC: Associated Publishers, 1922.
Wright, Nazera Sadiq. *Black Girlhood in the Nineteenth Century.* Urbana: University of Illinois Press, 2016.

Wyatt, Jean. "Patricia Hill Collins's *Black Sexual Politics* and the Genealogy of the Strong Black Woman." *Studies in Gender and Sexuality* 9, no. 1 (January 15, 2008): 52–67.

Young, Cynthia. *Soul Power: Culture, Radicalism, and the Making of a U.S. Third World Left*. Durham, NC: Duke University Press, 2006.

Young Lords Party (YLP). *Palante: Voices and Photographs of the Young Lords, 1969–1971*. Chicago, IL: Haymarket Books, 2011.

Young Lords Party, and Michael Abramson. *Palante: Young Lords Party*. Photographs by Michael Abramson, text by the Young Lords Party and Michael Abramson. New York: McGraw-Hill Book Company, 1971.

Zafar, Rafia. "Arturo Schomburg's Gastronomica." *African American Review* 54, no. 1–2 (2021): 159–165.

Zafar, Rafia. "The Negro Cooks Up His Past: Arturo Schomburg's Uncompleted Cookbook." In *Recipes for Respect: African American Meals and Meaning*, 79–90. Athens: University of Georgia Press, 2019.

Zamora, Omaris Z. "Transnational Renderings of *Negro/a/x/**." *Small Axe: A Caribbean Journal of Criticism* 26, no. 2 (July 1, 2022): 93–99.

Index

abjection, 91
Abraham Lincoln Brigade, 67–68
Abramson, Michael, 177n15
academic discourse, 77, 99, 189n124
Acevedo, Elizabeth, 79
Acosta-Belén, Edna, 51, 52, 73
activism, 49, 60, 73
Aesthetics of Excess (Hernández 2020), 131
Africa, 18, 24
African American jazz, 122
African diaspora: history of, 28; and Latinidad, 3; and Lucumi, 109, 111; and US narratives of Blackness, 5
Africanity: and Gloria Anzaldúa, 168n95; and Pura Belpré, 23; and Central America, 165n52; and erasure, 156, 157; and feminist spirituality, 18; and mestizaje, 55, 106; and Marta Moreno Vega, 104, 111–112, 122, 123, 124, 126, 191n19, 195n123; and Arturo Alfonso Schomburg, 27, 33–34, 40, 44, 45; and Piri Thomas, 75; and Young Lords, 51, 60, 62
Afro-Boricua identity, 55, 59, 63, 179n47, 181n84
Afro-Caribbean poets, 79
Afro-Central American writers, 161–162n15, 162n16, 163n25
Afro-diasporic Blackness, 29, 42
Afro-Dominicans, 154
AfroLatina life writing, 18, 23, 104, 158
AfroLatinidad: and Ariana Brown, 144; and Jaquira Díaz, 140; and Marta Moreno Vega, 107, 116; and postnationalism, 150–151; Puerto Rican construction of, 51; and Arturo Alfonso Schomburg, 38, 41–42, 46; and Piri Thomas, 185n25; and US narratives of Blackness, 5; and visibility, 1, 3–4
AfroLatinidades: construction of, 128, 153, 164n36, 170n29; and creative destruction, 80; defined, 4–5; and diasporic Black identity, 48, 104; and feminist spirituality, 103; and life writing, 13, 159; and masculinity, 18, 26, 90–91; and mestizaje, 10–11; and monstrosity, 132; and Marta Moreno Vega, 77; new forms of, 152; and queerness, 130; and Piri Thomas, 76; and US Black/white binary, 9; and white supremacy, 164n31; Omaris Zamora on, 202n2
AfroLatino writers, 7, 15, 18, 102, 190n6. *See also* specific writers
AfroLatinx life writing: and AfroLatinx studies, 5–6; and DNA ancestry tests, 153; and feminist

AfroLatinx life writing (*continued*) spirituality, 18; and gendered norms, 102; and mestizaje, 6, 7, 11; as papelitos guardados, 15; and politics, 16; and power structures, 11–13, 13; and Arturo Alfonso Schomburg, 46; as testimonio, 12; twenty-first century, 152; and visibility, 4, 7, 9, 153; and woman-of-color feminist theorists, 14–15
AfroLatinx studies, 5, 6, 7, 19, 29, 153–154, 201n149
afromestizaje, 14
Afro–Puerto Ricans: and activism, 49; and anti-Blackness, 141; and Blackness, 119–120; and early twentieth-century life writing, 178n23; and feminism, 28–29; and history, 60; liminal status of, 47, 56; and "observe and participate" autobiography, 73; and racial myth, 63; and representation, 50, 54; and socialist literary tradition, 51; and stereotypes, 107; and Piri Thomas, 79
Afro–Puerto Rican socialism, 48, 53–54
Alba, Marinieves, 161–162n15
Albizu Campos, Pedro, 51, 52, 60, 180–181n73
Alexander, M. Jacqui, 84, 115
Alonso, Manuel A., 55
The Altar of My Soul (Moreno Vega 2000), 107, 109–115, 116, 192–193n54
Amendment 17 in Cuba, 43
American Dirt (Cummins 2018), 131
American Negro Academy (ANA), 28
American Revolution, 34–36
Anacaona (cacique), 155–156
ancestry tests, 153–154, 154–155, 156–158, 201–202n1, 202n3, 203n20
"Angels in My Hometown Church" (Colón), 57
Anthony, Casey, 131
anti-Blackness: and academic mestizaje, 99–102; and Afro–Puerto Ricans, 56; and ancestry tests, 155; and ethnoracial identity, 94–95; and heritage, 89–90; and hypervisibility, 65–66; internalization of, 82, 119–120; and Latina/o/x community, 74; and mestizaje, 10; and Mexico, 149; and myth of racial harmony, 50; and Puerto Rico, 47–48, 61, 133; and secrecy, 118; transnational nature of, 43; and whitening, 141
Antillean independence movement, 27
Anzaldúa, Gloria: and Ariana Brown, 144; and Latinx studies, 13–14; and life writing, 12; and mestiza consciousness, 9; militance of, 151; and mosaic, 32
Aponte, Carlos, 60
archives: and AfroLatina writers, 15; and Black history, 28; and CENTRO, 48; and Arturo Alfonso Schomburg, 30, 46
Archives of Conjure (Otero 2020), 116
"Are You Still a Slave?" (hooks 2014), 129
Argentina, 141, 199n88
Arias, Arturo, 6, 9, 161n13, 164n33
Arrizón, Alicia, 9
Arroyo, Jossianna, 6, 21
art history, 39–41
"Art of Writing for Children" (Belpré undated), 24, 25
Ashe, Bertram, 161n3
"As I See It from Here" (Colón column), 51
assimilation, 91
"At the End of the Borderlands" (Brown 2021), 146
Attucks, Crispus, 26–27, 29, 34, 35, 36–37, 173n95
autobiographical manifestos, 64
auto/biography, 25, 26, 29, 32, 38, 48
Autobiography of Benjamin Franklin (1771–1790), 25
autohistoria, 14
autohistoria-teoría, 14, 15, 167n93

Baby Lollipops, 131, 137, 139–140, 198n66
Báez, Josefina, 151, 201n139

Balboa, 42
batá drums, 122–123, 124, 125, 126
Bauzá, Mario, 122
Beer, June, 177n10
Belpré, Pura: biography of, 169n19; and erasure, 25; and identity, 169–170n22; and jibaridad, 179n49; marriage of, 169n12; and masculinist power structures, 7; and mestizaje, 180n59; and Puerto Rico, 170n24, 177n18; and visibility, 17, 23–24; work of, 22–23, 49
Betances, Ramón Emeterio, 60, 171n46
Beyoncé, 112–113
Bignall, Simone, 27
biographical essays, 21–22
biography, 25, 29, 31, 32–33
biography studies, 27
Bird of Paradise (Cepeda 2013), 19, 154, 156–158
Bissette, Cyrille Charles Auguste, 32
Black art, 154
Black Arts Movement, 79
Black Central American writers, 161–162n15
Black feminism, 16. *See also* feminism
Black history, 29–32
Black Latinas Know Collective, 5, 6
Black Man (Brown 1863), 25
"Black Mother Woman" (Lorde), 2
black narrative modes, 61
Black nationalism, 81
Blackness: and abjection, 91; and AfroLatinx writers, 8; and Pedro Albizu Campos, 60; and Ariana Brown, 128, 200n104; and Central America, 163n25; conceptions of, 192n53; construction of, 47–48; definitions of, 96; and Dominicanidad, 202n15; and ethnoracial identity, 78; and Guatemala, 3; and hypervisibility, 65–66, 159; and identity, 17, 63, 94; and jibaridad, 59–60; and labor, 118; and Latinidad, 3, 5; in *Mama's Girl*, 2; and marielitos, 137–138; and mestizaje, 105–106; and monstrosity, 140; negotiation of, 92; and othering, 83; and Juan de Pareja, 40; and ruins, 147; and Arturo Alfonso Schomburg, 28–29; and Piri Thomas, 86; José Vasconcelos on, 165n56; and violence, 100; and visibility, 4, 76
Black Panamanians, 161n11
Black Panther 21, 179n41
Black Panther Party (BPP), 52, 55, 72
Black Power, 79, 97
Black studies, 5, 6, 8, 21, 30, 164n33
Black West Indians, 42
Black/white binary, 56–57
Blake, Felice, 184n7
blank space, 146
blanqueamiento, 55, 77, 98, 166n71. *See also* whitening
blurred visibility, 6
Bonilla-Silva, Eduardo, 91, 187n67
Borderlands / La Frontera (Anzaldúa 1987), 12, 14, 144, 151
borderlands theory, 14
Borders of Dominicanidad (García-Peña 2016), 14
Boriquén, 50
Boston Massacre, 26, 29, 35–36, 37–38, 173n95
bóvedas, 123–124
Brady, Mary Pat, 197n20
Brandon, George, 191n19
Braxton, Joanna, 12
Brigada Solidaria del Oeste, 74
"A Bright Child Asks a Question" (Colón), 56–57
Brown, Ariana: and Afro-Mexican history, 130; and Blackness, 200n104; and Chicana feminism, 14; and girlhood, 151–152; and masculinity, 150; and monstrosity, 131; and postnationalism, 149–151; and queer AfroLatinidad, 129; verse memoirs of, 18–19, 128, 144, 145, 146–147
Brown, Claude, 79–80
Brown, H. Rap/Jamil Abdullah Al-Amin, 92–93

Brown, Monica, 80–81, 186n47
Brown, Ruth Nicole, 151, 197–198n40
Brown, William Wells, 25
Brownness: and anti-Blackness, 14; and erasure, 57; and mestizaje, 9; and visibility, 4, 5
Bruce, John Edward, 25, 28
Bryant, Sherwin, 17, 47–48, 176n9

Cabeza de Vaca, Álvar Nuñez, 44
Cabral, Amilcar, 74, 107
Caine, Barbara, 30
call-and-response AfroLatinidad, 104, 124, 126, 190n4
Caminero-Santangelo, Marta, 99, 101
Campeche, José, 24, 39–40, 174n125
capitalism, 54
Cárdenas, Maritza E., 163n25
Cardona, Ana Maria, 137, 138, 139–140, 198n66, 198n69, 199n80
Caribbean colonies, 37
Caribbean Cultural Center African Diaspora Institute (CCCADI), 106–107
"Carmencita" (Colón 1961), 66–68
Casal, Lourdes: and ancestry, 154; and call-and-response AfroLatinidad, 104; on drumming, 122–123; and espiritismo, 115; and feminist spirituality, 18; and mestizaje, 105–106; and Marta Moreno Vega, 103; and Nigeria, 157, 203n24
Casper, Scott E., 25, 27
Castro, Juan E. de, 165n45
Castromán Soto, Margarita, 30
Catholic Church, 42, 45, 67
Catholicism, 106, 119
Central America: and Blackness, 3; and slavery, 37
Central American–Americanness, 8–9, 161n13
CENTRO, 48
Cepeda, Raquel: and ancestry, 202n9; and ancestry tests, 153–155; and Family Tree DNA, 202n19; and genealogy, 189n125; and oral history, 158; and scholarship, 19; and *Some Girls*, 203n31; and stereotypes, 156; travels of, 157
Cervantes, Marco A., 165n45
Chambers, Veronica, 1–3, 153, 161n4, 161n10, 161n14, 162n16, 162n18
Chicago Defender, 173n95
Chicana feminism, 14. *See also* feminism
Chicano Movement, 10
childhood, 84, 151
children's literature, 22, 23, 24
chonga body politics, 142
Christian, Barbara, 16
Cíbola, 44–45
cimarrones (maroons), 147
citizenship, 36, 51, 84
Clark, Mary Ann, 108, 116, 191n23
Cleaver, Eldridge, 79
Cohen, Jeffrey, 132, 134, 140
collective life stories, 53–54
colloquial speech, 69
Colón, Clara, 183n124
Colón, Jesús: and AfroLatinidad, 49; and anti-Blackness, 17, 48; and anti-Latina attitudes, 181n95; biography of, 51–52; childhood of, 64; and colorism, 23; and communism, 177n19; and crónicas, 179n43; and hypervisibility, 65–66; and life writing, 74; and mestizaje, 180n59; politics of, 47; and Puerto Ricans, 183n1; and Puerto Rico, 176n2; and religion, 190n6; and representation, 56–59; and Arturo Alfonso Schomburg, 171n55; sketches of, 54–55, 179n42, 180n62; Spanish-language writing of, 182n112; and Joseph Stalin, 178n23; and whiteness, 181n92; and Young Lords, 178n28
colonialism: and mestizaje, 9; and Puerto Rico, 47–48, 59; and Arturo Alfonso Schomburg, 27; and slavery, 176n9; and Taíno people, 155; and Young Lords, 17
color blindness, 43
colorism, 85, 89–90, 91, 118, 186n50

coming out, 129
communism, 67
Condition, Elevation, Emigration, and Destiny of the Colored People of the United States (Delany 1852), 25
conspiracy theories, 141
Cooper, Anna Julia, 96
Copeland, M. Shawn, 125
creative destruction, 76–77, 80, 84, 85, 92–93, 95, 102, 132
The Crisis, 25–26, 35, 39, 43
"Crispus Attucks—Free Patriot" (Schomburg 1935), 35, 37
"Cristo Era un Young Lord" (Young Lords), 53
crónicas, 22, 166n75, 172n64, 179n43
Crummell, Alexander, 28
Cruz, Angie, 88, 187n68
Cruz, Celia, 124–125
Cruz-Malavé, Arnaldo, 88, 90
Cuando los espiritús bailan mambo (Moreno Vega 2002), 107, 116
Cuba, 39, 43, 105–106, 109–110, 124
Cuban War of Independence, 43
cultural nationalism, 74
cultural remittances, 6
culture: and Afro–Puerto Rican literary tradition, 51, 64; and assimilation, 91; and autohistoria, 14; and Pura Belpré, 24; Lourdes Casal on, 105; and children's literature, 22; as fragments, 155; and genomic testing, 158; and identity, 76, 81, 86, 92, 94–96, 98; and mestizaje, 9–10; and monstrosity, 132, 134, 136; and Marta Moreno Vega, 112; and participant observation, 49–50; as political, 107; and queers of color, 130; and race, 115–116; and santería, 122
Cummins, Jeanine, 131
curandera historians, 110
Curtis, Benjamin Robbins, 36

The Daily Worker, 51
Das, Veena, 83
Davies, Carole Boyce, 14, 15, 53, 69, 85, 167n84, 168nn98–99

Dávila, Arlene, 55
Davis, Angela, 6, 164n39
Def, Mos, 59–60
Def Poetry Jam (Def 2002–2007), 59–60
Delany, Martin, 25
Delgadillo, Theresa, 167–168n94, 191n19, 192n27
diaspora Blackness, 3, 5, 6, 104
The Diaspora Strikes Back (Flores 2009), 6
diasporic Africanity, 18
Díaz, Jaquira: and Baby Lollipops case, 198n66; and girlhood, 141–144; and La Llorona, 134–137; and lesbianism, 140; marriage of, 199n91; and monstrosity, 18, 127, 128–129; origin story of, 133; parents of, 138–139; and queer AfroLatinidad, 129; and violence, 130, 131, 184n9
difference: and connection, 12, 32; and identity, 130
Di Iorio Sandín, Lyn, 84
DNA reveal videos, 158
domestic violence, 70
double-dutch, 1–2, 161n1
Down These Mean Streets (Thomas 1967): and AfroLatinidades, 77; and Barrio speech, 69; chronology of, 185n20; and colorism, 89; drafts of, 80–81, 88, 188n88; and identity, 86, 91, 92, 99; as influence, 131, 152; and marginality, 15; and mestizaje, 184n12; and monster theory, 196n6; and racial discourse, 187n57; reviews of, 79; and violence, 76, 84–85, 185n25; and visibility, 184n3; and *When the Spirits Dance Mambo*, 107
the dozens, 92–95, 96
Dred Scott, 43
Du Bois, W. E. B., 25, 77, 100, 101, 189n125, 190n138

"The Economic Contribution by the Negro to America" (Schomburg), 37
El gíbaro (Alonso 1845), 55
El Museo del Barrio, 106

El Nié, 151, 201n139
El pan nuestro de cada día (Our daily bread) (Frade 1905), 58–59
El pueblo se levanta, 59, 71–72, 182n105
"El puertorriqueño docil" (Marqués 1967), 61
Emerson, Ralph Waldo, 25, 38
"Entre todo el pueblo se escribe un poema / Pedro's Poetry" (YLP 1971), 59
erasure: of Africanity, 156, 157; and Afro-Dominicans, 154; and AfroLatina writers, 104; and AfroLatinidades, 3, 5; and AfroLatinx writers, 11, 25, 128, 153, 170n29; and archives, 21–22; and Pura Belpré, 23–24; Jesús Colón on, 57, 58, 59; and Indigenous people, 40, 44, 155; and Jewish people, 31; and mestizaje, 159; and minor feelings, 26; and monstrosity, 152; and Arturo Alfonso Schomburg, 32, 38; and Piri Thomas, 78, 184n15; and woman-of-color feminism, 7
Espaillat, Adriano, 163n27
Espicy Nipples y La Sombrilla Cuir, 74
espiritismo (spiritism), 115–116, 123, 124, 154
Estenoz, Evaristo, 43
Estevanico, 44, 45, 175n157
Esteves, Sandra María, 79
ethnic studies, 21
ethnoracial identity, 96
eugenics, 91
Every Child Is Born a Poet (Robinson and Thomas 2003), 187n72

family, 85, 86, 89–90, 91, 137, 154, 157–158
Family Tree DNA, 156, 202n11
Famous Men of the Negro Race (Hopkins 1900–1901), 25
femininity, 111–112
feminism, 12, 66–68, 192n27. *See also* Black feminism; Chicana feminism; Third World feminism
feminist socialism, 66

feminist spirituality, 18, 103, 104, 107, 110
Fennell, Saraciea J., 161–162n15, 163n25
Feracho, Lesley, 8, 165n46
Fernández Olmos, Margarite, 115
Fetta, Stephanie, 184n11
"Field Notes" (Brown 2021), 149
Figueroa, Sotero, 47
Figueroa-Vásquez, Yomaira C. (aka Yomaira Figueroa), 6, 8, 117, 165n49, 194n80
First Church Offensive, 59
First Spanish United Methodist Church, 182n105
Fleetwood, Nicole, 6, 8, 75
Flores, Juan, 4, 5, 6, 52, 176n1, 178n22
"Folklore of the Puerto Rican Child" (Belpré 1977?), 24, 170n25
Frade, Ramón, 58, 180n65
Franklin, Benjamin, 25
"Free Negroes in the Formation of the American Republic" (Schomburg), 36

gang organizations, 69–70, 81
García-Peña, Lorgia, 6, 14, 21, 151, 164n32, 190n3, 201n139
gender: and Jesús Colón, 48, 66; and double standards, 120–121; and life writing, 102; and orisha mythology, 113; and *Palante*, 59–60; racialized conceptions of, 64; and Young Lords, 70–73, 183n129
genealogies of empowerment, 159
"General Antonio Maceo" (Schomburg), 39
"General Evaristo Estenoz" (Schomburg), 43
genetic genealogy, 154
genomic life writing, 153–154
Georgie (Young Lord), 69
Gift of Black Folk (Du Bois 1924), 25
Gillespie, Dizzy, 122
Gilmore, Leigh, 129
girlhood: and Ariana Brown, 144, 151; and life writing, 129; literature of, 197n20; and Lucumí, 114–115; in

Mama's Girl, 2–3; and monstrosity, 131; in *Ordinary Girls*, 141–144; and santería, 110; in *When the Spirits Dance Mambo*, 117
Glissant, Edouard, 22
Gomez, Jewelle, 130, 196n12
González, Gloria (aka Gloria Gonzáles Fontanez), 52, 55
González, José Luis, 55, 176n7
González, Juan, 52, 55, 60, 63
González, Olivia, 137, 138, 139–140
Gordon, Avery F., 11, 136, 143, 198n57
Graciela, 124, 125
Great Man narrative, 13, 15, 27, 29, 38–45, 61, 75, 167n88, 170n32
Grillo, "Machito," 122
Guatemala, 162n23
Guidotti-Hernández, Nicole, 17, 82, 83, 84
Guillén, Nicolas, 164n38
Guridy, Frank, 177n10
Gusdorf, Georges, 13
Guzmán, Pablo "Yorúba," 49, 52, 55, 61–62, 68, 73

hair, 24, 61, 86, 91, 133, 187n56
Hale, Charles, 162n23
Ham, curse of, 98
Harlem, 52, 81, 122, 124
Harlem Renaissance, 28
Hartman, Saidiya, 18–19, 76, 128, 129, 132, 145, 165n49, 197n25, 197n28
Hecht, Joe, 67–68
hegemonic blackness, 92, 164n32, 190n3
The Help (Stockett 2009), 131
Hernández, Jillian, 131, 137–138, 142, 196n17
Herskovits, Melville J., 191n19
heteropatriarchy, 134
Hine, Darlene Clark, 118
hip-hop, 154, 203n26
history: and Afro-Caribbean religions, 105; and Pura Belpré, 169n19; and Ariana Brown, 148; and Jesús Colón, 57; and family, 157–158; and Great Man narrative, 170n32; and mestizaje, 155–156; and Arturo Alfonso Schomburg, 27–28, 29–33, 35, 36–42, 45, 46; and violence, 83, 134; and Young Lords, 52–53, 60, 62
"History of Boriken 7" (*Palante* 1971), 60
Hoffnung-Garskof, Jesse, 21
Holton, Adalaine, 21, 22, 28, 29, 41, 179n43
Homan, Margaret, 12
home, 86, 186n47
Hong, Cathy Park, 26, 54, 92, 131, 132, 147, 200n110
Hooker, Juliet, 177n10
hooks, bell, 15, 129, 143
Hopkins, Pauline, 25
Horn, Lars, 199n91
Howes, Craig, 12, 27, 167n86
Hoy, Vielka Cecilia, 3, 6–7
Hunsu, Folasade, 114
Hurricane María, 74
hybridity, 141
hypermasculinity, 79
hypervisibility: and AfroLatinidades, 4, 5, 128, 159, 170n29; and AfroLatinx life writing, 7; and AfroLatinx writers, 8, 12, 16, 153; and auto/biography, 48; and Jesús Colón, 57, 65–66; and feminist spirituality, 104; and monstrosity, 127; and *Ordinary Girls*, 133, 143; and queerness, 131; and scholarship, 6; and Arturo Alfonso Schomburg, 29; and spirituality, 104; and Piri Thomas, 77, 80, 83, 94, 184n2; and white supremacy, 11; and women's organizing, 71; and Yanga, 148, 149; and Young Lords, 48, 54–55

identity: and AfroLatinx writers, 6, 7–8; and Afro–Puerto Rican socialism, 53; and Pedro Albizu Campos, 60; and ancestry tests, 158; and Pura Belpré, 169–170n22; and Blackness, 3; and blacktinos, 196n18; and bodily experience, 77, 84; and Jesús Colón, 66–67; and culture, 96, 99; and dialogue, 94, 95; and

identity (*continued*)
  genomic life writing, 159; and Pablo "Yorúba" Guzmán, 61–62; and heritage, 78, 89–90; and home, 85; and jibaridad, 55, 63; and language, 92; and Latinidad, 5; and life writing, 48; and Lucumi, 111; in *Mama's Girl*, 2; and mestizaje, 9; and "observe and participate" autobiography, 50; and orisha mythology, 113; and political participation, 60; and postnationalism, 151; and queerness, 130; and racial self-identification, 101; and Arturo Alfonso Schomburg, 28–29, 46; and sexuality, 196n11; and Piri Thomas, 76–77; and violence, 83, 87, 93, 95; and visibility, 107; and Young Lords, 55
Ignatiev, Noel, 91
immigrant stories, 105–106
Independent Colored Party (Partido Independiente de Color, or PIC), 43
Indigenous erasure, 40
Indigenous identity, 155
"In Quest of Juan de Pareja" (Schomburg), 40–41
Insular Cases, 27
intellectualism, 99
interiority, 88–89
intersectionality, 113
intertextuality, 50
invisibility: and African explorers, 45; and AfroLatinidades, 5, 128; and AfroLatinx life writing, 7, 12; and auto/biography, 48; and Blackness, 24; and Central American–Americanness, 9; of Central American Blackness, 2, 9; and feminist spirituality, 104; and identity, 149; and labor, 7; and Lucumi, 103; and marginality, 15; mobilization of, 8; and scholarship, 6; and Arturo Alfonso Schomburg, 29; and white supremacy, 11
Irizarry, Ylce, 84

Irizarry Rodríguez, Jose M., 44
italics, 88–89

Jackson, Anna, 144–145
James, Winston, 28
Jefferson, Thomas, 34
Jesus Christ, 98–99
Jewish people, 31
jibaridad, 19, 48, 55, 58–59, 63, 179nn49–50, 181n84
"Jíbaro, My Pretty Nigger" (Luciano 1968), 59–60
Jim Crow laws, 95
Jiménez, Cha Cha, 49
Jiménez García, Marilisa, 23
Jiménez Román, Miriam, 4, 5, 6, 10
Jones, Jennifer A., 5, 164n36
Jones-Shafroth Act, 51
Jorge, Angela, 28–29
Jorgenson, Danny L., 49
"José Campeche 1752–1809" (Schomburg), 24, 39–40
Journal of Negro History, 26
Just Us (Rankine 2020), 145–146

Kachun, Mitch, 173n95
Kadar, Marlene, 21, 27
Kardec, Allan, 115
Kenyon Review, 127
King, Martin Luther Jr., 79
Kirkus Review, 2, 79
kitchen table histories, 117
Kleinman, Arthur, 83
Ku Klux Klan, 42–43

labor, 48, 66, 118
ladino identity, 3, 162n23
La Llorona, 129, 131, 134–137
language politics, 86
Lao-Montes, Agustin, 5, 6
La Patria, 47
"La Prieta" (Anzaldúa 1983), 14
La raza cósmica [*The Cosmic Race*] (Vasconcelos translated by Jaén 1997), 9
La relación y comentarios (Relation of Alvar Nuñez Cabeza de Vaca), 44

Las Dos Antillas, 27
La Sociedad de Albizu Campos, 52
Latina Feminist Group, 11, 14–15, 74, 108, 159
Latinidad: and AfroLatinx writers, 8; and anti-Blackness, 10; and Blackness, 3, 5; defined, 166n61; and whiteness, 85
Latino exceptionalism, 10
Latinx studies, 13–14
Laviera, Tato, 47, 79
lectores, 64
Lectures on Liberation (Davis 1970), 6
Lemonade (Beyoncé 2016), 112–113, 193n57
Lenin, Vladimir, 67
lesbianism, 140, 196n12
"Letter to Yanga, from Six-Year-Old Ariana" (Brown 2021), 147, 148
Levins Morales, Aurora, 74, 84, 110, 159
life writing: and AfroLatinx writers, 4; as creative destruction, 77–78; and feminist spirituality, 151; and Great Man narrative, 61; purpose of, 84; and religion, 110; responses to, 152; and social media, 159; studies of, 12; and violence, 83–84; and Young Lords, 48
life writing studies, 12, 27, 164n29, 167n86
Lipsitz, George, 91
"Little Things Are Big" (Colón 1961), 65–66
Locke, Alain, 29
Lomas, Laura, 47, 106
Look for Me in the Whirlwind (Black Panther 21), 179n41
López, Antonio, 164n31
López Oro, Paul Joseph, 6, 163n25
Lorde, Audre, 2, 6, 8, 12, 32, 130, 196n12
Los Angeles Times, 3
Luciano, Felipe, 52, 53, 55, 59–60
Lucumi: in *The Altar of My Soul*, 109–111, 112–114; and call-and-response AfroLatinidad, 18; and Casal, 105, 106; and Cuba, 6; and life writing, 103; and Moreno Vega, 104, 107; other terms for, 191n23; and syncretism, 191n19; terms for, 191n23; in *When the Spirits Dance Mambo*, 115–118, 123, 126, 191n19; and Yoruba philosophy, 108
Lucumi patakís (parables), 104, 110–114
Luis of Mozambique, 42
LUMA Energy protests, 74

Maceo, Antonio, 39, 40, 43
machismo, 72
Machito, 124, 125
Mahler, Anne Garland, 63
"Making of a Race" (Bruce 1922), 25
Mama's Girl (Chambers 1996), 1–3
Manchild in the Promised Land (Brown 1965), 79–80
marginality, 15, 39, 143
Mariel boatlift, 137–138
Marín, Francisco Gonzalo "Pachín," 47
Marisol and Magdalena (Chambers 1998), 2
maroon communities, 42
Marqués, René, 61
marriage, 22
Marshall, Elizabeth, 129
Martí, José, 172n64
Martínez, María Elena, 165n43
Martínez-Echazábal, Lourdes, 10, 106
Martír, Vanessa, 161–162n15
masculinism, 11, 15, 22, 38, 66, 102, 183n129
masculinity: and Black Power, 79; and bodily experience, 89; and creative destruction, 77; and interiority, 86; street practices of, 95; of street talk, 99; and Piri Thomas, 184n4, 184n7; and violence, 76
Masiki, Trent, 164n38
Matory, J. Lorand, 18
Mayflower, 38
McGill, Lisa D., 92
McLean, John, 36
mediation, 11, 148
Melendez, Miguel "Mickey," 52, 53, 63

mental illness, 136–137
Messy Girl (Brown 2017), 151, 201n143, 201n144
mestiza consciousness, 9, 168n95
mestizaje: academic, 99–102; and AfroLatinidades, 153; and AfroLatinx life writing, 11; and ancestry tests, 154, 155; and anti-Blackness, 14, 104; and call-and-response AfroLatinidad, 104; and Raquel Cepeda, 202n10; and colonial violence, 180n59; Jesús Colón on, 56–57; and Cuba, 165n54, 190n9; hegemonic, 105–106; histories of, 165–166n58; idealization of, 4; and monster theory, 19; perspectives on, 165n45; and Puerto Rico, 180n52; and racism, 43; and solidarity, 10; as a visibility structure, 6, 7, 9; and whitening, 55; and white supremacy, 164n31; and Yoruba philosophy, 111
Milian, Claudia, 6, 8–9, 162n20, 163n25
Millet, José, 116
Minh-ha, Trinh T., 14, 129, 168n99
minor feelings, 26, 54, 132, 197n25
Minor Feelings (Hong 2020), 131, 200n110
Mirabal, Nancy, 166n71, 190n9
Modestin, Yvette, 161–162n15, 163n25
monster theory, 128, 196n6, 198n71, 199n86
monstrosity, 127–129, 131–137, 139, 142
Monstrous Intimacies (Sharpe 2010), 128
Moody, Jocelyn, 12
Moore, Indya, 74
Moraga, Cherríe, 13–14
Morales, Iris, 52, 55, 70–72, 178n28, 182n121, 183n129
Moreno Vega, Marta: and AfroLatinidad, 77; and ancestry, 154; and Black Central American voices, 161–162n15; and Blackness, 112; and call-and-response AfroLatinidad, 104, 126; and Lourdes Casal, 103; on drumming, 123; and espiritismo, 115, 116,

124–125; and feminist spirituality, 18, 113; on Harlem music scene, 122; and identity, 120–121; and Lucumí, 106, 107, 109–110, 111, 117, 193nn60–61; and music, 195n123; and papelitos guardados, 108; and prophecy, 114; and santería, 117–118, 191n19; and secrecy, 119; and spiritual mestizaje, 167–168n94
Morrison, Toni, 33, 34, 173n90
Moya, Paula M. L., 15–16
mulataje, 166n59
multiculturalism, 24
Muñoz, José Esteban, 130, 131
Murillo, Edwin, 181n95
"Myself, First" (Brown 2020), 151
"My Wife Doesn't Work" (Colón 1961), 66

NAACP, 26
Nathans, Benjamin, 13
nationalism, 183n129
Nationalist Party (Puerto Rico), 51, 52
National Urban League, 26
Negro (Du Bois 1915), 25
Negro Brotherhood of Sevilla, 42–43, 44, 45
"The Negro Brotherhood of Sevilla" (Schomburg), 44
"The Negro Digs Up His Past" (Schomburg), 30, 31, 39
Negro in Our History (Woodson 1922), 25
Negro Makers of History (Woodson 1928), 25
Negro Society for Historical Research (NSHR), 28, 30
The New Negro (Locke 1925), 29, 30
New Negro ideology, 30
New York Amsterdam News, 35
New York City, 27–28, 62, 106
New York Public Library, 17, 22, 24, 28, 49, 169n12
New York Young Lords. *See* Young Lords
Neyra, Ren Ellis, 14
Nguyen, Viet Thanh, 17, 82–83, 128
nicknames, 118–119

Noel, Urayoán, 6, 184nn2–3, 184n8
nonviolence, 98–99
"Notes on Panamá and the Negro" (Schomburg), 41–42
Núñez, Victoria, 23
Nuyorican poetry, 6, 169n19, 184n2
Nuyorican Poets Cafe, 79
Nuyoricans, 62
Nwankwo, Ifeoma, 161n1

"observe and participate" autobiography, 49–51, 54, 64, 68–69, 73, 74
Oliver, Denise, 52, 55, 73, 179n47
Omi, Michael, 91
Operation Bootstrap, 78, 184–185n16
Opportunity, 25–26, 35, 41
Ordinary Girls (Díaz 2019): and Afro-diasporic tradition, 199n99; and girlhood, 141–144; and La Llorona, 18; and monstrosity, 127, 131–137; and queer AfroLatinidad, 152; and sexuality, 138–140; violence in, 3
orientalism, 156
"The Origin of Latin American Dances" (Colón), 52–53
orisha mythology, 111–114, 192n37, 192–193n54
Ortiz, Juan "Fi," 52
Ortiz, Ricardo L., 162n20
Oswald, Alice, 145
Otero, Solimar, 116
othering, 83
Oye, Boricua, 66

Padilla, Yajaira, 6, 164n33
Palante (Young Lords newsletter), 52, 60, 71
¡Palante, Siempre Palante! (Morales), 182n121
Palante: Young Lords Party (1971): and Blackness, 54–55; and gender, 70–71, 73; and history, 60; and masculinism, 17; and "observe and participate" autobiography, 50–51; and participant observation, 68–69; photos in, 62–63; and Pedro Pietri, 59; and revolutionary tradition, 61; structure of, 53
palenque communities, 42
Palmié, Stephan, 154–155
Panamá, 27, 41–42
Panama Canal, 42
papelitos guardados, 14–15, 108, 113, 121
Paravisini-Gebert, Lizabeth, 115
Pareja, Juan de, 40–41, 175n135
participant observation, 49, 68–69, 177n15
Patria, 172n64
Pelaez López, Alán, 147, 150, 162n20
Pérez, David, 52
Perez, Domino Renee, 134, 137
Pérez, Richie, 52, 55, 72–73, 73
Pérez-Torres, Rafael, 10–11, 165n45, 165–166n58
Perkins, Maureen, 13
Pero Like (YouTube channel), 158, 159
Pietri, Pedro, 59, 63, 180n69
"Pig of the Week" (Young Lords), 53
Platt Amendment, 43
Playing in the Dark (Morrison 1992), 33, 34
Poems and Letters (Wheatley 1915), 34
poetry, 79, 145
Portillo, Annette Angela, 12
postnationalism, 150–151
poverty, 62
Pozo, Chano, 122
prison, 79–80, 185n24
Puente, Tito, 122, 124
Puerto Rican folklore, 23, 24
"Puerto Rican Genocide!" (Young Lords), 53
A Puerto Rican in New York (Colón 1961), 17, 48, 51–52, 54, 55–57, 64–65, 177–178n21, 178n28
Puerto Rican nationalism, 81
"Puerto Rican Obituary" (Pietri 1971), 59, 60, 180n70
Puerto Ricans: liminal status of, 47; and Operation Bootstrap, 184–185n16; and representation, 56–59; and United States, 184n14; and voting, 178n22

Puerto Rico: and AfroLatino leadership, 61; and anti-Blackness, 17; and Pura Belpré, 170n24, 177n18; and Jesús Colón, 177n19; as commonwealth, 178n22; and Jaquira Díaz, 133; and espiritismo, 116; exploitation of, 74; and first uprising, 60; and mestizaje, 180n52; and Marta Moreno Vega, 117–118; and myth of racial harmony, 54; and nonwhiteness, 24; and tourism, 58; and US citizenship, 27; as US colony, 164n37, 176n2; and US imperialism, 51; and Young Lords, 53
Pullins, David, 175n135

Quashie, Kevin, 41, 85–86
queer AfroLatinidad, 18, 132, 144, 151, 152
Queer Latinidad (Rodríguez 2003), 130
queerness, 128, 129–131, 138, 139, 140–141, 151–152, 194n84
queers of color, 130
"Quick Story" (Brown 2021), 146–147
quietude, 41
Quinceañera Means Sweet 15 (Chambers 2001), 2

"Race for Theory" (Christian 1988), 16
racial democracy, 165–166n58
"Racial Integrity" (Schomburg 1913), 30–31
racialist science, 201–202n1
racialization: and ancestry tests, 153; and Black/white dichotomies, 105–106; and gender, 108; and girlhood, 197n20; and hair, 187n56; and interiority, 85–86; and monstrosity, 131–132; and participant observation, 65–66; and power structures, 11; and representation, 74; and stereotypes, 156; and street talk, 99
racism: and ancestry tests, 155; and anger, 89; and authentic Blackness, 95; internalization of, 93; and minor feelings, 54; and Nicaragua, 177n10; and pseudoscience, 91; and Puerto Rico, 57–58; and santería, 118; and US democracy, 67; and violence, 82
radical politics, 48
Rainbow Coalition, 52
Ramírez, Dixa, 8
Rangel, Charles, 163n27
Rankine, Claudia, 145–146, 200n114
Regla de Ocha, 115
religion, 66–67, 104, 109, 157, 190n6, 191n19
Remezcla, 74
representation: and AfroLatina writers, 165n49; and Afro–Puerto Ricans, 47, 74; and Pura Belpré, 24; and Ariana Brown, 148–149; and Jesús Colón, 56–59; and Dominicanidad, 202n15; and ghost stories, 143–144; and jibaridad, 55; and Marta Moreno Vega, 117; and participant observation, 50, 54; and queerness, 131, 196n4; and Piri Thomas, 84; and Young Lords, 61–63
Representative Men (Emerson 1850), 25, 38
respectability narratives, 71, 96, 131, 142, 196n17
revolutionary machismo, 183n129
Ribes Tovar, Federico, 180–181n73
Richardson, Jill Toliver, 186n47
#RickyRenuncia protests, 74
Rivail, H. Leon Denizard (aka Allan Kardec), 115
Rivera, Diego, 67
Robinson, Johnathon, 187n72
Rockefellers, 67
Rodríguez, Juana María, 130
Rodriguez, Ralph E., 15
Rosamond King, 14, 168n99
Rosario, Nelly, 158

Said, Edward, 156
Sana Sana (Brown 2020), 18–19, 129, 144, 148, 151, 200n118, 201n143
Sánchez, Marta E., 95, 98, 101

Sánchez González, Lisa, 21, 22, 23, 24, 30, 49, 87, 92
Sánchez Korrol, Virginia, 51, 52
santería, 103, 109, 110, 114, 117, 122, 167–168n94, 191n19, 191n23
Savior, Savior, Hold My Hand (Thomas 1972), 80, 185nn20–21
Schomburg, Arturo: and Africanity, 27; on Crispus Attucks, 173n95; and auto/biography, 30, 33–37, 46, 48; and Pura Belpré, 7, 23–24, 169n19; birthplace of, 171n45; and Black history, 31–32; as Black immigrant, 173n90; and crónicas, 172n64; debate over, 171n60; and W. E. B. Du Bois, 171n53; essays of, 25; and Fisk University, 171n54; and Great Man narrative, 38–45; on Haiti, 174n118; and identity, 26, 29; influences on, 171n46; interests of, 171n55; and life writing, 16–17; male-centeredness of, 172n70; and Juan de Pareja, 175n135; scholarship on, 21–22; and women, 169n11; work of, 28
Schomburg Center for Research in Black Culture, 28
Schomburg Collection, 28
scientific spirituality, 154
Scott v. Sanford, 35, 36
secrecy, 117–119, 139, 154, 194n84
Seven Long Times (Thomas 1974), 80, 82
sexuality, 102, 120, 139, 196n11
sexual violence, 95–96, 96–97, 133
Sharpe, Christina, 128, 133–134
Sheppard, Phillis Isabella, 103
Silencing the Past (Trouillot 1995), 11
Sinnette, Elinor Des Verney, 28
Sister Outsider (Lorde 1984), 12
slave narratives, 34
slavery: and Blackness, 17; and British colonies, 37; and colonialism, 176n9; history of, 174n115; and Latin America, 163n24; and monstrosity, 147–148; and Panama, 42; and Puerto Rico, 47–48
Smith, Sidonie, 11, 56, 64
social Darwinism, 91

socialism, 48, 53–54, 66–68, 71, 72, 177n10, 182n105
social media, 158–159
socioformal analysis, 15–16
solidarity, 9–10, 12, 96
soma, 184n11
Some Girls (Cepeda 2017), 19, 154, 155–156, 203n31
"Some Notable Colored Men from the West Indies" (Schomburg), 38
Soul on Ice (Cleaver 1968), 79
The Sovereignty of Quiet (Quashie 2012), 85–86
The Soviet Power (1939), 67
Spain, 24
Spanish Civil War, 67–68
Spanish Harlem, 106, 122
speaking near-by, 129
spiritual mestizaje, 167–168n94
Stalin, Joseph, 67, 178n23
stereotypes, 106–107, 111, 154, 156
Stockett, Kathryn, 131
Stories I Read to Children (Belpré 2013), 23
storytelling, 154
street talk, 81, 95, 99, 188n84
street vernacular, 69
subjectivity, 33–34
"Superpower" (Brown 2020), 148
Survey Graphic, 29
Svirsky, Marcelo, 27
syncretism, 191n19

Taíno Indians, 60, 155
Taney, Roger B., 35, 36, 43
Telling to Live (Latina Feminist Group 2001), 11, 108
"Tengo Puerto Rico en Mi Corazón" (Young Lords), 53
"Terrestrial Bodies" (Valdés 2019), 158
testimonio, 11, 12, 166n73, 166n75
theory in the flesh, 13–14
Third World feminism, 51, 55, 63–73, 182n121. *See also* feminism
13 Point Program, 63, 72
This Bridge Called My Back (Moraga and Anzaldúa 1983), 13

Thomas, Piri: archive of, 15, 77–84; and Pura Belpré, 169n19; and Brew, 188n88; on Christian racism, 185n23; chronology of, 185n20; and colorism, 187n54, 194n81; and Jaquira Díaz, 131; and *Every Child Is Born a Poet*, 187n72; heritage of, 184n15; and language, 92–98; language of, 69; and masculinity, 184n4, 184n7; memoirs of, 75–76; as outlaw figure, 185–186n29; and queer artists, 184n8; and violence, 17–18, 84–91, 185nn24–5; and visibility, 184nn2–3
Through the Eyes of Rebel Women (Morales 2016), 71, 182n121, 183n124
Tinajero, Araceli, 64
Torres, Arlene, 55, 61, 63
Torres, Ritchie, 163n27
Torres-Saillant, Silvio, 6, 55
tourism, 58
transculturation, 10
trauma porn, 131, 197n22
triple-consciousness, 4, 26
Troubling Vision (Fleetwood 2011), 8
Trouillot, Michel-Rolph, 11
true crime, 131
"Trujillo's Fair of Blood" (Colón), 52
Truth, Sojourner, 60
Tupamaros, 53
23andMe genealogists, 154, 158
Tyner, James A., 82

University of Saint Xavier, 45
Unspeakable Violence (Guidotti-Hernández 2011), 82
US Army, 140
US Blackness, 153
US citizenship, 27
US Civil Rights Movement, 56–57
US imperialism, 17, 27, 62, 83, 94

Valdés, Juana, 158
Valdés, Vanessa K.: and AfroLatinx studies, 6; and AfroLatinx subjectivity, 164n36; *Oshun's Daughters*, 192n47; and Juan de Pareja exhibit, 175n135; on Arturo Alfonso Schomburg, 21, 22, 28, 32, 43; on Schomburg's birthplace, 171n45; on Schomburg's influences, 171n47; on Schomburg's masculinist focus, 26, 169n8, 172n70; on Schomburg's narratives, 172n64
Vargas, Deborah, 199n93
Vasconcelos, José, 9, 165n56, 202n2
Vázquez, David J., 52
Velázquez, Diego, 41
verse biographies, 144–145
verse memoirs, 144–147
Victoria y Luna, Francisco Xavier, 44, 45
violence: and academic mestizaje, 100; and AfroLatinidad, 185n25; and *Bird of Paradise*, 203n37; and Jaquira Díaz, 140, 142, 199n74; in *Down These Mean Streets*, 79, 84–91, 92–99; and El Caserío, 133; as form of expression, 82; and identity, 76, 83, 184n9; and life writing, 77; in *Ordinary Girls*, 144; and prison, 185n24; and racism, 81; and Piri Thomas, 78, 80; and visibility, 17
visibility: and AfroLatinx life writing, 9; and AfroLatinx studies, 5; and Pura Belpré, 23; and Black Puerto Ricans, 79; and Ariana Brown, 149; and curandera historians, 110; Saidiya Hartman on, 165n49; and haunting, 136–137; and life writing, 162n18; and marginality, 15; and monster theory, 18; and narrative, 26; narratives of, 6–7; and power structures, 11–13; and surveillance, 197n28; and violence, 76, 132–133
A Voice from the South by a Black Woman of the South (Cooper 1892), 96
"A Voice through the Window" (Colón 1961), 64–65

Walker, Alice, 146, 147, 186n50
Watson, Julia, 11, 56
The Way It Was (Colón 1993), 17, 48, 52, 57–58

waywardness, 18, 128, 132, 197n27
We Are Owed. (Brown 2021): and *Borderlands / La Frontera*, 14; and girlhood, 129; and monstrosity, 144; and queer AfroLatinidad, 18–19, 152; as verse memoir, 145; and white space, 146–147, 200n118
"We Shall Overcome," 57
West, Gerald, 77, 99, 100–102
Wheatley, Phillis, 16, 17, 27, 29, 34–35, 46, 173n87
When the Spirits Dance Mambo (Moreno Vega 2004): and AfroLatinidad, 107; and bicultural identity, 194n85; and espiritismo, 116–117; impetus for, 108; and music, 115, 122–124, 195n123; and Ochun, 193n60; and secrecy, 118–121; and spiritual mestizaje, 167–168n94, 191n19; structure of, 114
Where Do We Go from Here (King 1967), 79
whiteness, 146, 155, 189n124, 201n131
whitening, 3, 9, 55, 77, 98, 141. *See also* blanqueamiento
white supremacy: and AfroLatinx life writing, 11; and AfroLatinx writers, 164n31; and ancestry tests, 158; and Pura Belpré, 24, 25; and José Campeche, 40; and history, 31, 33–34, 42–43; and life writing, 13; and Arturo Alfonso Schomburg, 22; and *Scott v. Sanford*, 36; and surveillance, 76; and violence, 132; and western hemisphere, 45; Omaris Zamora on, 202n2
white womanhood, 65–66, 181n92
Whitten, Norman Jr., 55, 61
Wild Tongues Can't Be Tamed (Fennell 2021), 161–162n15
Winant, Howard, 91
witchcraft, 118

Witnessing Girlhood (Gilmore and Marshall 2019), 129
woman-of-color feminist analysis, 7, 12, 14–15, 34
Women Warriors of the Afro-Latina Diaspora (Moreno Vega, Alba, and Modestin 2012), 161–162n15
Woodson, Carter G., 25, 26
Wynter, Sylvia, 22

X, Malcolm, 60

Yanga, Gaspar, 147–150, 151, 152, 200n121
"Yanga Builds Me a Panga" (Brown 2021), 147–148
YLP. *See* Young Lords
Yoruba people, 60
Yoruba philosophy, 108–109, 111, 112, 116, 123, 154
Young, Cynthia, 71–72
Young Lords: and Michael Abramson, 177n15; and AfroLatinidad, 49; and anti-Blackness, 17, 48; and Pura Belpré, 169n19; biography of, 53; and Jesús Colón, 178n28; and cultural nationalism, 192n29; and feminism, 70–73; and history, 60; and jibaridad, 59; and life writing, 74; and myth of racial harmony, 54–55; and participant observation, 68–69; politics of, 47; and Puerto Rico, 176n2; and revolutionary machismo, 183n129; and rhetoric of Christianity, 182n105; and 13 Point Plan, 63; women in, 182n121, 183n124; and YLO, 52
Young Lords Organization (YLO), 49, 52

Zafia, Rafar, 172n79
Zamora, Omaris Z., 4, 6, 63, 164n31, 202n2